Animal-Wise

ANIMAL-WISE:

The Spirit Language and Signs of Nature

Ted Andrews

DRAGONHAWK PUBLISHING   JACKSON, TENNESSEE

A Dragonhawk Publishing Book

Animal-Wise
Copyright © 1999 by Ted Andrews
All rights reserved.

First Edition

Cover Art: "Wolf Dreamer" by James Oberle

Editing, indexing, and book design by
Pagyn Alexander-Harding (IAAI, Hitterdal, MN) and
Diane Haugen (Whiskey Creek Document Design, Barnesville, MN)

ISBN 1-888767-34-0

Library of Congress Catalog Card Number: 98-84420

This book was designed and produced by
Dragonhawk Publishing
Jackson, TN
USA

Dedication

for
Kathy
and
in memory of those who blessed our lives while they lived:

Dusty and Freedom • red foxes

Confusion and Gus • red foxes

Beakless • red-tailed hawk

Humphrey • groundhog

Edgar • common crow

Buttons • red squirrel

Pockets • oppossum

Woody • wood duck

Lucky • guinea pig

Saki • barn owl

Bernice • barred owl

Juno • grcat horned owl

Stubby • short-eared owl

Beaker • Amcrican kestrel

Fog and Fergie • screech owls

Jaws • rose-breasted grosbeak

Ralph and Chuck • turkey vultures

Chester and Dudley • Canada geese

Oreo, Daisy, and Pepe • striped skunks

Lennie and Squiggie • most uncommon rats

TED ANDREWS

Table of Contents

LIST OF ILLUSTRATIONS

LIST OF EXERCISES

LIST OF TABLES

About the Animal Images

When Dragonhawk first contacted me about the page layout and book design for *Animal-Wise*, they had already decided not to include pictures of the animals. After all, trying to find over 150 black and white images of a variety of creatures, all in the same artistic style, seemed pretty nearly impossible.

Since I love a challenge almost as much as I do vintage etchings, I started thinking about where to look for images. I had Chapman's 1912 North American bird book, but wasn't sure where I could turn up the rest of the animals. Then I remembered an old, battered dictionary my kids had picked up at a flea market. In my search for vintage etchings, I usually pass these kinds of books up. Much of the front matter had been torn out, including the title page. Just the same, I did a quick check, and sure enough, there were many of the needed animals.

With some trepidation, I called Dragonhawk to let them know I could supply most of the pictures of the animals needed from my old books and they graciously took me up on the offer. With the exception of the birds, which mostly came from Chapman, the great majority of the animal images were taken from this battered old dictionary, a 1909 edition of a Websters edited by W. T.Harris. I managed to find the date on the one remaining scrap of the editor's comment page. Where pages were missing in this 1909 edition, I was able to fill some of the gaps with my 1872 Goodrich and Porter edition of Websters.

When I had no idea what an animal looked like, I found the images helpful even though dated, as well as the descriptive information. The words were sometimes a bit old-fashioned, but charming even though I know some of the Latin names have changed over time.

So if an animal image looks a tad strange to your modern eyes or a description sounds a little staid, remember the sources. I hope you enjoy them as much as I did!

Diane Haugen
Whiskey Creek Document Design
http://www.wcdd.com/index.html
218/962-3202

Introduction

Dream Song of the Eagle

Long before there was ever a long ago, a small village sat at the edge of a great woods. In this village a young girl was born, completely mute. She could not laugh. She could not cry. She could not speak or utter a sound. Because of this, she was often teased and shunned by both her family and the other people in the village. So the young girl did the only thing she knew to do to make herself feel better. She went to the woods. It was her safe spot…her haven. Only in the woods did she feel accepted. About the same time the young girl was born into the village, a young boy was born also. He could laugh, and shout, and speak—and make all manner of noise. But he did have something different about him as well.

The boy was a little clumsy…a little out of rhythm with everyone and everything in the village. He was often tripping over his own feet or those around him. Because of this, he too was often the object of a great deal of teasing and ridicule. Even his own family would often roll their eyes and comment that if dust got in his way, he would trip over it.

So he did what the young girl did as well. He went to the woods. It was one place where if he tripped or stumbled, no one ever seemed to mind. It was the one place he was not teased.

Because he and the girl shared this in common, they grew to be close friends. They would spend their days exploring the woods and seeking out new wonders. They would create games and adventures. They watched and studied everything they came across, and before long they knew more about the woods than anyone in their village had ever known.

One day while they were exploring a new area of the woods, they heard a rustling in the bushes to their left. They slowly walked over and gently moved the bushes back, and there lying on the ground was a young eagle that had been shot through the shoulder. The eagle looked at them with eyes filled with pain and fear, but it was too weak to even try to escape. The boy and girl just stood still, their eyes wide in amazement. They had never seen an eagle up close before.

Neither was sure what to do, and then the boy got an idea.

"I know," he said. "We'll bandage it and make it better. It will be our friend."

The girl just looked at him, not sure if that was something they should try to do. Then she motioned to the sky, telling her friend that maybe there might be a mother and father eagle that might come and take care of this one.

The boy ignored her gestures and motions. The seed had been planted. He had already decided that he would save the eagle and it would become his best friend. And he began to look for something to wrap the eagle in. The girl took a deep breath, knowing what her friend was like when he got something stuck in his head, and she began to look around for some sign of a mother and father eagle or a nest. Not far

from where they found the young injured eagle, she found the mother and father. They were laying behind an old tree...dead. Both had been killed. Her heart filled with sadness over the death of something so beautiful, wondering who could do such a horrible thing. Then she wiped the tears from her eyes and covered them with grasses and sticks. She turned away to tell her friend what she had found. She knew now that if the young eagle were to have a chance live it would be up to the two of them.

As she approached, he was carefully clearing away some of the brush around the eagle. She tapped him softly upon the shoulder, and he turned to look up at her. She shook her head and motioned softly with her hand. He frowned, understanding, and they both looked down at the eagle before them.

The girl removed the shawl she had tied around her waist, and together they lay the shawl over the eagle and carefully wrapped it. The eagle, weak with pain, did not struggle at all, and holding the bundled eagle between them, they began to carry it through the woods.

They carried the eagle to a meadow not far from where they found it. This meadow was the one place in all of the woods that was the most special to them. It was their true haven. To them it was their true home. There they bandaged the eagle and built a cage for it. When it wouldn't eat on its own, they force-fed it, afraid it would die if they didn't. And on the way back to the village, they decided to keep it all a secret. They decided to tell no one about their find.

Everyday they would rise early, making their way to the meadow. When they arrived at the meadow, they would change the eagle's bandages, clean its cage, and catch more food, trapping young mice and rabbits. Around the third day, it began to eat on its own, and the two began to breathe a little easier.

The two spent as much time in the meadow with the eagle as possible. Everyday the eagle seemed to grow stronger and healthier. It was eating on its own. It was alert. It was even trying to stretch its wings through the bandages.

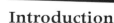

TED ANDREWS

Around the fourth week, they were up early as usual, making their way to the meadow. The sun had barely risen, and the grass was still wet with the dew. As they stepped into the meadow. They froze.

The cage was wide open and the eagle was gone!

They looked at each other and then began looking around the meadow. Both suspected that someone in the village had found out about their eagle and taken it away. As they looked around, their worry over someone from the village having taken it faded. There were no signs that anyone had ever been in the meadow other than themselves.

They were puzzled, and as they looked around trying to understand this mystery, the girl glanced up. And there she saw the eagle. High on a tree limb at the edge of the meadow above the cage, perched the eagle whose life they had saved. The bandage was off of its shoulder and draped over that limb.

The girl nudged her friend. He looked at her and then looked at her looking up. When both pairs of eyes were looking, the eagle solemnly bowed to them. Their eyes widened in amazement! They didn't know much about eagles, but they didn't think eagles bowed to people—much less children. But then it became stranger. The eagle fixed them both with his eyes and he began to speak.

"I wish to thank you, my young friends, for having saved my life, but now it is time for me to go."

Astounded that the eagle could speak, it was a moment before the boy answered, and then only at the nudging of the girl.

"Why?" he asked. "Why must you go? You can stay here with us!"

The eagle smiled and shook his head. "No, I'm sorry, my friends, but the people in your village have found out about me. They think you spend too much time here, and they intend to come here tomorrow and take me away."

Both the boy and the girl got tears in their eyes, saddened by his words.

"Don't be sad," the eagle continued. "You have performed a wonderful healing, and it is time for me

to go. I too have a home, and it is time to return to the Land of the Eagles."

Neither the boy nor the girl knew what to say to this magnificent bird. A lone tear rolled down the girl's cheeks. The boy sniffled, wiping his eyes, and then he got another idea!

"Take us with you! Let us go with you to the Land of the Eagles!" The eagle laughed softly.

"No, I'm sorry. The Land of the Eagles is a great journey. In fact, I have to fly through the heart of the sun itself."

We don't mind. No one really likes us here! We won't be any trouble."

The seed was planted, and the boy began to beg more. The girl urged him, seeing some hope in the request, her own eyes begging the eagle.

"No one likes us…they treat us terribly…they don't even care most of the time where we are…your back…."

As the boy begged on, the eagle closed his eyes and thought for a moment. When he opened them, the two became silent. The eagle fixed his eyes upon them and spoke again.

"I will give you the night to think about this. If you truly wish to make this journey, you must meet me here before the sun comes up tomorrow morning. But understand this: it is a long journey, and we will fly through the heart of the sun. If you make this journey, you may never be able to return again."

The two looked at the eagle, mimicking his solemn look, and then they looked at each other. Grins burst upon their faces, and the two turned and dashed out of the meadow, running back toward the village.

They sneaked into their homes and took what few belongings they thought they might need for their journey. Then they hid in the woods, spending the night so as not to be caught or delayed by anyone in the village. They hardly slept a wink the entire night. Long before the sun came up, they were awake and on their way to the meadow.

As they walked into the meadow, the sun was coming up over the horizon. On an old tree stump in the *middle of the meadow was the eagle whose life they had saved. He was stretching and flexing his wings, loosening them for the long journey ahead. As the children approached, he let his wings come to rest at his sides, and he bowed again to them.*

"I see you have made your decision," he said.

Both grinned widely and bobbed their heads up and down, up and down.

The eagle smiled briefly and then got more serious.

"You must understand several things," he said. "This is a very long journey, and we will fly through the heart of the sun. It won't be dangerous, but when we pass through the sun, you must close your eyes or the sun will be so bright that it will blind you. And also remember, that if you make this journey, you may never be able to return again."

The two looked at each other, and hesitation only crossed their faces for a brief moment. And again they both nodded.

"Then each of you climb upon one of my shoulders."

As they climbed onto his back, his weight shifted, adjusting to the children there. He bent his knees and spread his tremendous wings. Then he leaped up, beating his wings with great speed and force, trying to rise with the children on his back. At first it didn't seem as if he would be able to lift them, but inch by inch he began to climb with the children hanging on tightly. Soon he settled into a steady beat of his wings, strong and smooth. He circled the meadow and then began climbing.

As they reached treetop level, the children looked down off of the back of the eagle. They saw a line of villagers moving through the woods toward the meadow, and they knew that what the eagle had told them was true. They immediately began laughing, knowing they had gotten away.

That laughter carried down from the back of the eagle, and the villagers looked up. They saw the young boy and girl on the back of that eagle. They started hollering and shouting up at them, but by that time

the eagle had climbed so high their voices were lost in the wind. Still the eagle climbed higher.

Before long, the eagle and children disappeared into the heavens, and the eagle began the long journey toward the sun. He flew for what seemed an eternity to the children, and they began to wonder if they would be able to last. Then they approached the sun.

The eagle looked back over his shoulder at each of them, and he said, "Close your eyes." They closed their eyes, and the eagle passed through the heart of the sun!

As they came out the other side, their eyes opened and they looked about them in amazement. A golden sky surrounded them. Below them was a beautiful, rich green land. And soaring, diving, and screeching around them were thousands of eagles!

Slowly they began to circle down toward the land below. With a powerful flapping of its wings, the eagle landed softly in the grasses. The children slid off of his back and watched as all of the eagles dropped out of the sky and formed a circle about them on the ground.

Then together they all bowed to the young girl and boy. The eagle whose life they had saved stepped forward. He stood before them, not saying a word, and then with his wing he brushed under his beak and began to push it back. The children's eyes widened. This was nothing more than an eagle's head mask!

Next he shrugged his shoulders and a suit of feathers dropped off of him onto the ground. This wasn't an eagle at all!

Then all of the eagles surrounding them brushed back their eagle's head masks, shrugging off their own suit of feathers. The children stared, wide-eyed and then realized that this wasn't the Land of the Eagles.

This was the Land of the Spirit People!

The one whose life they saved looked at them and spoke softly and with great love: "in time, my young friends, we will make for you your own eagle's head mask. We will make for you your own suit of feathers. And we will teach you how to fly!"

The next year and a day was the happiest the two had ever lived. They got their own eagle's head mask and their own suit of feathers, and they were taught

how to fly. They would spend their days soaring and sailing through the clouds and over this beautiful land.

At the end of that year and a day, the boy got another idea: "Wouldn't it be great to go back to the village now. Wouldn't it be great to show them what we can do? They'd treat us differently. They'd love us now. We're eagle people. We can fly!"

The little girl shook her head vehemently. She wanted nothing to do with such an idea, but the seed was planted. The boy began to speak of it more and more.

"They'll treat us differently. We can fly. They won't make fun of us. They are our true family...."

The more he talked, the more he began to persuade the girl. Finally, he convinced her, and so one morning they arose before all of the others. They put on their suits of feathers and their eagle's head masks, and they took to the sky. Before long they disappeared into the heavens and began the long journey back through the sun to their village.

They paused at the sun, looking at each other, and then flew straight on. They passed through the sun's heart, and when they came out the other side, they were circling their own village.

It was morning in the village, and the people were just rising and lighting their cooking fires. They saw the shadows of two large birds circling on the ground. They looked up and saw two magnificent eagles soaring over head, descending toward the village. The villagers began running around, waking everyone up. This was a sign! This was something wondrous!

The villagers gathered, watching as the two eagles descended and landed softly in their midst. The villagers backed up, unsure of what to do, but amazed at the wondrous sign that had come to them.

The boy and the girl stood together—not moving—enjoying the moment. They looked at each other, and then each brushed a wing under the beak and pushed back the eagle's head mask.

The villagers gasped!

The two then shrugged their shoulders and the suits of feathers dropped off. No sooner had they taken

their suits off, though, and the garments turned to dust at their feet.

The villagers were stunned. These weren't eagles! These were the children! And they all began to speak at once.

"This is wonderful!"

"You are eagles!"

"Show us how you flew!"

"Yes, show us how you flew!"

The two children looked at each other and then they looked at the dust of their masks and suits. They didn't know what to say or to do. And because they didn't know what to do, they did nothing. When they did nothing, the mood of the crowd shifted. The people began to grumble.

"This is evil!" someone shouted from the back.

"Bad magic!" someone else answered.

Then someone picked up a stone and threw it at the two. The boy and the girl turned, their faces white with fear, and ran toward the woods. The villagers pursued, hollering, shouting, cussing, shaking their fists—angry enough to kill the children.

The children ran, dodging, dipping in and out of the trees, over hidden paths. The only thing that saved them was that they knew the woods better than anyone in the village had ever known..

Still the villagers hunted them. The children moved, running and hiding every day for a week before the villagers gave up their chase. Though the villagers no longer pursued them, the boy and the girl knew that they could never return to their village again. And the warning from the one whose life they saved whispered hauntingly in their heads.

Feeling more lost and alone than ever, they wandered the woods. They scavenged whatever food and berries they could find, and they slept in the hollows of old trees. They were alone. They knew their only choice was to leave their homeland forever. They decided though that before they would leave, they would make one last visit to their meadow.

As they stepped into the meadow, they saw what still remained of the cage they had built for the one

whose life they had saved. Their eyes went to that tree limb high above them, where the eagle had stood the day they discovered the empty cage. Snagged on a branch was a small strip of cloth that had been used to bandage its wing. Then their eyes raised to the sky, hoping to see their friend.

The sky was empty.

They both plopped down in the tall grasses of the meadow and began to cry, neither trying to hide it from the other. Long after the crying had stopped and the two sat silently staring at the grass in front of them, the girl's heart jumped. She looked over at her friend. He stared quietly at the ground, his face streaked from earlier tears. She glanced around the meadow, and a soft wisp of a breeze brushed across them. She raised her eyes to the sky. Far off was a tiny speck circling. She caught her breath, and her heart jumped again.

This time the boy felt her heart jump. He looked at her, and then looked at her looking up. He caught his own breath.

Slowly that speck began to circle down. When it reached treetop level, they both jumped up from the ground. It was the eagle! The one whose life they had saved!

They both began to cry again, as the eagle landed on that same tree limb high above them. The boy was jumping up and down, shouting, "Yes, we can go back! We can go back!"

The girl's face was filled with tears of hope and joy once more.

The eagle looked on them with sad eyes and then shook his head. "No, I'm sorry, my young friends, but you can never return again." He paused, and then continued.

The two paled at his words, feeling their hearts crash once more.

"But you did save my life, and because you saved my life, there is still something that I can give you."

With his beak, he reached in under his wing and dropped out from under it into the hands of the girl— a flute. He then fixed his attention on her.

"With this flute, you will learn to speak. The sound you make with it will call the wind, and the wind that you call will bring me from the other side of the sun to the sky above you. It is this Song of the Wind that I will bring to you in your dreams. But it will bring me no closer than the sky above."

Then he turned to the boy, and reaching under his other wing with his beak, he dropped out from under it into his hands a rattle.

"I will come also into your sleep. I will teach you a new rhythm, and I will sing you a song. When you can bring that rhythm and the ancient Song of the Eagles out of your sleep, it will be that song and that rhythm that will call me from the sky above to where I now stand."

He paused, and looked at both of them with great love.

"Only when the two of you can do this together, will I give you the last thing I have to give. I will teach you the language of animals. I will teach you how to talk with Nature!"

Before they could say a word, the eagle jumped, spreading his wings and began to climb and quickly disappeared into the heavens again.

The boy and girl looked at each other and then at what the eagle had dropped into their hands. The girl brought the flute to her mouth and blew softly, not knowing at all how to make it sound. Nothing came forth. It was silent.

The boy looked at the rattle in his hands and frowned, thinking, "This is a baby's toy. What am I going to do with this?"

That night while they slept, the eagle visited them. The girl's dreams were haunted with the soft song of the flute and winds blowing around her. The boy heard the sound of a rattle, like that of a snake. And he heard a song being chanted. When they awoke in the morning, they looked at each other and knew. What the eagle had told them was true. The girl began to experiment, trying to get a sound out of the flute. The boy tried to remember the rhythm of the rattle and the song that was chanted in his dreams, but it was to no

avail. No sooner would they open their eyes from the sleep, and the songs would fade back into the dreamtime. They could not bring them forth.

Many days passed, and the girl woke up early, the haunting song of the flute still a soft echo in her mind. She could hear her young friend next to her. She knew he was curled around the rattle, for she could hear it moving softly in his sleep. He was mumbling the dream song that was being sung to him. She decided that today would be the day.

With her eyes still closed, trying to hold the fading echoes of the flute sounds from her own sleep, she sat up and brought the flute to her lips. She placed her fingers over the holes, and blew softly.

Nothing.

She adjusted the flute and tried again.

Nothing.

She blew a little harder, steadier.

The flute sounded! It was a squeaky sound, but it was a sound!

She blew it again, and this time when it sounded, a breeze brushed across her.

It worked!

She blew a series of squeaks, each of which brought its own gust of breeze. She began to cry softly, and it was then that she heard the boy sitting up next to her. Each opened their eyes, and looked at each other. She blew the flute and a breeze brushed them both. He grinned at her, and the girl's eyes widened. The flute dropped away from her mouth. She stared at his hand. The boy looked down, and his hand was bouncing the rattle with a steady rhythm—almost of its own will.

He had the rhythm!

They began to laugh and cry at the same time. Now they understood what the eagle had told them. Only when they could do it together would he return.

Another week passed and still the girl was not able to bring the Song of the Wind from her sleep. She practiced and practiced, and though the sounds were smoother, she could not quite bring the true song from her sleep. She could create gusts and breezes, but noth-

Introduction   **Animal-Wise**

ing steady. And nothing like what came to her in her sleep.

The boy struggled also to bring his dream song into the waking time, but it wouldn't happen. He slept with the rattle in his hand. He carried it everywhere with him. Even though he had not tripped or stumbled once since he had the rhythm, when he awoke, the ancient words being sung to him would fade to nothingness.

Again the girl woke early one morning. The Song of the Wind was a little louder in her head, and she kept her eyes closed trying to hold onto it. She could hear the boy's rattle dancing in his hand while he slept. She could hear him mumbling ancient words being sung to him in his sleep.

She blocked him out, and reached slowly for her flute. She brought it up to her lips, listening intently to the song in her head. She took a deep breath and began to blow softly. The music was soft and smooth, and a breeze rose up immediately. She tried to ignore it, playing the music she heard more clearly with each breath. The breeze grew steady, and she began to smile while she played. She had the song!

The boy's rattle began to dance more clearly. The words from the song in his sleep began to be whispered. The wind grew stronger still. He sat up next to the girl, and though her eyes were still closed, she knew he was awake. The rattle moved and he began to whisper the ancient dream song to her.

Their eyes opened, and they grinned at each other. Slowly, while she continued to play and the boy sang softly the words that had been sung to him so often in his sleep. Their eyes were fixed on the sky above them.

Then, high in the heavens, a tiny speck appeared and began circling down. Their eyes began to tear, and they both stood up. The girl continued to play and the wind swirled around them. The boy looked directly up at the eagle and began to sing loudly and clearly. He began to sing the eagle down to the earth.

Slowly the eagle circled the treetops and then landed on the tree limb above them. The girl lowered

her flute, and the boy quit his song, tears on both their cheeks. They gripped each other's hands tightly. The winds died down around them. The eagle looked down from the tree at them with great love and pride, and he bowed to them once more.

"You have learned well, my young friends, but today the lessons truly begin. From this day forth I will teach you the language of Animals. I will teach you how to speak with the Nature. From this day forth your home will be among the woods and streams. Your family will be the creatures that abound within the world. Never more will you be outcast....

 # Notes

Introduction

Part I

Animal-Wise

*So important are animals to our spiritual lives
that we do not merely use animal imagery to embody religious themes;
rather, we discover spiritual values through animals.*
CHRISTOPHER MANES
Other Creations, p. 15

CHAPTER I

Understanding the Language of Animals

Everyone has a story of animals. Everyone has had some unique experience with them. Sometimes they are of domestic animals. Sometimes wild. Sometimes painful and sometimes wonderful. Everyone has been touched by animals in some way, either in life or in dreams, and always the difficulty is determining what it means.

In our modern world we have separated ourselves from Nature. It is something alien, something to be studied, and unfortunately, it is often something to be taken advantage of. What we fail to remember and realize though is that no matter how much we cloak ourselves in civilization, we are always part of the natural world. Everything that happens to us has repercussions upon Nature, and everything that happens to the natural world has repercussions upon us.

Because of this, it is important to try and understand Nature's language—to relate to Nature in a new way. The key to that new relationship is found in the animal realm. Every society has taught that the only way the Divine (no matter how you define that force within the world) could speak to humans was through Nature, and the only way humans could understand what the Divine was telling them about their lives was by studying Nature—especially the animals.

But how do we begin? How do we know whether the animal that has shown up in our life

has particular significance for us? It's not always easy. Nor is it always obvious. Learning anything new takes time, effort, and patience. Developing a new relationship demands even greater time, effort, and patience.

We begin by first recognizing and accepting that the animal has caught our attention for a reason. We do not have to believe the animal has a creative intelligence, but we can accept that some force, some archetypal energy is expressing itself through the animal. By studying and learning about the animal, we understand more about its spiritual significance to us and what it means in our life.

Maybe it is a specific message for us. Maybe the creature's appearance provides a clue to resolving a problem. Maybe it appeared to provide a course of action. Maybe this animal has the particular quality we need to develop at this time in our life. Maybe its appearance is just to remind us to keep a sense of wonder alive. Maybe it means all of these things— and more.

In understanding the language of animals and in developing that new relationship with Nature, we must develop the mindset that *everything has significance*. That significance is not always going to be crystal clear, and it may affect us on many levels. But everything we experience has some importance and significance for us.

We do live in a time in which most people are separated from the natural world. A recent poll estimated that the average person spends less than an hour a week outdoors. Often we get so

Animal

NIGHTLY ENCOUNTERS

Animals that come out at night are called nocturnal. They have a special layer of cells behind their retina that reflects light, giving the eyes more chance to use what little light there is. This layer is called *tapetum lucidum* and it is why nocturnal animals see so well in the dark. The reflection that we see from headlights or flashlights is called *eyeshine*. Different animals have different colored eyeshine, so even if we don't actually see the animal, we can help identify the animal through its eyeshine color.

- bullfrog (green) • night heron (red)
- oppossum (orange) • owl (yellow)
- raccoon (bright yellow)
- red fox (bright white)
- skunk (amber)

Wonders

wrapped up in the hustle and bustle of modern life that we lose our connection to Nature and thus we lose our sense of wonder at life. Often people forget that we can starve as much from a lack of wonder as we can a lack of food. Nature— especially through the animals within it—keeps our wonder alive. We rediscover our sense of wonder and we begin to believe once more.

Since the release of my book *Animal-Speak*, many people have shared their personal animal experiences. Workshops and lectures on the subject are usually packed with attendees, all attesting to the importance of animals in everyone's life. When we begin to examine Nature from the perspectives of science, of spirit, and of our personal relationship with it, we find ourselves becoming **animal-wise**.

Science vs St. Francis

➤ On an experiential level, it is difficult to imagine a life cut off from the creative wonders of nature. Our spiritual imagination responds in a unique way to living creatures. On an intuitive level, we always know there is a significance to animal experiences, even if we don't understand them. Zoologists try to rationalize their significance. Philosophers try to theorize about them, and the religious have always tried to spiritualize them. So where is the truth of their meaning? Do we need to become more animistic, as with many primitive societies, or should we focus strictly upon the scientific?

Modern society's reliance on reason has greatly diminished our relationship with animals. Reason enabled society to prosper, but it also promoted the non-importance of anything that was not human. The difficulty lies in balancing the zoological with the animistic views of Nature. It is for us a recurrence of an ancient battle— Science versus St. Francis. St. Francis, a twelfth century monk, expressed the belief that God's spirit lives in all of Nature—not just in humans.

This kind of animism is one approach to understanding the meaning of our animal encounters. It was a common belief in many shaman traditions around the world. Animism—sometimes called spiritism—is complex. At its core is the following perception:

> [the] phenomenal world—humans, animals, plants, and even non-biological entities such as stones, rivers, and cultural artifacts—is alive in the sense of being inspirited. Not only is the nonhuman world alive, but it is filled with articulate and at times intelligible subjects, able to communicate and interact with humans for good or ill.[1]

In anthropology, animism is the belief that all of Nature—the elements and the animals—have spirit. These spirits are closely connected to humans. Fetishes (feathers, skins, etc.) of the animals were protected and honored because they were bridges between the animal's spirit and the human. Often these beliefs became superstition, leading to the belief that harm to the fetish would in turn result in harm to the human.

Zoologists will often explain an animal's appearance only in terms of their science, describing the animal according to its biological behaviors and make-up. To zoologists, nothing is possible which cannot be proven or scientifically verified. This approach has great value, but it is not the complete explanation. If we truly wish to become *animal-wise*, we must combine the mysticism of the animism with the science of zoology without becoming superstitious or narrowly rational.

The scientific and the mystical viewpoints are not truly at odds when it comes to animals and Nature and their meaning in our life. They support and promote each other. Early shamans, priests, and priestesses knew this. They were

---

[1] Christopher Manes. *Other Creations* (New York: Doubleday), 1977, pp. 31-32.

mystics—magicians *and* scientists. They studied plants and animals, learning their characteristics and qualities. They also honored the spirit expressed in and through the animals and plants.

If we wish to truly become *animal-wise*, we must also blend the science with the spirit. We can study the metamorphic process of moths and butterflies and understand it scientifically, but we should also marvel at the handiwork of the Divine in a creature that can transform itself from caterpillar to butterfly.

Spirituality is not determined or limited by knowledge, reason, or creative intelligence. Our teachers are not merely the human ones. Our learning and guidance can come from sources other than human—Divine messages are not limited to coming to us only through those of "our kind." When we realize this, our world is no longer the same. Instead, it becomes filled with possibilities.

Later we will learn of four scientific observations that should be studied about every animal that comes into our lives. If nothing else is learned about these animals, these four things will help us understand their role in our lives and help our lives run more smoothly. But we should not stop with this zoological knowledge.

As much as possible within the confines of this text, I have tried to combine the science with the mystical from many traditions. My approach is universal, drawing upon my own naturalistic and mystical experiences and education. I have tried to incorporate the science with the mystical, the zoology with mythology, seeking out the common threads running through all traditions about the animals. I have provided outstanding behavioral characteristics and scientific qualities. When possible, I have tried to provide significant myths about the animals, showing how they work together. By reading the animal descriptions, you should come to a clearer understanding of how

Recent surveys indicate the average person in the U.S. spends less than an hour outdoors per week. Spending time outdoors is necessary for our physical, emotional, mental, and spiritual health.
We are not likely to have an actual animal encounter without spending some time outdoors!

the animals' qualities and characteristics reflect their spiritual keynotes.

People frequently ask me if I am Native American or if my interpretations and approaches are supposed to be predominantly Native American. My answer to both questions is no The book jackets of this and in my earlier work, *Animal-Speak* may give that indication. However, they were chosen for their Native American elements because in this country the native peoples are the primary keepers of the tradition of honoring animals and Nature. Remember, though, that other societies had their peoples who recognized and kept alive the teachings of animals and natures just as well.

The amazing thing is that when we compare the teachings of animals across various traditions, they are much more similar than different. This phenomena of common threads should be a reminder. Yes, the scientific knowledge helps us in our understanding, but just as important is the wisdom and balance and humility that comes when we use that knowledge as a doorway to the hidden teachings behind the world of animals, those from ancient traditions

Though we may scientifically understand more about animals and their behaviors than ever before, the sheer beauty of wild animals still fills us with amazement, with wonder. Our heart jumps. Our breath catches. Our pulse races. We have felt the breath of God within Nature and now upon our soul.

Understanding Animal Encounters

➤There are many types of animal encounters. This is important to understand, especially in the modern world where many people live within urban environments. Even in these urban environments there are a great many animal species that can be met.

Our modern cities are homes to a wide variety of mammals—mice, rats, squirrels, opossums,

raccoons, foxes, and coyotes. In some urban and suburban areas bears and even mountain lions sometime appear. Birds of every variety are found, from the tiny chickadee to hawks, vultures, owls, and eagles. And we have a multitude of insects, spiders and reptiles.

The animals are around us, no matter where we live, and so we are likely to have encounters, but they do not necessarily have to be face-to-face encounters. Every shamanic society taught that if we dream of an animal, it is the same as meeting it face-to-face when awake. It should be treated just as significantly. Maybe every time we turn on the television, there is a program on a particular animal. We open a magazine and there are photos of it. We can have a variety of encounters, and when we have several of them within a close time frame, we should pay attention.

Let's say, for example, that every night while driving home from work this past week you drove through clouds of skunk spray. This is an encounter. You get home and you turn on the Discovery channel and there is a program on skunks. You flip the channel to the cartoon network, and there is *Pepe LePew.* You walk into a store and there are stuffed skunk toys jumping out at you. These are encounters, and we have a responsibility to study them.

If we treat these meetings as significant, we must then do some studying. Skunks are part of a group of mammals called the *mustelids*—the weasel family. We are talking about weasels, ferrets, badgers, otters, wolverines, martins, and skunks. They all give off a strong musk fragrance. The skunk just gives it off more intensely.

Most animals have nothing to ever fear from a skunk. They usually have only one run-in with one. Rarely is this encounter deadly, but it is most memorable.

Skunks are fairly polite creatures. If they feel threatened or startled, they give warnings. The

first thing they do is raise their tails and pound their front feet on the ground. This warning. means, "Go away." If this display is not heeded, it gives a second warning. It turns its back to you. This means, "Really, I'm not kidding. Go away!"

The third thing it will do, if the second warning is not heeded, is look over its shoulder. And it looks for the face. It only needs a single glance of the face and then it sprays with great accuracy as much as 10 to 15 feet, 5 to 6 times.

If skunk has shown up in our lives, we may need to look at issues of boundaries. If our boundaries are being intruded upon, give a warning. Give it a second time, if necessary. And then let them have it.

The difficulty, though, is in determining the significance of our encounters. Is the animal just part of our normal environment? Or does it have a more direct message for us? And if it does, how do we interpret the meaning of animals within our lives? This is not always easy to determine. This book and its predecessor will help, but the answers are not always readily apparent. Learning any language can be time consuming, and when it comes to a symbolic language, we must guard against superstition.

Sometimes the answers will be apparent. That skunk that has shown up in our life may not have to do with boundaries. It may simply be saying we need to take a bath. Start with the obvious and then move to the more complex.

Animal

NATURAL FORECASTERS

By observing animal behaviors, we can get advance indications of weather changes. When my hawks become more ravenous with their food, eating more and more quickly when fed, it is always an indication their will be a change in the weather. The mistle thrush is known as the "storm cock" because it often sings from a tree top in windy weather. The arrival of swallows indicate summer is on its way. Some observations of animal weather casters have become a part of folklore:

- *When the swallows fly high, it will be dry.*
- *If the cows are lying down, it will rain.*
- *A good autumn for fruit means a hard winter to follow.*

Wonders

Most animals that show up will apply to our life on more than a superficial level. The meanings are frequently multidimensional, reflecting things going on in our life on several levels. Begin by asking some significant questions:

- When we have an encounter with the animal, examine what we were focused upon at that time. What were we doing or thinking about at that time?

- What have we been most focused upon in the couple of hours prior to the encounter? In the previous 24 hours?

- What major issues have been occurring within our life?

Sometimes it will be readily apparent as to what the animal applies. Other times it will require some effort. By studying the animal and its qualities in relation to people and issues in your life, we begin the process of determining its significance.

Sometimes our encounters are little more than environmental ones. The animals are a part of our living environment and thus our seeing them may not have a specific, spiritual message. This does not mean they aren't significant. Sometimes animals are a part of our life simply as reminders of the wonders that exist in Nature.

Do not disregard the importance of animals we see everyday in our environment. Those animals living in the same environment we do are doing so successfully. Thus, they can teach us how to live more successfully within that same environment.

How do we tell the difference between animals encountered because they are part of our own living environment and those that may actually be our spirit animals and totems and have a more specific importance to us at the time? Or are they one and the same thing? Experience is

the key, and sometimes it is just developing that "inner knowing." There are, though, two tangible signals that can help us.

1.   **Look for unusual and out-of-the-ordinary behaviors.**

      I am around a lot of animals every day—a wide variety of wild life. Because of this, I sometimes need the animal to stand out in a unique way through its appearance or behavior so that I know it is significanct.

2.   **If the animal is significant, it will make its presence known in different ways upon more than one occasion and these encounters will occur in close proximity to each other.**

      For example, seeing an owl is very rare. They are nocturnal and they are very well camouflaged. Hearing an owl is a much more common experience. To see an owl, especially during the day, is a real strong indicator that the animal has an important message for us. And if this happens several times over a week or so, then it is significant.

Animals and the Seasons

➤Pay close attention to the season in which you have your animal encounter. Some animals are procreative at specific times of the year and their appearance may indicate new fertility in some area. Some animals are more aggressive at certain times of the year. By studying your animal and its natural life cycles, you can determine much about the animal's role in your life and its message to you. (See Chapter 3 for more information on the animal's life cycle.)

Seasons do affect animals and how likely we are to have encounters with them. Each season has its own spirit or feel to it. Animals face unique conditions with each season and must adapt to

them accordingly. Examine how the animal that has appeared to you adapts to the season you are in. Most of the time, this adaptation will work for you in your own endeavors throughout this same season.

Animals face the same problems as plants in the winter. Water may be difficult to find; food is in short supply. In addition, warm-blooded creatures must conserve heat and must have shelter. How an animal survives the winter often provides directions as to how we can best manage through that season or when we feel winter has come upon us, whether it is by the calendar or not.

In the spring, as the days become longer, animals become more active. They prepare homes for young to be born. Migrant birds return to their breeding grounds. Cold-blooded creatures emerge from their winter hibernation as their body temperature rises with the surrounding warmth. Animals, active or appearing in the spring, often herald a coming forth, and provide clues how to initiate new activities.

In late spring and early summer, many animals hatch eggs or give birth to young which must be fed and guarded, and adults are frequently kept busy day and night. Examine your animal's activities during the summer and pattern your own after them. You will find less frustration in your life. Those animals which appear in the summer often reveal the best ways to help things grow and become stronger.

Autumn is the time of year when animals prepare for the winter and those coming into our life during this time of the year provide clues as to the best kind of preparations we can make for the upcoming winter. Animals instinctively know that food will become hard to find, so many animals store food to eat later in the winter. Most grow a thicker fur to help stay warm or build a winter home or den suitable for the cold months ahead.

Exercise

Still-Hunting

It is important that we learn to connect with Nature in a different way. Sometimes we shield ourselves so much that we lose the ability to experience fully. Sometimes we develop such a hectic lifestyle that we forget how to observe the subtleties of life. This is an exercise that can expand our perceptions and awareness of Nature and all of its inhabitants—plant, animal, and mineral. It develops our intuitive connections to all of the natural world.

Still-hunting was practiced in shaman traditions all over the world. Its primary purpose being to observe and learn. The still-hunter would go to a place he or she knew well or felt attracted to, whether a hillside, a meadow, a forest or a pond. There the individual would settle into a quiet, watchful mood. If the arrival had disturbed the wildlife around, the individual would wait patiently until everything returned to normal. Then the still-hunter opens himself or herself to learn from the natural world.

If we wish to become still hunters, we must let the place choose us. We should allow our intuition guide us to a place in order to learn a lesson. We must trust our mood, and once the place is selected, we must become as unobtrusive to the environment as possible. Still-hunting can be practiced anywhere, even in our own back yards. All that it requires is that we remain still and observe.

Let the world go on around you as if you weren't there. If you disturbed the environment upon your arrival, you must be patient. It may take some time before things settle, but it will as long as you remain settled and quiet.

1. **Feel and imagine yourself as part of the environment, a part of the natural surroundings.**

    Imagine yourself as the leaf rustling in the breeze. Feel the ticklish joy of the butterfly as it dances from flower to flower. Let the songs of the birds fill your heart, noting how it affects the body and where.

2. **Quietly observe the various sounds.**

    Note how the insects and animals respond to each other. If you must move and adjust your position for comfort, keep your movements slow and as infrequent as possible. The more still you are, the more likely we are to experience curious animals coming in for a closer look at you.

    Pay attention to how animals and plants use camouflage. Note how they move. Begin to keep a mental log of the number and kinds of insects, plants and animals that you experience.

    Even if you can't identify them at the time, when your still-hunting is over for the day, you can use books and other tools to help you identify them.

Keep a logbook of your still hunting experiences. Keep track of dates animals observed, and other unusual observations. Write down your moods—what you felt as you made your observations. Research fascinating facts about the creatures and plants you saw.

As you practice your still-hunting, you will find yourself becoming increasingly observant, recognizing by intuition the presence of creatures before they become visible to you. You will find yourself seeing more around you than you ever imagined. Remember that the greatest shamans are first and foremost great still-hunters.

Still-Hunting (cont.)

 **Notes**

CHAPTER 2

Spirit Animals and Totems

Part of the shamanic tradition is connecting to the energies of the earth and all life upon it. To assist with this, animal imagery is strongly utilized. In the East, it is said that the way to heaven is through the feet. By connecting with the energies and rhythms of the earth, we give greater impulse to our life.

Animals fascinate people because they provide a spiritual tie to the earth, and can become symbols of great power and energy. There is an unconscious recognition that animals reflect archetypal forces within the world, reminding us of the primal sources from which we came. We can use animal imagery to learn about ourselves and to actualize their related archetypal energies.

Animals serve a great purpose in our spiritual development. In many myths and tales, animals speak, deliver messages, and call the individual to the hero's path of awareness. Animals are a part of the initiation process, leading individuals in and out of the wildernesses of life.

Animal totems and guides assist us in breaking down barriers and opening up to the new. Carl Jung tells us that animals are representatives of the unconscious and all animals belong to Mother Earth. Part of the spiritual quest is to re-establish ties to the Great Mother which may be lost or forgotten within our life.

It is not enough to keep our images autistic and undeveloped. We must breathe new life into them by recognizing that all animal forms and images reflect archetypal forces. These forces have their own qualities and expressions which are evident through the natural behaviors and activities of the animal itself. The importance of this, especially in understanding the significance of our animal encounters, will be explored in the Chapter 3 on the four blessings of every animal.

Though most humans in today's world have lost or ignored the instinctive tie we have to the rhythm and patterns of Nature, each of us can still develop our intuitive ties to enhance our lives. Every animal reflects specific energy patterns and by aligning ourselves with the animal, we align ourselves with the energy pattern that works through it. When we use the animal and its imagery in something as simple as in meditation, we are asking to be drawn into harmony with it

Shamanism teaches us that all forms of life can teach us. By studying and reading about animals, birds, fish, insects, reptiles, amphibians, and more, we learn about the qualities they reflect in our self and our life. This is essential to understand when we discover our true, personal spirit animals and totems. The more we learn of our totems, the more we honor the archetypal energies that affect us through them. Remember that each species has its own unique qualities. An ant may not seem as glamorous as a bear, but an ant is industrious and has a strength that far exceeds its size.

Animal Wonders

PLAYING POSSUM

The Virginia Opossum is known for its ability to feign death in order to survive an attacker. At the approach of danger the opossum goes limp, drooping its head and will even loll its tongue from its open mouth. Although it seems dead and does not even flinch when bitten, the opossum's brain remains fully engaged, ready to seize any chance to escape. Opossums are not the only animals to use this escape tactic; Chameleons and some snakes "play dead" as well.

When we honor an animal, we are honoring the creative essence behind it. We do not have to believe that these animals embody creative intelligence, but there is an archetypal force behind them. When we open and attune to that essence, the force manifests more strongly. The animal then becomes our totem, our power, our medicine, and a symbol of a specific expression of archetypal energy we are inviting and manifesting within our life.

Myths and tales are filled with animal-people who teach, guide, and protect. From Aesop's fables to Navajo tales of Coyote the Trickster to Bushmen tales of the praying mantis, animals and creatures perform in the same way humans do. Although these stories are allegory on one level, they also stimulate the dynamic forces that operate through all kingdoms of life. It is this realization which helped many societies develop their animal mythologies to explain everything from creation to how dreams operate.

One of the most striking examples of this kinds of animal mythology is found in African Bushmen tales of the praying mantis. The stories of Mantis deal with the time when animals and birds were supernatural beings that later would become what they are today. Mantis was a kind of dreaming Bushman endowed with supernatural powers, along with human qualities. He taught the Kalahari Bushmen that big things come from the small, and thus they paid great attention to everything in their dreams.

Mantis worked his magic through other person-animals. When disaster was impending, Mantis would always have a dream that revealed what to do and the disaster would be averted. If danger threatened Mantis, it would form wings and fly to water. Water was a symbol of life to the Bushmen, but it is also an archetypal symbol for the dream world. Mantis had the ability to bring the dead back to life, and thus there arose a

Animal Imagery

strong belief that dreams could restore lives as well. Animals in myths and in life serve as symbols of those things which we have not expressed or even acknowledged. If we discover our spirit animals and totems, they can guide us in waking and dreaming.

➤Animal images and encounters are valid signposts within our life. Discovering the meanings is sometimes difficult, but there is no doubt that they stimulate some primordial part of our imagination. They help liberate the mind, opening us to possibilities beyond our daily routines. Through them, we become aware of what Jean Houston refers to as the *lure of becoming*.

There was a time when humanity saw itself as part of Nature and Nature as part of it. Dreaming and waking were inseparable. Animals and humans were inseparable. The natural and the supernatural do merge and blend. Shamans used the symbols and images of animals and Nature to express this unity and to instill a transpersonal kind of experience. Animal totems help us to see ourselves as part of the universe.

A totem is any natural object, being, or animal with which we feel closely associated and whose phenomena and energy are related to our life in some way. Some totems reflect energies operating for only short periods of time. Other totems remain with us from birth, through death, and beyond and become personal symbols and forces for integration, expression, and transformation.

Animals play a particularly strong role in our unconscious symbology, reflecting the emotional life of humanity, often mirroring back to us qualities of our own nature that must be overcome, controlled, and re-expressed as a tool of power. Animals are symbols of the archetypal power we can learn to draw upon when pure reason no longer serves us. Adopting the guise of

animals by wearing their skins and feathers or wearing a mask made to honor them symbolizes endowing ourselves with their primordial wisdom and instinct.

TERRESTRIAL ANIMALS are often symbols of fertility and creativity that must be re-manifested in our evolutionary process. Each species has its own characteristics and powers to remind us of the archetypal powers we must learn to manifest more consciously. They are bridges between the natural and the supernatural, awakening us to the realities of both.

BIRDS in myths and tales are often symbols of the soul. Their ability to fly reflects our ability to rise to new awareness by connecting the physical realms with those of the sky (heavens). Birds link the waking with the dreaming. We are all given to flights of fancy; a phrase often used to describe our dreams and imaginations. As totems and spirit animals, each bird has its own peculiar characteristics, but they all can be aids for inspiration, hope, and new ideas.

Animal

WISE
POLAR BEARS

Though polar bears need fresh drinking water just as humans do, fresh water is very difficult to find in the winter Artic lands and ice-covered seas, Polar bears discovered a way to exist surrounded by ice-covered, salty sea water. Since salt will eat through the ice in time, polar bears seek out old ice flows and drink from the puddles of sweet water on top. It is often believed that the early Arctic explorers were able to survive without fresh water sources by observing the polar bears at this activity.

Wonders

AQUATIC LIFE serves a role as a dynamic totem, connecting us to the reality of the dream life, sleeping or waking. Water is a symbol of the astral plane experience, much of which reflects itself in our dreams. The many myths of life springing from primordial waters return us to our origins. Water is the creative element, reflecting the feminine archetype of the Divine Mother.

It is the feminine, the intuitive, and the creative that is brought to life when we dream or

imagine. The moon, a symbol of the feminine, controls the tides upon the earth, and aquatic life teaches us about the tides at play in our own life on many levels.

Various fish and other forms of aquatic life make dynamic totems. Although they were left out of my earlier book, *Animal-Speak*, it was not for lack of their importance. In ancient myths, tales, and religious teachings they often symbolize guidance from our intuitive aspects. One of the most powerful totem fetishes is the shell. The shell reflects the powers of water and the feminine force and is often a symbol of the journey across the sea to a new life and the sounding forth of new life, like the trumpeting on a conch shell.

INSECTS AND ARACHNIDS are also a powerful part of Nature. They make strong totems and spirit animals, many having ancient mythological histories. Most people look upon insects as pests, but they serve a powerful purpose in the chain of life through their unique qualities, reflecting archetypal influences with which we can align.

REPTILES AND AMPHIBIANS are some of the most ancient creatures on this planet. As cold-blooded creatures, they are affected by whatever the temperature of the environment might be. Their appearance often tells us of our sensitivity to the world around us and our ability to adapt. Amphibians, living part of their life on land and part in water, inhabit two worlds and can help us develop our ability to blend realms (physical and spiritual, male and female, waking and sleeping).

Part of working with Nature and animals is to break down outworn preconceptions. Hopefully this book will help you with this.

Important Common Threads

➤When we examine what has been taught in different traditions about spirit animals and totems, we find amazing similarities, common threads that run through all traditions. These common threads provide tremendous insight into animals, Nature, and our relationship to them.

All traditions taught that each animal has a spirit. We do not have to believe that the animal has a creative intelligence, but we can accept that some spiritual force has brought that animal into our life, reflecting some archetypal energy. Oftentimes our spirit guides and angels will take the form of an animal to help us understand the role they will play in our life. Only by studying these animals will we truly come to know this.

All traditions taught that no animal is any better, any more spiritual than any other animal. Every animal has qualities that are unique, and the animal that has appeared in our life has done so because its qualities will work best for us at that time. In Western society there is a tendency to glamorize certain animals to think some are more spiritual and better than others are.

When I teach workshops on *Animal-Speak* and *The Animal-Wise Tarot*, I occasionally hear some participants say they don't like certain animals for their totems, such as vultures and ants. Although the vulture is not a glamorous animal, it serves an important function of cleaning the environment, feeding on the dead, and helping to prevent the spread of disease. The vulture's unique digestive system elicits a chemical that serves as a bactericide, enabling it to derive nutrition from what it is eating. In this way, vultures can teach us about life, death, rebirth, and ultimate fulfillment.

Ants are very strong and capable of more than their size would indicate. They also demonstrate great discipline and order within their communities, each having its own role and tasks. An ant's appearance as a totem could indicate a need to review more seriously our own spiritual role in life and how to express it within the mundane world. So when it comes to spirit animals and

Common Threads Among All Traditions

Each animal has a spirit.

No animal is any better or any more spiritual than any other animal.

Each animal has a power or medicine.

We can have more than one spirit animal and totem.

We must develop a relationship with the animal.

totems, we have to get rid of our preconceptions. Only by truly studying the animal can we do this.

All traditions taught that the animal has a power or medicine. Every animal has its own unique qualities and talents, using these abilities and skills for survival. An animal's appearance is a reminder to us that we have those same abilities. We may have an animal for a day, a month, or a lifetime. We may have an animal show up to help us make decisions or to show us the proper course of action, helping us to see the qualities we need to be developing right now.

All traditions taught that we could have more than one spirit animal and totem. We will have several LIFETIME or POWER animals. Our spirit animals will always be plural because nothing exists in Nature by itself. The interconnectedness of all things in the natural world is described as *trophism*—the grass absorbs the sunlight, the grasshopper feeds off the grass., the frog eats the grasshopper, the snake eats the frog, and the hawk eats the snake. Everything is tied to everything else. We always want to look at what the animal eats and what eats it.

All traditions taught that you must develop a relationship with the animal. You must honor it, Begin by learning as much about it as possible. What are its characteristics, behaviors, adaptations, etc.? You must find out what it can do and what it cannot do. Just because the animal has appeared in your life does not mean it is now your best friend. Building relationships takes time. You must find your own unique way of working with the animal and its qualities.

I have worked with hawks and other animals for a longtime, from both a hands-on and spiritual perspective. Yes, all hawks have similar qualities and characteristics, but in establishing your relationship with any hawk, you must find your own way of working with the animal. My way of working with hawks is unique. And yours must be

so as well. You must find how to apply the hawk energy and its qualities uniquely into your own life. Once you establish a good relationship with one animal, it opens the door for establishing relationships with others more easily. Every animal that comes into your life will add something new, something the others cannot provide.

Identifying Spirit Animals and Totems

➤ As we further examine what was taught in many traditions regarding spirit animals and totems, we also find similiarities in how to determine what our spirit animals and totems are. These common teachings hold true today and will provide a starting point in working more intimately with animals and all of Nature.

A totem is anything of the natural world that has significance for us. It can be an animal, a flower, a tree, a stone, or anything of Nature. In this book, we will focus on spirit animals and animal totems, the language of animals as messengers, and understanding their meaning in our lives.

In the native culture of the U.S. and among modern urban shamanic groups is the idea that to know one's true totem or spirit animal, we must perform a vision quest. This is a powerful ritual with many benefits, only one of which involves encountering our spirit animals. There are easier ways of determining and finding our own spirit animals. We can begin by examining the animals that have always fascinated us and and drawn our interest. An old axiom teaches, "like attracts like." We are drawn to the animal that resonates with us on some level. Particularly examine the animals you were drawn to as a child (whether from television, zoos, nature centers or other sources).

If you have children, examine the animals they are drawn to. Take them to a zoo or nature center. At the end of the visit, what animals are they most excited about having seen? If you have more than one child, they will frequently be drawn to

different animals. By studying and examining these animals, we are able to gain unique insight into our children's individual personalities and creativeness.

Every tradition also taught that if we dream of an animal, it is the same as having actually encountered it while awake. We need to treat the appearance of an animal in our dreams just as significantly. We should study it. The nice thing about dream animals is that by looking at where the dream scenario took place and who else was in it, we can get an idea as to what part of our life this animal applies.

Examine the animals in your own back yard or immediate environment. You are living in the same environment as they are. They can thus teach us how to live more successfully within those surroundings.

Most traditions around the world also taught that the animals we fear are also our potential totem guides. Our fears and doubts take the form of an animal, and until we come to terms with them, we are not whole. We cannot walk through life without casting a shadow. One of the best things to do in cases of a fear is to go to the children's section of the library. Most children's books on animals present their outstanding characteristics, and they do so while playing down the fear aspect. This doesn't mean we must learn to cuddle up with animals we might fear, but by studying them, we can learn how to apply their unique qualities within our own life.

Keep in mind that many of our fears of animals are social fears passed on to us through society. At the nature center, I always loved doing snake presentations. It provided a wonderful opportunity to break down misconceptions. One of the more common is the belief that snakes are slimy. They are not slimy; they have a shininess due to their scales.

Our snake presentations were sometimes per-formed in a room with a tile floor. I would have the kids rub the palms of their hands back and forth across the floor. These tile floors got a lot of traffic, gathered a lot of dirt, and when the kids held up their hands, they were always dirty (cre-ating groans of dismay from the parents and teachers). I would then take the tail of the snake and swipe it across the floor. Then I would wipe it with a white cloth. There would be no dirt on it! First of all, this shows the group that humans are slimier than snakes. And secondly, it helps teach them that if the snakes had any moisture on them, they would not be able to move and slither through the grass and dirt.

At the end of the program, we would always allow the kids to pet the snake to further dissipate those old beliefs. And every once in a while, when the snake was held out to an adult with the kids, we would hear, "Oh no, this is the kids time. Let them pet it." Well, this sends a message that a snake is still something to be feared. Parents and others indirectly pass on many of their fears to us in our society.

Nothing dissipates fear better than knowledge and wonder. Hopefully, through this book and its exercises, we all will come to understand the ani-mals we encounter more fully. We will recognize that feeling of wonder, the stirring of the soul, as it increasingly awakens to the archetypal forces of Nature.

Exercise

Establishing Animal Relationships

BENEFITS

- appreciation

- increased subtle recognition of animals

- opening the heart to the blessings of Nature

- increased opportunities to become an animal guardian

Many speak to me of wanting to attune more personally to animals and Nature. I am often asked if I do intensive one-on-one work with individuals (if I take personal students under my wing). My answer is always no. The reasons for this are many (most having to do with my not having much free time for my own personal studies, teachings, and writings and has nothing to do with "wanting to keep the secrets to myself.")

Although many may believe I have some special secret or gift for attuning to animals and Nature, it is nothing more than taking the time and energy to do so. This starts with opening the senses and heightening the powers of observation. There are no magickal tricks, per se. I did not find tablets from some divine source with secret animal communication knowledge inscribed upon them.

A recent survey estimated that the average person spends less than an hour per week outdoors. This is amazing to me. We live in a society in which people remain indoors for most of their activities. How many people do we know that have treadmills placed in front of a window so they can watch the outdoors from indoors while they run? Granted, weather does affect how much we can get outdoors, but there is no way to truly open to communing with animals and Nature without being outdoors.

Exercise

That doesn't mean our houseplants and pets have no benefit and can't help us, but if we truly wish to connect with wildlife on a deeper level, we have to go where the wildlife is, which can only be done by spending time outside (even in one's own backyard).

Fresh air is essential to our overall health, but it is essential for spiritual reasons as well. It opens the pores and our senses, strengthening and cleansing them. Being outdoors regularly is critical to heightening our senses, whether we live in a city or rural environment. Even if we live in the city, which houses a tremendous amount of wildlife, we can do a variety of things outdoors to help open our senses more fully and encourage greater experiences with animals.

Remember, Nature talks to us all of the time, and if we start listening and paying attention, we can gain some wonderful insight into our activities and our life processes. In the next chapter are exercises for getting answers and guidance through animals and Nature, but there are a number of things we can do to help re-establish our relationship with Mother Nature and strengthen the communications from her.

The following list provides simple ways of opening to the animal kingdom within your own living environment. It is a way of inviting the animals more strongly into your life. It will heighten your senses. You will become increasingly more aware of their presence through senses other than sight.

Perform some of these, and you will not only find yourself spending more time outdoors but also experiencing increasing animal wonders. Keep in mind that although the animals you experience as a result of some of these things may not be your power animal or totem, they are still important. By connecting with one aspect of Nature, it becomes increasingly easier to connect with all other aspects.

Establishing Animal Relationships (cont.)

1. **Involve yourself with some aspect of Nature more personally.**

   Plant a garden. Allow an area of your yard to grow wild so that the wild can take up residence within it. Become an amateur naturalist. Do some bird watching. Create a pond. Seek out marshlands. Take night hikes. Try to identify birds by their call and trees by their leaves.

   Take regular walks in Nature. You will be surprised at what you will encounter and experience with walks around your neighborhood or in parks. For many years, I lived in the city, but I always ran and walked my dogs around a certain route. About a year and a half before I moved, my wife discovered a family of albino squirrels in the area I had passed countless times without ever noticing. There is a tremendous amount of wildlife even in the city, but there is no chance of encountering any of it unless you get outside. What you encounter changes with each season!

2. **Support local animal shelters, humane societies, nature centers and zoos.**

   These non-profit organizations are always in need of assistance. For many years my wife and I volunteered at a nature center. Some think of it as glamorous, often believing that it will give them a chance to play and cuddle with animals. Often these individuals are disillusioned when they have to clean up animal droppings and perform other very unglamorous acts.

   Most centers need help so that they can do more of what they do best. They are often overworked and understaffed. We approached it from the perspective that we would do whatever was necessary to free up the full-time employees and interns. If you cannot volunteer time, then donate some money periodically.

3. **Study about animals and Nature.**

   One of the best things to do in opening to the animal world is to learn more about it. Study a different animal each week. In one year you will have learned a significant amount about 52 animals.

Exercise

Go to the library and get several books on the animal. Begin with animals found around your home or animals that have always fascinated you. You may even wish to keep a log on unusual and amazing facts about it.

4. **Meditate out in Nature.**

Send thoughts and prayers to Mother Nature, asking for signs and communications. Quiet the mind in your backyard or a nearby park and pay attention to what you feel, smell, hear, and see. Feel yourself become one with Nature. Try and feel the heartbeat of Nature resonating through you and your own heart beating to its rhythm.

Choose different environments for your meditations. Mediate under a tree or next to a pond. Sit quietly and contemplate the riverbed. Feel the warmth of the sun on a stone as you sit calmly. Lie back in the grass, breathing deeply of the sweet air and fragrance. Feel your body upon the Earth, balancing, grounding, and healing.

Perform walking meditations, especially at dawn and dusk. Feel the sacredness of the Earth and the softness of all life. With each step you will find yourself more attuned than ever before.

5. **Listen for and acknowledge Nature's daily greetings to you.**

When you are outside, even when just stepping out for a few moments, try to pay attention to what stands out for you. It may be a crow cawing to you. It may be a fragrance from a tree. Nature usually greets us in some way every time we step outside for a bit.

The more you acknowledge Nature with responses, the stronger the greetings become. If a bird speaks as you step out, mimic its greeting back to it. If a crow caws, caw back. If you are uncomfortable doing this, then just say something like, "Hello, friend crow." If the fragrance of a tree or flower catches your attention, greet it in return.

Some people are uncomfortable doing these kinds of things, worried about what others might say or think. I usually operate under the assumption that

Establishing Animal Relationships (cont.)

Exercise

Establishing Animal Relationships (cont.)

most people think I'm a little weird. (I know; it is hard to believe, isn't it?) If I am out walking and my neighbors see me saying hello to a tree, they usually just roll their eyes, pull their kids inside, and wait until I move on. But I don't worry about their response. I am being courteous and answering the greeting that was given to me.

6. **Plant a promise tree.**

    A tree is a living creature. It eats, rests, breathes, and even circulates its "blood" while providing a home and shelter for animal life. A tree also provides shade, prevents erosion of the soil, and is critical for habitat. Thus the planting of the tree is the planting of a promise to be a guardian of animals and Nature.

    As you care for and nourish the tree, the care and nourishment of Nature toward you will grow stronger. And even if the tree should die, your efforts will not be in vain. In Nature, even the dying trees provide shelter and food for insects and other plant life. When working with nature, every effort is a promise from you to Mother Nature and she always rewards the efforts.

7. **Read animal tales and myths from different traditions and countries.**

    In every society, there were individuals whose task it was to keep the ancient mysteries alive and to pass them on by word of mouth. These people were the storytellers. Through myths and tales, they guided individuals into new wonders and possibilities. They parted the veils of mysteries.

    By reading the tales and myths of animals from different parts of the world, several things will happen. First, you will begin to recognize common teachings about the animals and their qualities. Second, you will begin to see some of the spiritual qualities and thoughtforms that are associated with animals.

    Myths and tales touch us on many levels. They provide a tool for life direction and nudge us to ever-greater exploration of life's mysteries. They open us to possibilities. Through tales and myths of

animals, we open more fully to the colors of the archetypes they represent in our life.

8. Be ever grateful.

The other day I happened to glance out my front window on the way upstairs to my office. When I did, I froze. Shuffling across my front yard from out of the woods was a bevy of quail. I called to my wife and ran from window to window, pressing my face against the glass. I was like a little boy at Christmas.

Yes, I've seen quail before, but being surprised by them so close to the house just thrilled me. I watched, transfixed, as they moved as a group down the yard. Several times over the next week I encountered them. I returned from a trip to have the quail shuffle across my drive on their way back into the woods. As I was running with one of my dogs, I scared the group and it flew up out of the tall grasses in the field.

Each time I was just as excited as the first. My heart beat stronger. I felt lighter. And throughout the rest of the day I would pause in wonder, reflecting on them. Their appearance surprised me each time, but they also made my day a little more wonderful (a little more full of wonder).

That feeling is a feeling of gratefulness. When we have encounters, they stir wonder in us, and that stirring makes our day a little brighter and more fulfilled. That feeling we get is an expression of gratitude.

When we breathe deeply in the morning and enjoy the sweet air, whether we speak it or not, that appreciation is an expression of gratitude. Our excitement at spotting the hawk perched on the telephone pole or the woodpecker drumming on a nearby tree is a form of gratitude. If we take time to enjoy these moments, we express our gratitude.

The more we appreciate the little experiences of Nature and animals, the more frequently they come into our life. The experiences grow, increasing our wonder even more.

Exercise

Establishing Animal Relationships (cont.)

Exercise

BENEFITS

- stimulates dreams of animals

- uncovers animal totems

- discerns where the animal applies in your life

- increases vibrancy of dreams

- discovers the animal that can guide you through the dream world

Dream Totems

This meditation exercise will help you discover your animal totems through your dreams. It is a beneficial exercise for healing groups seeking their totem guides. The mythic imagery in this exercise will stimulate dream activity, especially when performed sometime in the evening or before going to sleep. Even if you fall asleep during this exercise, when performed for three days in a row, it will often stimulate dreams of animals . The people and places within the dream scenario provide clues as to where the animal energies should be applied within your life.

As in all meditations, music and fragrances can enhance the effects. Drums and rattles are connected to the heartbeat of the earth and are very important to incorporate in this shaman-type journey for the best results:

> In aboriginal drumming, it is the echo of the drumbeat that is important, for they say that the sound circulates around the mountaintops where the reverberation bumps the spirits surviving on cosmic planes, circles around the mountains back to the human world. And of course it helps the shaman to enter the expanded state of consciousness. Thus the drum is a tool for journeying in the dream time in order to perform certain kinds of work...[1]

---
[1] Dr. Nandisvara Nayake Thero. "The Dreamtime Mysticism and Liberation: Shamanism in Australia," in *Shamanism*. Shirley Nicholson, ed., (Wheaton, Illinois: Theosophical Publishing House, 1987), p.227.

The drumbeat should be slow and steady, and the participants should allow the drumbeat to lead them. Riding the drumbeat to the dream world is part of all shamanic experiences. With practice, it is easy to allow the drumbeat to escort you to the inner realms. You may even wish to use an audiotape of a drumbeat to assist in the dream work.

Individuals sometimes wonder if they are experiencing a true shamanic journey. The difference between a meditation and a true journey is the depth of the experience. In the journey, we are actually in it, feeling it and experiencing it first hand. It also will not always follow a prescribed pattern. On the other hand, in meditation exercises, we often observe ourselves experiencing the situation or imagine how it should be experienced. Imaging practices and meditation exercises lead to an ability to immerse ourselves fully into the midst of the experience. We become part, rather than just playing a part. The meditation aspects lead us to the control and experience of true shamanic journeys.

Make preparations before performing the exercise. You may wish to use a favorite fragrance (essential oil or incense). Make sure you will not be disturbed. If you have a drum or rattle, you may use it, or find a favorite drum selection. Make sure it is slow and steady. Perform a progressive relaxation, sending each part of the body warm and relaxed thoughts and feelings. The more relaxed you are, the better the exercise will work.

If you are using this exercise before bedtime, read through the scenario several times so it is firmly implanted in the mind. This way, if you fall asleep during the process, it will still work for you through the dream state.

As you relax, pull your energies and attention into yourself. You are going to go deep into yourself to find

Exercise

the totem that lives there to serve as your dream guide. Imagine yourself standing in a wide field. The air is still and there is calmness around you. The moon has already risen. It is dusk, that powerful time between day and night. It is the sacred time when the sun and moon share the sky. It is when day and night mingle. It is the intersection of light and dark, waking and sleeping.

Before you stands a tall oak tree. Its bark is gnarled and twisted. Its roots extend deep into the heart of the Earth. Its branches block your view of the sky as you stand beneath it. You are unable to see its uppermost branches.

There is a small opening at its base, just large enough to squeeze through if you bend slightly. With one last look toward the setting sun, you step carefully into the inner darkness of the tree. There is the smell of moss and moist wood. As you squeeze through the narrow opening, you find that it widens as you move further within as if it is adjusting to you. Soon you are able to stand erect, and you breathe a little easier.

Your hands reach out in the darkness, touching the inner side of the bark. It is warm to the touch and you are sure you can feel its lifeblood flowing through it. You pull your hands away from the bark and pause, catching your breath and summoning your courage to inch further into the darkness. It is then that you hear a faint sound.

At first the sound is hardly discernible. You hold perfectly still to insure that the sound is not your own movement. It is soft, but as you move forward, feeling your way into the darkness, the sound grows louder. It is the sound of a distant drum. In the darkness of the inner tree, the sound is hollow and primal. For a moment you imagine that it is the heartbeat of the Tree itself.

The beat is slow and steady, and yet its hollow tone touches the core of you. It coaxes you through the dark and deeper into the tree itself. It is hypnotic, and you know that it is sounding forth that which you have awaited a long time. You are not sure what it will be.

You have never been sure, but you know you will recognize the reality of it when confronted with it.

You go forward; knowing it is better to continue than to return. You are beginning to feel as if you are in a dream that has its own reality. As you move further in, you notice it grows lighter inside the tree. At first you are not sure whether it is due to your eyes adjusting to the darkness or whether something new is being introduced into this walking dream.

Ahead of you a soft torch is burning, illuminating the path you are upon. Now you can see that the path ahead is narrow. And you can see the inner sides of the tree. Its sides are steep and ridged with inner veins and arteries. You begin to understand. Lifeblood runs warmly through all living things. You find this comforting.

As you approach the torch, you find it is at the top of a steep, descending path. Sporadic torches, leading down into that which can only be experienced directly, illuminate it. You place your feet carefully, as the steps down are covered with a slick moss. Fortunately, the illumination grows brighter with each step downward.

The path spirals down, leading you deeper into the heart of the planet. You feel as if you are following the roots of the tree to the very core of the Earth, to the center of life. You know you are being led to a primal point of life and energy within yourself. You feel as if it is all to help you connect with your own roots.

The drumbeat has grown to a steady volume. It has become a part of your own rhythm—or you have become a part of it. You are not sure which is true. As you descend, another sound begins to reach you, enticing you even more deeply into the heart of life itself. It is the sound of running water. A stream maybe, or a waterfall. It is not quite discernible.

It is then that you see the end of this tunnel you have descended. Ahead of you is a cave-like opening. You step through the opening into sunshine that is warm and bright. It feels as if you have stepped out of the womb into new life.

Exercise

Sparkling sunlight and the soft greens of nature surround you. In the distance, a crystalline river runs through what appears to be the heart of the meadow. Wildflowers of every color and fragrance fill your senses with their beauty. The grass is emerald, and at the edge of the meadow is a forest of rich dark greens, the color of primeval Nature at its purest.

You move into the meadow, allowing the sun to fill your body with a fire that warms and soothes, chasing away all fears. You breathe deeply, filling your lungs with air that is sweet and fresh. You had almost forgotten how wonderful breathing could be.

You move to the edge of the river, and you watch hypnotically as it flows over rocks, creating eddies and spirals of myriad shapes. The sun glints off the water in rainbow hues. You look down the river and you see it widen and spill out into the deep blues of the ocean. All waters are here. You bend down and gently cup your hand, dipping it into the water, bringing the cool elixir to your mouth. It quenches your thirst and refreshes your body.

Next to the river is a large stone shaped a little like a chair. You sit down upon it, feeling how the sun has warmed it. From here you can take in the entire meadow. You are filled with a sense of peace. You do not remember the last time you felt this relaxed. Surely there could be no better place to get in touch with yourself. This is a place where dreams meet reality. Here you may connect with your inner core. Here you can discover the power that is yours to claim in life.

Your eyes look over the area (the river, the distant ocean, the meadow, and the forest). And then your breath catches. As if in response to your thoughts, there is a movement. It may come from the waters. It may come winging across the sky. It may emerge from the woods or rise up out of the tall grasses of the meadow. You sit, afraid to move, eyes widening with wonder as a beautiful animal appears in your vision. Its eyes seek you out and hold your gaze. As it looks into your eyes

and you into its, you realize that this magnificent creature has your eyes!

Never have you seen anything so wonderful, so unique. Such animals have always seemed so wild, so alien, so out of touch. But there is no fear. There is only recognition and wonder. Surely, this must be a dream!

Again, as if in response to your thoughts, it makes a sound, a movement, a gesture indicating its own unique power and strength. You are awestruck.

And then it disappears.

You stand, looking about you. Had you been dreaming? Was it all your imagination? Had you fallen asleep on the stone? You scan the woods, the meadow, and the skies. You look to the waters.

Nothing.

Had you done something to offend it? You are confused, unsure. It was so beautiful, so noble, such a unique expression of life. It deserved to be honored and respected—not just by you but by all of humanity.

A trumpeting that echoes through the meadow shatters your thoughts. You turn toward the mouth of the cave through which you came into the meadow. There, in the inner darkness of the opening, is the outline of your animal. Its image freezes briefly, its eyes holding yours once more. Then it fades, disappears once more.

You laugh with relief, beginning to understand. As you give it honor and respect, its energies will grow stronger in your life. Its energies are yours to claim, but they can only be claimed through honor, love, and respect.

As you reach the opening, there on the ground in front of you lies a large conch shell. This is a gift for you. It is a symbol of the calling forth of new energy and life. The trumpeting is a reminder that new life can be called forth to enable you to walk at one with Nature—in the waking and in the dreamtime.

You pick up the conch shell, and with a silent prayer of thanks, step back into the cave. Now it is well lit and its path is wide and clear. In the distance you

Exercise

Dream Totems (cont.)

Exercise

(cont.) Dream Totems

see your newfound guide, leading the way. Before long you see the light that leads you from the tree itself.

As you step from the tree, the sun is beginning to rise. It is now dawn, and the moon is still visible. Your guide is before you and as you look upon it, it shimmers and melts into you. With your next breath you feel it come alive within you, and there is no doubt that with every breath its essence and energy will become stronger in your life. You feel balanced and blessed. You are beginning to understand that as you claim your own power, as you connect with your true self, your path will become clearer and more easily managed.

You raise the conch shell to your mouth and you trumpet a new awakening. Three times the sound issues forth, and as it does, the scene around you fades, but it disappears from the inner vision only so it may be called forth into the outer. It fades from the dreamtime to trumpet within the waking.

Part I   **Animal-Wise**

CHAPTER 3

The Four Blessings of Every Creature

Over many years of teaching in both the psychic and holistic field, specifically when teaching the language of animals, I have found a tendency for many people to be superstitious or superficial when interpreting the meaning of animals and other aspects of Nature. What is sometimes lost, even among modern shaman groups, is the actual studying of the animals. And yet we are living in a time in which we know more about animals and their behaviors than at any other time in the history of humanity.

The actual scientific and behavioral study of animals does not mean that we lose the mystical aspect. Actually, it will deepen our wonder, making our interpretations so much more accurate. There is an old superstition about Valentine's Day concerning birds. Whatever bird we first see on February 14th will indicate what kind of person we will eventually marry. If it is a black bird or crow, the person will be serious, somber, and maybe a little mystical. If it is a goldfinch, the person will be wealthy. If it is a cardinal, the person will be full of vitality and sexuality. If it is a woodpecker, we will never get married.

This, of course, is a superstition and has nothing to do with the animal or any basic knowledge of it. Every society and tradition taught that if an animal showed up in our life (whether for real, in

a vision, or in a dream), our first responsibility was to study the animal and to learn as much about that animal as possible. Only then could we know its significance and meaning within our life. This doesn't mean that we should study every animal we see. In the course of a single day we may see numerous animals. But when we have encounters that repeat themselves, we should pay attention. These appearances are an indication this animal is important to some part of our life.

When we start having multiple encounters in a relatively short period of time, we should pay extra attention to them.Everything about the animal (its color, habitat, behaviors, and indigenous environment) has significance. The more we know about the animal, the more accurately we can interpret the meaning of its appearance. The animal has shown up in our life for a reason. Sometimes the reason is nothing more than a greeting. Sometimes it is the answer to our problems. Once we begin to realize that the encounter has significance for us, we must then work to determine what the significance is. This is where study comes in.

The Four Blessings

➤ There are four lessons every animal can teach us, lessons that are the animal's blessings to us and can serve as a mirror to show us what we need to do to be more successful. If we study and learn nothing else about the animal other than these four things, we will find out lives greatly enhanced.

Every animal has its own life cycle and rhythm.

➤ **1**. Study the life cycle and rhythm of the animal to learn the times it is more active, the times it is least active, and the times when it is more sexual and procreative. Some animals are *nocturnal* (night time) and some are *diurnal* (daytime). Determine the animal's natural life rhythms.

As late fall, early winter approaches, for example, the black bear will slow down its outer activity and go into its den. This is when the mother bear gives birth to the young (usually two, sometimes three cubs). In the spring she brings them out into the open. The young cubs will often stay with the mother for two years before they go off on their own.

If you have bears showing up in your life, as fall and winter approaches, slow down the outer activities. Go into your den and focus on two, maybe three projects. In the spring, bring them out into the open, but look for those projects to take maybe two years before they reach maturity and come to full fruition for you. This is the rhythm that will help us succeed and is one of the reasons the bear has shown up. When we use the rhythm of the animal, life flows more easily and with less frustration. We are putting our life into a more powerful, universal rhythm.

THE COYOTE

The coyote is one of the most adaptable and smartest of all animals whose territory has spread throughout the United States in spite of hunting and other concentrated efforts to limit its numbers and territory. These efforts have failed because of a lack of understanding of the coyote's adaptive behaviors. In the coyote pack, only the alpha male and female will breed. If either one or both of the alpha animals dies, the rest of the pack will breed uncontrollably. Thus the numbers increase, and the territory expands. This is one way the species ensures its survival.

➤ **2.** Study the adaptive behaviors of the animal. Some have physical adaptations; some have behavioral adaptations. For instance, the fox, particularly the desert fox, has very large ears. This physical adaptation dissipates excess body heat. If you have foxes in your life and are having difficulty with the heat, brush your hair behind your ears. You will notice a difference.

A mule deer never follows the same path to a water source. It knows if it does, it is more likely to end up as some predator's meal. If you have mule deer in your life, don't do the same thing in the same way twice. It won't work for you.

Every animal adapts to survive in the wild.

Crows work together to ward off predators. Whenever hawks or owls show up in crow territory, they will mob the owl to drive it away. Instinctively they know that if given a chance, that predator will have them for a meal. If it is an owl and it finds out where they roost, it will return at night when they cannot defend themselves. For those to whom crow appears, it is a reminder to us not to try and handle opposition and trouble by ourselves. We should enlist the aid of others. For the crow, there is power in numbers.

Remember that the animal has shown up in your life to tell you, "Look, these adaptive behaviors that I have are what will work best for you right now."

Every animal has certain potentials, abilities, and characteristics.

➤ 3. Study the basic potentials and skills of the animal. It has shown up in your life to say, "You have these same potentials and abilities, and these are what will work best for you at this time in your life."

A hawk that misses capturing a rabbit does not pretend it's a weasel and chase it on foot. It must learn to fly faster, strike harder and stronger. Be true to the qualities of the animal. Be true to yourself.

If the animal is a stalking predator such as a large cat, do not be letting others know of your plans. Be silent in your efforts and you will capture your prey (your goals).

All macaws are brightly colored, both the males and females. Potential mates are recognized and attracted by their vibrant, healthy feathers. If you have macaws in your life, dress or perform a little more colorfully to attract the attention necessary to accomplish your goals.

Spiders weave their web and then sit back and let the food come to them. They are economical in their efforts. If spiders have shown up in your life, spin your web and weave your plans; be pa-

THE MEANING OF ENVIRONMENTS

Landscapes and specific kinds of environments have had their own symbology, inhabited by certain kinds of plantlife and wildlife. By examining the landscapes and environments where certain animals live, we can gain even greater insight into the animal's role within our life.

DESERTS: hidden life; adaptation; ability to use resourcesavailable; hardiness and struggles; purification.

FORESTS: primal feminine; growth free of controls and constrictions; the unconscious mind; magnifying of creative forces.

GARDENS: Nature in miniature and controlled; abilities to create and nurture life; the opening of doors to Nature.

MARSHLAND: emotional stages of life; bringing fresh air into the emotional life; decomposition and new growth

MEADOWS: abundance and fertility; balance of life; place of silent and soft growth;: nourishment

MOUNTAINS: power and loftiness of spirit; discovering our own spiritual powers; outward expression and assertiveness; overcoming obstacles for spiritual attainment; communion with spirits.

OCEANS: the subconscious mind and the primal feminine; the womb, mother, and woman; new tides and depths of possibilities.

PLAINS: openness and freedom; journeys to new homes and possibilities; sensitivity and exposure to new winds and to subtle changes.

RIVERS: creation and the flow of time; gatherings for quenching thirst (spiritual or physical); process of evolution at play; past and future at play.

VALLEYS: fertility and new life; a neutral zone for developing our creativity; mythical home of priest and priestesses.

tient and let things come to you. Do not force them.

The animal is appearing to help you realize what will work most effectively for you. Its appearance is saying, "Pursue things the way I do them and you will more likely succeed."

Every animal shares the environment with other animals.

➤ **4.** The animal that has shown up will also teach us something about the relationships within our life. Take a look at the other animals with which it shares a particular environment. Is it an antagonistic relationship? Is it a tolerant one? Do they completely ignore each other? Then take a look at the people in your life. You will begin to see how best to treat some of the people within your own life's environment.

Animal

TOOL USERS

Humans and chimpanzees are not the only ones to use tools. Many other animals use them to find food, frighten enemies, and build homes. Sea otters will anchor themselves in long strands of sea kelp. They also use stones to open up shellfish. Egyptian vultures use stones to break open ostrich eggs. Cormorants overcome their natural buoyancy by swallowing pebbles when diving for fish. Baboons will throw stones in their own defense and South American spectacled bears use sticks to knock down fruits out of reach. When animals that use tools appear in our life, they teach us how to accomplish our own tasks more effectively.

Wonders

A wonderful example of how animals within the same environment treat each other can be found in the relationship of the badger and the coyote. Both live and hunt in the same territory, and they will frequently cooperate in their hunting. The coyote, with its tremendous sense of smell, can detect prey (mice, rabbits, etc.) when they are underground in tunnels and holes. The badger, with its tremendous digging ability, can dig out the prey even though it may not be able to detect its presence with its less sensitive nose. Thus the coyote smells and the badger digs. They then share the prey.

Look also at the animal's indigenous environment. Different environments reflect different

things. For example, wetlands and marshlands are actually areas of decomposition and new growth. They are places where there is a tearing down of old for new. Those animals found naturally within that environment will help us in tearing down old growth and moving into something new within our own life.

> Let's say, for example, that rabbits are showing up in our life. The rabbit is an animal with a very mixed symbology; most of it based on superstition and misconception. Among the Algonquin Natives it was kind of a demi-god. In Egypt, the rabbit was a hieroglyph that represented the soul or being. To the ancient Hebrew, it was considered unclean because it was so prolific. It did what rabbits do best—procreate rapidly. To the ancient Chinese and Japanese, there was not a man in the moon but rather a hare in the moon.

> When we study the rabbit, we find that of all of these interpretations, it is the Asian that is the closest to Nature. Young rabbits are capable of being out on their own at 28 days. Twenty-eight days is the lunar cycle. When rabbits appear in our life, there is a cycle or rhythm of 28 days (or one month) at play.

> All animals adapt to survive in the wild, and the rabbit is no exception. Rabbits, mice, and rats are the most common prey animals and most predators recognize prey by movement. The rabbit's ability to freeze is an adaptive behavior that enables it to go undetected and avoid becoming some predator's meal.

I love it when rabbits show up in my life. It is always an indication that I will not have to invest a great deal of time and energy into something before I see results. If something is occurring in my life when rabbits appear and I am not sure

The Four Blessings in Action

FIRST BLESSING
(rabbit's life cycle and rhythm)

SECOND BLESSING
(how rabbits adapt)

what to do, I freeze. I do nothing. It doesn't take more than 28 days before I know exactly what I must do.

THIRD BLESSING
(rabbit's potentials and abilities)

➤ And rabbits do not do things in a step-by-step fashion. They move in little hops and jumps. So even if I have to backtrack, I can do it in jumps and leaps and I will quickly make up lost ground. This ability to move in hops and jumps, backtracking as needed, is a rabbit's natural ability and potential.

FOURTH BLESSING
(rabbit's environment)

➤ Rabbits are found in most land environments. Because they are one of the most common prey animals, they relate to their environment by being very prolific. They will have several litters in a year to ensure their survival as a species. If rabbits are showing up in your life, be involved in as many creative projects as possible within your own environment. Some may not make it, but some will!

```
┌─────────────────────────────────────────┐
│                 BENEFITS                  │
│  •  learn to recognize communications of  │
│     Nature                                │
│                                           │
│  •  develop intuition                     │
│                                           │
│  •  strengthen relationship with animals  │
│                                           │
│  •  increase knowledge of animals         │
└─────────────────────────────────────────┘
```

Exercise

Getting Simple Animal Answers

1. **Ask for communications whenever you start something new.**

One of the best things about my travels are the opportunities to see animals on the longer trips, and whenever I teach a new subject for the first time, I especially look to see what animal shows up on that trip. About eight years ago, I was teaching my first workshop on making spirit animal masks and how to use them in healing and meditation.

The workshop was about an hour and a half from where I lived. On the trip there I did not see a single animal. I did not see a bird, a mammal, or an insect. I did not even see the hawks that always watch out for me when I travel. This was most strange, and needless to say I was more than a bit concerned.

When I arrived at the workshop in the early evening, everything was set with a group of about 40 people in attendance. We made beautiful masks. We did a wonderful healing meditation with them, and by the time I left, I was very confused. As I pulled away, and started down the road, my headlights caught the eyeshine of an animal. I slowed down; assuming it was a dog or cat. As I reached the corner, there was a raccoon sitting up on the sewer grate watching me as I drove by.

Now I was completely lost. I was more than halfway home when I had one of my sometimes-

(cont.) Getting Simple Animal Answers

frequent forehead slapping, experiences. Raccoon! Masks! Duh! Raccoons have a natural mask. Their paws are also quite agile and capable of subtle manipulations. Well, we were using our "paws" to make masks. They are also nocturnal, and so it was not appropriate for me to see them before I arrived at the workshop. Now every time I teach that workshop, raccoons are there at some point. A totem that guides the seminar.

When you start something new, take a few minutes to meditate or pray, asking for guidance from some aspect of nature to watch over the activity. Ask that it make itself known so that you can honor it. When we start to ask, we get our answers.

2. Take answer walks in Nature.

If you have a problem, take a walk to find out your answer. Remember, Nature is talking to us all of the time. Most of the time, we miss the communications. If we have a problem or need some guidance, sit and meditate upon it, praying for Nature to provide you with a message.

Then take a walk in the woods or in a park. Even take a walk in your neighborhood. Do not talk to others. Reflect on your problem or situation. Make sure the walk lasts about half an hour.

At the end of the walk, what aspect of Nature stood out or kept coming up? Was there a particular fragrance? Maybe you kept smelling pines. Pine fragrance is calming to emotions and feelings of guilt. It may be telling you that you are getting too emotional about the problem. A study of the plant or tree will provide some clues as to its meaning.

Was there a particular bird or animal that caught your attention? Maybe a blue jay was calling off and on. Blue jays often indicate assertiveness, reflecting proper and improper uses of power. It might indicate a need to take advantage of an opportunity or to assert yourself more.

Do not worry that you might be imagining it all. The particular aspect of Nature would not be catching your attention or coming to mind if it did not have significance for you.

Be specific in your questions. The more specific you get as to what you should do, the better and more specific the answer will be. Ask what behavior you should demonstrate in a situation. Then observe what behaviors you most see in the animals on your walk. When you start applying these answers and when you then study the animal, you will gain even more insight and you will start to recognize more and more subtle communications.

3. **Use animal cards for your answers.**

Another simple way of getting quick and accurate answers is through the use of animal cards. These can be purchased or made. Two sets that are wonderful to use, but must be purchased are *The Medicine Cards* by Jamie Sams and David Carson and my own *The Animal-Wise Tarot*.

Making your own can be quite effective and empowering, although it does take more time and energy. Begin with a deck of blank index cards. On one side of the card, draw or paste a picture of an animal. On the other side write down some of the important characteristics and behaviors of the animal. You might want to begin with its life cycle and adaptive behaviors.

At first, make cards for your favorite animals. Then branch out. Make sure you have animals of all types (insects, mammals, birds, reptiles, etc). Make at least 30 so that there is a wide variety of possibilities and thus a greater ability to get clear answers.

When you have a problem, meditate upon it while shuffling the cards and ask your question. Then draw a card from your deck for your answer. Again, the more specific you are with your question, the more specific the answer will be.

Exercise

Getting Simple Animal Answers (cont.)

TED ANDREWS   Part I

Notes

CHAPTER 4

Beastly Behaviors

Cranes dance, alligators roar, prairie dogs kiss, and pandas turn somersaults.

Animals display a tremendous variety of behaviors that can help us to understand their meaning in our lives if we know what those actions mean. This kind of understanding will also help prevent us from becoming superstitious and help us recognize an important element in animal language.

➤ Animals communicate in a variety of ways. They use sounds, gestures, and postures for a many different purposes. Some also use touch and the sense of smell to communicate as well. Each type of animal uses its own unique communication method to alert for danger, to indicate locations of food, to assert territoriality, for mating, and to keep family groups together.

Vocal communication is common among animals. Birds sing for many reasons. Their song reflects territory, warnings, and mating intentions. There is flock chatter as well as chatter and song an animal mother uses to keep in touch with her young. Mammals use vocal communications too, varying with each species. Cats purr to show contentment. Wolves snarl, bark, and employ other sounds to communicate with each other. Fish communicate with sounds, such as the grunting noise of the catfish. These noises often serve to keep schools together in the darkness of the water and to draw a mate.

TED ANDREWS

How Animals Communicate

Part I

**How Animal
Communicate**

vocal sounds

gestures, postures,
and movements

scent

Animals use gestures, postures, and other movements to communicate messages. Understanding the reasons for these behaviors can help us in understanding the message to us. Male fiddler crabs wave their claws in a beckoning gesture to female fiddlers. Rabbits thump the ground to warn of dangers. Worker bees dance to let other workers know where to find nectar and and how far it is. If the nectar is near, they perform a round dance. If it is far, they wiggle-waggle in a figure eight. The speed of the dance conveys the distance to the nectar.

Animals also use scent to send messages and to mark their territory. Foxes have a strong scent in their urine to mark their turf. Fish and other animals release scent when injured or frightened. Minnows can smell their enemies from a distance. When the opossum plays dead, it releases a musk scent to add to the illusion of its suddenly dying. Insects are also very scent oriented. Ants leave a chemical trail, and many insects release subtle pheromones that draw a mate through the sense of smell.

Studying the way an animal uses its senses and various movements to communicate can provide great insight into what the animal might mean to us. A spider has eight eyes, but it does not see very well. It senses the world around it primarily through subtle fibers on its legs. If a spider has shown up in your life, trust what you feel. What you see and hear may not be a true communication. The strongest sense of the animal is often an indication of the one that is becoming stronger and more reliable to you at that time.

The Art of Camouflage

➤ Unless an animal has a very special defense or a special escape, it will always use camouflage to conceal itself from its enemy or any other perceived danger. Camouflage also enables many animals to hunt for food more effectively. By studying the way our spirit animals and totems use camouflage, we can often see the best way to avoid trouble and the best way to capturing our own goals more effectively.

Most people are aware that the average back yard male bird is usually more brightly colored than the female, but the female is often a bit larger than the male. This is because the female, for the most part, protects the nest. Thus it is more important for her to be more camouflaged and stronger. If the female bird appears, we may need to be more cautious in protecting "our nest with young ones" whether it is our family or our newly hatched activities.

This coloring factor does not hold true for birds of prey. Because these birds are hunters, they are all camouflaged. Although the only true way of determining male and female among birds of prey is through blood testing, the female is almost always larger than the male. The male does the hunting when there is nesting involved, but the female guards the nest. I have a female and a male red-tailed hawk that I use in educational programs with the schools. The female is much larger than the male and I often tell the kids that "although the male birds are often prettier, the females are bigger and can always whoop 'em."

➤ **1.** There are different kinds of camouflage, and a study of your animal's method will help you to employ the process in your own life more successfully. One kind of camouflage is resemblance where the animal tends to merge with its background, looking like everything else. Most often, this is seen in grazing animals. Their earthy colors merge with the plains, and since most predators only see in shades of gray, the animal does not stand out.

Many grazing animals also gather in large groups, making it more difficult for a predator to single one out. This kind of camouflage allows

Types of Camouflage Used

resemblance

countershading

disruptive coloring

change colors

imitation

RESEMBLANCE

the animals to graze and grow to adulthood in peace and safety. Sometimes a grazing animal coming into our life can indicate a time to do as most others have done, a time to use the patterns of others to lay our own foundation in endeavors. The time for separating ourselves from the rest will come later.

COUNTER-SHADING

➤ **2.** Many animals conceal themselves through countershading, where the animal is darker on top than underneath. Light usually comes from above, casting a shadow below. The darker area above absorbs part of the light, causing the shadows to disappear and the animal merges with the background. Zebras and many hawks have this characteristic.

If animals that use this type of camouflage appear as a warning, it can often reflect that our presence and activities are not as hidden as may think. Animals like this are often an indication that we should not make our light too visible too soon. It is sometimes a sign to do the opposite of what others have done or are doing. This opposite direction in our endeavors is likely to be more successful at this time.

DISRUPTIVE COLORING

➤ **3.** Some animals use disruptive coloring with contrasting colors and patterns. This draws attention away from the whole shape, breaking up the outline of the whole body. Fish, snakes, and many ground-nesting birds use this type of camouflage. In a natural background, they will seem to disappear. This kind of misdirection is particularly effective when you are tackling several activities or goals or if there are others who may interfere with your endeavors or hinder them.

➤ **4.** Some animals change colors as a form of camouflage. Pigments are redistributed according to changes in temperature and perceived threat. Animals like the chameleon and flounder are able to change their pigments to look more like their background. These types of animals can teach us how to blend and shift our energies. They are the natural shapeshifters and they often signal a need to learn to shift our energies, to change how we have been approaching things. We may need to be more flexible at this time and try doing things in a different way.

➤ **5.** Yet another form of camouflage is that of imitation, where the animal looks like its environment. Stick bugs and leaf insects are the best examples of this. Sometimes a form of mimicry is used. Some insects resemble another animal that may be protected by a chemical or a smell. The warning colors or appearances of the insects they resemble benefit the mimicking insect.

It is said that imitation is the highest form of flattery. Animals that use imitation can remind us about using methods and techniques which have had success in our types of endeavors. These animals often show up in the beginning of new endeavors when individuals are initiating new lines of work and creative activities and they may not be sure of the most successful way to accomplish them.

➤ An animal's first need is for food. The second is to mate to ensure the survival of the species. Animal guides can provide great insight into relationships and even sexual activities. Every animal has times in which it is more procreative, and these times often reflect a rhythm in which our own creative energies are higher. Animals also have their own unique mating rituals (some elaborate, some deceptive and some quite simple.)

CHANGE COLORS

IMITATION

Courtship and Mating

Some animals are very monogamous, but many are not. If your totem is not a monogamous creature, this should not be interpreted that you are free to be as sexually active as you wish. We are not animals. We can use them as guides and teachers, but we should always live responsibly. If the animals teach us anything, it is that there is no such thing as "casual sex."

On the other hand, by examining how the animal relates to its opposite sex as well as its unique mating rituals and nesting behaviors, we can often find what is more likely to be effective for us in our own life. We can learn how to communicate more effectively within relationships and even open doors to establishing a relationship that will work best for us. We can also gain greater insight into the best ways of giving birth to new endeavors.

For herds, flocks, and other animals living in groups, finding a mate is not difficult. There is often a hierarchy that might have to be contended with, but there is at least great opportunity. In some groups, only some individuals will mate. Among wolves, there is usually an alpha male and an alpha female. These are the ones who will mate. The alpha male may not be the best hunter, just who won the right to mate. Although it may perform the mating, it will give over its leadership position to the best hunter

Animal

FUN WITH CAMOUFLAGE

Animals can teach us some unusual lessons when we examine the ways in which they camouflage and dress themselves. Many animals, such as snakes and insects, appear poisonous by having a yellow and black coloring. Could this be telling us that if we wish to appear poisonous to others, we should wear yellow and black? The peacock has tremendously beautiful feathering. It puts on quite a display of these feathers when it wishes to attract the attention of a female. Does this mean we must dress to the nines to get the girl? Green tree frogs are often relatively quiet compared to other frog groups. They hang back and remain quiet, patiently waiting for food or a mate. Could this mean we should be careful of the quiet ones?

Wonders

when the hunt begins. What is best for the survival of the pack comes first.

It is the solitary animal that has the most difficult time. Often the sense through which that animal attracts a mate is what will often attract us. Some animals use all of the senses, but many rely primarily upon one.

Many animals find a mate through the sense of smell. Female moths release pheromones, which will lure males from over a half-mile away. Not even the smell of rotten eggs will cover up this smell from other moths. Many female fish release a chemical into the water that can be detected by the male of the species. If your animal is one that uses scent, it often indicates your own sensitivity to smells, and that animal can probably guide you in greater knowledge of the use of aromas and fragrances. In this case, you might find that studying aromatherapy and the use of essential oils might be a powerful resource for you.

Animal

MATING IN ELEPHANT SEALS

The mating ritual of elephant seals are very powerful. A single male will try and mate with as many females as possible. The bull male will often have to fight with other males for the right to mate. These fights can be dangerous from various perspectives. Woundings can cause death. The fights and lack of eating while the sex drive is high can burn up critical stores of fat, affecting the survival of the seal. Several slightly askew and humorous interpretations might be made of the elephant seal mating rituals:

- if you want lots of women, you must be big, mean, and have lots of fat to burn, and
- if you are not interested in sex, do what the female elephant seal does— she whacks the male's penis with her flipper.

Wonders

Some animals use sound to court a mate. Some birds sing. Male crickets and grasshoppers create sounds to attract a female. Animals that use sound can teach us how to use our words and our voice, one of our most creative instruments, to have a greater impact upon others, not just for personal relationships but as a tool in every part of our life.

Some animals use sight, and some animals use all of the senses. While fireflies use only flickers of light to attract mates, many other animals use combinations of the senses. Males of various species display courage to the females, make handsome displays, and even present females with gifts. These kind of visual displays are most important in the bird kingdom. Mammals use scent and display. Males will usually fight, but not to the finish, and the females look to males who appear strong and established.

By studying the way an animal courts, we have cues to the best ways for us to court new situations, romantic or otherwise. We can also use animals for understanding our present relationships. Begin by determining the animal totem of the individual. Then study that animal. How does it respond to certain courtship rituals? How does it relate to others of its kind? Look especially for unique characteristics of the animal's mating rites. If the person has a totem that is a herd animal, then like that animal, this is probably a person who is very sociable or perhaps needs a lot of company and interaction.

If we know the animal of someone we are romantically interested in, study the way that animal chooses a mate. It will provide insight as to the best approach to open the doors of communication. For example, if it is a bird person with whom we are interested, then we should use displays. Birds respond strongly to handsome shows. Males strut, dance, and sing. Who knows? It may lead to a wonderful relationship.

BENEFITS

- heightening the sense of smell

- developing subtlety of perception

- attuning to animals and Nature

Many animals mark their territories or boundaries by leaving scent. This scent may be urine, feces, or glandular, such as musk. It is a way for marking their direction so they can find their way home (the "Hansel and Gretel Response") that also serves as a warning to others of its kind that this territory is taken.

Most mammals have a highly developed sense of smell. Although the human sense of smell is not as keen as that of other mammals, this exercise has a lot of subtle benefits, not the least of which is to awaken a deeper respect for an animal's use of the sense of smell.

This exercise must be performed outdoors and another person must participate.

1. **Using a bottle of a strong-smelling liquid, such as vinegar or vanilla, have your partner shake a trail of drops across an open space while you are not looking**

   In essence, he or she is marking a territory. Then try and follow the trail by crawling about and sniffing hard.

2. **Mark the point where you find the trail and then start again. Keep marking when you smell the trail and see if you can locate and follow the territory of your partner.**

   You will be surprised at not only the variety of smells encountered, but also you will begin to understand the strength of animal sensory organs. As you learn to attune to them, your own senses will strengthen.

Notes

CHAPTER 5

Creating the Inner Totem Pole

The carved column called the totem pole is the art form most popularly associated with the Northwest Coast Indians. These poles were covered with carved faces from top to bottom, faces that represented all kinds of creatures from different worlds. They depicted lineage, protection, clan, and more. Each face— each animal—had its significance.

We cannot hope to explore all of the aspects and intricacies of the totem pole in this book, but their creation is a sacred act that brought wholeness and balance to the tribe. It was a tangible prayer. The totem pole carvers used pictures to tell stories, often using and carving the images of symbolic creatures into cedar poles.

In some traditions, totem poles were actual doorways into homes or they were placed beside doorways to protect the home and its occupants. In the Haida tradition, the home was given a name to signify that it had a life and spirit of its own. The home often had a totem pole with a ceremonial entryway through its base, but had another doorway for everyday use. The figures on the totem pole reflected characteristics attributed to the members of the home or clan and to the spirit of the home. The images represented the spiritual forces that would protect the home and its inhabitants and could be called upon throughout life.

The Human Chakra System

➤ Like the totem pole, the human body is a bridge, with our feet upon the Earth and our heads in the Heavens. Running through our body is a central pillar of energy. In ancient Qabalistic traditions, the central pillar is called the Middle Pillar of Balance. In Eastern traditions, it is called *susumna*—the balance of male and female, the pole through which our energy flows and manifests.

Within our body are energy centers, often referred to as chakras, that are the primary mediators of all energy within the body and coming into it. Although often thought of as metaphysical "mumbo jumbo," modern science is demonstrating that in the traditional locations of these major centers, there is a higher degree of electromagnetic emanations from the body than in other areas.

The chakras are connected to the functions of the physical body primarily through the endocrine glands and the spinal or nervous system. Different chakras are linked to the functions of specific physiological systems and organs, as well as levels of consciousness. These energy centers respond to color, light, sound, and other stimuli. By learning to interact with them, we can learn to impact physiological conditions and tap our more creative abilities.

Each chakra or energy center in the body mediates various expressions of our energy—physiologically, emotionally, mentally, and spiritually. One way of empowering our own chakra centers and its expressions of energy is by discovering the animal totem or spirit of the center. When we discover the animal that reflects the expression of energy through our major chakra centers, we create an inner totem pole that we can use for healing, spirit contact, balance, and strength, thereby giving us greater insight into our individual energy systems and our natural abilities.

THE HUMAN CHAKRA SYSTEM

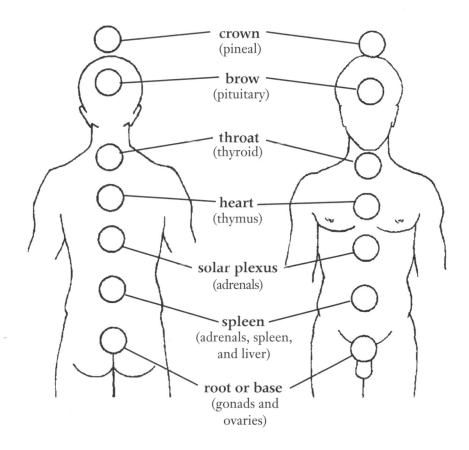

crown
(pineal)

brow
(pituitary)

throat
(thyroid)

heart
(thymus)

solar plexus
(adrenals)

spleen
(adrenals, spleen,
and liver)

root or base
(gonads and
ovaries)

*The chakras mediate all energy coming into, going out of,
and traveling within the human body. They link to levels
of the subconscious mind for distributing our physical,
emotional, mental, and spiritual functions. The seven
major chakras have physical points located along the
median, or central pole, of the body. They work within
the body through the spine and glandular system. The
feet are also a point of great chakra activity. Although
considered minor, the feet chakra serve a vital functiopn
in keeping us grounded and linked to the earth.*

The Inner Totem Pole

➤ The animal of the different chakra centers can help us work with our individual energies and abilities with greater effectiveness. The brow chakra, for example, is linked to vision and dreams and the animal of that center will help us with our higher perceptions, often serving as a dream guide. The throat chakra is linked to vocal expression and assertion of will. An individual who is shy and has difficulty speaking could draw upon the animal of the throat center to find a more natural way of communicating—one that reflects how the animal communicates and expresses itself.

The base chakra (located at the base of the spine) is linked to the functions of the circulatory system and is central to our basic life force (energy levels) and our creativity. The base chakra is also tied to the level of the subconscious mind that contains knowledge of past life talents and abilities that we may awaken and draw upon within this life. The animal of this center reveals what those talents are. By working with that animal, we reawaken those talents more quickly and easily.

For instance, if the animal for our base center was a groundhog, we can learn much about our reawakening and redeveloping own abilities. The groundhog is a semi-hibernating animal with the ability to awaken throughout the winter and feed if necessary. Its normal body temperature is somewhere around 96 degrees Fahrenheit. When it goes into winter sleep, its temperature drops from that 96 degrees to somewhere between 36 and 42 degrees Fahrenheit and its heartbeat slows to about 5-10 beats per minute and its breathing rate to one breath per minute. The groundhog's metabolism slows so it can survive.

This knowledge of the groundhog can reveal much about what we may have developed in the past. By learning to align and attune to the

groundhog, our own ability to control physiological functions will reawaken. Like the
groundhog, we can learn to go into altered states,
we can learn to control our metabolism so that
we can survive a harsh time or environment. For
us it is the key to successful survival.

The base chakra is also strongly affected by
certain emotional conditions, our own or those of
others, that can affect our blood pressure. Learning to attune to the groundhog will help us maintain control of our physiological processes, keep
our blood pressure steady and even slow it down
as necessary regardless of the emotional environment we are in. Most likely we are already instinctively doing this. If not, we may need to
attune to that totem to reawaken that ability or
manifest it more strongly.

Creating the inner totem pole can be a powerful form of initiation into new levels of understanding and communication with all of Nature
and with animals in particular.

Two exercises, "Discover Your Spirit Animals" and "Awakening the Chakra Totems" can
be used to help with the process of creating an inner totem pole. Both exercises are located at the
end of this chapter.

➤ The unveiling and strengthening of the inner
totem pole is best accomplished over a one-year
period. There is always the question as to when
this year of initiation should begin. This is an
individual decision. Some begin on their birth-
day, as it is a powerful time of the year. Some
begin just when they feel the time is right. I first
did this many years ago beginning with the autumn equinox, allowing the unveiling and unfolding of the inner totem pole to take the
rhythm of the ancient "Year of the Soul."

In the ancient Year of the Soul, autumn marks
the beginning, a time of harvesting and sowing

The Year
of the
Inner
Totem Pole

THE INNER
TOTEM POLE

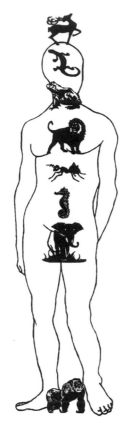

seeds. Seeds sown in the fall germinate in the winter, sprout in the spring, and come to fruition in the summer. Seeds we plant in the fall will come to fruition by the following fall. Things we clean out of our lives in the fall of the year will be replaced by something more beneficial by the following fall. We use the natural universal rhythms to accelerate our growth.

The autumn has always been a powerful time for me. Every fall I either take on a new study, a new endeavor, or a new expression of an old activity. This serves to keep me being ever creative. But this is what worked for me. The right time to begin is when you feel it is right.

For this year of initiation, you will need one month for awakening and working with each of the eight chakra totems. The remaining four months are used to work on bringing the totems into harmony with you and your life. We do not have the time in this book to cover all of the intricacies of this process, but the last four months of the year are used for keeping the chakra totems strong and balanced. Four is the rhythm of nature and the elements. The four-month period is a time of learning to harmonize your inner totems within your life environment, calling upon the animal guides and guardians, and of learning to work with them daily, as they are expressions of yourself.

When you begin, allow a period of time between working on each chakra totem. I recommend at least one month between the chakras. Some people start this activity on the first day of each month and others begin at the new moon. This gives them a full month to study and work with the animal, establishing a good relationship with the totem of that particular chakra.

Remember that when we work with the animal and its image, we are accessing archetypal energies, stimulating them, and releasing them to play out within our life. By allowing a month between each animal, we do not activate too much too soon. We are less likely to be overwhelmed and more likely to remain balanced throughout the process.

That month should be spent learning about the animal. Explore its biology and mythology. Find photos or pictures of it. Begin creating a shield that will eventually contain all eight of the animals. Meditate on it. Hold conversations with it. Take walks in nature with it. See and feel it within you. The more you do with it that first month, the stronger the connection will become. This is especially important with the first animal.

➤ **1.** As we create the inner totem pole, we start by unveiling the animal associated with the feet chakra so we are more grounded and then working our way up. The "Discover Your Spirit Animal" exercise included in this section is written specifically for that purpose, although the exercise can be easily modified for other chakras. Perform the exercise three days in a row. Three is a creative rhythm, and it helps to more fully awaken the animal's energy.

Let the animal appear no matter what it is. Remember that no animal is any more powerful or spiritual than any other animal. Even though a mouse may not seem glamorous to some, it has abilities and skills that cannot be matched by other animals. Part of our growing process is learning to see ourselves truly. The animal that appears helps us with that.

After the animal appears upon the first working of this exercise, make sure that it appears in the second and third time as well. We are helping out our creative imagination. The wonderful thing about this exercise is that you will get confirmation of the animal within 7-10 days of your third exercise process and repeated confirmation

START WITH THE FEET CHAKRA

throughout that first month. These confirmations may come in a variety of ways through:

- dream encounters with the animal

- actual encounters with the animal

- images of the animal catching your attention repeatedly (in TV, magazines, art, etc.)

- appearances of the animal's natural predator or prey in the wild

These are all signs that you have uncovered the correct animal for the chakra you are working on. It also confirms that the energy of the animal is awakened and working in your life. Enhance that play of energy by studying the animal, acknowledging its presence, visualizing it within you, and through any other means you may think of.

However, if at the end of seven days there has been no confirmation, perform the exercise three days in a row again. If you do not receive several confirmations within seven days following the third working of the exercise, then the animal is not part of your inner totem pole. Do not be discouraged by this. The animal may have to do with other activities within your life. Remember that there are other animals that help us and guide us at different times in our life. It might even reflect that you are trying to choose the animals you wish when you have already been chosen. It may be denial or a lack of recognition.

I once guided a group through this exercise, and at the end, a young lady raised her hand. She complained of it being a frustrating experience because the entire time she was waiting for her animal to appear, a butterfly kept flitting around her face distracting her. And no matter what she did, it wouldn't leave her alone.

Insects are animals. They are not often glamorized, but they have magnificent qualities. Our totems may be part of that family of "creepy crawlies." We will probably have mammals, insects, birds, and others. Do not limit yourself. Keep in mind the idea that whatever is your totem will manifest.

➤ **2.** Once we have uncovered all of the animals and have unveiled the inner totem pole—we should see them working together within us. A healthy valley, meadow, or any balanced natural environment will have a variety of wildlife, varieties that are not any more dominant than any other. See yourself as a balanced environment in which the creatures live together, each adding to the balance, strength, and health of the environment that is you.

Once we have unveiled our inner totem pole, we can then draw upon the animals more strongly. Visualize the chakra centers regularly. See and feel the animal within that chakra. Imagine it strong and helping you with whatever is associated with that center.

Within one year, you will find yourself more balanced, healthier, and more attuned to nature and animals than you ever imagined. When you are outdoors, you will increasingly recognize when animals are greeting you and will find yourself increasingly aware of the animal communications around you and understand them. And this is just the beginning.

WORKING
WITH THE
COMPLETED
INNER
TOTEM POLE

🐾 Feet Center 🐾

Colors	*Fragrances*	*Gifts*
earth tones, browns, deep greens	cedar, clay, sandalwood, musk	opening doors, movement into new worlds and new terrain

Strengthens
courage, openness to new, commitments

Overcomes
hesitations, procrastination, instability in our life

Chakra Totems

THE CHAKRA

It has been said that the way to heaven is through the feet. In other words, it is through our practical, day-to-day activities that move us along the spiritual path. Everything spiritual must be expressed through the physical. Although the chakra center of the feet is often considered a minor center, but it is extremely important when creating the inner totem pole and for establishing and maintaining our innate link to all of Nature.

Our feet are our support system, enabling us to stand and to move, and linking us to the earth, keeping us grounded. Our feet are our symbols of stability and firmness.

ABOUT THE TOTEM

The totem for this center will help us maintain perspective. It is this animal that can help us remain practical in our endeavors, of doing what is necessary, helping us in fulfilling our daily obligations and to survive in the real world more easily.

When we feel our foundations giving away, we should call upon this spirit animal for help. This animal guide will help us to move when appropriate and to hold still when it is not. If we are giving away our own ground needlessly, this is the spirit animal to call on. It is the animal that will help us to get a firmer hold on life. Mimicking the way this animal walks and stands is a powerful way to awaken its energies in you.

This animal is a wonderful guide to the lower worlds in traditional shamanism. It is the animal to call upon whenever you are entering through new doors in your life or are wishing help in opening doors in your life.

❧ Base Center ❧

Colors	*Fragrances*	*Gifts*
reds, reddish browns	cinnamon, sage	past life abilities, overcoming fears, awakening the kundalini

Strengthens

physical energy,
common sense,
prosperity

Overcomes

obsessive worries, recklessness,
impulsiveness, aggression

THE CHAKRA

The base chakra center is the seat of the kundalini, the creative life force and the source of our life-promoting energies. Located at the coccyx, the base chakra affects the circulatory and the reproductive systems of the body and is also a link to our sexual energies, rhythms, and organs.

The base chakra is also a center tied to a level of the subconscious mind that holds the knowledge of past lives. When stimulated and awakened, it often reveals past-life talents and issues.

ABOUT THE TOTEM

The totem of this center is often one with which we have had connections in previous lives, and the talents of the animal were also often developed by us in the past. Thus these talents can be reawakened and used in our present life as well.

A study of this animal's biology will reveal much about our own energy rhythms and cycles, times in which we can be more creative. The maturation and reproductive cycle of this animal can reveal much about our own cycles.

By working with this animal, we can become more secure. Drawing upon this animal in times and situations of insecurity will be a tremendous asset. This is the animal to call upon when confronting aggression or if we are being too reckless. This totem will reveal where we are most secure and will guide us to safe spots, physically and emotionally.

Chakra Totems (cont.)

❧ Spleen Center ❧

Colors

oranges, rust and
autumn colors,
indigos

Fragrances

juniper, pine,
patchouli, gardenia

Gifts

creative joy,
sexual energies,
healing touch,
psychism

Strengthens

independence, self-awareness,
detoxifying of body and life

Overcomes

overcome impulsiveness,
following, and mistrust

(cont.) Chakra Totems

THE CHAKRA

The spleen chakra
center is linked to reproduction, but it has stronger ties to the eliminative
processes, aiding in
detoxifying the body. On
other levels, it is linked to
our emotional well being
and to creative sensations.

This center is also
linked to that level of
consciousness affecting
dreams, some out-of-body
experiences, and psychic
experiences.

ABOUT THE TOTEM

The totem for this center can assist us in
spirit communication and in making our
dreams more lucid and vibrant. This
totem can also guide us into the astral
realms and can be called upon to enhance
our own psychic sensitivities and healing
touch. By examining the instinctual
aspects of the animal, we can heighten
our own extrasensory instincts.

It is through this totem that we can
learn to find joy in the little things of life.
We can call upon this animal to help us
get rid of troublesome and toxic situations and people, reflecting the most
effective way to handle such situations—
especially by examining how the animal
protects itself and its home and how it
plays.

The totem of this center helps us in
overcoming loss and a fear of loss. This
animal can also aid us in issues of mistrust. By looking at its environment, its
position in the predator and prey status,
and how it relates to animals within its
own environment, we can discern more
easily who to trust and when.

We can also work with the totem of
this center to become more independent,
gaining the courage to eliminate what is
not good for us, making ourselves
stronger.

Part I   **Animal-Wise**

❧ Solar Plexus Center ❧

Colors

yellows,
citrine, peach,
yellowish greens

Fragrances

wisteria, mints,
rosemary

Gifts

psychic touch, insight
into other's talents,
opening to new
knowledge, artistic
inspiration

Strengthens
rational thought,
optimism, truthfulness

Overcomes
emotionalism, impatience,
criticalness, bullying

THE CHAKRA

The solar plexus chakra center has links to the digestion system of the body, mind, and soul. This chakra aids in digestive functions and also influences the adrenals, helping the body assimilate nutrients as well as ideas and experiences. The animal of this center helps us realize the power of mind—the power of our own thoughts in creating the world around us.

This center is also linked to the ability for clairsentience and general psychic experiences and therefore the animal of this center is our psychic guide. Many psychics use an animal as their guardian and guide when working with the public.

ABOUT THE TOTEM

This totem aids in this process and can serve as gatekeeper when working with spirits so as not to be overwhelmed by them. This animal can also aid us in developing mediumship.

The totem of this center also protects us against psychic dangers and helps us in finding the knowledge we need from our life experiences. This animal can lead us to the truths we need to see. Through this animal guide, we can come to understand non-physical purposes. We gain perception into the talents of others.

This animal totem also brings patience into our lives, helping us overcome imbalances in our own life or others'. It can be called upon at times when there is bullying and over criticalness within our life, helping us deal more effectively with over emotionalism, whether our own or that of others around us. This animal totem leads us to our own power in all situations.

Chakra Totems (cont.)

❧ Heart Center ❧

Colors

greens, pinks,
golden yellow

Fragrances

rose, lilac, lily

Gifts

healing, balance,
wision into others,
guidance in sacred
quests

Strengthens

spiritual reverence,
idealism, compassion

Overcomes

doubts and insecurity,
pride, anger, jealousy

(cont.) Chakra Totems

THE CHAKRA

The heart chakra is
associated with that level
of the subconscious mind
that affects the circulatory
system, the cardiac aspects
of the body, and the
immune system. The
chakra also has links to the
process of tissue regeneration and is central to
balance and healing on all
levels.

ABOUT THE TOTEM

The animal totem of this center will
help us in healing—ourselves or others.
Holistic healers will find that working
with this animal guide will help in
assessing imbalances and in finding the
right healing modalities to employ.

This center is also associated with
higher expressions of love and compassion. The totem of the heart helps us in
developing and expressing these qualities
more effectively. The animal totem of
this center helps us in overcoming anger
(of others or us) and in overcoming
emotional insecurities.

The spirit totem of the heart is a
wonderful guide to call upon during our
sacred quests in life. This guide awakens
our own inner vision so that we can more
easily read the hearts of others and can
guide us to new ideals.

The animal of the heart helps to keep
the child within alive and active in our
life. Through this animal comes healing,
and guidance in our life paths so that we
discover the reality of miracles and grace.

❧ Throat Center ❧

Colors	Fragrances	Gifts
blue, silver, turquiose	wisteria, eucalyptus, bay	creative expression, strength of will, hidden knowledge

Strengthens	Overcomes
open-mindedness, facing of karma, all communicaitons	apathy, wcak will forcc, resistance to change

THE CHAKRA

The throat chakra is linked to a level of the subconscious mind that affects the respiratory activities of the body. In Eastern traditions, the throat center is tied to the functions of the throat, ears, lungs (particularly the upper lobes), sinuses, and other aspects of respiration.

This chakra also influences the body's metabolism and our ability to express ourselves.

ABOUT THE TOTEM

The animal of this center helps us to awaken our own unique, creative expressions and communications.

The totem of this center often helps in developing clairaudience, the hearing of spirit, whether it is external to us or within our own minds. This is the animal that often teaches us our own unique ways of developing telepathy, especially of reading the thoughts of others.

Through this animal we can develop strength of will and proper expressions of that will within our life. Study how this animal asserts itself and find similar ways of expressing will in your own life to open doors.

This animal can help us to be flexibile to life situations, aiding us when there is resistance to change in us or in our life. We can call upon this animal when dealing with apathy and blame.

The spirit animal of this center helps us open to secret knowledge and creative expression that can lead to opportunities for increased wealth and prosperity. This animal can guide us in our willingness and ability to face our karma and can also give us the courage to express ourselves more truly and creatively.

Chakra Totems (cont.)

❧ Brow Center ❧

Colors	*Fragrances*	*Gifts*
indigo, black, gray	sage, eucalyptus, cedar, myrrh	clairvoyance, spirit contact, invisibility, birth, dream activity

Strengthens

faith, discipline, nurturing ability, vision

Overcomes

fear of future, worries, impatience

Chakra Totems (cont.)

THE CHAKRA

The brow chakra center is linked to a level of the subconscious mind that affects the glandular system of the body. By directing and influencing our major glands, this center has an impact upon our immune system. It also affects the synapses of the brain and has links to the eyes, sinuses, and facial attributes of the body.

In traditional metaphysics, the brow chakra is also the center for higher perceptions and the seat of the body's feminine and magnetic aspects.

ABOUT THE TOTEM

This center's animal can help us develop vision into the health of others, sometimes even manifesting as an X-ray vision. The totem of this center strengthens our natural clairvoyance and inner vision and helps us learn to use dream time.

This animal often guides us through the dream world and shows us how to manifest our dreams, helping us with our spirit communication so we can experience more clearly what might otherwise be hidden or invisible to us.

This totem aids us in overcoming impatience, worries, and fears of the future, helping us to control the creative imagination so that it works for us rather than against us. It helps us understand our sacrifices at deeper levels. The totem of this center assists us in learning that there is strength in silence and shows us how to give birth and initiate activities that will assist in creating the new.

The totem of this center helps us see things concealed around us that are still affecting or influencing us. How this animal uses camouflage will aid us in becoming covert in our activities and even invisible to those around us if need be. Through this guide comes greater devotion to life and our own creative, birth-giving powers.

☙ Crown Center ☙

Colors

violet, purple,
crystalline white

Fragrances

frankincense,
sage, musk

Gifts

initiation, devotioin to
higher causes,
increased wonder,
protection

Strengthens

creative imagination,
stellar influences,
acceptance of change

Overcomes

procrastination,
superstitiousness,
shame, lack of sympathy

THE CHAKRA

The crown chakra is
linked to a level of the
subconscious mind that
affects the nervous and
skeletal systems of the
body, including all nerve
passages and electrical
synapses. The crown
chakra works to balance
the functions and activities
of the brain hemispheres.
In essence, when the
hemispheres are balanced
and working together, we
learn more quickly and
retain what we learn
longer.

ABOUT THE TOTEM

The animal of this center helps us in
controlling our own nervous energies so
we can use them more effectively. The
skeletal system, the bones, form the
framework for the body. and support
movement and soft tissue. Through this
animal, our own movement is facilitated
and we can gain extra support and
protection in our activities. The totem of
this center helps move us past shame
(which has its origins outside of us) and
into empowerment from within.

This animal helps us to overcome
procrastination, bringing us clarity so we
do not become superstitious. Through
this totem we can move past self-denial
and embrace our own creative power.
This animal teaches us of the significance
of who we are.

This animal totem awakens greater
spiritual and artistic inspiration and we
are more able to put life into a balanced
perspective. Through this animal, we
discover new methods of initiating
endeavors and learn we are powerful and
magical in ways we may have denied or
long forgotten. Through this guide we
gain perspective on our individual
spiritual path, recognizing it more
clearly.

Chakra Totems (cont.)

Exercise

BENEFITS

- empowerment

- discovery of personal totems and spirit guides

- healing

- balance and attunement to Earth

This exercise[1] is effective for uncovering and awakening the totem animals of our chakras. Another wonderful exercise is the one provided earlier for uncovering totems through your dreams and it can be easily adapted for the purpose of creating the inner totem pole. One way of working with them is using the dream totem exercise for the lower four chakra centers and the following exercise for the upper four. Do not be afraid to experiment with them, as they both contain archetypal imagery that will benefit you.

Begin by making sure you will be undisturbed. Phones should be off the hook, and use fragrance and candles to set the mood. Choose the fragrance associated with the chakra and a candle of the correct color. If you have soft, unintrusive music it may help. Using the steady drumbeat rhythms discussed earlier is effective. Also effective is the music composed for the audiocassette version of this exercise. The music was composed specifically to enhance the imagery and overall experience.

Discover Your Spirit Animals

---

[1] Available on audio tape from your local bookstore.

1. Perform a progressive relaxation, sending warm soothing to every part of your body.

    Take your time with this, as the more relaxed you are the more effective the exercise will be.

2. As you breathe slowly, relaxing, visualize the color of the candle and the chakra forming a small crystalline sphere of light in the appropriate area of the body.

    Feel that part of your body warm and tingling, and from the center of that chakra, there appears a tiny spark of light.

As you focus upon that spark of light in your mind's eye, it begins to shimmer and dance, growing brighter with each breath that you take. As you relax, breathing deeply, you feel a cool brush of air across your face and body. And in your mind's eye images begin to appear.

A meadow begins to form around. You feel the Earth solid beneath your feet. The air is cool and sweet. Their is the fragrance of new mown hay and spring flowers. The sun is warm upon the face and body.

As you look around you see that this meadow is surrounded by tall stately trees. At one end of this meadow is a path lined with flowers and stones of every color and kind, leading up to a distant mountain. The crest of the mountain is lost among the clouds. On the opposite side of the meadow, the path continues, leading down to a distant valley. As you look down toward that valley, you see your present home there.

And you begin to understand.

This meadow is a plateau, an intersection of time and space. It is where the finite and the infinite come together where the physical and the spiritual meet. Here nature and human are one. And knowing this is freeing to the senses. For here there is only to be.

Exercise

And then you feel that brush of air across the face and body yet again.

Then a shadow passes over you, and you feel that brush of air again. As you look across the meadow you see the shadow of what appears to be a large bird. As the shadow circles the meadow and over you, you feel that brush of air again. You watch the shadow, and every time it passes over you, you feel that brush of air as if powerful wings are fanning you.

You raise your eyes to the sky and far off you see a bird circling overhead. You are amazed. You are also quite sure that it must be immense to be able to cast a shadow from such a distance.

As you watch it, it descends and circles the tops of the trees. You are awe struck. It is so large and so magnificent. As you gaze up at it, its shadow now filling the meadow, it hovers. And before you can respond, it swoops down and grasps, holding you firmly but gently, and it begins to carry you up and out of this meadow.

Those tremendous wings beat, sending gusts of wind past you. As you look down toward the meadow, you see the grasses waving in response to the currents created by its wings, and for just a moment you are sure that they are waving good-bye to you. Still the bird climbs higher, leaving the meadow far behind.

The air becomes cooler, but it is not uncomfortable as you are carried higher and higher. You realize you are being carried in the direction of that distant mountain. Swirls of cloud brush you and before long you are circling high above that distant mountain.

Then the beating of the wings stops, and this magnificent bird begins to soar, riding upon the winds. Slowly it circles, gliding. Slowly it begins to descend toward the mountain crest. As you look down toward it, you see a large nest at its very crest.

You catch your breath as you descend, drawing closer to that nest. You are afraid that you will hit it too hard, but with a powerful flapping of its wings, the bird hovers over the nest and lays you gently within it.

With more powerful strokes of its wings, it rises once more and disappears into the sky.

You are standing in this nest, at what you are sure is the top of the world. You move to the edge and look down, but the view is dizzying and you step back, breathing deeply to relax. The winds begin to rise around you, swirling æ rising and falling.

As you continue to breathe deeply, you begin to hear faint whispers in that wind. As you relax those whispers harmonize and a clear voice issues forth from those winds.

"You are part of Nature. You within Nature and are touched by all of Nature...when you learn to attune to the animals æ to the other creatures that live within it, you will become more sensitive to all environments. You will learn which environments to avoid and which to embrace. You will find yourself awakened and empowered. You will once more be animal-wise."

And then the voice fades into the wind, but it grows stronger around you. You move once more to the edge of the nest, standing upon its side. You breathe deeply the air moving around your body. You see the wind as crystalline spirals of energy. Every cell within you seems to be breathing, and with each breath you feel yourself becoming lighter and lighter.

You extend your arms outward, like an eagle spreading its wings. You feel what every bird has ever felt when it prepared to fly from the nest the first time. You breathe deeply, and you step off.

There is a soft drop and then the wind catches you and lifts you, sending you upward. You begin to relax into the wind, soaring with it. Riding upon it not against. Never have you felt so free.

As you relax into the currents, you realize you have begun a slow gentle spiral down toward that meadow. As you look down, everything is brighter. There is a shine that wasn't there before. Slowly and gently the currents carry you toward that meadow.

As you get closer, you realize that there is now a tree standing in the middle of this meadow. Its roots

(cont.) Discover Your Spirit Animals

extend deep into the heart of the Earth and its upper branches seem to reach out toward you. Gently you reach out with your hand, brushing the top of that tree to slow your descent and you land softly on the grasses at its base.

You are filled with wonder at the journey you have just taken. You look around you and everything looks so much more alive! And then there is a subtle movement from the opposite side of this tree. Your breath catches and you watch as there appears a magnificent creature. You are again filled with wonder, realizing that this is the animal of your feet chakra. It will connect you to all things of the earth.

As you gaze upon it, you are filled with awe at its beauty and energy. And then you realize that this creature has your eyes. It is your eyes that are looking out from it at you. And in that moment it begins to shimmer and with your next breath it melts into you. You feel it coming alive within you, growing stronger with every breath you take. You feel a tingling in the area of your feet. You feel the pulse of the Earth. You feel yourself being connected.

You breathe deeply and close your eyes, offering a prayer of thanks for that which you have just experienced and for that which will unfold in the days ahead. You see the chakra within you bright and strong connecting you to the Earth. You see and feel that animal alive within you.

As you open your eyes you are amazed to find that tree gone. In its place is a wooden staff. Its upper third is carved into eight sections. In the bottom section is a carving of the animal that now breathes within you. You reach out and take the staff in hand, placing your palm against the carving of the animal. You close your eyes and breathe deeply as a soft tingling runs through your body. A brush of air passes across you and you feel a wave of joy and strength fills you.

You raise the staff above your head and speak a prayer of thanks and honor to this creature. And you breathe deeply, feeling more whole than you have felt in ages.

As you open your eyes yet again, you see that the meadow is fading from the vision. The distant mountain. The valley below. The meadow itself. Yet the staff is strong in your hands, and the animal alive within you. You breathe deep and again there is that brush of air, and it fills you with promise. And as the images fade from the inner vision, you realize that they do so only to be born into the outer life.

Exercise

Discover Your Spirit Animals (cont.)

Awakening the Chakra Totems

Exercise

┌─────────────────────────────────────┐
│   BENEFITS   │
│   │
│   • attuning to totems   │
│   │
│   • strengthening of health   │
│   │
│   • empowering individual chakras │
│   │
│   • honoring the animals and ourselves │
└─────────────────────────────────────┘

Once we have discovered the spirit animals and totems for our major chakras, we must awaken them more strongly within us. This is done in the same way we work with any spirit animal. We begin by studying the animal itself, learning as much about it as possible, including its own unique physiological processes and systems, examining them in relationship to the same system in us. We should also study and learn about the chakra centers through which the animal will most likely express its energies in your life.

There are other activities to awaken the animal in your chakra centers:

• Visualize the animal within you in that area of your body.

• Visualize the animal encircled in the color of the chakra center.

• When meditating upon the animal, use colors and fragrances that will awaken and stimulate the chakra center.

• Imagine yourself as a living totem pole, seeing the animals alive within you.

• If you wish to activate the animal more strongly, allow your body to fill with the color radiance of the chakra center. As you breathe, feel the animal growing within you, filling your entire body with its image.

Feel it breathe when you breathe, knowing that with each breath it becomes stronger and more beneficial to you.

• Make a medicine staff. Carve and paint on it the animals for each chakra near the top of the staff so that when you walk with it in Nature, your hand can rest on the image of the totemæa conscious reminder.

• Learn to make the sounds of the animal to call it. Most libraries of recordings of animal sounds. Do not worry if you do not do it well. Just the act of trying to communicate with its sounds will call it to attention and activate its energies within you.

Exercise

Awakenign the Chakra Totems (cont.)

Part II

The Kingdom of Birds

And perhaps just as God made man in his own image and likeness, so also did he make the remaining creatures after certain other heavenly images as a likeness.
ORIGEN

If I keep a green bough in my heart, the singing bird will come.
CHINESE PROVERB

CHAPTER 6

Songs of the Birds

Birds were often considered the closest relatives to humans because they walk around on two legs like we do. The truth is, though, that most humans pay little attention to the presence of birds, even when most societies at one time or another taught that all birds were messengers with some symbolism associated with them. Usually they were considered divine messengers.

All birds are governed by instinct with a unique ability to react automatically and quickly to whatever data is present. This same ability to respond automatically and quickly to stimuli within our own environments is part of what every bird can teach us. The individual species will let us know what and how specific the response should be.

The thousands of species of birds have many characteristics in common. Most birds are designed for lightness, having hollow bones, which is essential to flight. There are, in fact, only a few birds that cannot fly. Birds also are distinguished from other groups of animals by their feathers, which facilitate their flight but also insulates and protects. Feathers are actually specialized skin scales. Like the fur and scales of other animals, feathers serve a variety of purposes, from insulation to balance to flight.

Because birds move between the earth and the heavens, they were universally considered divine messengers.

All birds have excellent vision, giving them the ability to judge distances. Migration is also common among birds. While mammals may travel over a large territory for food, birds will migrate to an entirely different zone. Birds teach us how to see what is ahead and how to make the necessary migrations and movements in our life.

Birds also have an accelerated metabolism to accommodate flight, and thus birds can teach us how to accelerate our own metabolic rate, primarily through breathing techniques. This is what links birds to the element of air and all of its symbolic associations such as being linked to the suit of swords in the traditional tarot.[1]

The Significance of Air

➤For those to whom birds appear, working with the element of air can be very important. For our own well being, we must all have regular fresh air. Going outside and performing breathing exercises is essential. Breath and air are critical to life, and birds hold the healing and spiritual secrets to both. Birds show us how to use breath to move between realms, to lift our perspective, and to open our vision. They show us how to rise to new heights in all of our endeavors and how to be grounded even while we reach for the stars.

Birds are often considered some of the most important messengers whose role in many ancient traditions is to help humans understand the world around them and the spiritual forces playing upon them.

To keep the symbols in order, Pueblo ornithology must study and relate to the birds themselves, but the system is not primarily designed to make sense of an outer world, because the natural world is presumed to be the sense. The

---

[1] Ted Andrews. *The Animal-Wise Tarot* (Jackson, TN: Dragonhawk Publishing), 1998.

order and perfection of nature may therefore be drawn into less stable society, where it will impart meaning to transitory human affairs.[2]

By observing a bird's habitat and flight behaviors, we can determine much of what can be gained from them. Habitats and behaviors provide suggestions and insight into their ties to our life situations and our life behaviors. Some birds' habitats and flight indicate they are tied to the earth and thus they often have messages tied to our own earthiness and the practical aspects of life, reminding us of a need to stay connected to the earth. Others suggest an energy of learning to soar and ride upon winds.

Bird feathers have often been signs to humans. They have also been messages to the gods and other abstract spirit forces. Birds have always had magical properties that can be put to human use. They are our extended kin and thus share common desires with us. Because of this, their powers are easily recognized and when honored, they easily manifest.[3]

➤Air is as essential to life as water. Air is an active, creative element that is symbolic of thought, memory, and even freedom. Air separates Earth and Heaven, and thus it symbolizes higher mind and inspiration, the link between physical con-

Birds, as messengers, help humans understand the world around them and the spiritual forces playing upon them.

Birds and the Initiation of Air

---

[2] Tyler Hamilton, *Pueblo Birds and Myths*, (Flagstaff, AZ: Northland Publishing, 1991), p. xi.

[3] Please keep in mind that most birds are protected under the Migratory Bird Act. When it comes to possessing feathers and parts of migratory birds—especially birds of prey, it is illegal both on federal and state levels. You do NOT need a hawk feather to connect with or relate to a hawk. Any feather will connect you to any member of the bird kingdom.

One of the most creative and honoring ways of working with feathers is to take something like a chicken feather and paint it to look like a hawk's feather, or any other bird's feather. The creative process aligns you with the bird.

sciousness and spiritual consciousness through knowledge and inspiration.

Through air, we assimilate power. The coming and going of air in the breathing process reflects the involution and evolution of life. The initiation of air is tied to the mental and intellectual energies of life, involving the understanding and working with the powers of the mind, the opening to new expressions of wisdom. Air in motion—mind in motion—is a force we must learn to use. Our thoughts have power.

An old adage tells of "strength through knowledge." Through the element of air— through applied knowledge—we learn to build bridges between realms within our life. Knowledge gives us the ability to overcome struggles and helps us to develop self-mastery. The initiation of air involves discovering strength through overcoming.

With the air as their domain, all birds are the air's representatives. Since they move between the earth and the sky, between one realm and the next, and overcome gravity, birds can teach us how to lift ourselves up, how to rise above struggles. Through them we learn to make our wishes reality and learn to empower our thoughts.

If there is a predominance of air or animals of air within our lives, we may need more mental stimulation. They are present to show us how to bridge to new levels or go beyond struggles through the right inspiration and wisdom. Birds can reflects issues of intellectual freedom and a need to visit the mountains in order to replenish ourselves—a need to strengthen our connections to the element of air.

Part II   **The Kingdom of Birds**

CHAPTER 7

Dictionary of Birds

In this chapter, you can find specific information about the following birds:

- albatross
- bittern
- black vulture
- bluebird
- bobwhite
- burrowing owl
- caracara
- cockatoo
- condor
- conures
- cormorant
- emu
- flamingo
- goshawk
- great blue heron
- grebe
- gyrfalcon
- harrier hawk
- harris hawk
- ibis
- junco
- killdeer
- kite
- lark
- long-eared owl
- macaw
- merlin
- nighthawk
- osprey
- parakeet
- puffin
- sandhill crane
- sapsucker
- secretary bird
- sharp-shinned hawk
- shorteared owl
- tufted titmous
- white crane

Remember that all birds have qualities in common. Most fly and thus are often messengers between realms, people, and even states of being. Each species of birds has its own unique colors, calls, and behaviors, and it is through studying their individual characteristics that we come to a more specific understanding of what the message is that they bring.

It is difficult to label and define the powers and qualities of any single bird or animal of any kind. We can, though, by studying the animal's behaviors, qualities, and habitats, discover a prominent aspect that will help us to define its meaning for us. As with all animal encounters, begin by studying the animal, and ask yourself important questions:

- What were you doing or thinking at the time of the encounter?

- What has been most on your mind for the past 24 hours prior to the encounter?

The answers to these will often provide good clues as to where in your life the bird's message applies.

Albatross

KEYNOTE

• be alert for signs and omens

• extended success through exploration and maturity

➤ The albatross is a large seabird with mostly white with black parts. It has a powerful, hooked bill and is probably most famous for its appearance in the Coleridge's poem called "The Rhyme of the Ancient Mariner," in which it became a bird of ill omen. To have an albatross about one's neck is a phrase depicting trouble and bad luck surrounding oneself and one's activities. The albatross is a bird of omen, but not necessarily of ill-fated endeavors.

The albatross breeds mostly on Antarctica and oceanic islands and they do not breed until they are at least seven years old. This reflects much about the cycle of maturity for those to whom the albatross appears. Personal, business, and other endeavors—especially all creative activities and undertakings—will usually take seven years before they become truly productive for you.

That seven-year period is an educational and preparation time, time to lay the groundwork. If this maturation is not rushed and is done carefully, then the endeavors set in motion during this time will bear fruit for many years and there will be a permanence to them not experienced by others. The albatross can live to be 70 years old, reflecting the extended success that manifests through proper maturity and development.

The albatross is a bird of the sea, the ancient archetype of creativity, inspiration, mothering, and nurturing energies. The fact that it spends most of its life around the sea and feeding upon the marine life reveals the need for those to whom the albatross appears to be involved in creative and artistic endeavors.

The best known of its species is "the wandering albatross," one of the largest, with a twelve-foot wingspan. Like most albatross, it is an expert glider and can stay airborne for long periods of time. The albatross is a patient bird and those to

Albatross
(cont.)

whom it has appeared must be patient and be willing to glide for long periods of time. It is not unusual to find that albatross people have a period of as much as seven years in which they seem lost and unfocused, perhaps even appearing not to have goals, but they know there is something out there in the world for them. Once they find it, it will last and sustain them through the rest of their life.

Albatross people do not seem to know what to do. They are dreamers, always effortlessly seeking what will inspire and awaken them for more than just the moment. Many albatross people spend more time in school than other people, often changing their areas of study. Some seem to wander from job to job without goals or direction. Those around the albatross must be patient, for the albatross is always an omen of inspiration and ultimate success if searching continues.

To those whom the albatross appears come lessons in conserving and using our energies in the most beneficial manner. The albatross is a reminder that sometimes we have to commit fully in order to know if something is right. And even if it is not, the albatross promises that without some commitment, we will never succeed.

When the albatross appears, it is a sign of something on the horizon for us. We must seek it out, trusting, and allowing the winds to carry us to that promised horizon.

Are we settling for less than we should rather than continuing our searches for what excites and inspires us?

Are we fearful of committing to something or someone?

Are we not committing to anything?

WANDERING ALBATROSS
(*Diomedea exulans*)
Any of several web-footed birds related to the petrels... They are the largest of sea birds, capable of long-continued flight, and are often seen at great distances from land.

Harris, p. 51

The largest known species, the Wandering Albatross, which has been made famous by Coleridge's "Rime of the Ancient Mariner," measures from twelve to fourteen feet in expanse of wing, and, like other members of this family, is a tireless ocean wanderer.

Chapman, p. 61

Bittern

KEYNOTE

• **signs are apparent**

• **promise of gentle rains if we heed the signs**

AMERICAN BITTERN
(*Botaurus lentiginosus*)
A glossy black streak on
either side of the neck.

Are we ignoring the signs?

Are we hiding things that we shouldn't?

Are we making promises that we shouldn't?

Are others making promises around us that won't be kept?

Are we being deceived?

Are we not trusting and protecting our heart?

➤Among the Pueblo peoples, the bittern is a bird often associated with water (whether a pool, marsh, stream, or river), and thus linked to rain. Rain was essential and critical to life for the Pueblo, and thus the birds of water and rain held a special role. Because many of the water birds migrate, in their mythology they are often associated with bringing the rains.

The bittern is of the heron family, but has a shorter and thicker neck. Thus, herons should be studied as well. Bitterns are brown and mottled with a white chin and a black cap. Birds and animals with black caps reflect hidden insight.

The appearance of the bittern is a message about a promise being made to us or by us which is often missed because this is a bird that gets little attention. The appearance of the bittern is usually an indication to pay attention to the little things, the warnings and hints, the subtle psychic nudges that we get and usually ignore.

The bittern reminds us that there is more going on around us than what is readily apparent, and we should not ignore the clues. The most familiar species in Europe is known for its booming call, often likened to the bellowing of a bull. Bitterns often appear when we have been ignoring the signs. It's as if to say, in a booming voice, "If I know what is going on, if I can read the signs, so should you!"

The bittern is a bird of the reeds, a place of old and new growth. When it appears, there is a promise of new growth through clearing out the old. By heeding the signs about what troubles us, we open ourselves to solutions. If we are having troubles and difficulties and are unsure of or unaccepting of the messages we are receiving, the bittern promises clarification with signs that are true, regardless of appearances.

The bittern urges that we make a promise to ourselves first, and everything will fall into our life like a gentle rain that brings new growth.

Black Vulture

> All vultures are garbage men. They clean up the dead animals out of the environment. They are amazing creatures, beautiful in flight, though often labeled as comical and gross. Nonetheless, all vultures are tied to the energies of life, death, and rebirth. They all reflect transformation in some fashion.

Although often thought of as a bird of prey, recent discoveries and DNA studies indicate that the vulture is more closely related to the crane family than to other birds of prey. It is unique in that it rarely kills what it eats, although it will attack the young and hurt them. One example of this is in the southern areas where green turtles break out of their nests and struggle to make it to the sea. Black vultures will gather beside the nests, picking off the young as they emerge. Turtles that hatch out at night do not encounter this danger.

The turtle, long a symbol for the earth and new life, meets death and rebirth through the vulture. Although it may seem cruel and harsh to some, it is the cycle of life that is reflected in the turtle and in the vulture. Life, death, and rebirth are inseparable. If we breathe, we will encounter death and transformation. The vulture reminds us to be patient and continue on, soaring as they do, trusting the instinct that says nourishment will be there for us.

While the turkey vulture has a highly developed sense of smell, the black vulture finds food by sight alone. They often rely on their turkey vulture cousin's rare sense of smell to find them food. Then they hiss and aggressively drive off the turkey vultures so they may feed. The black vulture reminds us to truly pay attention to what is happening before our eyes. Phrases such as: "I can't believe my eyes" or "Surely they would not do that right in front of me" should be discarded. Seeing is believing. Trust what you see and what you "imagine" you see.

KEYNOTE

- transformation
- life, death, and rebirth
- ultimate fulfillment

BLACK VULTURE
(*Catharista urubu*)
Head and neck unfeathered, black, plumage black, under surface of wings silvery.

Black Vulture (cont.)

Are we not trusting in what we see—physically or psychically?

Are we worrying too much about keeping up with the Jones's rather than just taking care of business, as we know best to do?

Are we getting too stressed over what might be?

Are we not trusting in the rhythms of life and allowing its winds to carry us to what we need or to carry what we need to us?

Black vultures fly later in the day so that they can ride warmer thermals. They also fly higher than their turkey cousins do. They also have a peculiar habit of bowing wings under their body while in flight, with the tips almost touching. It almost appears as if they are stretching to relieve stress. For individuals to whom the black vulture appears, stretching, especially the upper body, will be critical to alleviate stress and tension.

Black vultures lay eggs without a nest. This often reflects the ability to be creative without a lot of preparation. Black vulture people are not necessarily "nesting" people. This does not mean that they are bad parents. In actuality, they are very good parents, but they do not concern themselves with the superfluous. The young are loved and cared for, but they are not indulged, making the young strong and self-sufficient. This is reflected in humans for whom the black vulture is a totem.

When the black vulture appears, we must learn to relax into the rhythm of life. We should not push. We should soar until what we need presents itself. Once it does, we may have to hiss and fight, but we must claim it as it comes to us.

Remember, the black vulture is a sign of transformation and ultimate fulfillment if we allow the transformations to play themselves out. For wherever there is death, there will also be life.

Bluebird

KEYNOTE

- transformation
- passage into happiness and fertility

►In an ancient Pima tale, the bluebird is described as having been an ugly color, but then one day it found a sacred lake where no water ever flowed in or out. The bird bathed in it four times every morning for four mornings, singing a sacred song. On that fourth morning, it came out of the river with no feathers at all. When it bathed itself again on the fifth morning, it came out of the sacred lake with its blue feathers. The bluebird became a symbol of transformation through sacred song and sacred acts.

In the Pueblo tradition, great importance is placed upon rituals and ceremonies honoring the six directions. In the Niman Kachina ceremony, the bluebird represented the southwest direction. The southeast and southwest directions represented the rising and setting of the shortest day; thus the bluebird was a symbol of the setting on the shortest day of the year, the winter solstice. Hence the bluebird is considered a winter bird, but it often indicates that each day that follows will have greater sunshine.

The bluebird is also often considered a spring bird, representing the movement out of winter into spring. It is a bird of transition, of passage—from winter to summer, from child to adult, night to day, barrenness to fertility.

In the north the appearance of the bluebird heralds the coming of spring. Its habitat is one of open fields with scattered trees and is one of the few birds that has benefited by the spread of agriculture, and thus it is often a sign that we will also benefit from the agriculture within our own life. The things we have planted and the seeds we have sown will come to fruition.

Among the Pueblo, bluebird feathers were used to promote snow and ice, moisture that will bring new growth. Because of this and other similar associations, the bluebird is also related to fertility on all levels.

EASTERN BLUEBIRD
(*Sialia sialis*)
Above, including wings and tail, brigh blue; throat and breast rusty borwn, belly whitish.

Bluebird
(cont.)

The bluebird is a guardian of all passages and transitions that we make or are about to make. We speak often of the bluebird of happiness, and this is rightly so. It makes our movements more fertile, productive, and protected so that we can attain the happiness we need in life. Additional information on the bluebird can be found in the book *Animal-Speak*.

When the bluebirds show up, we are about to see a change in the climate. Darkness will soon fade and more sunshine will arrive. Our own fertility in our endeavors will increase, and our passages and movement in all endeavors will be protected. Those things or people who had hindered our endeavors will find themselves bogged down in their own "ice and snow."

Animal

BIRD FATHERS

Males of most bird species help their mates to feed the chicks. Some even sit on the eggs, relieving the mother. Some of their behaviors can be quite amazing. Two examples are the bluebird and sandgrouse.

Bluebird males show a favoritism for feeding the daughters, possibly because the males are perceived as a threat. Young females will eventually leave the areas of birth in search of a mate. Young males settle close to and compete with the father for territory and mates.

The sandgrouse of southern Africa can soak up eight times the weight of its chest feathers in water. Chicks born in this desert area can drink the cargo of water the father has had to fly so far to get for them.

Wonders

Bobwhite

➤The bobwhite is a member of the quail family and speaks its own name. There has always been a tremendous mysticism surrounding names. A common belief was that to know something or someone's true name was to have power over it or the person. To name something was to make it your own. When the bobwhite appears, it is time to sing your own name and to claim what is yours. More information on names can be found in my earlier work, *The Magical Name*.

As a member of the quail family, bobwhites are bound to the earth in their habits. They are lively birds, always on the move, and if possible they are more likely to run to safety than to fly. They are often found in groups of 10-15 called coveys or bevies. When disturbed, they will rise up and scatter with a loud roar of wingbeats, re-grouping later.

Like most quail, they will roost together in tight circles, tails toward the center and heads facing out, enabling them to respond more quickly when disturbed. If startled, they can quickly fly up and confuse predators that appear.

If the bobwhite has appeared, we may need to be more protected of what is truly ours. If we feel something is threatened or about to be disturbed, we should respond explosively. The bobwhite reminds us to work with others who are like-minded for our greatest success.

KEYNOTE

- **protect secrets**
- **sacred naming**

BOBWHITE OR QUAIL
(*Dolinus virginianus*)
Throat, forehead and line over eye white in male, buff in female.

Are we being too open about our activities?

Do we need to be more secretive?

Do we need to express ourselves more clearly?

Are we trying to make our names known in an inappropriate manner?

Burrowing Owl

KEYNOTE

- priestly responsibilities

- links to the spirits and to the underworld

- keeping our sense of humor in regards to things spiritual

➤All owls have had many misconceptions and legends develop about them and all are associated with life and death. They have been thought of as the reincarnation of the dead and a sign of fertility and pregnancy. Many people placed an owl feather in the bed of a baby to help it sleep during the day.

The burrowing owl is very different from most species of owls. Even from a mythical aspect, its significance is often ambiguous. Among the Pueblo peoples seven owls have spiritual significance, but only three are treated with any special importance: the screech owl, the great horned owl, and the burrowing owl.

To the Pueblo, the burrowing owl knew how to chase away clouds and rain because it had learned how to do this to prevent its burrow from being flooded. When rains were flooding its home, the owl forced the tip beetle to disgorge its terrible smell into a bag. Then the owl drummed, beating on the bag, releasing the smell into the air, chasing away the rain clouds and the rain gods.

While most owls are nocturnal, the burrowing owl is very active during the day. It is often found nesting in the burrows of other animals, and most frequently shares its habitat with prairie dogs. For those to whom the burrowing owl appears, the prairie dog should also be studied, as it is one of your totems as well.

The Zuni's labeled the burrowing owl as "The Priest of the Prairie Dogs." When the burrowing owl appears, there will arise occasions in which we find ourselves having to assume the role of priest or priestess in some area of life. This may be formal or informal, as in the case of increasingly providing spiritual guidance.

It also has a habit of nodding and bobbing around, sometimes making very theatrical displays. Thus it sometimes fluctuates between the

image of a priest and that of a clown. Because of this, it is a reminder of our need to keep our sense of humor, especially about things in the spiritual realm. Often as I travel and teach, I encounter people who are so serious about their "spiritual path" that they actually put people off. They seem to be lost in the misconception that suffering and martyrdom are the road to spirituality. Humor is essential to life and health. Nowhere is it more essential than in our spiritual activities.

If we have lost our ability to see the humor in our life path and ourselves, it is time for a change. The burrowing owl is a reminder not to take ourselves so seriously. We should always retain the ability to poke a little fun at our path and ourselves. It keeps us grounded and it keeps the ego in check.

While most owls nest in trees, the burrowing owl is a ground dweller, usually living underground. Because of this, it is often a connection to the dead and the darkness—the underworld. A more substantial connection with spirits will be occurring. This is also a further reminder to keep us grounded and down to earth in our spiritual activities, studies, and explorations. The spiritual path is not one that leads up into some blinding light into which all of our troubles are dissolved. Rather, it is a path that leads to finding the light within and shining out into our world.

BURROWING OWL
(*Speotyto cunicularia hypogoea*)
Tarsi bare behind.
Spotted above with buffy;
belly barred; chin and
breast-patch white.

Caracara

KEYNOTE

- adaptability
- making use of available resources

GUADALUPE CARACARA

(*Polyborus lutosus*)

Rump and upper tail-coverts dull brownish buff broadly barred with dull brown; tail brownish buff with broad bars of grayish brown bordered by narrower zigzag bars or lines of dusky.

➤ The caracara is the national bird of Mexico that walks on long thin legs and has flat claws. This vulture-like scavenger even flies among vultures, following vultures for carrion, often robbing them of their meal by forcing them to disgorge. For this reason, the caracara was often called king buzzard or the king of the buzzards.

When the caracara appears, it often reflects some awakening link to the Mexican and Hispanic community, or it may reflect past life issues from a time in this locale that are resurfacing to be finally resolved.

The caracara is a great flyer, but it can also run swiftly, reflecting its ability to survive as a hunter in dual realms—the land and air. One of this bird's lessons for us is adaptability.

No other bird of prey has such a varied diet. It scratches like a chicken for worms and insects, or it will catch and eat skunks (the favorite food of great horned owls and not eaten often by other birds of prey). They also eat prairie dogs, opossums, other rodents, and will even eat turtle, carrying them by gripping the edge of their shells with their eagle-like beaks. The caracara also teaches us to make use of what is available to us, reminding us that we have access to more than we may realize.

The caracara is not a migratory bird and will build a nest that can be quite large. They are often seen in pairs, and for those who have a caracara as a totem, close companionship with at least one person is often a quality. Both the male and female participate in the incubation of the eggs, reflecting again the closeness of that singular relationship.

The caracara's name is derived from its call, which it utters from a conspicuous location, usually during mating season. Unless frightened or startled, it is otherwise a silent bird. When excited, though, its bright red face will turn yellow, and for those to whom the caracara is a totem, it

will be difficult to disguise emotions. Facial expressions and atypical vocalizations will always give away the emotions and thoughts

When the caracara appears, there are always issues surrounding adaptability or a lack of adaptability within our life. The caracara reminds us that the resources we need to succeed are available to us, but we must adapt to take advantage of them to their fullest.

Are we being too rigid?

Do we need to try new things?

Do we need to trust in the one who is closest to us?

Are we not taking advantage of the opportunities that are presenting themselves?

THE
AMAZING EAGLE

The eagle is a most adaptable bird of prey. In order to survive, it has developed seven successful methods of obtaining food. In fact, its only major obstacle in life is the human one.

- It hunts while in flight, able to dive at 200 mph to capture prey.

- It hunts from a perch, conserving energy and being conspicuous to let other eagles know this is its territory.

- It hunts on the ground, sometimes sneaking into thickets to flush hiding animals.

- It wades into shallow water for fish.

- It will sometimes participate in cooperative hunting with another eagle, one flushing the prey out into the clutches of the other.

- It will also steal another animal's kill, often snatching food from ospreys and otters.

- It will also scavenge unattended carcasses.

Cockatoo

KEYNOTE

- courtship
- strengthening bonds in relationships

PINK COCKATOO
(*Cacatua leadbeateri*)
Any of various parrots, almost exclusively confined to the Australian region...some of which are favorite cage birds, though they do not learn to speak much.

Is one person doing all of the work in the relationship?

Are the displays and demonstrations superficial and inconsistent?

Is this person in our life truly demonstrating responsibility and concern for home and family?

➤A relative of the parrot family, this beautiful bird is native to Australia. Most are white with pink or yellowed tinges, and their crests are colored. They are different from other parrots in that they do have a crest. They are similar in that they are also good mimics, and most have some magnificent qualities.

A specific ritualized courtship among this species is one of their most outstanding characteristics. The displaying of the colorful primary feathers to the female is just a small part. The male will actually feed the female to demonstrate his ability to care for her and any young.

After these introductory courtship displays and flights, other forms of behavior follow which strengthen the bond between the partners. The most important is mutual feeding and is usually initiated by the male. The incubation and care of the eggs is truly shared by the male, with the male often sitting on the eggs. Because of this, the appearance of the cockatoo during any phase of a romance or engagement (especially in the early stages) was a good sign of a caring and responsible mate.

Long betrothal periods and courtships used to be common in most societies, serving several functions. First, it helped determine whether the two were truly suitable for each other. Second, longer courtships helped to establish a stronger bond between the couple, enabling the couple to truly determine their compatibility beyond initial passions. Cockatoos remind us that relationships require great effort and demonstrations on the part of all concerned. If it does not, then there are likely to be problems down the road. Efforts and displays must be mutually consistent. A one time or occasional display is not enough.

If cockatoos have appeared in your life, there is a need to examine the mutual bonds and strengths of relationships—in those just developing or even long-standing ones as well.

Condor

KEYNOTE

- ancient mysteries of life and death
- communion with the spirits
- soaring above our limitations

➤The condor is a relative of the vulture, a larger and more powerful version. Like the vulture, they are experts at soaring. A number of years ago I was fortunate to witness a free-flying demonstration of a captive California vulture. The size and power of this bird was amazing.

The vulture, buzzard, and condor often signified the divine power of disposing that which is dangerous to health and life. They were frequently adopted as symbols of the disintegrative process, which accomplishes good while destroying. Some traditions interpreted this as evil, but their true energy is one of rebirth in the mystery of life and death.

All condors have excellent eyesight and can spot a carcass from a great distance. When one drops to the ground suddenly, others quickly follow, for they know it has found food. The appearance of condors often reflects greater spiritual vision and leadership that will be followed.

Mythically, the vulture and condor are links to the ancient griffin. The griffin was often given the features of a variety of animals, but it was always a protector, particularly of Nature and all of her spirits. To encounter a griffin was to meet a guardian of sky and earth and usually meant that great magic and power would awaken within our own life.

Condors, like griffins, lend their immense strength and readiness for whatever task may present itself for those to whom it appears, becoming a guardian like a griffin. Once it enters our life, it never leaves, although it may seem absent at times. Condors signal a time of rebirth and lifting up of the spirit, a time of action and salvation through linking the physical with the spiritual in powerful new ways.

Condors have ruffs at their neck where the body bridges the head, symbolic of the links between worlds and between the physical and the

CALIFORNIA VULTURE
(*Gymnogyps californianus*)
Head and neck orange, blue, and red, unfeathered; feathers around neck and on underparts narrow and stiffened; greater wing-coverts tipped with white; under wing-coverts white.

Condor
(cont.)

spiritual, between life and death. The Andean condor differs from its relative, the California condor, in that it has a ruff that is white, emphasizing the bridge of light between realms.

Condors prefer living in remote environments such as high mountains. Mountains are ancient symbols of spirit, and the animals found within them naturally help us to rise to our own spiritual powers. To climb a mountain is to rise above the obstacles in our life to achieve the greatness of our spirit. No animal reflects this principle more than the magnificent condor.

They are symbols of rising above the limitations of life, of spiritual elevation and communion with the spirits. Their love of the remote often reminds us that we need times of more remote isolation to come to terms with life. Their appearance might also mean we need the spiritual heights to lift us from the physical drudgeries of life. If we are to soar above our troubles, we must do so through spirit.

Most people are familiar with both endangered species of condor—the California and the Andean. Efforts are currently underway to release the California condor back into the wild. Very close to extinction, it has been making a slow but steady comeback in captivity. The Andean condor is also now very rare in the wild. The few remaining birds are living in the Andes of Columbia, Chile, Ecuador, and Peru.

The California condor is the largest North American bird, with a wingspan of about nine feet. It is black with a white lining on the underside of its wings. On the edge of extinction, its range once extended from Baja, California, to British Columbia. While shooting was a major problem, the spread of agriculture and grazing lands have limited its food supply. It must eat about two pounds of meat per day, and farmers and ranchers usually remove dead domestic animals from the farm environment.

The California condor nests every other year, but any disturbance may cause the bird to leap from its nest, injuring the eggs or young. If we are to give new birth to our spirit, we must have times of remoteness and even reclusiveness for our well being and ourselves.

The California condor was considered an important source of supernatural powers whose energies were invoked for healing. In one ceremony, the shaman would stick a condor feather down the throat of a person to counteract disease. The Sierra Miwok Indians, the Sisquoc, Tecuya, Inaja, and other tribes had sacred ceremonies to honor the condor. The first condor born in captivity was named "Moloku," the Miwok name for condor and an animal these people honored with its own dance.

The Andean condor is the world's largest flying bird, weighing about 25 pounds, with a wingspan of around 12 feet. Villagers in Peru often shot this species or used it in a brutal ceremony called the *arrangue del condor* in which its body is suspended from a frame. Horsemen would then ride past, punching the bird with their fists until the condor died.

The ritual killing of condors as a means to supernatural power or to open doorways into spiritual realms was performed among a variety of peoples. Sometimes the ritual death was mimicked with the bird being released and not actually killed. In most of these ceremonies, the purpose was to heal and to overcome death.

The Andean condor soars over slopes and coastal plains, but it returns to roost and nest in the mountains. Mountains provide enough updraft for them to take off and soar. The Andean condor reminds us that we are spirit first and must always return to our source.

If the condor appears, we are entering a time of greater protection, especially in things of the spirit.

Are we focusing too much on things of the physical?

Are we getting too flighty and need to be grounded?

Are we not taking time for ourselves?

Are we focusing too much on the negative and not on the positive?

Are we ignoring our communications from spirit?

Are we relying solely on spirit for our accomplishments?

Conures

KEYNOTE

- deepening relationships
- family and young require attention and careful expressions

➤ Conures are part of the parakeet family. There are many varieties and they are often kept as pets. Known for their loud voices, their screeching is what makes them and most parrots difficult pets to have in apartment environments. They also delight in destroying and chewing woods. For little birds, they have powerful beaks. "His bark is worse than his bite" definitely does not apply with conures.

In the wild, the very colorful conures are found in tropical areas of Central and South America. A study of their qualities of color will provide some insight into their individual energies. Two of the more commonly known species are the Sun and Jandaya conures.

The male Sun conure spends only the night in the nest and both parents feed the young. In eight weeks, the young are completely independent and even among most conures, the young become quite independent very quickly, often a reflection of their significance. Creative endeavors usually mature and become independent quickly, often indicating a rhythm of eight weeks at play within our life.

Another common conure is the Jandaya, whose head and nape is a bright yellow with an underside orange red. The wings are mostly green, and like their relatives the Sun conure, they can be quite loud and vocal. Unlike the Sun conure, the males will spend the night and most of the day in the nest. Both parents feed the young. This is a reminder for those in relationships, family, or business to share in the care of the young—whether children or projects.

In nearly all species of parrots and parakeets, the beak is an amazing instrument and is used almost like a third foot when climbing. Thus all parakeets show us how to accomplish tasks with what we have available. The beak is designed for removing husks and breaking up plant food. For those to whom the conure appears, this upper

mandible with its special mobility reflects increased ability at discerning and "getting to the heart of matters."

Between its loud screeching and its beak, we gain some special insight to all species of this and other similar birds. The jaw and mouth are essential to expression and digestion. The voice is our most creative instrument. We can use it to make a person feel as if they are standing in the shadows of the divine or wish they had never been born. Conures reflect this ability, reminding us that our words will have an increasingly greater effect. Things written or spoken more gently will be experienced more gently. Things spoken or written more harshly will be more devastating. Learning to control how we express ourselves will become more and more important.

Conure's nests have great significance as a "true home" because it is used year round, not used just during the breeding season. In the wild, even the fledged young will return to it regularly to roost. What we say and how we say it will have a great impact upon our children and their independence. The foundation will be used by others who will learn from us.

When conures show up, we must be careful to choose our words and activities carefully. They will have a greater impact upon those who are closest to us. Conures are wonderful signs of potentially deepening relationships and responsibilities. The bonding between most pairs is very deep and they often feed each other outside of the breeding season. They reflect greater opportunities for balance, especially in home life. Although greater balance is developing in these areas, the home will require greater attention and more careful expressions of caring than ever before.

Conures
(cont.)

CARAOLINA PAROQUET
(*Conurus carolinensis*)
Forehead and cheeks deep orange, rest of head yellow.

Range formerly easter United States, north to Maryland, Great Lakes, and Iowa; west to Colorado, Oklahoma and eastern Texas; now restricted to southern Florida and parts of Indian Territory.

Are we being too critical or harsh?

Do we need to take our responsibilities more seriously?

Are others around us not fulfilling theirs?

Cormorant

KEYNOTE

- time to dive in deeper
- new birth

CORMORANT
(*Phalacrocorax cargo*)
Chin and sides of throat whitish; back glossy brownish, *distinctly* margined with black; below, uniform shining black.

Are we hesitating acting on our ideas?

Are we diving in without thought or reason?

Are we ignoring our opportunities for new birth?

Do we need to take advantage of new learning opportunities?

➤ Found all over the world, there are over 30 species of cormorants. The common cormorant is also called the great or black cormorant. They have glossy black plumage with a white patch on the chin and cheeks. Their webbed feet, upright stance, and long necks suggest they lead a completely or mostly aquatic life, but they rarely fly out to sea. They are found mostly along coasts or inland waters.

They are expert divers and swimmers and can show us how to dive in and to swim where we wouldn't think it possible—in almost any environment within our life. The cormorant must swallow pebbles to make itself heavy enough to stay under water. When it appears in our life there will come a teaching or a new opportunity that will enable us to accomplish what didn't seem possible.

In Japan, the cormorants are trained for fishing. A metal ring is placed around their necks to prevent them from swallowing their catch. This is a reminder that we must learn to enjoy our accomplishments, our catches in life, and not allow others to distract us from the enjoyment of our accomplishments.

When the cormorant is an individual's totem, the person will have a knack for accomplishing in unique ways what others could not seem to do. When it appears in our life as a message, it is a reminder for us to dive in to what we have been hesitating about. Remember that the cormorant teaches us how to dive into the waters of life creatively especially if we wish a new birth.

➤ The emu is a tall, flightless bird from Australia, rivaled only in its size by the ostrich. It is a bird of the deserts and plains and thus the significance of these environments should also be studied. These are both places of great openness, and so the emu often teaches us in some way about the openness of our lives to others.

This is further reinforced by the fact that aside from the breeding season, emus live in nomadic flocks. They wander in small groups, raiding crops and waterholes, finding food, water, and shelter wherever they can. Individuals with emus as totems or for whom the emu appears as a message often find themselves wandering in their lives, but able to survive successfully and easily during these nomadic journeys. These may be actual journeys or they may be movements from job to job, person to person, etc. The emu often reflects the wandering spirit that is already strong or being awakened in these individuals.

As mentioned, except during the breeding season, they live a nomadic life with small groups. It is not unusual when the emu appears to find ourselves joining with others of a like mind on some spiritual journey.

One of the most unusual characteristics of the emu occurs in the raising of the young when the role of the male becomes primary. The male builds the nest, incubates the eggs, and raises the young. They epitomize the "Mr. Mom Syndrome" and they do it successfully. It is not unusual to find responsible single fathers having an emu as their totem.

Emu

KEYNOTE

- **wandering spirit**
- **responsible fatherhood during the journeys of life**

EMU
(*Dromaeus novae-hollandiae*)
A large Australian ratite bird....Next to the ostrich, to which they are closely related, the emus are the largest existing birds.

Are we wandering aimlessly or do we have a destination?

Are we fulfilling our responsibilities while we pursue our spiritual and personal quests?

Do we need to look for like-minded individuals for support?

Flamingo

KEYNOTE

- **healing and filtering through the lessons of the heart**

- **flirtatiousness**

FLAMINGO
(*Phoenicopterus ruber*)
Rosy red, ligher on back; primaries and secondaries black.

➤ The flamingo is an unusual bird in that its neck and legs are proportionally longer than any other bird. With plumage tinged with pink, except for its black flight feathers, it ranges from the Bahamas to the tip of South America and from southern Europe to South Africa, flamingos are native to some of the most uninhabitable wetlands on the earth—places too remote, salty, and alkaline to attract predators and thus they are able to raise their families in relative peace.

Their unusual body proportions enable them to feed in a peculiar manner, with their heads upside down in foul, alkaline, or salty water. They filter out the water from the blue-green algae in much the same manner the baleen whales filter food through their mouths. As they feed, water is filtered through comblike bristles in the bill to extract the tiny plants and animals from it. Food is swallowed after the water has been expelled.

This filtering of food is related to the primary symbol of the ancient Qabala, the Tree of Life. There are ten levels on the Tree of Life and each level on the tree has four worlds or dimensions. One of the four worlds is Yetzirah, or the world of formation, where the energy of things begins to take shape or form. It is in this realm that the choirs of angels are found who work to manifest energy into reality. At the heart of the Tree of Life is the level known as Tiphareth, the center for healing. Tiphareth, in the world of Yetzirah, has the color of salmon pink like that of the flamingo. Like the flamingo, this is where the filtering for the energies of new healing begin to occur. We begin to see what will benefit us and our hearts and what will not. Like the flamingo, we begin to filter through the things of the heart, especially that which may not be of benefit.

In this world are found the ancient Malachim, a group of angels known as the miracle workers who work under the guidance of the archangel Raphael, the keeper of the Holy Grail, which

Flamingo
(cont.)

lives within the heart of us all. Through the flamingo, we open to that which is most sacred to
our hearts.

Pink in color therapy is used to heal skin conditions. Our skin is our largest sensory organ, and
when the flamingo appears, our physical senses
will be heightened. The flamingo is often a totem
for those who psychically use touch or psychometry. *How To Develop And Use Psychic Touch* will
help those with flamingo totems to use touch to
heighten their psychism and healing abilities
while staying grounded.

Flamingos are almost never alone, and thus
the company of others is often necessary for
those to whom the flamingo is a totem or messenger. However, it can also indicate a need to
become less isolated.

Much of their group behavior has a sexual element to it, which helps the birds to synchronize
their libidos during breeding season so mating
and birth occurs at the most opportune time. It is
not unusual for flamingo people to behave in
a similar manner, often being flirtatious
over long periods of time to stimulate and
align their libidos with others. And in
the flamingo community, there is often communal care of the young
while the parents seek out food.

When the flamingo appears as
a messenger or as a totem, we are
entering a time of cleansing and
filtering to find what nourishes
and heals the heart. It is a time to
follow the heart in all of our endeavors, in spite of the environment
we find ourselves in. In areas of romance and things of the heart, the flamingo reminds us of the need to be a little
more flirtatious if we wish to see results over
time.

Are we discerning about that which is most beneficial to us or are we just accepting whatever comes our way?

Are we ignoring the things we love to do?

Do we need to pursue what is in our heart?

Are we ignoring what we are feeling?

Do we need to explore our own healing gifts and abilities?

Do we need to let others know how we feel?

Animal Wonders

LEFT-FOOTED

Raptors and parrots use their feet to hold food or to catch prey. Most seem to be left-footed.

Black shouldered kite catch prey with their left foot twice as often as with the right. When they do use both feet, they strike first with the left.

Goshawk

KEYNOTE

skillful and relentless pursuit and maneuvering

AMERICAN GOSHAWK
(*Accipiter atricapillus*)
Above bluish slate; crown darker; a whitish line over the eye to the nape; below *finely* marked with gray and white.

Are we afraid to pursue what is available to us at this time?

Are we not trusting in our own power of spirit?

Are we giving up the pursuit too quickly?

➤ The goshawk is a large, gray hawk that looks similar to the American kestral. Hawks are often divided into two common groups—accipiters and buteos. While buteos are soaring hawks, accipiters are medium-sized, short-winged, long-legged hawks with a low, darting flight pattern. The goshawk is the largest North American accipiter and even though its wings are large, it is an extremely good flyer, with a skillful ability to pursue prey through heavily wooded areas.

The goshawk is usually gray with a white eye stripe. This ghostlike hawk maneuvers with the grace of spirit. It often indicates new spirit contact within your life that will provide guidance in accomplishing your goals and maneuvering through any troubled waters that will appear or are already stirred up within your life. This magnificent hawk shows us the power of our own spirit and reminds us of our ability to achieve our hopes and dreams. Its message is always: "Remember who you truly are."

Individuals for whom this bird appears must trust in their own ability to maneuver in all that is going on. Planning may not work. This is a time to trust your instincts in the correct moves. Trust in spirit at this time, but remember that spirit just directs. Your efforts must be employed and applied as well.

Usually found in northern and mountain forests, goshawks are primarily bird eaters, although they prey on a variety of small mammals and birds including pheasants, squirrels, pigeons, and even the occasional fox. They often concentrate their hunting on the most plentiful prey in the area. Goshawks teach us to seek a variety of things to feed ourselves, physically and spiritually. They also remind us we must often focus on what is most plentiful at the time rather than that which may not be as plentiful or accessible.

The goshawk reminds us that if we can dream it, we can achieve it.

➤ The great blue heron is part of a group of wading birds which includes other herons, bitterns, and egrets. It is common to marshlands and shallow waters, usually wading to feed in the shallows. Often considered the king of the marshes, its appearance is a sign to assert our authority and counsel. Now more than ever we will be heard and followed. The great blue heron heralds a time in which our advice and counsel is most accurate and well received.

The legs of the great blue heron are its outstanding characteristic, as are the legs of all waders. Though thin, herons can perch easily on just one. The heron's long, thin legs remind us we don't need massive pillars to balance us, but we do have to be able to stand on our own. The heron's appearance now is a sign that we can do so. Now is the time to assert and become our own authority, the time to take charge, a time others will find us more reliable and more committed. Not a time to be impatient, this a time to act. Others reassess their former opinions of us now, realizing they may have been mistaken

The great blue heron stands tall within the water, yet is a powerful and graceful flyer as well. Stalking in a careful stride when hunting, it spears its prey quickly and directly with its long beak, reminding us that now is the time to assert outselves and explore new areas and activities, to move aggressively toward our opportunities. When heron appears, we know what is best for us now and should follow our own inner prompting rather than the prompting of others.

The great blue heron epitomizes the jack-of-all-trades, comfortable on land, in the air, and in water. Because it is adept in all environments, the heron reminds us of the need to follow our own path in life. Or, it may indicate that we are dabbling in too many areas, trying to assert ourselves too much and spreading ourselves too thin. The heron's appearance may also reflect a little too

Great Blue Heron

KEYNOTE

assertive authority and counsel

GREAT BLUE HERON
(*Ardea berodias*)
Center of crown white, head
crested; legs blackish.

Are we trying to live a traditional style that is not working?

Are we trying to be too "alternative" in our approach to life?

Are we trying to keep up with the Jones's?

Are we being too rigid?

Are we being too unstructured?

Are we not asserting or asserting too strongly?

Great Blue Heron
(cont.)

much structure and authority. Maybe we are being too strict with others and ourselves. It is important to assert, but assertiveness can become aggression and bullying if it is not watched or balanced. The heron's appearance may indicated that either we or someone around us may be acting too aggressively and bullyingly. There is an environment of unfair decisions being made.

Great blue herons are fairly solitary creatures, seeming quite comfortable in their own manner of living. Though they gather in colonies when breeding, they stand out in their uniqueness.

Grebe

KEYNOTE

creative environments essential to growth

WESTERN GREBE
(*Aechmophorus occidentalis*)
Crown and hindneck black; back grayish brown; sides of head and under parts white.

➤ Grebes are very elegant water birds generally found on lakes and reservoirs. These diving and swimming birds are similar to ducks except that they have a pointed bill rather than a flattened one. Some stay in one place year round, but a few species do migrate. In fact, some species of these birds do not fly much at all and must run across the top of water to take off.

When on the ground, grebes are often clumsy and move with difficulty. This is reminder of the importance of the creative and artistic environment to those whom the grebe appears. These people will often feel out of place and awkward except in certain environments.

Water is the environment of the emotional, creative, artistic, the psychic. Dreams and water energy is essential to the well being of grebe people. However, these people must exercise caution and not to become too emotional, remembering that there must be some grounding. Otherwise, grebe people are likely to become the temperamental artist.

For the most part, grebes feed, court, sleep, and carry their young around on the water. When threatened, they will dive beneath the surface, even with their young on their back. Since

Grebe
(cont.)

the young cannot dive until they are several weeks old, both parents take turns carrying them around. It is not unusual to find that when the grebe is a totem for artistic people, they are often very careful about exposing their young creations too soon.

At one time, it was thought that grebes were related to loons, and so a study of loons and loon behavior may help you in understanding the grebe. They neither dive as deeply nor stay under as long as longs, but, like the loon, the appearance of the grebe always indicates more intense dream activity, which includes lucid dreaming.

Grebes are great divers, living off of small fish and such in their environment. As with all diving birds and animals, they teach us how to dive into the creative waters of life, serving as a reminder that we must come to the surface, must come out of those creative waters, from time to time.

The grebe has an unusual habit of eating their own feathers and feeding them to the young. The ball of feathers is thought to aid in digestion in more than one way. It protects the walls of the stomach and plugs the stomach outlet so that fish bones dissolve before passing into the intestines. This is often an indication greater care to prevent indigestion problems may be of concern to those to whom the grebe appears. Usually these digestion problems for grebe people are the result of unbalanced emotions and stifled creativity.

ANTING

Anting is a strange behavior of perching birds, particularly in jays and starlings, but also in robins, hummingbirds, flickers, and sparrows.

The bird po sitions itself over an ants' nest or a line of foraging ants. The bird picks up the ants and rubs their bodies against its feathers. Sometimes through squatting they allow the ants to climb into their plumage.

The formic acid from the ants helps kill parasitic feather lice. If we observe a bird in this activity, it may indicate we need to cleanse ourselves or some aspect of our life from parasites or parasitic activities around us.

Are we ignoring our creative impulses?

Are we in an environment that is stifling to our emotions and creativity?

Are we ignoring our dreams?

Do we need to express our creativity more productively?

Gyrfalcon

KEYNOTE

- sacred gift and knightly codes
- slow and steady brings fastest progress

WHITE GYRFALCON

(*FALCO RUSTICOLUS*)

Tarsus feathered in front nearly to toes; only outer primary notched. Under tail coverts *pure* white.

➤ The gyrfalcon is the largest and one of the most majestic of all falcons. Found in the Arctic tundra, almost solely in Canada, Northern Europe, and Scandinavia, it is well adapted to this northern climate. The gyrfalcon does not migrate, keeping to the harsh environment even in winter with belly feathers long enough to keep its feet warm.

Its favorite food is the Arctic Hare, but it will also hunt ptarmigan, lemmings, and sea birds. It nests on rock ledges, giving it a wider vision, reflective of its closeness to spirit. When the gyrfalcon appears, our own intuitive and spiritual vision will grow, especially in perceiving opportunities and the best paths to progress.

The Gyrfalcon has ancient and sacred ties to spirit. The name is thought to come from the slang Latin, meaning "sacred Falcon." In the past, it was considered a knightly gift in falconry.

It has two primary forms, a white and dark one. The dark form has two tones, with a dark hood. The white form has a regal coloring that has been compared to the back of a snow leopard with which it shares many of the same qualities, and thus studying the snow leopard can provide additional insight.

The gyrfalcon has wing beats that are slow and deep, but they produce a deceptively rapid flight. This slow deep movement also helps to conserve energy in a climate where food may not be as readily available. The gyrfalcon teaches how to conserve and steady our movements for the fastest progress.

This is the bird of the knight's quest—regardless of that quest. It is a reminder to keep the knightly code sacred at this time for our greatest benefit. When the gyrfalcon appears, there is a sacred gift about to come into our life. Our efforts and code of behavior will be rewarded. Though our progress may have been slow, it is about to accelerate.

►The harrier is a hawk of the marsh and wetland areas. Like many falcons, it has a dark-hooded head. Also like falcons, it is an extremely gifted flyer—fast and skilled at aerobatics

The harrier is most active at dawn and dusk. These are sacred times, intersections in the worlds and dimensions, neither morning nor night. These are times when the veils between the physical and spiritual are thinner and the doors between these dimensions are more open. Thus the harrier is always an indication of spirit messages, often from a family member who has passed on, frequently of the opposite sex.

The concept that a message from a family member who has passed on is further reinforced by the harrier's indigenous environment being the marsh and wetlands. These, like "tween times," are "tween places" where the physical and spiritual intersect more intensely. Marshlands are neither entirely water nor land. They are in between.

During mating, the male performs great aerobatic feats to court the female; it loops and dives, displaying its skills to impress the female. The harrier nests on the ground, and during the nesting, the male hunts for the female and the young, fulfilling responsibilities to its family unit. The female harrier prefers eating mammals, while the male prefers eating birds.

Nesting on the ground is a strong reminder that when we work with the less substantial realms, we must stay grounded. We can work with the spirit, but we must live in the physical. That is where our responsibilities lie. No matter how skilled we may be, we must stay grounded when we work with the psychic and spiritual worlds and fulfill our responsibilities by taking care of our daily obligations.

Harrier Hawk

KEYNOTE

- spirit messages
- staying grounded when working with the psychic

HARRIER OR MARSH HAWK
(*Circus budsonius*)
Upper tail-coverts and base of tail white.

Harris Hawk

KEYNOTE

**cooperative pursuit
and hunting**

HARRIS HAWK
(*Parabuteo unicinctus harrisi*)
Longer upper tail-coverts,
base and tip of tail white.

*Are you trying to do
everything yourself?*

*Do you need to
let others help?*

*Are you or others around
you being uncooperative?*

➤A number of years ago, a falconer in Colorado by the name of Kin Quitugua took me on one of his Hawkquest educational programs. His primary birds were Harris Hawks, which he used to hunt and to educate the public. He also used them to help rehabilitate releasable birds of prey. At the time, he was using his hawks to help teach a golden eagle how to hunt.

He allowed me to fist his bird called C.C. and I was so amazed at the behavior of his hawks that I almost forgot to release C.C. during the demonstration.[1] One would fly from above to scare out the rabbits, while the other came from below. This cooperative hunting technique is unique among birds of prey, and is the primary lesson of this species, teaching us that cooperation is needed for the greatest success.

Harris hawks are not loners like so many birds of prey. They breed in small groups and hunt in teams. Then they share the prey. Their hunting parties are usually family groups. The group hunting is an adaptive behavior. Harris hawks live in desert areas where prey is more scarce but often larger than in other environments. So in order to survive as a species, group hunting was adopted over the years.

One of their more amazing behaviors is their stack perching. In the desert there are few trees to perch on, and so the Harris hawks will often stand and perch on each other's shoulders on top of a cactus.

When the Harris hawk appears, it is time to get help from like-minded individuals. Larger goals are best accomplished with the assistance of others. Bigger goals will be accomplished more effectively if we do not try and do it all ourselves.

Reassess your goals. Remember that, as with all hawks, Harris hawks have tremendous vision and they are able to see larger prey and goals.

---

[1] To *fist* a bird is a falcony term the means to put the bird on the hand.

The Kingdom of Birds

Trust in your vision, but also trust in others' abilities to help you accomplish your goals. Everyone benefits when there is cooperation and working together.

►The ibis is a wading bird related to the spoonbill. Found in marshes, wetlands and mudflats, ibis have long spindly legs and long necks, both of which help them to maneuver in shallow waters and feed upon small aquatic animals.

This bird tucks its head under its wing when it sleeps, and when it does this, it resembles the shape of the heart. According to the Greek scholar Aelian, it also had a stride that was exactly one cubit, a unit of measurement used in building temples. Because of this, it was always considered a sacred bird.

The ibis was particularly sacred in Egypt because of its ability to eat snakes—even poisonous ones. The snake was an animal of transformation, life, death, and rebirth. To eat a snake was to have power over it and thus the ibis was considered a bird of great healing and magic.

The ibis is related to Thoth, the Egyptian god of wisdom, medicine, and magic, who is the brother of Isis and Osiris. It was believed that Thoth hovered or flew over the Egyptian people in the form of an ibis, and he taught them the occult sciences and arts. Whenever the ibis appears, there will come opportunities to learn new healing techniques and wisdom, along with other sacred arts. New mysteries are about to open up in our life and it is time to wade into them a little more.

Harris Hawk
(cont.)

Ibis

KEYNOTE

healing and magic

WOOD IBIS
(*Tantalus loculator*)
Head and neck bare; white, primaries, secondaries and tail blackish.

Junco

KEYNOTE

- **revealing facial expressions**
- **replenishing**

SLATE-COLORED JUNCO
(*Junco hyemalis*)
Head and back gray, the crown sometimes slightly darker, the feathers usually more or less tipped with brownish; breast and sides *gray*; belly white; third outer tail-feather with white.

➤ This small, migrating bird is slate gray with white outer tail feathers that flash conspicuously in flight. It is widespread and there are many varieties, the most common being the dark-eyed junco, distinguished from the others with a darker, masklike appearance around the eyes. It also has a pale bill that contrasts with its dark face.

This contrast in appearance is part of what shows up in those to whom the junco is a totem or messenger. Watch the faces of others around you, as their expressions will reveal more than their words will. Also be careful of your own facial expressions as they may give away more than you desire.

There are four species of dark-eyed juncos, and all have pink or pinkish bills. This can be a reminder to be softer in our expressions. It sometimes indicate we may see a softer and more revealing side to those who are normally more hidden from us.

The junco is often called the snowbird, making long migrations. For those to whom this bird is a totem, such long moves may also occur. The Pueblo people also referred to the junco as a snowbird, believing it brought the snows south in the winter with them, providing moisture to dry areas. They were honored for this.

The appearance of the junco indicates a period of replenishing. New waters are coming that will replenish us and our lives. Opportunities to stimulate new growth will occur.

Killdeer

KEYNOTE

guardianship of creative acts

➤The killdeer is usually considered a water bird in mythologies, with all of the traditional symbology of water and its connection to creativity and birth. They will live around any kind of water, from mud puddles to lakes. In New Mexico, they often retreat from the northern part of the state in midwinter but return by March, making their time of greatest power spring through autumn.

Killdeer, of the plover family, normally nests in open country, always near water. Black and white stripes camouflage the bird on its nest, and thus protecting and guarding what it gives birth to more easily. If disturbed, they will leave the eggs and draw intruders away by spreading their tails and flapping their wings to make themselves conspicuous. This reminds us it is not enough to give birth to things, but we must guard and protect our creative acts until they mature. We must sometimes mislead and misdirect threats or perceived threats for the benefit of our creations.

The killdeer usually derives its name in various languages from its high pitched cry. A Pueblo story tells how coyote, when stealing fire, tosses the embers to an unknown bird before being caught. The bird took the fire, and even though it burned its hands, cried out its name—killdeer. But it did not let go of the fire, so the bird is also associated with fire as well as water, therefore showing us how to handle opposing forces and withstanding their intensities.

During nesting season, killdeer will often do a broken wing act to lead intruders away from their nests, usually just hollows on the ground. Intruders are lead from the nest thinking the bird is wounded prey. When killdeer appears, there is the ability to lead and misdirect danger. It may signal a need to do so at this time in order to protect what's in your nest—which is in your offspring. Killdeer attend to the order of creativity and have connections to its guardianship.

KILLDEER
(*Oxyechus vociferus*)
Rump and upper tail-coverts rusty. In adults, above grayish brown and rusty; below white with *two* black rings.

Killdeer
(cont.)

Killdeer are sentinels to the water sources because none can approach their waters without arousing their cries. If killdeer have appeared in your life, take extra care to protect and hide your creations at this time. Do not expose them too soon to the outer world and its threats. Use some deception if necessary to protect what is yours.

Kite

KEYNOTE

- adaptability and flexibility
- opening to the underworld

SWALLOW-TAILED KITE
(*Elanoides forficatus*)
Back purplish black, wings and tail blue-black.

➤Kites are part of the falcon family and there are a variety of them. They are fast and skilled flyers, able to perform great aerial acrobatics and ballet, and most kites are found in swamps and marshes. Some also gather and hunt in open country, and many kites hunt while flying, taking advantage of opportunities when they appear.

The swallow-tailed kite has a long, deep, forked tail and snow white underparts. Its habitat is the swamp, an area often associated with spirits and the underworld; therefore, it can show us how to maneuver within this realm. Many mediums have the swallow-tailed kite as a guide when they begin to develop their ability to communicate with "the dead." Swallow-tailed kites drink in air in a swallowing pattern and can teach us how to develop unique breathing techniques to open our psychic sensitivities and abilities for recognizing and communicating with spirit.

Other common kites are the black-shouldered kite and Mississippi kite. The black-shouldered kite has grayish black primary feathers. They frequently gather in marshes and open country, and when it is riding the winds, it seems motionless. The Mississippi kite is the true social butterfly, often seen performing leisurely somersaults with many of its friends.

The snail kite is endangered in the U.S. Unlike many birds of prey that have adapted their eating habits for survival, the snail kite continues to feed only upon a rare snail found in swamps and marshes. With the loss of their wetland and

Kite

(cont.)

environmental home, this snail is diminishing in great numbers. As it does, so does the snail kite.

Kites make flying look easy. Any time a kite shows up, it is an indication of a need to develop flexibility and adaptability. Kites are messages to use our skills. They remind us that the world of spirits is opening to us, and although many people often struggle to develop these skills, they will seem to come much easier with the help of the kite.

Are we trying to do more than we can?

Are we not performing in our most creative ways?

Are we limiting our possibilities like a snail kite, refusing to adapt?

EVERGLADE KITE OR
SNAIL HAWK
(*Rostrhamus sociabilis*)
Longer upper tail-coverts and base of tail white. Adults slatey black; end of tail with brownish and whitish bands.

Lark

KEYNOTE

- sacred songs of harmony and luck
- the bardic tradition awakening

HORNED LARK
(*Otocoris alpestris*)

Hind toe-nail much the longest. Throat and line over eye distinctly *yellow*; black feathers over eye lengthened, forming when raised little tufts; breast-patch, sides of throat, line over eye and forecrown black, more or less tipped, especially on head, with yellowish or brownish; back brownish.

►There are 78 species of larks found throughout the world, except in parts of South America and Antarctica. They are small, perching birds with long, pointed wings who live in open grasslands, and they are most known for their musical song. The unusual aspect of their song is that they sing while in flight. The skylark in particular is known for this quality as it soars upward.

The mysticism of song and its effects—physically, psychologically, and spiritually—is great. This bird links us to the ancient bards.

> In every society, in every part of the world, there were individuals whose task it was to keep the ancient mysteries alive and to pass them on by word of mouth. These individuals were historians, musicians, and healers. They are what we now group under the generic term of "bard."[1]

This included such groups as the African Griot, The Norse Skalds, The Anglo-Saxon Gleemen, The Navajo Singers, The Russian Kaleki, The Japanese Zenza, and The English Bards, to name just a few.

For those to whom the lark appears, the mysteries and science of sound, music, and voice will become increasingly important and the shamanic aspects of song and sorcery will become unveiled. This is reflected in a lot of the superstitions surrounding this bird. It was considered a sacred bird throughout the Shetland Islands and thus harming the lark while it was on its nest would bring a person bad luck. The lark also has three black spots on its tongue, and thus for every lark eaten, you would incur three curses.

When the lark appears, the creative power of the voice awakens and stories and song (telling and singing as well as hearing) will become important. Words spoken will take on greater

---

[1] Ted Andrews. *Sacred Sounds* (St. Paul, MN: Llewellyn Publications, 1993), p. 115.

Lark
(cont.)

power and magic. Things spoken lovingly will be felt more lovingly. Things spoken harshly will cut more deeply. The power of the voice is awakening.

It has been said that the angels sing everyday for us, but to hear the song of the angels we must first be able to hear the song within our own hearts. When the lark appears, our own sacred song is being awakened in our life.

Long-Eared Owl

KEYNOTE

silent and assertive defense

AMERICAN
LONG-EARED OWL
(*Asia wilsonianus*)
Ear-tufts long; eyes yellow.
Abopve varied with gray;
belly barred.

➤ The long-eared owl is a slender, medium-sized, grayish owl. Like the great horned owl, it also has feather tufts, but longer. Thus its name. The feather tufts are close together and directly over the facial discs of this owl. No one is truly sure what purposes the tufts serve. Theories vary from the idea that it is for courtship appearance to threatening displays to camouflaged secretiveness.

The long wings of this owl give it a large appearance when in flight, but the flight is very graceful. Individuals to whom the long-eared owl appears often have deceptive appearances, being much more creative and productive than may be realized. They are often an indication of a need to focus on the creation and protection of endeavors rather than the environment in which the creation is taking place. The grace and recognition will come in time.

It is a "fly by night" owl, never building its own nest, but rather using deserted squirrel and crow nests, yet it is still a powerful parent. The long-eared owl is fierce in defending its young, preventing attack by displaying a great "wounded bird act" to draw away intruders.

This bird tells us that it is not the place where we give birth that is important but that we do give birth and that we fiercely defend what we birth. It is a sign that protection of our creative endeavors is most important.

Even among owls, this one is seldom seen. It is extremely nocturnal, and during the day remains quiet and very well hidden. Nocturnal birds and animals usually reflect a tremendously active dream life from which comes great inspiration. This is especially true of the long-eared owl. When this bird appears, nighttime is going to be a more productive and creative time.

Macaw

➤ All macaws are members of the parrot family and have brilliantly colored feathers—scarlet, military, blue and gold, and green-winged. These colorful birds are intelligent, perceptive, brave, and alert. Though they always appear calm, they rarely miss anything that goes on around them, as if everything around them is being exposed to new sunlight.

KEYNOTE

- sharp vision and spiritual perception
- new sunshine and healing

Archaeological evidence reveals that macaws were imported by the Pueblo peoples and they are now native to Mexico and Central America. Their feathers were as important in Pueblo ritual and ceremony as were the feathers of eagles and turkeys. Evidence seems to indicate that Pueblos had a preference for the bright red feathers of the military and scarlet varieties.

The military macaw was honored for its ability to descend to the ground in May in parts of Mexico and eat poisonous ava nuts. Macaws were a sign of new light that would swallow up the dark around an individual or group, reflecting the return of the healing powers of the sun.

The blue and gold is a larger species of macaw. Its blue and yellow feathers signify balance and were often associated with the directions of north (yellow) and west (blue), reflecting the direction to look for healing and balance. Mythologically, all macaws are linked to curative and healing powers, especially of the sun. Although there is never just a single keynote for any bird, macaws are first and foremost birds of the sun.

BLUE AND YELLOW MACAW
(*Ara ararauna*)
Any of numerous parrots, chiefly of the genus *Ara*, now confined to South and Central American, but formerly also represented in the West Indies. They are among the largest of parrots, and have a very long tail, a naked space around the eyes, and a strong hooked bill with which they crack hard nuts.

Scarlet macaw is found in rainforest areas of Mexico, Central America, and South America and their bright plumage is a favorite of natives to the area. They can live a long time, estimated at 75 to 90 years, and their appearance always indicates the beginning of a long period of greater spiritual depth, creativity, and heightened perceptions, all becoming sharper and more accurate. We should trust our perceptions, no matter how bizarre or strange they may be.

Macaw
(cont.)

In the Amazon, the scarlet macaw is linked to natives known as the Jaguar People, who believe they came from the stars. When it came time for them to return to the heavens, scarlet macaw was sent to gether them up. Some were accidentlally left behind, and when the gods discovered this, the scarlet macaw was banished to Earth to serve as guardian and messenger for these people until the gods returned to return them to the stars.

Macaws are also very emotional birds. It has been theorized that scarlet macaws have the emotional development of a two-to-three-year-old child. They respond to emotions around them in creative ways.

Although macaws mimic human speech, they have an intricate body language and a variety of vocalizations that reflect a heightened ability to communicate more colorfully and effectively. When the macaw appears in our lives, people will pay attention and listen as never before. People will seek out our counsel, and we are likely to find new creative ways of expressing our perceptions and performing the counseling.

Macaws have powerful beaks, used to break open nuts, and they can show us how to crack open the fruit of life. In the wild, they often are found to eat and dig in a particular kind of clay, and it is theorized that there are minerals within it essential to their health. For those to whom the macaw appears, an examination of our mineral intake may be important now.

The macaw often reminds us to look at health issues. If there are health problems, they may be emotionally related. We live in a time in which we know that emotions affect physiological processes. Balancing the emotions will benefit physical imbalances as well. Learning to control the emotions is important now. The appearance of the scarlet macaw may also reflect a need for some sunshine and some color in our life or that color therapy could be of benefit.

➤ Merlins, like the mythical character, are magical birds. The merlin is a "pigeon hawk." Actually a member of the falcon family, it has a slate blue crown and black back and mimics the flight of pigeons to sneak up on unwary prey. It also will use its flying maneuvers to startle flocks of birds and then in seemingly magical displays of flying, snatch stragglers from the air.

Its ability to mimic pigeons to capture prey indicates what this bird's message is. Sometimes we must appear as something we are not in order to capture what we need or want, weaving a little shapeshifting magic, creating an illusion in order to accomplish our goals.

The merlin can also appear if we need to look for someone around us who may not be what he or she appears to be. We may find ourselves in a vulnerable position and should be cautious about becoming someone's prey.

The merlin in falconry was a preference of noble ladies. The merlin is easily trainable and was then often returned back to the wild after a season of hunting. Because of this, the merlin is a reminder to weave and use a little magic for the time being. It is an indication new and often temporary doors of learning will open. We should take advantage of these opportunities, undertake some quick training and accomplish what we need at the moment because our learning will come quickly and will serve its purpose for the time.

Now is the time to shapeshift our life and ourselves a little for the greatest benefits.

Merlin

KEYNOTE

quick and magical maneuvers and shapeshiftings

RICHARDSON MERLIN
(*Falco richardsonii*)
Resembles the black merlin, but is pal er and has the central tail feather crossed by six light bars, counting the terminal one.

Are others around you appearing as they are not?

Are we doing all we can to help ourselves?

Are we using our magic inappropriately?

Are we not using the magic that we should?

Are we allowing ourselves to be vulnerable?

Night-hawk

KEYNOTE

diligence and persistence

NIGHTHAWK
(*Chordeiles virginianus*)
Primaries blackish with a
white bar and no rusty spots;
darkest of our Nighthawks

➤The nighthawk is not really a hawk or a bird of prey in the hawk or falcon family. It is actually a swisher, a member of the whip-poor-will family, of which there are a number of varieties. I spoke of the swisher in my book *Animal-Speak*, but over the years so many have asked about the "nighthawk" that I am including a little more here. I strongly recommend reading and studying the information on the swisher in the previous work.

The nighthawk is a *crepuscular* bird, meaning that it is most active at twilight where its form is recognizable as it is often seen sweeping by with stiff wings. It is a diligent and persistent hunter of insects, and thus it teaches us to be the same. Nothing succeeds like persistence.

Among the Hopi, it was called "Rain Flopper" because it makes a sound during courtship that seemed to imitate thunder to them. It was a sacred bird to have around, especially for newly made fields created to capture run-off. It was a sign of success and plenty.

When the nighthawk appears, we need to ask ourselves some important questions.

Are we truly going after what we seek?

Are we persisting?

If we wish the rains of abundance in our lives, are we willing to do our par t to bring them?

➤ Often mistaken for immature bald eagles, the osprey is a fish hawk with an eye stripe with white feathers on its head and a white underside. Found near water and coastlines, it is the only raptor with a reversible outer toe for an extra firm grip and with footpads that have spicules for grasping slippery fish. This bird of prey can show us how to grasp and hold onto what we go after.

Ospreys build a huge stick nest, some weighing up to half a ton. It uses a shrill whistle and defends its nest aggressively against intruders, even against other osprey hunting in its territory.

The courtship ritual is powerful. The male performs a fish dance, flying up and down in front of the female, bringing fish to her, demonstrating to the female what a great provider it can be. In competition for a mate, it can perform amazing and frightening feats. It will lock talons with other osprey and do a freefall spin until one or the other breaks away.

The osprey sometimes submerges completely under the water to capture fish. It has an enlarged cere that can cover its nostrils in water. The diving into waters to grasp food can be symbolic of diving into the creative waters of life to awaken and draw forth what will nourish us.

To the Pueblo people, this was known as a water eagle, more skillful at diving into water and catching fish than the bald eagle. The osprey, like the eagle, has a head of white feathers, but it has a dark facial mask. Unlike the bald eagle, it usually has a white breast as well.

When the osprey appears, it is time to check our commitments to those people and things closest to us and the commitment of others to us. Remember that ospreys are active hunters.

KEYNOTE

assertive hunting and actions

AMERICAN OSPREY
OR FISH HAWK
(*Pandiaon haliaetus carolinensis*)
Nape white; feet large; no bars on primaries. Below white with few or no spots on breast.

Are we truly going after what we desire?

Are we giving it our all?

Are we diving in and hooding back?

How far are we will to go to achieve what we seek?

Parakeet

KEYNOTE

messenger and companion

➤ The parakeet or "budgie" is an Australian member of the parrot family. In the wild, they are a grass green with a bright yellow head and long tapering blue tails They can mimic other sounds, including human speech, and thus they were often thought of as the messengers from other realms and distant places. They are extremely social, travelling in flocks and are always with others of its kind. Hence its other keynote—companionship.

When the parakeet appears, one of two things is usually going on in our life. Either we are about to have some new companionship, or it is time to get away from the crowd and spend some time alone. The message is always about whom we are or are not associating with.

The parakeet is a traditional messenger symbol not unlike the crow. In Egypt it was a symbol of the soul. The Persian poet, Farrid Ud-Din Attar, tells a tale of the parrot/parakeet that seeks out the waters of immortality and how it encounters various companions.

There are many species of parakeets, and each has its own unique qualities. But even with their uniqueness, they are always the messenger companions.

The Kingdom of Birds

Puffin

KEYNOTE

prayer and humor are the tools we need for abundance

➤ Puffins are small auks, sea birds, usually about 12 inches tall that live in northern waters. Their bills are very large and triangular shaped and colored with bright yellow, red and blue stripes. The plumage is black with white underneath and the legs are bright orange. Overall, it gives them a comical and almost clownlike appearance.

Their colors are reminiscent of the Qabalistic Tree of Life upon which all things become possible. The white is the hidden or spiritual side to life on earths (the black). The three colors of the bill are three colors of specific spheres on the Tree of life. The Yellow is Tiphareth (Temple of the Heart, child's prayer). The orange/red is Geburah (Temple of Strength and Work) and the blue is Chesed (The Temple of Abundance). The puffin is a reminder to combine work, prayer, and fun for abundance.

Their scientific name, *fratercula*, translates as little brother, but it is sometimes interpreted as "little friar" from the bird's habit of clasping its feet together as though in prayer when it rises from the sea. Proper prayer is essential to manifesting anything in life. Puffins swim underwater, using their wings while searching for food, and they can hold as many as 30 small fish in their mouth. They remind us that there is an abundance available to us, but we must learn to dive in, trusting in our prayers and our efforts.

Puffins are also reminders that humor is essential to our physical health, our spiritual health, and just as important as prayer. When we are in spiritual waters, we should pray and meditate, but we should have fun as well, and be careful not to take ourselves or our spiritual path too seriously. Many of the people I meet in my travels could learn much from the puffin, as some seem to believe that there is no room for humor and fun when on the spiritual path.

PUFFIN
(*Fratercula arctica*)
Above, and foreneck blackish; cheeks and under parts white; bill in summer touched with bright red.

Puffin
(cont.)

These birds live in burrows of loose soil at the tops of cliffs or on islands, both of which are magical places associated with the wonders of the spirit world. Puffins are curious animals who can awaken our own curiosity about things of the spirit. When they appear as totems or messengers, there will be increased contact with spirit that may sometimes be humorous but very real.

Puffins show us how to work, pray and have fun, and by combining all three, we open to greater abundance within our life. If they have appeared in our life, we need to look at which of these three things we are not doing and thus should do more of.

➤ Sandhill cranes are waterbirds that often eat other water symbols, such as fish and frogs. All cranes have qualities in common, and thus some study of cranes, in general, is recommended.

Sandhill cranes are high flyers, always announcing their presence with loud calls. Hence, they are often considered noble guardians, calling out loudly to forewarn. If they appear in our life, there is usually something we need to watch out for and attend to more carefully.

Many of their natural behaviors further reinforce the perception of them as guardians in the traditional sense. When threatened, an annoyed crane aims its spearlike bill and rushes toward intruders, occasionally nipping them.

In their preening, they also do a bit of feather painting. Sandhills comb their feathers, coating them with oil in the same manner as other birds and then painting them a rusty brown with a mixture of grass and mud. This gives them a somewhat camouflaged appearance.

These behaviors convey the impression of standing guard and driving off intruders from the environment. The migrations of sandhill cranes parallel the journeys of the sun, moving from north to south, reminding us that there are times to change and move the guard. When sandhill cranes appear, there is usually some hidden protection around us, energy of secret and noble guardianship. Sometimes it's a sign we may need to be the hidden protector of someone else. Sometimes it's a warning to watch our possessions and ourselves a little more closely.

Most photos of sandhills reveal only the adult birds, probably because the young are often scarce and the parents are secretive in rearing them. This further reflects the energies of protectiveness and guardianship associated with these cranes. Extra care to protect our young—children or projects—should be taken.

Sandhill Crane

KEYNOTE

- noble and secret guardianship
- the dance of life

SANDHILL CRANE
(*Grus mexicana*)
Similar to the little brown crane, but larger.

Sandhill Crane
(cont.)

The Zuni Indian perspective further reinforces the notion of secretive guardianship. Among the Zuni, the sandhill crane was a source of great secret magic and the feathers could only be used by members of the "Galaxy Society." The meaning and actual use of the feathers have been well-kept, closed secrets.

The noise of thousands of cranes together is legendary, conveying an almost ancient and untamed quality. Their incredibly loud whoops coordinate their movements, defend territories, find mates, and keep lifelong mates together, all functions of a traditional guard at the gates.

The sandhill crane is famous for its dancing, which is inspiring in that it seems to express a joy at life. Around the world no dance has probably been more imitated among native peoples, who danced in response to its migration to celebrate the seasons, for protection, and for fertility.

The sandhill crane's mating dance is very much like a ballet with three predominant displays: an upright wing stretch, a horizontal head pump (a bowing), and what is sometimes referred to as a vertical toss. In this display, the crane lowers its heads, grabs a stick or vegetation, and then flings it in the air as it raises its head back up. The crane then begins a bowing with a vertical leap, the heart of crane dancing. In the spring, mating pairs perform this, but it usually inspires all of the other cranes to participate as well. Each bird coils and then springs up, sometimes as high as 15 feet, holding its head high and flapping its wings 4 to 5 times before coming down.

The enthusiasm among the cranes is contagious and serves a reminder that we should celebrate and dance for what is ours. Guardianship is important, but it does not mean that we hide from life. Life is meant to be danced and celebrated. When we are safe, then it is time to dance. When cranes appear, it is usually time for us to join in the dance of life.

Sapsucker

> All woodpeckers from around the world have great mythology surrounding them. Their rhythmic drumming reflects new rhythms of change within a person's life and they can be a weather bird, connected to the thunder. Different species have their own unique qualities, but all have something to do with new rhythms at play within our life.

Sapsuckers are part of the woodpecker family with a special feeding process. As with all woodpeckers, they drill small, shallow holes into trees. They differ from other types of woodpeckers in that the trees are usually live, and they are not just digging for insects in dead and rotting wood. As their name suggests, they lap up the sap that exudes from the holes they drill. Insects get caught in the sap and thus they come back later to the holes to feed on them as well. The holes do not harm the trees, and thus the sapsucker shows us how to find and extract nutrition and nourishment from the resources around us without harming them or depleting them. They show us the hidden beauty and nectar of life.

The yellow-bellied sapsucker has a barred black and white plumage. In the male, the head is a scarlet color, reflecting the ability to use our head creatively to find the nutrition and resources we need. The male usually has a red throat as well, while the female has a white throat. The throat is the area of expression and the early place of digestion, *i.e.* swallowing. It is the bridge between the heart and the head. Because of this, the sapsucker reminds us that we must be creative in our expressions and follow our own hearts and minds—our own rhythms—in life.

Remember that the sapsucker reminds us that now is the time to dig the sweetness out from the shell. To open up the flow a little more fully.

KEYNOTE

- **extracting hidden nourishment**

- **look and dig beneath the surface**

YELLOW-BELIED SAPSUCKER
(*Sphyrapicus varius*)
Crown and throat red; a *whitish* band from eye to eye across nape; belly washed with yellow; breast patch black.

Are we following our own rhythms?

Are we finding things difficult to digest?

Are we following our own hearts and mind?

Are we extracting all that we can from the resources available to us?

Secretary Bird

KEYNOTE

- trust in your uniqueness

- customs and behaviors must be appropriate

SECRETARY BIRD

(*Serpentarius serpentarious*)

A large long-legged raptorial bird of Africa (chiefly South Africa). It has a powerful hooked beak, a crest of long feathers, and a long tail. Its general color is blue gray, with black wing quills, thighs, abdomen, and bars on the tail. It feeds largely upon reptiles, and is often tamed to rid premises of them.

➤ The secretary bird is from the African plains and stands over four feet tall, with a wing-span of two feet. It gets its name from the similarity of its crest feathers to that of a quill pen sticking out from behind a secretary's or clerk's ear.

The secretary bird is the only bird of prey with extremely long stork-like legs and an extremely long, stiff tail. Flying very well, it is an expert at soaring, and unlike other birds of prey, it easily chases down its prey on foot, seldom flying.

The secretary bird spends most of its time striding calmly along the African grasslands in search of prey, such as arthropods, rodents, lizards, and even snakes. It has a reputation as a snake killer, but it does not actively seek them. It kills its prey with its bill or with blows from its strong feet, swallowing it whole.

The secretary bird has a specific courtship ritual that involves sending and reacting to specific behavioral signals from its potential mate. This includes a ritualized head bowing. If either the male or female behaves inappropriately, they may fail to breed in that year.

When the secretary bird appears, it is a reminder that we must use what we have and do things in the manner best for us. The secretary bird reminds us to stand tall in our uniqueness because ultimately that is what will serve us best, but it is also a reminder not to exaggerate that uniqueness just for the sake of display and attention.

Are we trying to be something we are not?

Do we need to pay attention to proper customs and behaviors?

Are others around us ignoring and dishonoring our own customs?

Do we need to more strongly strike out in our own unique manner?

Are we trying to be too unique and too alternative?

➤ The sharp-shinned hawk is one of several hawks often found within the cities and suburbs. This hawk is very quick flyer, and will often come into yards to prey on small birds, darting through trees and across lawns, seizing an unwary bird, and carrying it off in its talons.

This woodland hawk is an accipiter with short wings and long tails, which distinguish it from its soaring relatives, the buteos, which have broader and longer wings and shorter tails. The short, rounded wings give it great maneuverability in woodlands and serves to remind us that we will be able to maneuver through the situations going on around us with much greater ease than we may have imaged.

Among the Pueblo, it was considered a lesser hawk, but being swift and tireless, it served as an inspiration for youths. It was a relative of Kisa, a Hunting Hawk deity of the Hopi. In one of their legends, it gives to the Hopi the throwing stick or boomerang with magical qualities for hunting small prey. The stick was modeled after the curved wing of the smaller hawks.

The sharp-shinned hawk lays its eggs with a unique sense of timing. They are laid so that the fully-fledged young leave the nest in time to practice their hunting skills on the young of small songbirds and other small species of birds. This sense of opportune timing is often found among those who have the sharp-shinned hawk as a totem. They have a knack for timing activities appropriately and most beneficially.

As with all hawks, it has excellent eyesight, seeing about seven times better than humans. When this fast and agile flyer appears, it helps us to see opportunities ahead and remind us to act quickly to take advantage of them, often telling us that now is the time to act on the opportunities we perceive.

Sharp-Shinned Hawk

KEYNOTE

- vision, perception, and quick action
- impeccable timing

SHARP-SHINNED HAWK
(Accipiter velox)
Tail *square* at end. Above slatey gray; crown darker; below barred white and rusty brown.

Are we not pursuing strong enough that which has presented itself to us?

Are we not looking far enough ahead?

Are we hesitating to act?

Remember that timing is everything.

Short-eared Owl

KEYNOTE

aggressive pursuit of skills and goals

SHORT-EARED OWL
(*Asio accipitrinus*)
Ear tufts short; eyes yellow. No gray above, belly *streaked*.

➤The short-eared owl is a tawny, medium-sized owl with piercing yellow eyes. No owl can truly rotate its head completely. All birds, though, do have extra vertebrae in the neck, giving them the ability to rotate as much as 270 degrees and even a bit more.

The short-eared owl is extremely adept at the head rotation, enhancing its alertness and perception. This is probably so as it is—unlike the majority of owls—a daytime hunter. It hunts also at night, but mostly during the day. Its medicine or power is active both day and night.

It shares the marshes with the harrier hawks and, as skilled a flyer as the harrier may be, the short-eared owl is even more skilled. The two can sometimes be observed chasing each other as if involved in good-natured flying competitions. Individuals with a short-eared owl as a totem usually have a friend or competitor in an important role within their lives. A study of the harrier hawk is also important and will benefit these people.

While the great blue heron often is considered the king of the marshlands, the short-eared owl can truly rule it. It is aggressive and fiery. The scientific name used to be *Asio flammeus*, and it has flamelike markings, relfecting its fiery personality.

The short-eared owl roosts and nests on the ground. It is unique among owls in that it will meticulously build its home. This is often an indication of a need to carefully develop your skills and talents. Build your life solidly, taking the time to do so correctly. Develop your life skills consciously.

The Kingdom of Birds

➤The titmouse family is a group of small, dull, or brown colored birds. The "tit" comes from the 14th century English word for anything little. The "mouse" was a general name for any small, dull-colored bird of that same century. The chickadee, also related, should be studied as well.

The tufted titmouse has a pointed crest, although it is not always raised. A crest is like a crown, and all birds with crests reflect a need to recognize our own nobility. Nobility revolves around fulfilling our responsibilities to ourselves and to others with dedication and commitment. With its pointed tuft of head feathers and its large eyes, this small bird is very striking. Its tuft of feathers is raised most often when it is asserting its territory, about to drive another bird from the feeder, or when trying to attract a mate.

A gray bird with paler underside, its coloring reflects the covering of clouds. Oftentimes we get so wrapped up in our daily obligations we forget what magnificent creatures we are. The titmouse reminds us to look behind the clouds of our life. There is nobility in taking care of our responsibilities that is often forgotten and ignored in the modern world. When the tufted titmouse appears, there will occur a clearing of the clouds and there some recognition of your efforts.

When a pair raises two families in a summer, the young titmice of the first brood will help feed the second. Because of this, the titmouse is often a reminder of familial responsibilities. Once titmice use a nest box, they may often continue to use. Thus they teach the importance of family traditions, that there is a familial responsibility in life that reflects the nobility of the human soul.

If the titmouse has shown up in your life, remember the nobility of the little things you do. They may seem unglamorous at times, but they serve a great function. Fulfilling them develops and reflects great character. It is through the little things in life that we grow the most.

Tufted Titmouse

KEYNOTE

the simple nobility of fulfilling family responsibilities and traditions

TUFTED TITMOUSE
(*Baeolophus bicolor*)
Head crested; forehead *black*;
above gray; below whitish,
sides rusty.

Are you forgetting the importance of the things you are doing?

Have you forgotten the reasons you first un – dertook a task?

Do you need to get back to your foundations and traditions?

Are you looking too much toward the great things rather than allowing the little things to grow into the great?

White Crane

KEYNOTE

- longevity
- honor
- spiritual justice

WHOOPING CRANE
(*Grus americana*)
White; skin on top of head
dull red; primaries black.

➤ "Honorable Lord Crane" is the ancient symbol of spiritual justice and longevity whose appearance can help us to draw upon our own innate waters, our intuitive faculty, awakening freshness within tradition for new growth.

The crane is both a solar symbol and a herald for death. This contrast is significant in that cranes teach the need for both life and death as part of the same process. Crane always heralds the end or change of old ways so that a new expression can be born within them.

As a wading bird, white cranes can comfortably move between water, land, earth, and sky. They can open doors between all worlds, realms, times and traditions, stimulating new tangible, spiritual experiences, revealing how death is just a transition, not an end.

In more ancient times, the hierophants, the priests and priestesses, were schooled in walking between worlds, with all that this implies. Because of its link between worlds, cranes can awaken past lives, revealing how ancient we truly are and how the past is affecting our present. This can bring a new understanding of our karma, life issues, sacrifices we have made or are making, and how the laws of spiritual justice play out within our life.

Crane always awakens us to the ancient ones—the beings of Spirit and its various realms—including that of the Faerie. Now is the time to draw upon ancient teachings and to find ways of re-expressing them within the modern world and within current life.

In the wild, the crane often lays two eggs, but usually only rears one. The parents are very secretive in rearing their vulnerable young. A crane's appearance may indicate that we are not applying the focus we should or that we need to develop a new sense of secrecy in regards to something being given birth to within our life. The crane can reflect for both men and women

a need to give more time and attention to the children, literally or figuratively. Crane reminds us not to scatter our energies and to celebrate our creative resources and to keep them alive, that thorugh propoer focus, what we give birth to will have a long, honorable life.

A crane might also reveal where we are too rigid in our beliefs and traditions, conforming to them without knowing why or for what benefit other than "that is the way it has always been done." We may want to examine our perspectives, reviewing where we have been following the traditions of the past that have perhaps outlived their usefulness. Or, the crane may be reminding us that there is a benefit from following past traditions, but only when given fresh expression and perspectives.

The white crane reminds us that spiritual justice will play itself out within the mundane world, but not necessarily according to how we believe it should. We need to remember that justice will unfold in the time, manner, and means that is best.

Part III

The Kingdom
of Mammals

Every wolf and lion's howl
Raises from Hell a Human Soul
WILLIAM BLAKE

Perhaps scientific knowledge and the power it brings
were not as important as wisdom and balance and
humility in the face of the teachings
hidden in the world of nature.
CHRISTOPHER MANES
Other Creations

CHAPTER 8

The Communications of Mammals

Mammals are our closest relatives among all animals. There are roughly 4300 species and over 400 on the North American continent alone. Found in all environments, they each have their own unique characteristics.

Mammals are distinguished from other types of animals primarily by their feeding of their young with milk from the mother's body. Mammals are all warm-blooded, and with the exception of a few whales, have a certain amount of hair or fur. They all breathe air through lungs, and except for the duck-billed platypus and some other echidnas, give birth to live young.

Although most species of mammals have four legs and live upon the land, whales and dolphins, one of the most common species of mammals, live in the sea. All the other mammals live upon the land, and thus they are symbolically associated with the element of earth, since mammals help us in staying grounded and with the practical aspects of life. Mammals are frequently the keys to accomplishing our daily life goals and for guiding us to our true potentials and their proper expression within our life. Like the milk mammals feed their young, the Earth provides us the nourishment required.

Many mammals lead a nomadic life in search of food, but unlike birds and many other animals,

Mammals provide keys to guide us in accomplishing our daily goals and for guiding up to our true life potential and their proper expresion within our lives.

they do not truly migrate. This is often a reminder that we must seek out our sustenance, sometimes altering our patterns and expanding where we put our efforts in order to lead a successful life. Mammals show us how best to accomplish this.

The Significance of Mammals

➤All mammals have a highly developed sense of smell. It is one of the most—if not the most—important sense. They can smell and distinguish thousands of aromas. Members of the same species mark their territory so that others can smell it and know the presence of others of its kind.

Mammals can help us learn how to establish new territories (boundaries) as well as alerting us when we have wandered into unfamiliar and unproductive realms. They very often can show us new territories and to recognize others of like mind and spirit in the same arena of life.

The sense of smell is related to discrimination and discernment. Because of this, mammal totems always teach us something about discernment or lack of discernment in some area of our life. They remind us to be discriminating in all of our activities with others. Animals with strong scent often help us to discern our gifts and powers more clearly. Mammals, through their sense of smell, help us to recognize our own abilities.

The sense of smell is also related to sexuality and there is a direct link between fragrance and sexual responses, which are related to our creative energies and endeavors. Mammals also help us to use our sexual rhythms and times more creatively and productively. Sometimes they reveal when we are not using these energies appropriately as well.

Mammals and the Initiation of Earth

➤Anything of the earth implies form, shape, weight, and material substance. The initiation of the earth element involves learning how to free ourselves from those limitations by working with them. This means becoming adept at controlling our physical body and our physical life by developing ways to work with matter creatively.

The element of earth has many expressions. Its lesson is understanding that all energies must express themselves through the physical. The earth element teaches us to recognize our innate power and energies within and express them in the outer world. Mammals, the animals of this element, help us to recognize our potentials and show us how best to express them within our daily life.

The initiation of the element of earth involves learning to recognize the power or mammals—their qualities—within us and to apply them successfully within our own lives in the outer world.

When this element and its associated animals show up, there arises the challenge of coping with the stimulating energies of the world. Issues surface around meeting the material obligations and maintaining balance while doing so. One of the best ways of strengthening our connection to the earth element is through mammals. Working with them, we find physical balance within life. Even getting our bare feet into the mud and grass, making a physical connection with the Earth, or finding time to be around plants and trees is very effective for strengthening the earth element within our life.

Through mammals, we open ourselves to the wonders of Mother Earth. We learn about our journey upon her and how best to express our potentials throughout that adventure. Mammals teach us to keep our feet upon the ground.

Notes

CHAPTER 9

Dictionary of Mammals

All mammals have certain qualities in common. They all have flexible body parts: a head, body, and two pairs of limbs. Only mammals have hair, which helps them to keep warm. There are exceptions, such as the naked mole rat, but almost all mammals do have hair. Mammals are also warm-blooded, meaning that they are always the same temperature inside. All mammals also drink milk, a combination of water, fat, sugar, protein, and minerals. Milk is an ancient symbol of the mothering, nurturing qualities of life.

Because of these qualities, when we have a mammal as a totem, we should examine our flexibility, our ability to maintain a steady "temperature" in life's situations. We should also examine the amount of basic nourishment we are giving and receiving in various avenues of our life—physically, emotionally, mentally, and spiritually. It would benefit us to learn how to use our abilities to nurture others and ourselves in the same way milk nurtured us in our early years.

Still, there is a tremendous diversity among the various species. They are like humans and since we are mammals as well, often their messages to us are more individual and personal, reflecting our own potentials and abilities. The individual animal, though, must be studied to understand the specific messages to and for us.

Animals covered in this chapter include:
- aardvark
- apes and monkeys
- arctic fox
- baboons
- beluga
- boar
- camel
- capybara
- caribou
- cheetah
- chimpanzee
- chipmunk
- dingo
- eland
- ferret
- gazelle
- gibbon
- gorilla
- guinea pig
- hedgehog
- hippopotamus
- humpback whale
- hyena
- impala
- jackal
- jaguar
- kangaroo
- koala
- lemur
- llama
- mole
- musk ox
- muskrat
- orangutan
- panda
- polar bear
- shrew
- Siberian tiger
- wallaby
- walrus
- wolverine
- zebra

Aardvark

KEYNOTE

unearthing and extracting the hidden

AARD-VARK
(*Orycteropus capensis*)
Either of two African mammals...found in Africa. They grow about five feet long, including the tail, and burrow in the ground, feeding entirely on ants, which they catch with the long, slimy tongue.

Are we going to extremes?

➤ The aardvark gets its name from the Afrikaans word meaning "earth pig."[1] It is a burrowing animal with feet that have very strong digging claws, four in front and five in back. An aardvark has a long snout and claws, enabling it to root out and smell food sources.

Aardvarks, because of their sense of smell, help us to trust our own instincts as to what we can dig out for ourselves. The sense of smell is discernment, and aardvark people have a wonderful ability to smell successful ventures and those that may not be. Learning to trust "what smells right and what smells fishy" is part of what the aardvark teaches.

The aardvark is a nocturnal animal that feeds primarily on termites. It is so powerful with its claws and digging that it can easily rip through the extremely hard walls of termite nests. It has tenacity and the ability to unearth its food. For those with the aardvark as totems, termites should be studied as well. Termites are social insects and although often considered destructive, they do teach how groups can become more productive by behaving like a single living organism. Their social aspect is a direct contrast to the solitary quality of the aardvark.

If aardvark has appeared, now is the time to dig deeper and faster. There is food and protection beneath the surface (aardvarks bury themselves in dirt to avoid predators). They are reminders that what has been hidden will be unearthed if we continue to dig. What we uncover will nourish us and feed us on a variety of levels. We might also need to look at how isolated or social we are becoming.

---

[1] Michael Chinery, ed. *Illustrated Encyclopedia of Animals.* (New York: Kingfisher Books, 1992), p. 8.

➤ Probably because apes and monkeys are closest to us in form and behavior, they fascinate humans more than most other animals. Their anatomies and behaviors are similar, particularly among the apes, and they often have a range of emotional expressions quite identical to humans.

Apes and monkeys often have confusing interpretations. They are, in fact, very different species. Each grouping has its own unique qualities. Some of the specific members of each are covered in this book, but what is provided here is only the very basic information.

All apes and monkeys are able to express aggression, submission, and other messages with a variety of vocalizations, expressions, and body language. Their body language and displays are subtle and varied. In fact, most disputes among all of the species are settled through expressions and displays and not through actual fights.

For anyone to whom an ape or monkey appears, there are issues of proper communication at hand. Learning "apespeak" is often part of the message. We must become more clear and distinct in how and what we communicate to others through our words, actions, and body language. This is not a time for subtle messages.

Apes and monkeys are also skilled tool users. Chimpanzees will use chewed-up leaves as a sponge to soak up water. Sticks are used to draw termites and insects out of rotten wood for eating. Orangutans use large leaves as makeshift umbrellas. Monkeys and apes teach us to be innovative and use the tools available to us at the time to accomplish what we must.

All primates have clusters of touch receptors in their fingertips which help them with delicate grooming tasks and other expressions. All primates teach us to use our sense of touch for healing and expressions of love.

Apes and Monkeys

KEYNOTE

communication and expression

BARBARY APE
(*Macaca inua*)
An ape...of North Africa and Gibralter Rock, being the only monkey inhabiting Europe. It is often trained by showmen.

CAPUCHIN
(*Cebus capucinus*)
A long-tailed South American monkey...having the forehead naked and wrinkled, with the hair on the crown reflexed and resembling a monk's cowl.

Apes and Monkeys (cont.)

Apes differ from monkeys in a variety of ways. Apes are nearest to humans in structure and development. Unlike monkeys, they do not have a tail. They also walk upright at times. In Asia, there are two main groups of apes—orangutans and gibbons. In Africa, there is the chimpanzee and the gorilla.

In myths and tales, apes and monkeys were often related to sprites, fairies, and sorcerers. They were often seen as "familiar" beasts, and to chase one through the forests would lead you into other realms and dimensions. There are also many myths about ape and monkey gods and goddesses—gorilla guardians and baboon protectors. In some African tales the baboon is a comic figure, much like the Native American coyote, sometimes wise and sometimes foolish, often outwitting himself. Among the Swahili, the monkey is wise and clever.

The monkey plays a leading part in many mythic stories found in the Tibetan, Chinese, and Indian traditions. Gods in Chinese legends often appear in the form of monkeys. Many temples were built in India and China to honor the monkey and monkey gods.

In the Chinese zodiac the monkey is the ninth creature and is credited with the power of granting good health, success, and protection. Often associated with mischievousness and imagination, monkeys have great physical dexterity and they represent men-

Animal

BONDING AND TIES

While some animals are solitary, others can be quite sociable. Many animals groom each other to keep each other free of pests and to strengthen and maintain family and group bonds. The more sociable groups demonstrate strong bonds and emotions that go beyond instinct, even mourning the loss of others in their family or group. This is often very noticeable among mammals.

Elephants greet with caresses and rumbles even after only a few hours aprat. After many days of separation, reunions can be quite noisey. Whole families of elephants will mourn the loss of one of their own.

Chimpanzees make special efforts after disputes to kiss and comfort one another.

Wonders

tal dexterity and wittiness as well. Those born in the sign of the monkey are quite inquisitive.

One of the outstanding characteristics of the monkey is its tail, which is symbolically linked to the sexual energies and creativity. The tail or tail end is the seat of the life force. The monkey's tail is often used to help it balance itself as it plays and climbs among the trees. It can hang from it and utilize it in amazing ways.

South American spider monkeys have a small patch of sensitive skin on the underside of their tails. This spot is as sensitive to touch as its hands and feet, and thus the spider monkey's tail can be manipulated to pick up objects and food around it. Because of this, "monkey" people have a wonderfully unique ways of expressing and incorporating their creativity into their lives.

All primates are intelligent and communicative. They teach us to be so as well within our own life. They are social and expressive in all they do. If members of these families have appeared, it is time to examine how we are expressing and communicating or if we even are communicating.

Arctic Fox

KEYNOTE

- **shapeshifting**
- **seasonal transformations**

ARCTIC, OR WHITE, FOX
(*Vulpes lagopus*)
A small fox...of the arctic regions of both hemispheres. Its fur, which is blue-gray or brownish in summer and white in winter, is valuable.

➤ Masters of camouflage and quiet, all foxes are shapeshifters. They can be three feet from us in the wild and we not know they are near us. They have a long history of magical and mystical associations. In China, foxes become wizards and wizards become foxes. Among many Native Americans, the fox is associated with healing and shapeshifting.

Most foxes have color variations in their coat to serve as camouflage, enabling them to remain relatively unseen. The Arctic fox is the only member of the fox family whose fur actually changes color with the seasons. Its coat becomes white during the winter months, helping it to blend into the white snow of the north more effectively. This kind of camouflage allows the fox to remain unseen by potential prey.

Often this is a reminder to us that we must change our "colors," our approaches, with the seasons as well. What worked this past season will not work for us in the upcoming one. A change in climate requires a change in approach or coloring. Otherwise, what we wish to capture will escape us.

The seasonal changes in light triggers a hormonal change in some animals, which in turn stimulates an appropriate change of color in the fur for the season. As winter approaches, the Arctic fox's fur changes from a brown and gray to white. This indicates a sensitivity to light for those to whom this animal is a messenger or totem. Working with light and color as a healing modality may be effective.

If the Arctic fox has appeared in your life, review *Aminal-Speak* where I discussed at great length the fox, especially the practice of being a fox by learning to adjust the human aura. Learning to develop the art of camouflage is critical for anyone with a fox totem and is especially important from a seasonal perspective for those to whom the Arctic fox appears.

Unlike other foxes, they have more rounded ears to protect and insulate themselves from the harsh cold of the winters. Its appearance often is a reminder that the harshness of what others are saying or have said will not be as effective as what they may imagine. We will have extra insulation.

Arctic foxes need more than a change of fur color and insulation to survive the harsh environments of the Arctic lands. Arctic foxes will often secret (hide) their prey. They have great memories for finding it again and could not survive without these previously buried food stores to rely on. The icy climate keeps their caches of prey well refrigerated.

This instinctual planning for the future is also what the Arctic fox teaches, reminding us to not only adapt to the environment and seasons, but also plan for the future. We should store and prepare, just in case things become harsher than we may have anticipated.

Since food supply is an essential in cold weather territories, the sharing of spoils among different animals within the same territory is common. In the arctic region, polar bears support the arctic fox by allowing the fox to finish the parts of a captured seal the bear does not want. Arctic foxes are often found tagging along with polar bears to share in the polar bears' bounty:

> Perhaps [the polar bear] finds some satisfaction in the companionship of the small fox. A few seagulls, too, are permanent members of the company.[2]

When the arctic fox appears, we can anticipate that events are shapeshifting around us and it will teach us to prepare and to use our shapeshifting abilities to get what we need to survive the coming seasons.

Arctic Fox
(cont.)

Are we ready to adapt to them?

Are we prepared for most eventualities?

Are we adjusting ourselves to meet the needs of the time and place?

---

[2] Christopher Manes. *Other Creations* (New York: Doubleday), 1977, pp. 31–32.

Baboon

KEYNOTE

- maintain sacred space
- groundedness

CHACMA BABOON

(Papio porcarius)

Any of certain large Old World apes....Baboons have doglike muzles, large canine teeth, cheek pouches, a short tail, and naked callosities on the buttocks. They inhabit Africa and Arabia.

➤Baboons are monkeys that have forsaken a life in the trees to live on the ground. Although they are quite comfortable in trees if they choose to be and they still sleep in them for protection, they spend most of their waking time on the ground.

They appear in myth and lore throughout Africa, often taking on characteristics that are both comical and wise. In many ways, they are sometimes depicted like the coyote among the Native Americans, as both wise and foolish, and even outsmarting themselves sometimes. In northeast Africa and Arabia, the hamadryad baboon is considered sacred.

Baboons live in close family groups called *troops*. Their chief enemies are lions and leopards, and when threatened, they move to the trees and will throw rocks and sticks to protect themselves. When they are safe from an attack or danger, they bark defiantly, throw stones, and if forced to, will turn on their predators. Ethiopian baboons are well equipped for defense with large canine teeth.

For extra protection, young baboons ride around on their mother's back. Other baboons that are part of the troop will playfully caress these young baboons. Baboon troops are extremely protective of their environments from outsiders. This is a reminder to those whom the baboon is a messenger. Protect your creations and endeavors. Caress them and guard them.

For the male olive baboon, there is a constant struggle for status, and it is within the troop itself that most struggles are encountered. A young male rises in the troop by displacing seniors. It is not just the highest ranked male who mates. All may do it at any time, although only the highest-ranking male will mate with a female when she is ovulating.

Often the appearance of the baboon is a reminder to keep our issues within our "family"

Baboon
(cont.)

group, whether it is the actual family or metaphorical family. Outsiders are not going to help. Baboons remind us of the sacredness of the family and of resolving things within the family.

Are we keeping sacred space and times for ourselves? Are we allowing our space to be intruded upon? Are we allowing others in that should not be allowed? Do we need to take a closer look at resolving family problems ourselves, rather than leaving them to others? Baboons remind us of the importance of maintaining a sacred space for that which is most important to us whether it is our family, work, or our creative efforts.

GRIZZLY LORE

Among the Modoc is the story of the daughter of the Chief of the Sky Spirits. This young girl became separated and lost from her father, but she was found by a grizzly bear. He carried her home with him and his When she became a young woman, she married the eldest son. They had many babies who were not as hairy as the grizzlies, but neither did they look like their mother. As she grew older and began to die, she sent one ofher many grandchildren in search of her father.

Though angry at first at what she had created, he saw the wonders of this new race of people. The Sky Spirit's grandchildren were the first Indians. They were the ancestors of all the Indian peoples.

Beluga

KEYNOTE

spirit of the waters

BELUGA, OR WHITE WHALE

(*Delphinapterus leucas*)

A cetacean…of the dolphin family, which becomes about ten feet long, and is white when adult; the white whale. It occurs chiefly in northern seas and esp. in the lower St. Lawrence River.

Are we too focused in the physical?

Are we too focused in the spiritual?

Are we ignoring our own sacred songs?

Are we ignoring the siren calls to the spirit path?

➤ The beluga is a white whale, related to the dolphin and sometimes known as the ghost or spirit whale. Early fisherman often thought of it as a ghost in the waters because of its pale white coloring. Like the manatee, it was often perceived to be a mermaid or other such spirit of the ocean.

Belugas can reach 20 feet in length. They are found in arctic waters, but they will occasionally swim up rivers as well. This toothed whale feeds primarily upon fish, shrimp, and crabs. Their chief enemy is the orca, and thus it should be studied as well.

Belugas talk to each other in a series of whistles, and because of their whistling abilities, belugas were rumored to be sirens of the sea, tempting sailors into the unknown, and even death. They were also known as "sea canaries," and it is not unusual for those to whom the beluga comes as a totem or messenger to have the ability to whistle and sing in ways that are both haunting and soothing, but always healing.

The Huichol Indians and other traditions speak of whistling for one's spirit as a way of calling the spirits and for finding one's own when separated or lost. When the beluga appears, there will soon arise opportunities to find our spirit or spiritual path. Their appearance can herald a time of greater or clearer contact with spirit, usually through the sense of hearing.

The beluga is a guide and a guardian into the Faerie Realms of water and can lead us to underwater treasures and kingdoms. It opens us to all of the most positive aspects of what water symbolizes—creativity, lucid dreaming, imagination, and new dimensions.

Belugas usually travel in groups of twelve, and the symbolism and significance of the number twelve should be studied as well. Rhythms of twelve will often be a play—twelve hours, twelve days, twelve months, twelve friends, and even twelve blessings in the coming twelve months.

➤ The boar and pig have sometimes had an ambivalent meaning. If a sow crossed your path, it was a sign of disappointments coming your way. If a sow crossed your path with a litter, it was a sign of good luck. Boars were a symbol of fidelity and strength, but also of intrepidness and irrational urges. Sacred in Babylon and in the Celtic tradition, boars were associated with distinction and positive character. The savior god of India, Vishnu, once incarnated as a boar.

The Celtic moon goddess is sometimes depicted as the sow, the shining one. Many of the Celts venerated the boar as sacred to prophesy, protection, and magical powers. Druids referred to themselves as boars because they dwelt in the woods as solitaries.

In other places the boar had similar meanings. In Scandinavia, the god and goddess Frey and Freyja both rode boars and provided protection for warriors. The maternal sow was often a symbol of the Earth goddess. The Tibetan adamantine sow is the Queen of Heaven, the Moon, and Fertility. The female boar and pig were often fertility symbols because of their large litters. "Lucky pig charms" were made in Europe and America for fertility and prosperity as well as lustiness in the home.

The wild boar is forerunner of the domestic pig. Different societies had their own species of boar. Most people in the US are familiar with the European wild boar, but the Chinese and Indian wild boars are closely related to it. These are sometimes classified as the Eurasian wild boar.

Wild boars and their relatives are wonderfully adaptive to thick, underbrush environments. Because of this, they can show us how to maneuver quickly and powerfully through areas of congestion within our own life.

Boars range from gray to brown to black, and have bristles and sparse hairs on their bodies protecting them against the thick brush in which

Boar

(including wart hogs and pigs)

KEYNOTE

- fertility
- fidelity
- strength
- family protection

WART HOG
Any wild hog of the genus *Macrocephalus*...of northeast Africa, having two pairs of rough warty excrecences on the face and large protruding tusks.

Boar
(cont.)

Are we or others around us being unfaithful?

Do we need to assert our family strengths?

Do we need a show of fidelity, especially to our children?

When members of the boar family appear, it is time to hold true to our standards of strength, faith and family.

Are we not using our creative abilities? Do we need to look for more fertile life activities?

they live. This makes them wonderful animals for helping us when we need some thicker skin, when facing the innuendoes, accusations, or any negative words and projections of others.

The wild boar also has a disc-like snout it uses for rooting. The boar can grow to 5 feet (150 cm) and can weigh up to 400 pounds (180 kg). The tusks may grow as much as 12 inches and are used for protection and for digging food. The boar and pig are excellent animals to help us sniff out and root out treasures and delights. When the boar shows up, it is always a reminder that if we want the treasures, we must dig them out for ourselves, relying on our own strengths.

Warthogs have a shovel-shaped head with tusks and are part of the boar and pig family found in mostly open fields in Africa south of the Sahara. Males have two lumps or warts on each side of the snout near the tusks.

Warthogs can inflict severe wounds with their tusks, just as boars can. For the most part, though, they are rather inoffensive, but are powerfully protective of babies. The lion is its predominant predator and should be studied as well.

Boars are surprisingly fast and powerfully strong and usually live in small family groups in open woodland, although the old males remain solitary. The old males are unceasingly protective of the young and in European heraldry, the boar is powerful symbol of strength and family.

In the Chinese zodiac, the boar or pig is one of the twelve signs and is associated with a cheerful and patient disposition. Boar people are encouraging to others and very honest, sometimes to the point of being naive. The boar person is generous and diligent in pursuits, especially in of the good life for their family. The boar is sometimes a symbol for sexuality. "Eating roast pork" is a Chinese metaphor for sexual intercourse.

When the boar appears, it is time to examine our fidelity and protection of the family.

➤ The camel is traditionally considered a relative of the ancient dragons and other winged serpents. In the *Zohar*, the serpent in the Garden of Eden is described as a kind of "flying camel" and similar allusions are found in ancient Persia, but not all of the references are negative ones.

The camel is a desert animal of Asia and Africa that is primarily used for transportation and journeys because of its ability to travel great lengths with little water. The appearance of the camel is often a reminder that the journey ahead may be difficult, but we will be able to survive it and we will have the "waters" necessary to complete the journey successfully.

With long eyelashes to protect its eyes from wind-blown sand, camels are well equipped for life upon the desert. Their nostrils close easily and their broad feet enable them to walk over the sand's shifting surfaces. A camel sweats very little, thus retaining its water. When the camel is a totem, we are able to accomplish and succeed in environments that often amaze others and ourselves. It is a reminder that although the sands may be shifting around us, we will have the ability to remain steady amidst them.

Camels can drink 53 gallons of water at a time. This is the equivalent of 440 lbs. of water per day. The water they drink passes directly from the stomach into body tissues. On the desert, they will get water from desert plants, but they can go on a dry diet for several weeks. A camel may lose one fourth of its body weight in water without showing any distress.

The camel stores fat in its hump, which is essential for it to go for such great periods of time. The hump is also full of hydrogen atoms, As the camel breathes in oxygen, the oxygen combines with the hydrogen atoms to make H_2O (water). The hump can weigh as much as 100 pounds, and is a reservoir of energy, a reminder that our own energy reservoir is greater than we may believe.

Camel

KEYNOTE

- replenishment
- surviving during parched times and journeys

DROMEDARY
(*Camelus dromedarious*)
Orig., a camel of unusual speed bred and trained especially for riding; now, more often, the Arabian or one-humped camel.

Camel
(cont.)

BACTRIAN CAMEL

Either of two species of large ruminant mammals used in the desert regions of Asia and Africa for carrying burdens and for riding. They are peculiarly adapted for life in the desert, being able to live on the tough thorny plants of such regions, and having thick callous soles to the feet, the hoofs being small and situated at the ends of the two toes. They can go many days without drinking, having cavities, or diverticula of the stomach closed by sphincter muscles, in which a supply of water may be stored up. The existing species are the Arabian (*Camelus dromedarious*), often called the dromedary, having one large hump on the back, and the Bactrian (*C. bactrianus*), an Asiatic species having two humps. The Arabian camel is no longer found in a wild state, except where it has escaped from domestication.

Camels also have a high degree of endorphin activity. Endorphins are released in the body during times of exercise, creating a kind of natural high or sense of "euphoria." Those with camels as totems have a wonderful ability to remain positive amid the harshest of times and experiences. Theirs is the innate philosophy of "the glass is half full."

Camels sleep in 3-minute spans of time and for a total of only 20 minutes per night. Camel people often have unusual sleep habits. Individuals who learn to use "power naps" often have a camel or an animal with similar sleeping abilities as part of their totem shield.

When the camel appears, the journey may become difficult, but we will have all that we need to complete it successfully. It is a sign that we will be replenished and the journey will be successful. The way may be difficult and the world may seem to shift around us, but if we remain positive, all will work out for us. We will accomplish what others would find impossible.

➤ Sometimes growing to be over a yard long, the capybara is the largest living rodent. A native to South America, the capybara has a pig-like appearance and the guinea pig is a distant relative, and should be studied as well.

Capybaras are often found near water. They browse upon water plants and grasses. They swim and dive very well and are at home in the water. When threatened, they will often seek safety in the water. They use their slightly webbed feet to swim, and their stored fat helps give them extra buoyancy.

Their greatest enemies are the crocodile and the jaguar, and both of these should be studied as well. They help balance the capybara's docility, and help teach those with this animal as a totem or messenger how and when to become more aggressive, helping teach the capybara individual how and when to set aside the docility.

When the capybara appears, it is time to seek out safe emotional and spiritual waters. If life is troubling and hectic, seek refuge in the familiar. Look for environments with natural waters and activities that are emotionally soothing, at least for a short time. Intense emotional and spiritual stress can disrupt the health of the capybara person. Because of this, it is more important to seek out familiar emotional and spiritual comforts rather than explore the new. The capybara teaches us to find comfort and refuge in familiar surroundings.

Capybara

KEYNOTE

seek refuge and safety in emotional and spiritual waters

CAPYBARA
(Hydrochoerus hydrochaerus)
A large South American rodent…living on the margins of lakes and rivers and largely aquatic in habit. It is the largest existing rodent, being over four feet long and half that in height. In form it somewhat resembles the Guinea pig, to which it is related. The tail is entirely absent and the feet are partially webbed; the fur is coarse and rough. Its flesh is edible.

Are we moving into environments for which we are unprepared?

Are we becoming too emotional in regards to present situations?

Are we ignoring our spiritual development?

Caribou

KEYNOTE

migration, travel, and movement are necessary now

CARIBOU

(Rangifer caribou)

Any of several species or varieties of reindeer found in northern North American and Greenland. The larger forms inhabit wooded localities and are distinguished as woodland caribou. The best known of these (*Rangifer caribou*) was formerly found in many of the northern states, but being easily killed has been long since exterminated in most of them. The smaller forms inhabiting open country are called *Barren Ground Caribou*.

➤ A member of the deer family, the caribou is the wild counterpart to the domesticated and semi-domesticated reindeer. Caribou are found in the north in harsh and open tundra areas where movement and migration is one of their adaptations for survival:

> All animals have an instinctive perception of changes in temperature and just as men seek shelter in homes in winter, or as men of great possessions spend their summer in cool places and their winter in sunny ones, so also animals that can do so shift their habit at various seasons.[1]

Caribou of North America travel over 3100 miles (5000km) in a year, the longest animal migration of any mammal. This amazing journey follows a traditional path from their summer wintering grounds to the northern tundra where they can give birth without threat from wolves.

Every summer, though, they are harassed and attacked by a variety of flies and other pests. Millions of flies plague the caribou, and their only defense is to hide from them. Flies find the caribou through the carbon dioxide in their breath and attack the caribou's belly and legs where the skin is thinnest and blood vessels are closest to the surface. For the young and weak, this is debilitating. However, the migration helps. By gathering in large groups in the open tundra, the fly attacks are less concentrated. In forested areas, it is often better to go it alone or with a small group, although wolves are more likely to attack then.

When caribou appear, it is time to act. Yes, there is danger in making decisions and choices, but the danger and problems are greater if we do not. Now is the time to act, choosing the lesser of two evils. Work with a group, because there is safety and protection in numbers. Are we remain-

---

[1] Aristotle. *History of Animals.*

ing too idle? Are we afraid to move or act? Safety, security and new birth can only come through action. If we do not move and act, the irritations and problems will only intensify, and the stress can be debilitating.

Caribou mate in late October and early November. The young are then born in early June and have time to grow strong before the next winter. The fall season is thus a powerful and creative time for those to whom the caribou is a totem or messenger. Fall and spring are the best times to make a major move within our life or life circumstances.

Caribou promise success through movement, through actions. They also assure us that although our journeys may be lengthy, as long as we do not go it alone the entire time, we will succeed.

Animal Wonders

GRIZZLY MILK

All mammals feed their young with milk which is a combination of water, fat, sugar, protein, and minerals. Grizzly bear milk is one of the richest milks among mammals. It must be to sustain the cubs and help them to develop fat to keep them warm. Grizzly bear milk is as rich as pure whipping cream, and this is what helps the young cubs to become big.

Cheetah

KEYNOTE

speed and flexibility

CHEETAH
(*Acinonyx jubatus*)

An animal of the cat family...found in India, Persia, etc., as well as in much of Africa, which is often tamed and trained to hunt antelopes and other game. It differs from the typical cats and approaches the dogs in several respects.

The legs are long and adapted for prolonged running, and the claws are slightly if at all retractile. It is of the size of a leopard, and has small black spots on the body. The African race has been regarded by some as a distinct species (*C. lanigera*).

➤ With its slim, streamlined body, small head, and long legs, the cheetah is built for speed. It can shoot forward from a standstill to 45 miles per hour in three seconds—nearly as fast as racing cars and faster than most sports cars. At full speed, a cheetah can reach 63 mph, but can maintain that speed for only a short distance.

The cheetah has a supple spine, which enables it to increase the length of its stride to about 23 feet and extend the reach of both fore legs and hind legs. This flexibility is essential to work on for anyone to whom cheetah appears because stretching and flexibility of the body and spirit is essential to a healthy and fulfilled life for them.

The cheetah cannot fully retract its claws, which adds to its maneuverability, allowing a firmer grip on the ground for quick starts and sharp turns. For those to whom it appears, the cheetah's maneuverability is a reminder that we must be able to respond quickly, instantly, and with great flexibility, especially to opportunities that present themselves.

After a chase, successful or not, the cheetah must rest, usually fifteen minutes is all that is necessary. During a chase, its temperature can soar from 101 to 105 degrees and if it were maintained, would create brain damage. If the cheetah captures its prey, the cheetah chokes it to death. For those to whom the cheetah is a totem, great rest should follow periods of intense effort as well. Cheetah people must be careful not to overheat and over-exhaust their energies.

Unlike other wild cats, the cheetah hunts by day. This is partly due to sharing the territory with the lion, the cheetah's greatest enemy. Lions hunt at night and will seek out young cheetahs and try to kill them. Lions perceive cheetahs as future competitors for their other prey. Another reason the cheetah hunts during the day is because it can rely on its speed to bring down smaller prey. Hunt during the day, the cheetah has adapted to the bright sun and heat of the African savanna.

Cheetahs have dark stripes under their eyes to help shade them from the sun. These tear stripes almost look like mascara that has run down their faces from crying. Often the early lives of those with cheetah totems were quite tearful at times. Even if the crying had been done on the inside, the tear stripes of the cheetah reveals that those to whom it is a totem have a great capacity to feel and respond quickly to the hurt of others.

This competition with lions and the resulting threats upon the cheetah's young is also reflected in the tear stripe. Often cheetah mothers will lose their young to lions. It appears harsh and cruel. Young cheetahs must struggle to survive. The tear stripe is a reminder of the struggles we have had and the tears we have shed to attain our goals and achieve our successes. We must never forget what brought us to where we are.

A young cheetah's mane may serve as camouflage and it also serves to help the mother to grip her cubs for carrying them. Another theory too is that the cheetah's mane makes the cubs look more like the much fiercer and stronger honey badger, deterrent to potential predators. Once the cheetah cubs are big enough to follow the mother around, they take great interest in her hunts. When half grown, the cubs practice their own hunting skills on captured prey.

When the cheetah appears, it is time to protect our young. We may be in environments that are unsafe at times. That to which we give birth must be watched over carefully as others may try to harm it. Find a time in which you can work more easily and with fewer threats. Rely on your speed and flexibility.

Young male cheetahs (around 18 months) frequently band together in defense of their territory and may eventually be pushed out by another group or even by one determined adult.

Cheetah
(cont.)

Have we forgotten our own hurts?

Are we ignoring the hurts of others?

Are we ignoring our opportunities to help ease the hurts of others?

Are we hesitating in acting?

Are we holding back?

Have we forgotten that if we respond with speed and flexibility, we will eventually succeed?

Cheetah
(cont.)

Conflicts can be quite fierce and some male cheetahs of the same litter stay together for life. Again, it reflects a small social and bonding "family" common to people with cheetahs as totems and messengers. A cheetah relies mostly on itself and a select few to which it has bonded.

Male and female cheetahs will often live apart, with the females being nomadic, searching for prey and safe places to rear cubs. The females lead solitary lives, rarely interacting with other females. Cheetah women usually have closer men friends than women, but all cheetah people are somewhat solitary and thus never quite understood.

When the cheetah appears, it is time for all-out efforts and not a time to pace oneself—always act swiftly and with great flexibility.

Chimpan-zee

KEYNOTE

- innovative abilities
- use of tools

➤Thanks to Jane Goodall, we know more about chimpanzees than ever. Many of the myths and misconceptions about this wonderful animal have been shattered. New light and new admiration for their wonderful intelligence and abilities has been fostered.

Chimpanzees are one of the great apes, nearest in intelligence to humans, along with the gorilla. They are found in the tropical rain forests of Africa. At night they sleep in nests made of branches and vines. They also walk on all fours, but they can run on three. This combination of moving about the ground and sleeping in the trees reminds us that we need both qualities in our life—earth and heaven, physical and spiritual.

Chimpanzees are expert toolmakers. They use sticks to extract honey, ants, and termites. They use stones to crack open nuts or to use as missiles in defense. They will also make sponges from chewed leaves to extract water from sources not easily accessible. They use what they have to accomplish their tasks. Because of this, they remind us that with a little insight and imagination, we already have what we need to accomplish the tasks in our own life—physical or spiritual.

Chimpanzees are social animals, and they exhibit almost as wide a range of emotions as humans do. They remind us of the importance of a social life for our emotional health and well being. Chimpanzees groom each other, reminding us of our need to care for those in our family, immediate or extended. The males have a social order, and for those human males who have a chimpanzee as a totem or messenger, it will be particularly important to have male companions of their own.

Chimpanzees are self-aware animals. An animal is considered self-aware if it recognizes itself in a mirror. They are also emotional. After disputes, chimpanzees make a special effort to kiss and comfort one another. Chimpanzees remind us to be more aware of ourselves and how we affect those around us.

Mother chimps are very caring and protective of their young. When the young are born, they will usually stay with the mother for two years. If a chimpanzee is our totem or messenger, we may need to look at a two-year cycle at play within our life. What we give birth to must be nurtured for almost two years before it matures and moves on its own. The nurturing and caring, though, as with chimps, is rewarding and beneficial.

Chimpanzees eat as much as seven hours per day and their diet includes fruit, leaves, roots, ants, and other assorted vegetation. They have no trouble eating all sorts of fruits that contain virulent poisons locked in their seeds. Their thick muscular lips and bony palates allow them to mash the fruit without crushing the seeds. Chimpanzees show us how to creatively extract the juice of life with no harm.

Chimpanzee (cont.)

CHIMPANZEE, FEMALE

An anthropoid ape (*Simia satyrus*, syn. *Anthropopithecus troglodytes*) of the equatorial forests of Africa, smaller and more completely arboreal in habit than the gorilla and of a less ferocious disposition, being easily tamed when taken young. The head is rounder than that of the gorilla, and its ears are large. It rarely stands erect, and habitually uses its arms in walking, resting on the knuckles.

Chimpanzee
(cont.)

Some animals resort to some kind of medicine when feeling ill. Chimpanzees are one of these. They link the eating of certain plants with relief from sickness. They will occasionally eat a few leaves of the aspilia plant (like sunflowers) in the early morning, massaging them but not chewing them. These leaves contain a chemical that combats infection from bacteria, fungi, and worms. The massaging allows the chemical to be released into the body through the mouth tissues.

They also eat plants of the spiderwort and vermonia families, which are antibacterial and help boost the immune system. The spiderwort's milky sap is a remedy for earaches and fevers. Chimpanzees are often messengers to eat more healthy, natural foods. Often those with chimpanzees as totems work with herbs in some way.

Primates frequently use deception to get food and mates. Some even seem to do things out of spite. Among most monkeys and apes, the powerful dominant male in a troop expects to have a monopoly on all females and all mating opportunities. The females, though, may be interested in other males, so furtive mating often occurs out of the sight of the dominant male. Females seeking a clandestine mate will get "left behind" as the troop is on the move. The desired male will have the same thing happen, but it will also use its hands to to hide the erect penis so the dominant male cannot suspect.

This chimpanzee behavior shows a weakness in the structured societies of primates, but it is sometimes necessary for the survival of the species. If everyone were dishonest, the society would disintegrate. On the other hand, checking the truth of everything would be time consuming. To assume that there are no ulterior motives and that everyone is behaving honestly saves a lot of time, but it makes it possible for occasional cheats to profit at the expense of others. In closely knit, family-connected groups, there is less deception. Sometimes it is better to turn a blind eye to what is going on around us. This is also why chimpanzees live in groups that change constantly, and they remind us of the need for change.

Counterdeception, in which one animal guesses another's ploy and outwits it, indicates an ability to see an event from another's point of view. Chimpanzees will incorporate strategic thinking; planned offensives, and counter deceptions to gain the fruits they desire.

When the chimpanzee shows up as a totem or messenger, it is time to look at ourselves more closely. They often reflect our own lives.

Chimpanzees always bring multiple and often complex messages, but this is because they also bring multiple gifts and opportunities to use those gifts as well. They herald an awakening of new activities, new life strategies, and creative tools to help us on our path ahead.

Chimpanzee
(cont.)

Do we need to be more social and involved with others around us?

Are others being deceptive around us?

Are we being deceptive?

Do we need to hide what we are about to accomplish our tasks?

Are we using the tools available to us?

Are we being creative and intelligent in our activities and endeavors?

Chipmunk

KEYNOTE

• **treasures of the earth**

• **storage, work, and play**

CHIPMUNK

(*Tamias striatus*)

Any of numerous small striped American rodents of the genus *Tamias*, of the squirrel family, terrestrial in habit, and intermediate between the typical squirrels and the spermophiles. They are often called *ground squirrels* and *striped squirrels*. The common species of the eastern United States is *T. striatus*. In the West there are numerous species, some of them exceedingly abundant in certain localities.

➤ Chipmunks are related to squirrels and in fact, they are a species of common ground squirrels, which includes about twenty different types. They have very similar characteristics and behaviors to squirrels and thus the squirrel should be studied too. Chipmunks are small (four ounces) with dark reddish brown stripes on their back and they live in wooded areas.

The western chipmunk stores food in the summer and sleeps through most of the winter. Many species of chipmunks have cheek pouches in which they carry berries and nuts. Then they store them in their burrows.

Chipmunks live in underground burrow systems, usually in open pastures and woodland. When building their underground homes, chipmunks fill their cheeks with soil and eventually carry the soil out and dump it elsewhere so the entrance to the burrow isn't so obvious. By depositing the soil somewhere else, chipmunks can camouflage their homes from potential invaders such as weasels, snakes, and foxes.

Burrows sometimes extend up to twenty feet and can be quite complex with several exits and many storage chambers filled with nuts and seeds. For the chipmunk, the burrow is a place of safety, homes in which litters of blind, defenseless young are born. Young chipmunks will spend the first six weeks of their life in the burrow—their most vulnerable time.

When the chipmunk appears, it is important to keep our creations protected and out of sight. Usually a six-week period is the most vulnerable time when new projects are initiated and new endeavors started. Mother chipmunks are known to defend their homes and young even against rattlesnakes. For those to whom the chipmunk is a totem, a study of the rattlesnake should also be undertaken.

Chipmunks also teach us how to read the voices of others. Their hearing is so acute they can tell a lot about the snakes from their rattles. The sound of the rattle changes according to how warm or lively the snake is. Larger snakes have a deeper rattle. If the snake sounds sluggish or small, the chipmunk stands its grounds and drives it fiercely from the burrow.

Chipmunks have a chit-like alarm call and have several other calls, including a single, high-pitched note repeated about 130 times per minute. They can produce these calls even with their cheeks stuffed full of food. Sometimes chipmunks will start to call in unison and it sounds like a chorus singing.

When the chipmunk appears, trust what you hear in the other person's voice in spite of the actual words. The timbre and quality of speech will reveal more about the person than other clues. Chipmunks always give us reason to examine our lives.

Are we ignoring what we are hearing?

Do we need to balance work and play?

Do we need to be careful about what our own voice conveys about us?

Do we need to prepare and protect our endeavors, at least through the early stages?

Are we or our creative projects threatened?

Do we need to dig beneath the surface in order to protect our activities and ourselves?

Dingo

KEYNOTE

- relentlessness succeeds
- cautiousness in all activities

DINGO
(Canis dingo)

A wild dog...found in Australia, but supposed to have been introduced by man at a very early period. It has a wolflike face, bushy tail, and unsually a reddish brown color. It is very destructive to sheep.

Are we giving up too easily?

Are we looking for the quick and easy?

Are we leaping before we look?

Do we not trust what smells right or what smells fishy around us?

Have we become so cautious that we are not moving at all?

Are we trying to accomplish our endeavors by ourselves and not trusting in the bonds that we have formed to help us?

➤ The dingo is a medium sized, wild dog of Australia that is often found in packs. This is unusual in that the dingo is a placental animal, one of the few found in Australia.

In the wild, dingoes hunt in packs, often choosing young wallabies and kangaroos as their prey. If available though they will take sheep and cattle, and it is because of this they are often hunted intensely by humans. In spite of this, the species continues to adapt and survive.

Dingoes are relentless hunters, pursuing their prey, wearing it down. In this activity is one of the most important messages for those to whom the dingo appears as a totem or messenger. Persistence pays off. Continue in your pursuit. Relentlessness in efforts will bring rewards and success.

This is an extremely adaptable animal, in many ways similar to the coyote in the United States. It is intelligent, and in spite of efforts to reduce its numbers its territory grows. The efforts to decrease the dingo population have taught this quick learner to be ever cautious in its pursuits and activities. This animal often appears at times when we need to be much more cautious in our activities. They teach us how to pursue relentlessly, but cautiously.

As with all members of the canine family, the dingo has a highly developed sense of smell. Sight and hearing are also good, but they rely on their sense of smell, especially when hunting. Trusting in what "smell's right" is often important to the success of the hunt.

If the dingo has appeared as a messenger, it is time to take a look at how we are approaching our endeavors. Remember, the dingo teaches us relentless pursuit and persistence as the key to success.

➤ Found in the African savanna lands, some forest areas, and desert fringes, the eland is one of the largest of the antelopes.

Both sexes have spiral horns, and there is a well-developed dewlap (loose skin) hanging below the throat. Horns and antlers are often considered antennae to the spirit world. The dewlap is often associated with hidden communication. Thus the eland is often an animal that heralds a time of strong and clear spirit communication.

To the Bushmen of Africa, the eland is the first and favorite creature of a god called Kaggen. In one tale, this being soaked his son-in-law's shoe in water, giving it honey to eat and fondling it lovingly, returning daily to watch the shoe grow into an eland. In another version, Kaggen's wife gave birth to the first eland.

The eland was to the Bushmen a Master Animal and could only be killed in a special way. The hunter must identify himself with the animal and throughout the animal's dying, special magical observances were performed. This intentional identification was to create a kind of shape-shifting in which the hunter performs a powerful eland dance. Through the sacred eland rites, the Bushmen established and maintained communication with their god. Through the hunt, killing, and honoring of the eland, the cycle of sacrificing life to promote further life was ritually expressed.

The songs and dances of the eland ritual endowed the individual with supernatural power. This power would overcome them at some point, and sliding into trance, their spirits would fly along the threads of spider silk to the sky to commune with the spirits of the dead.

Elands live in herds and the bulls warn others of possible danger through deep barks. The herd then takes flight with the bulls at the rear. Elands are very fast, able to reach speeds of 40 miles per hour. They move in great bounding leaps. Because of this, elands often remind us to respond

Eland

KEYNOTE

- strong spirit communications
- divine messages and warnings
- quick responses to alerts

ELAND
(*Taurotragus oryx*)
The largest of the South African antelopes... the males sometimes standing six feet in height and weighing over 1,500 pounds. The eland was formerly found in immense herds on the plains of South Africa, but, being of heavy build and comparatively slow, has been practically exterminated. In western equaatorial Africa a closely related form (*T. derbianus*), having dark stripes not present in the South African eland, is still found in considerable numbers.

Eland
(cont.)

quickly and to use great leaps if necessary when trouble or problems arise.

The appearance of elands as totems or messengers often indicates great clear spiritual messages, generally as alerts and warnings. Meditative states will become deeper. Dance and ritual as a means of honoring and opening the doors to spirit communication will work more successfully at this time.

Remember that the Bushmen use physical activities such as dance to connect with the spirit. We must learn to work from both realms.

SQUIRREL NESTS

During the winter months, a squirrel makes a drey (nest) close to the tree trunk. In the spring, a new one is built farther out in the branches. This is where the young are born and raised.

If squirrels appear to you, in the winter you might want to keep your activities sheltered and solidly balanced (trunk of the tree)., In the spring, you might want to move your new activities away from areas of your usual ones to protect them from predators and other dangers until they are more mature (the second nest for y oung in the outer branches).

Are we thankful for that which we have achieved or are achieving?

Do we need to act more quickly?

Are we heeding our inner voice?

Do we need to pay attention to our dream communications?

Are we too focused on the spiritual and not staying grounded?

Are we ignoring the physical as we work to achieve the spiritual?

➤Ferrets, graceful and solitary animals, are some of the smallest members of the weasel family, which includes weasels, martins, skunks, badgers, and wolverines. The ferret is a great hunter with a slim, agile body enabling it to follow prey into openings that other animals could not do. It has a highly developed sense of smell and can teach us to trust our senses, even if it means going alone.

Ferrets were once believed to be a cure for the whooping cough. Milk was poured into a saucer and a ferret was allowed to drink part. The rest was given to the patient. One reason this was believed to work was because ferrets and weasels are quiet hunters. Thus many people believed that ferrets couldn't cough so this must be a cure for coughing.

Ferrets sometimes teach us how to squeeze through tight fixes that we couldn't otherwise manage. They can also show us how through silent observation we can uncover what is secret or hidden around us without anyone else finding out. Ferrets as messengers and totems often reflect hidden things about to be revealed if we are silent and observing.

Ferrets, as with all members of the weasel family, can be ferocious if threatened or frightened. They show us how to be aggressive if we need be, but they show us also how to be playful as well. Finding the balance between playfulness and ferocity is part of what the ferret teaches.

Ferret

KEYNOTE

- stealth and agility in healing and protection
- uncovering the hidden

FERRET
(*Putorius furo*)
An animal of the weasel family (*Putorius furo*), closely related to, and perhaps a domesticated variety of, the polecat (*Putorius putorius*). It is about fourteen inches long, of a pale yellow or white color, with red eyes. It is a native of Africa, but is kept in Europe and America for hunting rabbits and sometimes rats.

Do you need to develop your observational skills?

Are you being too open about your activities?

Are you trying to squeeze into things that you shouldn't?

Are you or others keeping secrets (and being as secretive as we belive?

Are we balancing play and serious work?

Do we need to become a little more ferocious in activities and endeavors?

Are we expressing too much ferocity in our activities and endeavors?

Gazelle

KEYNOTE

- trust intuition and respond quickly to avoid trouble or complications

- follow through on all you do

- overconfidence creates complications

➤ The slender and graceful gazelle, part of the antelope family, is found in Asia and northern and eastern Africa. The Thomson's gazelle is the most commonly known and at one time great herds of these once roamed the African savanna.

The gazelle is one of the ancient emblems of the soul. From primitive times, it frequently was depicted in flight from danger or in the jaws of a lion, leopard, or panther. Similar images were used in art to symbolize the persecution of passions, and sometimes they even represented self-destructive aspects.

Males have sweeping horns and females either have small spikes or no horns at all. Horns are often symbols of higher perceptions. It is not unusual for those with gazelles as totems and messengers to have great leaps of visionary insights. Remember, though, that the vision of something is not the same as the real thing. If we wish to manifest the vision, we must employ effort and sometimes suffer droughts in some areas of our lives to achieve the dream.

All antelope, including gazelles, are usually specialized for living within their particular environment. Gazelles thrive in dry country and can go without drinking for long periods of time. This hints at the stamina and persistence sometimes required in life's situations. We may find ourselves at times doing without what would replenish us. Although things may seem to be drying up around us, when the gazelle appears, we will be able to survive the droughts more easily and effectively than most.

Gazelles are fawn colored, enabling them to blend into their environment and among each other more easily. This makes it more difficult for them to be picked out by predators, an important behavior for those to whom the gazelle appears. Now is not a time to stand out. Doing so will create problems or complications.

Gazelle
(cont.)

GAZELLE
(*Gazella dorcas*)

Any of numerous small graceful and very swift antelopes constituting the genus *Gazella* and allied genera. The gazelles are celebrated for the luster and soft expressioin of their eyes. Their horns are transversely ringed and usually present in both sexes. Among the best-known species are the common gazelle of northern Africa (*G. dorcas*), the Persian gazelle (*G. subgutturosa*), the Indian gazelle (*G. benetti*), and the springbok (*Antidorcas euchore*).

For anyone with a gazelle as a totem, there may be a need to insulate and blend into the crowd a little more at this time in order to accomplish what needs to be done more successfully. Sometimes, though, the gazelle's appearance may indicate a need to come out of hiding. Take a look at the past several months. Have you been more exposed or more hidden?

Gazelles, impalas, and springboks will *pronk* or *stot* (leap straight up in the air) if they see a predator. Some believe this is a way of letting the predator know it has been spotted and it will be a hard chase. Others believe it is to see over the tall grasses so it will know the best way to run. Still others believe it is warning to other members of the herd.

When it does run, the gazelle tries to get a good jump and zigzags wildly, making it impossible for the predator to reach full speed. The cheetah's top speed is nearly twenty miles per hour faster than that of the gazelle, but with the gazelle zigzagging, the cheetah can never reach top speed. Keeping pursuers, competitors, and antagonists in your life off balance is the best defense. When confronted, do not run blindly. Get a head start and zigzag, changing your direction frequently.

Sometimes when endangered, gazelles do not use their natural speed and leaping ability to escape. They will instead dart around for several hundred yards and then stop to look back at their enemy. Sometimes they discover their enemy is still behind them and the time taken to stop and look was all that was needed for the predator to pounce. Leaving things half done, uncompleted, and stopping to rest before the work is truly done may create complications and problems.

When gazelle appears as a totem or messenger, it promises great vision and great ability to achieve that goal in environments where others would suffer.

Are we counting our chickens before they are hatched?

Are we not following through on our visions?

Are we giving up when it becomes difficult?

Are we hesitating once we have committed ourselves?

Are we overconfident?

Gibbon

KEYNOTE

- **extended and graceful reach**
- **close family ties**

GIBBON
(*Hylobates agilis*)

Any of several apes constituting the genus *Hylobates*. They are the lowest of the anthropoid apes, and the smallest and most perfectly arboreal in habits of that group. Their arms are very long, and they have small but distinct ischial callosities, but no tail or cheek pouches. They are found in southeastern Asia and the East Indies.

Is it time to make some new leaps?

Are we using all of our skills?

Do we need to support the family more?

Does the family need to support you more?

Are we allowing fear to hold us back?

➤ The gibbon and its relative, the siamangs, are the smallest of the apes, and found mostly in Southeast Asia. It's the only ape to habitually walk upright,. It's arms, are almost one and a half times longer than its legs.

Gibbons can swing so rapidly they sometimes appear to fly, occasionally leaping as far as 50 feet in a downward direction. They are so well coordinated they have even been known to catch flying birds as they swing.

When the gibbon appears, it's time to extend your reach. Take on new projects. Jump for new areas. You will find yourself able to do so with great ease. Those with a lifetime gibbon totem have a knack to always leap successfully on new opportunities, accomplishing things others find amazing. Gibbons like to move, and they are the best acrobats of all the apes.

Gibbons do not like water, rarely crossing a water barrier, so zoos often keep them displayed surrounded by water. For an animal so skilled and acrobatic, this seems an unusual fear. Those with a gibbon totem, usually have some personal fear that seems unreasonable. Others cannot comprehend how someone so skilled and capable could have such a "silly" fear, but it is real nonetheless. Gibbon people just leap around it.

Gibbons live in small groups, usually consisting of a mated pair (for life) and three to four of their offspring. When the gibbon appears as a spirit messenger or totem, the family unit will be very important—whether biological or some other close unit in their lives. Food is readily shared and fights rarely occur. Family members join together to protect their territory. Every day they hoot and holler loudly to let other gibbons know they are there and where their territory, is, again reflecting group unity and support.

Remember, gibbons are amazing animals, and the only thing holding them back in whatever they do is what they allow to hold them back.

Gorilla

- **strength**
- **nobility**
- **generosity**

➤The powerful gorilla is the largest of the apes, with broad chests, muscular necks, and strong hands and feet. Although they are often described as savage beasts, these very peaceful and gentle creatures have great nobility in them, frequently demonstrated by their behaviors toward each other within their community. When the gorilla appears, it signals the awakening of a more primal strength and acknowledgement of our innate nobility.

Gorillas remind us of the nobility of living and performing, of noble qualities that humans do not always express as well. Living in groups called *troops*, they care for each other, demonstrating almost as wide a range of emotions as humans do, including affection, mourning, protection, and caring for each other.

When gorilla appears, it is a confirmation that our industry—our endeavors—is solid and steady. They walk upon all fours, and adults seldom climb trees, reminding us that the more spiritual act is to stay grounded and handle our responsibilties.

The gorilla is a teacher and its appearance is often an indication that a teacher will appear, (usually a man) who is humble but gifted and who will help us in our endeavors. The individual is usually someone who has achieved a certain status but is not overcome by his position in life.

When gorilla appears, sometimes it is a confirmation that our own strengths—our inner strength and nobility—are about to be recognized. The idea of "nice guys finish last" does not hold true here. The gorilla reminds us of the nobility of proper living for one's family and community and for that we are about to be recognized and honored. .

The gorilla has no natural enemy in the wild. Leopards may take young gorillas if they can, but gorillas watch over each other's young. When gorilla shows up, we may not be watching over

GORILLA
(*Gorilla gorilla*, syn. *G. savagei*)
The largest known anthropoid ape...an inhabitant of a small area of the forest region of equatorial West Africa. It is closely related to the chimpanzee, but much larger, the males being much more powerful than a man, although (as they usually stand) not so tall, with massive bones, broad shoulders, very long arms, and strong jaws with tusklike canine teeth. The female is considerably smaller. There are thirteen pairs of ribs, the nose has a prominent median ridge, the ears are small, and the face is covered with black, nearly bare skin. The gorilla...lives in small family groups. They are less arboreal than the chimpanzee and do not usually walk erect.

Gorilla
(cont.)

our activities as carefully as we should be. It can be a sign we are being careless.

Territories often overlap, but when troops meet, rarely is any aggression shown. If gorilla appears, a threat is being perceived where there is none. We, or someone around us, may be too materialistic and too territorial and troubles or complications can result from this.

Within the gorilla troop, there are dominant roles, each troop being led by an old male. When gorilla appears, there are problems in leadership around us. It may have to do with our own leadership or the leadership of someone else in some area of our life. There may be someone trying to take charge who is not qualified or who is abusing the position of authority. Is it ourselves or is it someone around us?

Are we being too aggressive?

Are we trying to assert an authority we do not have?

Is someone else?

Are we fulfilling our responsibility to the family or community?

Are we looking out only for our own needs?

Are we being selfish and bullying?

MATERNAL CARING

Mammals, unlike most other species, care for their young, a principal preoccupation of mothers. When grazing on steep slopes, female mountain goats always position themselves below their kids to block their fall if they slip. Female capybaras will often nurse young that are not their own. And many other examples exist in every species.

Maybe what mammals can teach us most is how to care and nurture those nearest and dearest to us.

➤The native people of South America ate wild cavies, or guinea pigs, until around 5000 BC when the Incas domesticated them. Guinea pigs were used in religious ceremonies and as food.

When the Spanish conquered the Incas, they brought guinea pigs back to Europe and they became a popular pet among aristocrats during the 1600s. Even today, in South America guinea pigs are still believed to have the power to remove illness, appease spirits, and help people pass from one stage of life to another.

One theory as to how the guinea pig got its name is that its meat tastes like pork, another that it looks like a miniature pig, and yet another that guinea is a mispronunciation of Guyana, where European traders acquired the animal.

The guinea pig is a cavy, a rodent related to the capybara. For those to whom the guinea pig has appeared as a totem or messenger, a study of the capybara would also be beneficial.

The guinea pig, as with all rodents, can reproduce quickly. Living in social groups called herds, females can bear young when only one month old. Because they have no natural defense, they use the herd for protection. They create trails between their burrows so they can always find cover when danger approaches. Often animals with burrow systems are those whose spirits helps us bridge to new realms—whether safety, healing, or spiritual ones.

When the guinea pig appears, new realms will open up. People who think more like you, no matter how different your beliefs, will come forward. There will be more communing and participation in spiritual activities and sacred rites of passage.

If the guinea pig has appeared in your life, it's time to explore some new possibilities, time to initiate or reopen spiritual doors and passages of sacred communion. Those of like mind can join together for great healing work.

Guinea Pig

KEYNOTE

sacred and social communing and healing

GUINEA PIG

A stout, short-tailed, short-eared cavy about six inches long, which is domesticated and kept as a pet in most parts of the world, and extensively used in bacteriological experiments. It is usually black, white, and tawny in color, but many fancy varieties, commonly called cavies...are raised. Some have very long hair. The guinea pig is very prolific. It is of South American origin, and is supposed to be a domesticated form of the restless caby (C. aperea) of Guinea and Brazil, which has hair of a grayish color.

Are you ignoring your early spiritual and religious associations?

Do you need to reintegrate them?

Are you being too solitary in your spiritual practices?

Do you need to seek out groups who can help with your healing work?

Are you ignoring the opportunities to involve yourself in healing activities?

Hedgehog

KEYNOTE

- **inquisitiveness and curiosity**
- **misunderstanding**
- **defensiveness**

EUROPEAN HEDGEHOG
(*Erinaceus europaeus*)

Any of certain Old World insectivorous mammals constituting the genus *Erinaceus*, esp. the European species, *E. europaeus*. They have the hair on the upper part of the body mixed with prickles or spines. They are able to roll themselves up so as to present the spines outwardly in every direction. The hedgehog is nocturnal in its habits, feeding chiefly upon insects, slugs, etc.

➤ Hedgehog Day was celebrated in Rome in a festival on February 2. Over the centuries it would become Americanized into Groundhog Day for the forecasting of the weather. The Roman writer Pliny spoke of how hedgehogs rolled themselves on apples, sticking their quills into them and then carrying them back to their burrows.

Hedgehogs were killed by the thousands in some parts of Europe. During the reign of Queen Elizabeth I, it was believed that this creature was responsible for destruction to farm crops and for carrying the plague. A bounty of three pence was paid for every hedgehog killed.

In European folklore, they were accused of suckling dairy cows. Even Shakespeare in *A Midsummer Night's Dream* had little positive to say about them:

> You spotted snakes with double tongue,
> Thorny hedgehogs, be not seen;
> Newts and blindworms do no wrong;
> Come not near our Fairy Queen.

Today the hedgehog is protected in most countries and is treated with a little more understanding. Often when the hedgehog appears we find ourselves in positions where others around us just don't seem to understand who we are and what we are doing. We seem very alone, as if others are overlooking who we are beyond the outer covering. This can make us want to roll up into a ball and hide a little. Sometimes it also indicates that we may not understand fully others that are presently in our life, and there may be a need to be more sensitive.

In cartoons and books, the hedgehog is often depicted as a whimsical creature with a natural curiosity and inquisitiveness about it. When it appears in our life, our own sense of curiosity about the world around us will increase. Now is a time to explore, but with a little cautiousness.

Hedgehogs have been around since the age of the dinosaurs, and its natural habitat ranged from southern Europe to South Africa. Two main types exist today, the European and the African. In the wild, their range is about 500-1000 feet surrounding their burrows. Gardeners love hedgehogs because they will consume 1/3 of their weight each day in slugs, snails, and insects. These solitary insectivores are wonderful companions to gardening environments.

The hedgehog has a natural set of defenses that will discourage most predators. Its quills are actually stiff hollowed hairs. The hedgehog can roll itself up into a ball so that the quills crisscross for a strong defense against anyone touching it.

The defensive posture of rolling into a ball is one of its most peculiar characteristics. In *Alice in Wonderland*, the mad queen used a rolled-up hedgehog as her croquet ball. At times in our life, we all need to roll ourselves up in a ball and be more protective.

The hedgehog teaches us to explore and follow our natural curiosity, but it also shows us how to be more protective of ourselves as well. Even though others may not understand our peculiar habits or us, we have a wonderful way of stimulating the curiosity and inquisitiveness within their natures. We cannot have a hedgehog as part of our life without touching others in unique and wonderful ways.

Do we need to be more defensive about the pests in our life?

Are we too open and exposed?

Do we need to pull ourselves in a ball and be more protective?

Are we being too defensive and not allowing anyone to touch us?

If no one can touch us, then we cannot be hurt.

Are we protecting our emotions and heart?

Hippo-potamus

KEYNOTE

- creative power to shapeshift one's life
- sacred baptism

HIPPOPOTAMUS
(*Hippopotamus amphibius*)

The popular as well as...the generic name of a very large artiodactyl mammal...allied to the hogs, which was formerly found in the rivers of most parts of Africa, and is still common in the more remote districts. The feet are four-toed, the skin is bare and very thick, and the legs are very short. Next to the elephants it is the bulkiest existing quadruped, becoming at least 14 feel long. It is largely aquatic in habits, and can swim well and remain long under water. The hippopotamus feeds chiefly on aquatic plants, but also seeks its food on land and is sometimes destructive to cultivated crops. In western Africa a smaller species is found, which has been made the type of a separate genus or subgenus and called *Charopsis liberiensis*.

➤ In Africa are many tales of the hippopotamus. In one, a great warrior woman shapeshifts to become a hippopotamus to defeat a monster trying to destroy her village. In another, the hare pairs the elephant against the hippo in a humorous test of strength and wit. It is a creature of great myth and folklore, and as a totem or spirit messenger, its medicine is always powerful.

Weighing as much as four tons, the hippopotamus is the second largest mammal, rivaling the rhinoceros. It once lived throughout Africa, but it is now found only in protected areas.

Hippopotamus means "river horse," which is appropriate since it spends most of its day in lakes and rivers or basking in the sands next to them. At night, it comes to land to feed on grasses. Its association with water is its most symbolic aspect. Water is the ancient realm of birth, power, creation, imagination, healing, and artistic sensibilities. It is the place of sacred baptism, a rite involving water and the awakening of our higher sensibilities. It enables lucid dreaming and greater conscious spirit contact. When the hippo appears, this opportunity will manifest itself within the year. Now is the time to prepare.

The hippo can remain under water for up to five minutes and its eyes and nostrils are high on the head so that it can stay in the water with just its nostrils on the surface, seeming almost invisible within the water. The hippopotamus is a link to the spiritual, artistic, and healing realms of water. It teaches how to be strong within them, and anytime this animal appears as a messenger, the creative and artistic energies will grow stronger.

With this animal comes the "artistic temperament" as well. During mating season the males are extremely aggressive. Fights are vigorous and large gashes are inflicted with the tusks. Learning to control the powerful creative energies will be part of what must be developed for those to whom this great animal is a totem.

Hippos live in large groups, and unlike many other species of animals, the females choose their mates. For many to whom the hippo is a totem or messenger, there will be a feeling or belief that their path in life was chosen for them and there is no choice but to follow it.

The hippo's only enemy is the crocodile, and thus it should be studied as well. The crocodile though is truly only a threat to the young. An adult can easily bite the crocodile in two. This reflects the great power that can be drawn upon if necessary to protect creative endeavors from outside threats, whether real or perceived.

When the hippopotamus appears, we should also do some self-examination. It is time to immerse oneself more powerfully, more fully, into the spiritual, artistic, or healing environments.

Hippopotamus (cont.)

Are we hesitating following our own path?

Are we hesitant to immerse ourselves in the creative process?

Are we not controlling or directing our creative energies appropriately?

Are we too temperamental?

Do we need to draw out our power from the waters of life?

Humpback Whale

KEYNOTE

song of new birth

PACIFIC HUMPBACK
(*Megaptera versabilis*)

Any whalebone whale of
the genus *Megaptera*,
related to the rorquals,
but having very long
flippers. The color is
black above and white
below, and they attain a
large size, but their
whalebone and oil are
inferior. The number of
species is uncertain. That
of the Atlantic is *M. nodosa*,
that of the Pacific
(doubtfully distinct) is
M. versabilis.

*Are we using our vocal
powers constructively?*

*Are we being unmindful
of what we say and
how we say it?*

*Are we hearing what is
said beneath the words
of others?*

*Are we acting upon our
inspirations?*

*Are we ready to sing
forth a new birth
in our life?*

➤ Most whales are divided into two categories: toothed and baleen. Toothed whales have sharp teeth by which they catch and eat fish and other marine animals. Baleen whales do not have teeth. Their mouths are lined with bony plates of hard keratin. They strain seawater through these plates, feeding on plankton or the sea life within it. The humpback whale is a baleen.

It is most noted for its wonderful song, the beautiful sounds sung by males. Each breeding season brings with it corresponding changes in the whales' songs, reflecting the ability of the whale to teach us how to create through song and sounds—adjusting it to the time, place, and individual.

Singing is one of our most powerful and creative acts, linking us to the underlying substance and being, and is a means by which we can enter into a relationship with our most spiritual powers and abilities. It awakens our healing energies.

Whales have a form of echo-location or sonar. This sensitivity to sound links the humpback whale to the primal creative sounds of life. Sound is the creative force of life. Humpback whale teaches us how to direct it and respond to its feedback. This can be used to tap hidden levels of our mind and even to accelerate the manifesting our goals.

Unlike the sociable sperm whale, the humpback whale lives in a very loose and changing group of about four to ten whales where the most stable and longest lasting relationship is between mother and calf. They remain close to each other for up to a year. When the humpback appears, there is usually a year cycle at play in which our creative powers of sound and voice will develop. We will find ways to use our voice more effectively in all aspects of our life.

Humpbacks usually give birth to one whale. The umbilical cord is snapped and the young instinctively come to the surface for their first breath. The mother urges the baby to the surface, pushing the young upwards. These first seconds are crucial because until it fills its lungs with air, the calf's body is heavier than the water and it is in danger of sinking and drowning.

Often those who have humpbacks as a totem also have someone who is there at new undertakings, pushing and nudging them to go higher. It is a reminder too that although the first year of a "new birth" may be difficult, greater strength and independence comes quickly after.

MARATHON
MAMMALS

Many mammals have abilities that are amazing and which hint at what they can teach us to accomplish in areas of our own life.

- A puma can leap 15 to 20 feet straight up.

- Even though it weighs over 3000 pounds, a rhinocerous can run nearlly 30 miles per hour.

- A pronghorn antelope can run 35 miles per hour for many miles.

- A chimpanzee can lift six times its own body weight.

- The gray whale migrates 26,000 miles eery year from feeding grounds to breeding grounds and back again.

The amazing things animals accomplish reflect greater possibilities for outselves than we may have ever imagined.

Hyena

KEYNOTE

- **formidable instincts and abilities**

- **develop clan and communal life**

STRIPED HYENA

(*Hyaena hyaena*)

Any of several large and strong but nocturnal carnivorous mammals constituting the family Hyaenidae. They have a long thick neck, large head, powerful jaws, rough coat, and four-toed feet with nonretractile claws. The hyenas are nocturnal and feed largely on carrion. There are three living species, the striped hyena (*H. hyaena*) of parts of Africa and southern Asia east to India, the spotted hyena (*H. crocuta*, or *Crocuta crocuta*) of Africa south of the Sahara, and the brown hyena (*H. brunnea*) of South Africa, also various more or less related extinct forms.

➤ Hyenas are dog-like creatures of Africa and Asia and are often scorned for their funny looks and their scavenging habits, but they are in reality formidable hunters, taking on formidable prey. They have keen noses for hunting, and actually hunt more prey than scavenge. They will chase off lions, and a fully-grown hyena is capable of tackling a wildebeest on its own.

Spotted hyenas do almost everything together in packs. Still, the females give birth alone, staying away from their clan for at least a week before moving the litter into the communal den. It is safer, for adult males will eat the young. It also enables time for the mother and young to bond. It is often a reminder in our modern times of a need to have time alone with our children, especially in the early days. It will make them stronger, more confident, and formidable adults.

In more ancient times, the first month or so after a new birth was a time when only the immediate family had contact with the mother and child. This sheltered the young from outside disease and influence, and it strengthened the bond of the family.

For those to whom the hyena appears, the clan, be it biological or otherwise, will become more important. Tasks will be accomplished more easily and effectively. Protection and safety will be found in clan-type alliances—especially in business.

All females in the spotted hyena clan breed and they will suckle their young for up to 18 months. In order to feed her young for such a length of time, there must be a gorging at pack kills. In a single year, a nursing mother may travel up to 4000 miles to and from her pups. The mother usually only raises two pups on her own and each mother has her own call to her pups, which will respond in kind.

The jaws and stomach of the hyena are extremely strong, so strong that it is capable of devouring a whole wildebeest carcass. This includes the bones, hooves, and horn. When the hyena appears, our ability to digest more, to take in more experiences and opportunities, will increase.

Our jaws will become stronger in the sense of our words and communications. Things said more softly and lovingly will be felt more lovingly. Things said more harshly and cutting will cut more deeply. We will need to be careful of what we say, how we say it, and to whom we say it.

Hyenas have extremely highly developed noses:

> The nasal membrane surface is 50 times bigger than a human's. This gives it a sensitivity to smell that allows communication approaching the subtlety of human speech. From a single patch of urine, a hyena can tell what type of animal secreted it, even if the patch is several hours old. And if the urine was passed by one of its own clan, it can tell which animal it was.[3]

The sense of smell is associated with discrimination and discernment. When the hyena appears as a messenger, we will find our ability to discern and discriminate growing stronger. We will be clearer on what to do, when to do it, who to trust, who to believe, and more. We will learn to trust "what smells right" as opposed to "what smells fishy." Our inner sense of smell will be more acute than what we see or hear, and it will be important to trust it.

The hyena is a truly formidable animal, but we should examine our present situation when it appears. Our instincts will be strong and accurate and our clan support for our endeavors will be so as well.

Hyena
(cont.)

Do we trust our own perceptions?

Do we need to be more discerning and discriminating?

Are we not acting on our impressions?

Are we not pursuing the opportunities that "we smell" in the offing?

Do we need to help our family and friends more?

Are we getting help from them as well?

---

[3] John Palmer, ed. *Exploring the Secrets of Nature.* (New York: Reader's Digest Association, 1994), p. 317.

Impala

KEYNOTE

great leaps with grace

Are we hesitating to make the leaps available to us?

Are we ignoring our opportunities?

Are we ignoring our impressions and what we think we are hearing?

Do we need to be more alert to problems?

Are we trying to be too much of an individual?

Are we going against the crowd just to be an individual?

Are we allowing the group to prevent us from taking the leaps?

➤ The impala is a graceful antelope, and if it has appeared as a messenger or totem, consult the information on antelopes from my earlier book Animal-Speak. It will help to also consult the previous information on the gazelle, as they share very similar qualities.

Unlike their relative the gazelle, though, the impala likes being near water and avoids the open country. Its hearing is very acute, and at the slightest odd sound, it will raise its head, alert to any possible danger. When the impala appears as a messenger, listen closely to the voice expressions of others. Listen to what isn't being said. Trust in those feelings.

At the approach of a predator, the impala will bound straight up into the air and release scent from its hind glands. This alerts other impalas and warns them of the danger. The herd runs together, following the scent of the first. By running in a herd, they are safer, as an individual runner is much more vulnerable.

The main predator for the impala is the leopard, and it should be studied as well. When it captures an impala, it is usually one that has separated from the herd. Leopards will drag the impala carcass up into a tree to store it and secure it from scavengers. With the impala and leopard, there is predator and prey, the contrary medicine that brings balance when both are employed.

The impala runs with great, graceful, and bounding leaps and is able to jump higher and further than what appears possible. When the impala appears in our life, we should not hesitate to make the leaps and bounds we are considering. We will make them and with much more grace and ease than even we imagined possible.

➤ Jackals are scavengers and all scavengers are connected to the process of life, death, and rebirth. They remove the body from nature so that it can be born again and they aid in helping individuals move between the world of the living and the world of the dead.

In Egypt, the jackal was sacred to Anubis, the guardian between worlds—the living and the dead, the waking and the sleeping. The jackal is the guide dog that also guards against lower forces. Anubis guards the spirit, or ba, whenever it is away from the body, thus protecting the traveler whether in spirit or body.

When the jackal appears, there will be protection and guidance from hidden dangers, complications, and problems in our travels—whether of body, mind, or spirit. It is an indication that new realms will be crossed, and any adversity will not be allowed to overcome us. We are not alone.

Found in wooded and savanna country of Asia and Africa, jackals are a close relative to the dog and wolf. This wolf is usually seen in pairs, but jackals hunt in packs. When the jackal appears as a totem or messenger, we will have guardianship with us. For those endeavors we undertake it will seem as if "a pack of jackals" is working for us.

Young jackals stay with their parents the first year and hunt in family packs. Working together, they are more successful in their endeavors. When we start into new realms, it is good to initially enter them with those who are of like spirit. Our efforts will be more successful than if we go it all alone, especially in the initial stages.

The jackal has a highly developed sense of smell, but it also has excellent eyesight, and hearing. When it appears in our life, our psychic perceptions will become increasingly acute to warn us of adversity or to alert us to opportunity.

Jackal

KEYNOTE

guidance and guardianship in new realms and endeavors

JACKAL
(Canis aureus)
Any of several wild dogs of the Old World, esp. *Canis aureus* of southeastern Europe, southern Asia, and northern Africa. They are smaller, usually more yellowish, and hunt in packs at night. Jackals feed on carrion and small animals, including poultry. They can be tamed, and by some are believed to be the progenitors of domestic dogs.

Jaguar

KEYNOTE

reclaiming power and fruits of labor

JAGUAR
(Felis onca)

A large powerful feline animal…ranging from Texas to Paraguay. It has a larger head, heavier body, and shorter, thicker legs than the leopard or the cougar. It is brownish yellow or buff, marked with black spots, each primary spot surrounded by a somewhat broken ring of smaller ones. It chiefly inhabits forests and preys especially on the capybara and tapir.

➤ The jaguar, also known as a panther, is related to the leopard family of large cats and lives in tropical forests. Little is known about their habits, but the jaguar, like larger cats, is a stalker and its primary prey is the capybara and peccary. This patient stalker waits until its prey is close enough to strike strongly and hard. When jaguar appears, our patience is about to be rewarded, but we must strike when the opportunity presents itself.

Jaguars also have great power and can climb, run, and even swim better than a tiger They will often bite through the temporal lobe of their prey and have even been known to shear off the heads of other animals with a single swipe of their claws. Because of this, when jaguar appears, we should trust in our own instinctsæ—not that of others—to know how best to attack. Also, because they stalk, it is important for those with this animal appearing not to let others know of their plans. Otherwise the opportunity to reclaim what is rightfully ours may be missed.

Jaguars have also been seen hanging over streams and flipping fish out of the water with their paws. This is a reminder of the ability to do things not necessarily believed or that the situations surrounding us are not what they appear to be. We may be disappointed with the results of our efforts at this time. The jealousy of others or ourselves may be undermining our efforts. Our own insecurities and timidness about acting when the opportunity presents itself may be hindering us.

They breed at any time during the year, and they usually have two to four cubs per year. When the jaguar shows up, we have an opportunity to give birth to new things two to four times in the coming year. The Arawak people say that everything has jaguar—that nothing can exist without it. Stories abound of revenge, abductions, and even great cures through the use of jaguar power. If jaguar has shown up as a messenger, we may need to be cautious about others stealing our power—our opportunities. We may be letting others know of our plans and intentions and thus giving away our strengths and possibilities.

Because it functions so well in so many environments, the jaguar is a symbol of mastery over dimensions where others cannot survive. This animal has great mysticism and significance, and its appearance heralds good opportunities from various directions, providing time for reclaiming our own power.

Whether our power was lost, stolen, or broken, there is arising a time to reclaim it and express it again, even more strongly and solidly than if we had not lost it to begin with. Our efforts and patience are about to be rewarded much more greatly than we had anticipated. We will now be able to enjoy the fruits of our long labors.

When the jaguar appears as a messenger, we need to ask ourselves if we are letting others know of our plans before we get a chance to act upon them, Remember, the jaguar stalks silently. The time to discuss it with others is after we have captured the prize.

In reclaiming our power, or reclaiming what we lost, the jaguar gives us the ability to go beyond what has been imagined and to pursue the opportunities with discipline and control. It heralds the blessing of the hero's quest and the promise of the return to the hero's path within our life.

Are we acting too aggressively in our undertakings?

Are we responding too intensely?

Do we need to temper responses so as not to unintentionally wound others?

Are we giving our power— and thus our rewards— to someone else?

Are we letting the past stop us from accomplishments in the present?

Are we being too impatient in achieving our goals?

Kangaroo

KEYNOTE

time to move forward, not back

➤ When Captain Cook first saw the kangaroo in Australia, he asked the aborigines what that strange looking animal was. Their response to him was, "kangaroo," which means "I don't understand you."

There are 57 species of kangaroo and they are probably the most famous of jumping animals. They are nocturnal, marsupials, and plant eaters. The adult male is called a *boomer* and the female is called a *doe*.

All marsupials, or pouched animals, give birth to immature young that complete their development outside the womb in the mother's pouch. Every marsupial tells us that we need to give birth prematurely. We then help what we have given birth to in developing outside the womb. Experience becomes the best teacher.

The kangaroo often reflects several possible time cycles at play within our life. Like all marsupials, the moment it is born, the young kangaroo, called a *joey*, (approximately 1 inch in length) must undertake the hazardous journey to its mother's pouch. After only five weeks in the womb, it must crawl six to eight inches to find one of the four nipples in its mother's pouch—its home for the next 18 months or so. When the joey appears, it is often an indication that we have only five weeks to give birth to something we have been thinking about.

The joey may stay in the pouch for 9 months before it first appears outside, but it may move in and out for up to 18 months. After we give birth to our project, it may be nine months before our work begins to "mature" and benefit us.

When the kangaroo appears, a 9-month cycle is at play, indicating a time to emerge and move forward. There is a safety net of yet another 9 months in which we can move back and forth without committing fully. Then there will be no choice. It is time to move forward. It is time to come out of the pouch and safety of what is familiar. In most cases, the joey vacates the pouch as early as 7 months and for good at 11 months.

It is unknown how the joey is able to find its mother's nipple at such a young age, especially since it's blind. The theory is that it relies on smell. Once the joey finds the nipple, it clamps its mouth over it and the nipple swells to fix the mouth firmly in place. There it remains for about a month until the baby has developed enough to be able to release itself. Often when young joeys appear to people, it is an indication of more growth still to come, reflecting the need to learn to disconnect from the things of childhood. It often reminds us that we must continually nurse what we may have given birth to prematurely.

A mother kangaroo that nurses two young-sters of differing ages will produce two different types of milk. The younger member gets milk with very little fat. The older sibling who has left the pouch will get an increased amount of fat. Kangaroos often indicate a need to adjust our "diet" according to our needs and activities. What worked for as in the beginning won't con-tinue to do so as we mature—physically or in various endeavors.

The primary predator of the kangaroo is the dingo, and thus it should be studied as well. If it is the joey that has appeared in your life, we would do well by studying the wedge-tailed eagle, as it is the number-one predator of them. Usually if in danger, the kangaroo will try and be still and quiet

In defense and in competition with other members, particularly among the males for fe-males, kangaroos will use their heavy tails to bal-ance themselves while they kick and "box" with their hind and fore legs, respectively. The tail is also used as a counterbalance when hopping.

The kangaroo tail is an amazing appendage. It can be as long as the rest of its body, and when hopping it balances the body so the kangaroo

Kangaroo
(cont.)

GIANT KANGAROO
(*Macropus giganteus*)

Any of the herbivorous leaping marsupial mammals of the family Macropodidae, of Australia, New Guinea, and adjacent islands; esp., those of the genus *Macropus*. The largest and best-known species are the giant kangaroo (*M. giganteus*) and the red kangaroo (*M. rufus*), which are about five feet long, excluding the tail. They have a small head, large ears, very long and powerful hind legs, and a long thick tail, which is used as a support in standing or walking. The relatively small fore legs are not used for progression. The two larger hind toes are armed with heavy nails, forming the animal's only means of defense. Kangaroos are often hunted with dogs, and their flesh was largely eaten by the aboriginal Australians. Related to the kangaroos of the genus *Macropus* are the wallabies, rock kangaroos, hare kangaroos, tree kangaroos, bettongs, and musk kangaroos.

Kangaroo
(cont.)

Are we not moving forward?

Do we need to go ahead, even if it seems premature?

Are we refusing to disconnect from things of childhood?

Are we heeding our previous experiences?

Are we trying to reverse, when we can only truly go forward?

Are we nursing what we have birthed?

Do we need to balance our creative activities?

Are we staying grounded?

Are we giving up too easily?

does not fall on its face. It also serves as a built-in chair. The large tail is a symbol of power and strength inherent for those to whom the kangaroo is a messenger or totem. Learning to balance the powerful creative energies will be part of the task. Kangaroos can teach us to use the tail, an ancient symbol of creative and sexual life force, to move quickly and make great leaps in our creativity.

Strength and agility are two qualities associated with the kangaroo. In one hop, a gray kangaroo can jump a distance of 44 feet, and when it really gets going it can leap as high as 11 feet off the ground. It can hop faster than horses can run, although a kangaroo cannot hop backwards. This is especially important; when kangaroo appears, it is time to leap forward. You will have the stamina and strength to continue on. Do not try and go back.

A kangaroo uses less energy as it moves faster and faster. They actually "recycle" their energy. A large tendon in the leg stretches like a rubber band. When the kangaroo leaves the ground, the tendon "snaps back" helping to lift the animal into the air. For those with the kangaroo as a spirit messenger, movement may be smaller in the beginning, but as you begin to progress, the movement will become faster and greater. This allows the kangaroo to travel great distances without getting tired. Getting the initial momentum will be the difficult part in endeavors for those with this totem, but once achieved, progress will come quickly and the stamina will be great.

Kangaroos live in desert climates, and they can actually live on less water than camels. When we start something new, we may have to do without for a long period, but we will survive. If we keep our stamina up, we will succeed, and once things start to move, it will be with great leaps.

➤ Most people call the koala a "koala bear," but it is not even remotely related to bears. Like the kangaroo, the koala is a marsupial, a pouched animal that gives birth prematurely to its young. All marsupials teach us the importance of giving birth prematurely and then developing and nurturing the young out of the womb. For example, ideas for endeavors should be brought out early on and then nursed along outside through experience.

Koalas, nocturnal animals, live in different parts of eastern Australia and feed mainly on certain kinds of eucalyptus leaves, each species eating a different variety. For anyone to whom the koala is a totem, a study of the healing aspects of eucalyptus would be beneficial.

Eucalyptus is a fragrance that has tremendous healing qualities. It has a penetrating aroma benefitial in treating conditions of the lungs, kidneys, liver, and nasal passages. It helps the eliminative system dispel toxins, and is calming to highly charged emotional states.

Eucalyptus leaves are poisonous to most mammals, but the koala has special stomachs that can break down the poisonous oils in the leaves, so it can eat as much as two pounds of eucalyptus leaves per day. They also get most of their water needs from the leaves.

When the koala appears in our life as a totem and messenger, it is often an indication of a need to keep the emotions in control. We may be becoming too sensitive, too emotional. Others around us might be as well. Now is the time not to give in to emotionally charged situations.

Often when the koala appears, there may even be some toxic emotional situations around us. It is time to cleanse them, digest them, and move away from them. Climb above them if possible. Koalas teach us how to detoxify our lives—physically, emotionally, mentally, and spiritually. They can teach us about healing toxic situations. When

Koala

KEYNOTE

- time to calm down and relax and detoxify your life
- promise of relief

KOALA

(*Phascolarctos cinereus*)

An Australian arboreal marsupial…called also *bear* or *native bear*. It is about two feet long, with no obvious tail, large hairy ears, thick ashy gray fur, and sharp claws. It is awkward and sluggish, and feeds upon eucalyptus leaves. The single young is early removed from the pouch and carried on the parent's back.

Koala
(cont.)

*Are our emotions
out of control?*

*Are we feeling
too sensitive?*

*Are others around us too
emotionally charged?*

*Do we need to retreat
from others in our life
for a while?*

*Are we not hanging on
and we should be?*

*Do we need to insulate
ourselves a little more?*

koalas appear, we need to take a look at our emotional life

Koalas have a wonderful climbing ability. Their arms and shoulders are very muscular, enabling them to climb to heights of safety. Arms and shoulders are symbolic of carrying things, often burdens. When the koala appears, we have probably been carrying an emotional burden or someone close to us has.

Koalas have special hands that help them hang on tight and climb trees. They actually have two thumbs on each hand, which enables them to grip. The koala is a reminder that we are stronger than we imagined and we will be able to hang on through whatever situation is occurring in our life. Maintain our hold for calm is coming. The koala promises relief from the tensions and emotions and stresses in our life—if we hang on.

Koalas have a fur that is warm, thick, and very insulating. This further reinforces the idea that we may need to insulate ourselves from the emotions and stresses around us. Some of them may become toxic to us if we do not.

Koalas don't often come down from their trees and if koalas are our totem or messenger, we need a place of safety, a home we can always go to. Koala people are very sensitive and need to have a place where they can be alone, safe, and not feel stressed. They are often people who are comfortable being by themselves. And they are always unique individuals.

Often shy, koala people are very empathic. They are sensitive to the emotions of others and their environments. Because others and the environment in which they find themselves easily effect empathic people, they need time alone to disassociate from the energies that have touched them throughout the day.

Lemur

➤ In the Madagascar forests, the haunting, weird-calling sound that echoes comes from the lemur, known as the ghost of the forest. Lemurs are related to but more primitive than monkeys, and their name actually means "ghost."

They have bushy tails and large eyes that give them a haunted kind of expression. There are three main groups of lemurs, and all are confined to Madagascar. The most commonly recognized is the ring-tailed lemur, noticeable for its banded tale it usually carries in the air, like a flag, to signal its presence to others.

When the lemur appears, so too will spirits. We will begin to see and hear the presence of spirits and ghosts more clearly. They will not be harmful, but their presence may be a little startling to us because of their accompanying phenomena. We will see forms and shadows moving or hear whispers and seemingly haunted sounds. As we work to connect more clearly, they will become more distinct. Sometimes they herald the return of an "imaginary" childhood friend.

When the lemur appears, the opening to the spirit realm with answers that can come from it alone begin to manifest.

Are you ignoring the phenomena?

Do you trust what you hear?

Are you haunted by the past and need clarification?

KEYNOTE

- clairaudience
- spirit contact
- ghostly presence

LEMUR
(*Lemur albifrons*)

Any of numerous arboreal, chiefly nocturnal mammals allied to the monkeys, but usually regarded as constituting a distinct suborder, Lemuroides. In general form and habits they resemble monkeys, but nearly all have a sharp foxlike muzzle, large eyes, and very soft woolly fur. The tail, thought sometimes rudimentary, is usually long and furry, but never prehensile. The brain is relatively small, and differs from that of monkeys in having the cerebellum exposed. The placenta is nondeciduate. As in monkeys, the mammae are pectoral and the thumbs and toes opposable. Most lemurs are confined to Madagascar and adjacent islands, but representatives occur in Africa and the Oriental region. Fossil forms have been found in Europe, Asia, and America.

Llama

KEYNOTE

surefootedness

LLAMA
(Lama huanacos)

Any yof several wild and
domesticated
South American ruminants
allied to the camels, but
smaller and without a hump;
esp., the domesticated variety
of the guanaco
(*L. huanacos*), used for
centruies as a beast of burden
in the Andes. It is about three
feet high at the shoulder and
varies in color from black to
white. Its coat is long and
woolly, but coarser than in
the alpaca, which is otherwise
very similar.

➤ The llama is a domestic member of the camel family, and thus the camel should be studied as well whenever the llama appears as a totem and messenger. A beast of burden in Peru and other parts of South America, the llama is well adapted to work in high altitudes.

The llama is always surefooted on steep mountain trails, and in this is found its keynote. When the llama appears, we will find our footing is secure. We will be able to maneuver through the environments that are steep and otherwise somewhat treacherous. If we have been feeling insecure about our footing in various situations, we can relax.

The llama can be stubborn, though, when it is tired or if it feels its load is too heavy. When the llama appears, we should examine whether we are being stubborn or just cautious. Llamas teach us to climb slowly and securely in our endeavors and its appearance heralds security in our efforts.

Are we carrying too muchof a load?

Are we hesitating to make our moves?

Are we feeling insecure?

Do things feel unstable around us?

*Are we being too stubborn and refusing to move,
even though it may result in new achievements?*

Are others putting too much of a load upon us?

Are we doing this to others?

➤ According to Pliny in his Natural History, the mole was the animal that magicians admired the most because its entrails always revealed the fates accurately. He also taught that if a person swallows the heart of a mole while it was still beating, the person would receive the gift of prophecy. The mole was used in magical rites to make a woman dance naked and to heal toothaches, epilepsy, and other diseases as well. To have a purse of moleskin would insure that you would always have money to put in it.

None of these old superstitions have anything to do with the reality of this animal's true meaning. There are around 20 species of moles, and they range throughout most of the world—North America, Europe, and Asia.

As a burrowing animal, the mole is well adapted to life underground; placcs beneath the earth were often considered mysterious, leading to the land of the dead and to great treasures. The mole shows us how to dig out our own treasures in life through our own efforts. In shamanism, they can be guides into the Underworld.

The mole has a cylindrical body with front feet that are extremely broad and function as diggers for its tunnels, where it spends most of its life. Often, for those to whom the mole is a messenger or totem, there is a natural ability to dig beneath the surface of things, to analyze and uncover the hidden.

The mole's skin has more organs for touch than any other animal. For those to whom the mole is a totem, the sense of touch is already or will soon become greatly heightened. To mole individuals, there will often occur two responses, because of this sensitivity. The pleasure response from touch will increase, or the individual will try to be more standoffish because of the increased sensitivity. Psychic touch will be a major part of this and should be relied upon by those to whom

Mole

KEYNOTE

- **heightened senses (especially touch)**

- **luck in endeavors through our own efforts**

SHREW MOLE

Any of numerous Insectivora belonging to various genera, chiefly of the family Talpidae, mostly found in temperate parts of Europe, Asia, and North America. They have minute eyes often covered with skin, small concealed ears, very soft and often iridescent fur, and strong fossorial fore feet. They live almost entirely under ground, making extensive galleries and feeding on small life, esp. earthworms. The common European mole is *Talpa europea*. The common species of the eastern United States is *Scalopus aquaticus*, which has partially webbed feet. The star-nosed more (*Condylura cristata*) of the same region has a long thick tail and a fleshy starlike appendage on the snout. From its burrowing habits t is called a *moldwarp*, or *mold-turner*. The name is also applied in North American, to the shrew, a small burrowing animal of the genus *Sorex*.

Mole
(cont.)

Do you trust what you feel?

Are you ignoring your feelings?

Are you becoming too sensitive?

Are you not working to make your own luck?

Are you sitting back, waiting for things to come to you?

this animal appears. Do not trust what you see or hear as much as what you feel.

Increasingly, those with the mole as a messenger will find that their own sense of touch will let them know what is true. Trusting in what is felt, no matter how strange the impression, may become important. Individuals with moles as guides often find that when they touch certain people, strange and sometimes disturbing images come to mind. Usually the initial response is "Now why would I ever think that of this person?" Learning to trust this sense of touch, regardless of the logic of the impression, will be important. Sooner or later, the truth will reveal itself.

Moles dig their own ventilation shafts so that they have fresh air. For those to whom the mole is a totem, it will be extremely important for their health to get plenty of fresh air.

Moles feed primarily upon earthworms, one of the great natural treasures of fertile soil. Because of this, the mole helps us to seek out treasures of fertile soil in areas of our life to nourish us. Remember that the mole is a digger of tunnels, constantly searching for his treasures that he ultimately finds.

➤ One of the most ancient and primitive looking mammals is the musk ox, with its large head and shaggy fur. Though they seem to look like oxen, they are probably more closely related to sheep and goats.

Usuallly found in small herds, the musk ox lives in the Arctic tundra, one of the harshest environments, and has been able to live there successfully. This is a reminder often for those to whom it comes as a messenger that there will be protection in the harshness of the environment in which we are finding ourselves. It is a powerful animal that hints at the primal strength that is opening to us if we need it for protection.

The musk ox enemy is the arctic wolf, and thus it should be studied as well. The wolves rarely try to take a healthy adult, but try instead to snatch a calf. This is often a message of a need to protect our young, our creative endeavors.

When threatened, the musk oxen form a tight circle, with the young in the middle for protection. This huddle is often called a *phalanx* because of its resemblance to the battle formation of ancient Macedonia. (Sometimes the musk ox appearance indicates past life issues associated with a time in Macedonia may be at play or coming into play within your life.) With their heads and horns lowered, the adults face outwards. They guard the young, trying to gore and even trample the attackers.

Gathering in a tight circle with the adults facing outwards is also used to protect the young against blizzards. When the musk ox appears, it is time to protect our young. It is also a message that we should not try and do it ourselves. Greatest success occurs through having the family or group band together.

When the musk ox appears, it is time to draw upon ancient and primal strengths to protect what is ours.

Musk Ox

KEYNOTE

**primitive and ancient
protection in groups**

MUSK OX
(*Ovibos moschatus*)
A hollow-horned ungulate...circumpolar in distribution during the Pleistocene period, but now confined to Greenland and the barren grounds of North America. It is intermediate between the sheep and the oxen in size and in many characters. [sic] The horns of the male are heavy, rugose, and apposed at the base and curve outward and downward and then slightly upward at the tips. Those on the females are more slender. The thick, long, shaggy pelage is dark grayish brown or blackish with a light saddle marking.

Are we trying to do everything ourselves?

Are we not protecting our creative young?

Do we need to get some assistance from others?

Are we afraid to use the strength and power we have available to us?

Muskrat

KEYNOTE

maneuvering through emotional, astral, and spiritual waters

MUSKRAT
(*Fiber zibethicus*)
An abundant aquatic rodent...found throughout the United States and Canada. It is as large as a small cat and has the tail long, scaly, and laterally compressed, the hind feet webbed, and the fur dark glossy brown. Muskrats live in holes in banks or in dome-shaped houses which they make of rushes and mud; they have small glands emitting a musky odor.

➤ The muskrat is a member of the rodent family. Although often seen as related to rats and mice, it is actually a large water vole. Voles are commonly mistaken for rats and mice, but they have blunter snouts. Meadow voles also have shorter tails. For those to whom the muskrat appears, it would be wise to study the section on voles as well.

It is appropriate to think of the muskrat as a small beaver in that they share similar qualities. Like the beaver, the muskrat has a thick layer of waterproof underhairs and long, shiny guard hairs. They also build lodges and dig burrows for their home like the beaver. But it's long, rat-like tail helps to distinguish it from its larger cousin. If intruders appear, it will slap its narrow tail (scaly and flattened from side to side) on the surface of the water to warn neighbors just like a beaver. The difference, though, is that because its tail is much narrower than a beaver's, the sound is not nearly as intense.

Muskrats are excellent swimmers and are almost always found near water. With hind feet that are partly webbed, it is well adapted for swimming. It also dives well and is able to stay submerged for 12-17 minutes. They can teach us how to immerse ourselves in things for great periods of time. Muskrat people often require time where they can go deep into themselves and although this may worry loved ones, they will eventually emerge. It is necessary for them in order to develop their own strength and to tap ever-deeper resources within. It is also not unusual for muskrat people to lose track of time when working upon something creative.

Because of its association with water (an ancient symbol for the creative, the astral and spiritual) muskrats are great dream guides. Their appearance often indicates a time in which dreams will be more lucid and colorful and it is not unusual for conscious out-of-body experiences to occur when muskrat shows up.

The muskrat is often seen as a pest because of the burrows they dig into the bank sides, but its tremendous appetite for water plants creates open water in marshy areas that will provide perfect habitat for migrating fowl. They will also eat crayfish, mussels, and the occasional fish.

The muskrat gets its name from the Algonquin word for animal, musquash. It has two musk glands located near the anus at the base of the tail. The scent is deposited on a scent post (usually a twist of grass at the water's edge) to announce its willingness to mate, and in males to mark their territory.

Although several muskrats may share a single lodge, they can be very territorial, defending their burrows and ponds intensely. They smell and hear superbly, but they do not always see very well. When muskrats appear, it is important not to trust what you see, but what sounds and smells right to you. Listen and you will hear undercurrents in the voices of others that will provide tremendous insight. You will detect underlying emotions.

Muskrats are always connected to emotions in some way because of their association with water. They can teach us how to maneuver through them, to recognize their subtleties, and to derive strength and nutrition from them without being drowned. This is especially reflected in their unique incisors that are located outside the lips, allowing them to gnaw on plants in water without drowning. Muskrats can be quite scrappy and vocal, but they also know how to dig their own safe burrows into whatever emotional environments they work and live in.

Are you paying attention to your dreams?

Are you approaching emotional issues in your life from a superficial perspective?

Are you afraid to submerge yourself in new waters Ä new endeavors?

Are you wallowing in emotions?

Are you making the most of the situation at hand, finding your own burrows?

Are you taking time for yourself alone?

Are you hesitating to dive into new spiritual waters?

Orangutan

KEYNOTE

**cleverness and skill
at presentation**

ORANG-UTAN

An anthropoid ape (*Pongo pygmaeus*, syn. *Simia satyrus*) found in the low, swampy forests of Borneo and Sumatra. It is about two thrids as large as the gorilla, and is distinguished by its small ears, brown skin, and long, sparse, reddish brown hair. The adult male stands about four feet high and may weigh as much as 250 pounds. The arms are very long. The face, hands, and feet are naked, and in old mlaes flattened expansions of the cheeks are developed. It is chiefly herbivorous and lives almost exclusively in tree tops, where it constructs rude temporary nests of leaves and branches in which to sleep.

Are we doing things in the same way as always?

Do we need to look for new possibilities?

Do we need to change our appearance to accomplish what we must more successfully?

➤ Orangutans are natural escape artists who are extremely clever with their hands and their ability to feign and distract. They teach us how to be cleverer and even how to put on the best face to accomplish what we must more successfully. Orangutans are also very expressive with their faces, and those to whom this is a significant animal will find their own facial expressions becoming more colorful and important in communication.

Orangutans are only found in Southeast Asia, on the islands of Borneo and Sumatra. Unlike other apes, they live alone most of the time. Mothers and their young are the exceptions. They often keep their young with them for six to ten years and it is this six to ten year cycle that comes into play for those to whom the orangutan is a totem or messenger. The mother carries the young most of the time until a new baby arrives. This reflects the strong bond with one's mother for those who have an orangutan as a totem.

As male orangutans grow older, their faces change a great deal. This is a reminder that as we mature in our tasks and various situations in life, our face will change. We must change the face we put forward to others.

Orangutans are the largest mammal on earth surviving mainly on fruit. Because of this, fruit will be critical to the health of those who have orangutans as messengers or totems. To locate widely dispersed fruit trees, orangutans need a thorough knowledge of their environment and the various seasons. They teach us to know more about our own surroundings and read the signs there more effectively. We come to read the changing "faces" around us more clearly as well.

Orangutans teach us clever uses of what is available to us. For example, they will often use a large leaf as a makeshift umbrella. When the orangutan appears, it is time to be cleverer about how we express ourselves and how we use what is available to us.

Panda

KEYNOTE

- **gentle strength**
- **nourishment**
- **sensitivity**

➤ The giant panda is a placental mammal, nourishing young within the uterus through an umbilical cord. Though the adult is quite large, the babies are the smallest of the placental young. The mother is almost a thousand times larger than its mouse-sized cub, which at birth weighs about three to four ounces.

The cub is completely helpless, and the large mother has to feed, warm, and stimulate it to defecate. The mother rarely leaves it during its first three weeks. Pandas often give birth to twins, but the demands of raising such tiny creatures are usually too great and most of the time only one will survive. Even in captivity, one is immediately rejected.

A panda must eat up to 14 hours a day to keep its energy levels high. Its diet consists of 99 percent bamboo so bamboo is always a totem as well for panda people. Pandas also have an extra thumb for gripping the bamboo, and they must strip off the outer hard bark to get to the soft insides. Because of this, the panda teaches us how to get to the meat of the matters surrounding us. Their appearance can often affirm we are focusing on the real issues, or it may indicate we need to strip back the outer surfaces to see what is underneath.

A study of the significance of bamboo will also provide some insight. Bamboo has strength and flexibility. It has had many uses through the ages, often considered one of the most important natural products. Bamboo shoots are a delicacy; wine often being spiced with bamboo leaves. Bamboo discs were sometimes used for money. The Chinese counterpart of the hobbyhorse was usually made of bamboo and symbolized youth. During the Han dynasty in China, prescriptive herbal remedies were discovered in the province of Gansu written on bamboo strips .

An old Chinese saying states that the leaves of the bamboo drop because its heart is empty, but

Are you trying to do too many things at once?

Are you looking for short cuts?

Are you staying focused on the tasks or are you being distracted?

Panda
(cont.)

an empty heart is also the same as being modest. The bamboo and panda reflect a quiet, unassuming essence—one that is modest and yet quite strong. Bamboo and panda are emblems of modesty and strength and thus are often associated with the goddess Kwan Yin.

Panda's raise one cub at a time, and they usually only have four in their entire lifetime. For those to whom the panda is a totem, it will be most important not to take on more creative activities than you can handle. Like pandas, you should focus on one at a time, raising and developing it, before the next. We must nourish fully one project before initiating another.

For those to whom the panda appears there are great tasks ahead. The early stages will be the most difficult, and it will be important not to split your attention in whatever you endeavor. Remain focused on one thing at a time. Follow it to completion and then move on to something else.

HEALING DIETS

Many animals, especially mammals, supplement their diet with healing minerals and plants. No one is truly sure whether this occurs through instinct or experience.

Mountain gorillas will make use of volcanic ash, rich in calcium and potassium, and they occasionally eat salt-rich soil. Elephants also seek out salt-rich volcanic rocks. Chimpanzees eat spiderwort without chewing it. Its milky sap is a remedy for earaches and fevers.

➤To the Eskimos, the polar bear is "Nanook" and is believed to have great supernatural powers. To the Inuit people, polar bears embody the living spirit of the North at the top of the world. The polar bear is a shaman, a liaison with the spirit world, keeping the wisdom of the ages. He was a teacher to the native peoples, showing them how to hunt, navigate, and survive in the Arctic.

These fearsome and independent animals were hunted for food and skins, and for generations were considered relatives, embodying and reflecting the great spirit of the people. All bears can swim and walk like human (heel to toe), and so they were often considered the closest kin to humans. Many traditions have myths of humans and bears living together, bears walking around as people, and people becoming bears. Some traditions teach that the bear is a ghost or spirit of a relative who has passed on and with whom there is unfinished work.

The senses of bears are extremely acute. Their sense of smell is better than a dog's, and their hearing just as sharp. It's believed that unlike other animals, bears see color. They also have prehensile lips, agile and unattached to the gums, enabling them to eat a variety of foods otherwise unattainable. Bears often indicate that our senses and our appetites are growing stronger.

Polar bears are one of the largest land carnivores. And it is one of the most outstanding hunters of the bear family. These white bears have no fear and they have no enemies or predators except humans. They are more powerful, more dangerous, and in many ways more gentle than any other bear. They embody power in strength and gentleness, in all extremes.

Polar bears prey mainly on seals, hunting them on the ice. They rely on a steady, stealthy approach and a highly developed sense of smell.

Polar Bear

KEYNOTE

great teachings and supernatural power in physical and spiritual realms

POLAR BEAR
A large bear, (*Ursus*, or *Thalarctos*, *maritimus*) inhabiting the Arctic regions of both the Old and the New World. It attains a length of about nine feet and often weights more than 1,000 pounds. It frequents the shores and ice floes, and swims well, living largely on seals. It differs from other bears in its creamy white color, long neck, narrow skull, and small molar teeth.

Polar Bear
(cont.)

Polar bears have a hundred times more sensors in their nose cavity than humans. They can sniff out a seal under two feet of snow from 20 miles away. When they approach, they do it slowly, often lying in wait, appearing to be an ice chunk to draw seals out. They must do this because seals are experts at detecting movement above them on the ice. Such hunts are more successful alone, so polar bears remain relatively unaccompanied and solitary.

Mating time is one of the few times they seek company. The female digs a den in November and the cubs are born during the arctic winter. The den's interior, warmed by the mother's body, is warmer than the outside. When the female gives birth to the cubs, she is particularly careful to avoid males because she knows that the bigger and stronger male will attack her to get to her cubs. She keeps her den meticulously clean. She passes very little urine and feces, living mostly off of her fat. Stimulated by increasing amounts of light, in March she emerges with the cubs.

Polar bears move equally well on land and in water. They can run up to 18 miles per hour on ice and as fast as 40 miles per hour on land. They can cover 100 miles in a stretch nonstop in the water. They move between water and land with ease, and thus they are teachers of how to move from one realm to the next and back again with great ease and power.

They can adjust their metabolism, as with many bears, to conserve energy and body heat.

Animal Wonders

WATER

All animals need water to survive, but some have earned a great reputation for their ability to go without water for great periods of time. While most people think the camel is best at going without water, a rat or a giraffe can do so longer than a camel can.

When asleep, their pulse rates slow to eight beats per minute, and they can awaken in a moment into a kind of "walking hibernation." The polar bear teaches us to control our metabolism, to move between realms, and to conserve our own energies and efforts.

The mother bear is very loving and caring toward her young. The cubs will stay with the mother from two to five years learning what it means to be a polar bear. When the polar bear appears as a totem or guide, a tremendous period of learning and power is being born. The teaching and learning may take two to five years, but in the process you will learn how to move between realms, manifest your great strength, and pursue what you need deliberately and powerfully.

Polar bears can almost magically appear and disappear out of nowhere. They are the travelers and guides between worlds. They walk the path between the spirit and the physical, unafraid and unrestricted. Even though the adult bears are fierce, they will exhibit behavior that can only be interpreted as play and can teach us how to be both fierce and playful within our lives.

Sometimes two bears will form friendships that last for weeks or even years. The friendly bears may feed and travel together or even form "play groups." It is not unusual as we start on a power journey that brief and even lasting friendships with those on a similar path may arise.

When the polar bear travels into our life, a new and powerful spiritual journey is about to be undertaken with the potential to awaken our greatest abilities in all extremes of life.

Polar Bear
(cont.)

Are we following the crowd or do we need to step out on our own?

Are we willing to face realms tha t we have dreamed of but never truly experienced?

Are we willing to take the time to develop our powers and abilities, no matter how primal?

Are we being too aggressive in our endeavors?

Is it time to learn new techniques to accomplish what we wish, to be able to move into new realms with great strength?

Shrew

KEYNOTE

- **vision in the dark**

- **acute hearing and smell**

- **early weaning**

SHREW

Any of numerous small mammals of the family Soricidae, mouselike in form, but belonging to the order Insectifora and most closely related to the moles. Among them are the smallest of all mammals, some being scarcely two inches in length. They have a long pointed snout, very small eyes, and velvety fur. They are chiefly nocturnal, feeding mostly on worms and insects.

Are you taking things on first sight?

Are you ignoring inner promptings?

Are you hanging onto things that no longer nourish you?

Do you need to bemore organized?

➤ The shrew was considered to be an evil creature by Pliny, the ancient Roman author of Natural History. To meet a shrew when heading out on a journey was an omen of evil and bad luck. In the 1700s, many believed that if a shrew walked over an animal or human, the creature would be inflicted with great anguish. On the other hand, some people believed they could cure rheumatism by carrying a dead shrew in their pocket.

Shrews are mouselike animals found in most parts of the world. They have very poor eyesight and in some species they are blind. They do have great hearing and a very acute sense of smell. The shrew teaches us not to trust what we see. Trusting in what we hear, especially in the undertones and expressions used will be more reliable. Even more reliable still is trusting what smells right and what doesn't. Trusting our inner vision rather than the outer is what shrews teach best.

Shrews have a constantly high demand for energy. Each day a shrew must eat its own weight in food—up to a half an ounce. This task is most difficult for shrews in the winter because there is a shortage of food and many die in the winter because of this. The only way shrews can survive cold winters is to keep eating to provide themselves with energy.

If shrew has shown up in your life, you must prepare for the winter. You must find ways to nourish yourself and your life. Winter will not be a good time to start or expand projects or endeavors. A shrew's life span is about a year, and thus the cycle of its energy in our life when it appears will be about the same.

As soon as possible, baby shrews begin supplementing their mother's milk with insects. Shrews are not very big and feeding a litter is draining to the mother. For those to whom the shrew is a totem or messenger, we may need to wean ourselves as quickly as possibly from someone or something around us.

Shrew families travel in a single file, each member holding onto the previous member's tail. In this way, the mother shrew can keep track of her young. Part of the shrew's lessons has to do with organization and keeping track of all that we initiate.

Animal Wonders

MASTER BUILDERS

Mole rats contruct entire subterranean homes that have storerooms, halls, bedrooms, a separate bathroom, and a mating chamber. When its bathroom is filled, it seals it off from the rest of the house.

A titmouse in Africa builds such a sturdy home that Masai tribesmen use their nests for purses and carrying cases.

A female weaverbird will not mate with a male who builds a shoddy nest. If spurned, the male must take the nest apart and completely rebuilt it to win the female's affections.

Siberian Tiger

KEYNOTE

- **passion**
- **power and sensuality**
- **stamina**

➤ All tigers are known for their power and ferocity. Siberian tigers are the most magnificent. The Siberian is the largest of the tigers, sometimes exceeding ten feet in length and weighing more than 700 pounds. It originated in the northern part of East Asia and is still found in the snowbound forests of Eastern Russia and northeast China, but their numbers are diminishing greatly, and they are endangered in the wild.

Tigers are fierce, stalking predators. They can sprint, but they do not pursue prey for very long. They are also very protective of their dens. Recent observations indicate that mother Siberians will actually hunt any animal—including humans—that intrude on their dens, especially if young are in it. They will try to eliminate any possibility of such an intrusion again.

Tigers are surprisingly strong swimmers and actually seem to enjoy the water, unlike most cats. This ability to move in both realms indicates the power and opportunities likely to open. When searching for food, Siberians have marathon ability as well as swimming ability, covering great distances in a their search for food. Males have been known to walk more than 600 miles in twenty days or so. They teach us stamina and persistence in all we does, and it is this that can be drawn upon in our own endeavors.

All cats use their whiskers as feelers to detect air currents. These enable cats to find their way or judge the shape and size of obstacles if it is too dark or if their vision is impaired. The whiskers

Animal Wonders

SPEED TRIALS

The fastest animal on four legs is the cheetah and it can accelerate to 45 mph in 2 seconds, racing over short distances at a speed of 700 mph.

Frigate birds, howver, can fly at a speed of 260 mph. The swordfish (fastest fish in the sea) can swim at 68 mph. A bottlenose dolphin, though, can dive to a depth of 3000 feet in 2 minutes. A rhino can charge at a speed of 30 mph and a hippo run faster than man.

On the other hand, it taks a snail an hour to travel a little less than .0004 of a mile.

of Siberian tigers are very sensitive. They will use them to size each other up in preparation for fights.

Tigers also have a unique organ in their mouth called a *flehmen*. Through a peculiar grimace, they expose the organ which can detect the scent of other tigers. When the tiger appears as a messenger, we should trust what we sense about others, especially others who seem to be interested in the same things we are. Keep ideas and endeavors to oneself. All tigers remind us to go after our prey quietly.

The Chinese recognize the tiger as passionate and powerful, and sometimes unpredictable. If the Siberian has come into your life, you can expect an expansion of your powers and sensibilities. New adventures will occur.

Siberian Tiger (cont.)

Is it time to follow your passions?

Are you being to vocal about what you hope to do?

Are you expressing your passions and powers inappropriately?

Walrus

KEYNOTE

- **uncovering the hidden**

- **powerful psychic touch**

WALRUS

A very large marine mammal (*Odobenus rosmarus*) of the Arctic Ocean, allied to the seals but forming a distinct family, Odobenidae. In the male the upper canine teeth form greatly elongated protruding tusks and the neck and shoulders are very thick and heavy. Individuals often weigh over a ton....The animals have been much hunted, and are now rare except in the far north.

Do you trust what you feel?

Are you being too isolated and hidden from others?

Do you need to be more sociable?

Do you need to dig out a little, finding what feels right for you?

Is it time to examine what may be hidden around you?

➤ Walruses are pinnipeds or "fin feet," as are seals and sea lions. They are marine mammals. They live in two environments, land and water, and for those, to whom the walrus has appeared, there will be two distinct environments manifesting within their lives.

Unlike other pinnipeds, the walrus has long white tusks, which are really just two teeth in the upper jaw that grow very large, continue to grow as long as the walrus is alive. These are used as weapons and as tools to dig in the mud for food. Stirring up the mud reveals where shellfish are hiding. For those to whom the walrus is a totem, there will come opportunities to uncover what is hidden, to find hidden treasures in the things around us.

Walruses like to gather in large groups, and for those to whom it is a messenger there will arise a greater need and desire to be in among more people of like mind. In the water, the group is called a herd. On the land, they are called a rookery.

Walruses have amazing whiskers and their popular "moustaches" serve as feelers in the dark at the bottom of the ocean. Their main means of finding food is through touch. They feel around in the mud for food with their stiff whiskers.

There is a form of psychometry or psychic touch in which the individual places an object against the face. The individual is able to pick up impressions from the object through what is felt in the face cheeks and forehead. Often to those to whom the walrus comes, there is a powerful ability to do this more and more, especially in uncovering hidden things.

Adult males live apart from the herd except during breeding season. Males will fight for the right to breed, and males and females will fight to protect the young. Although they look clumsy on land, they can move as easily and as quickly as humans can.

Wolverine

➤ The wolverine is the largest member of the weasel family, the most ferocious of all mammals. The wolverine is a cross between the badger and a small bear, wearing a shaggy coat of dark fur with a pale band on each side. It can get as large as four feet in length (1.2 meters) and will weigh around 60 pounds (27 kg.).

Wolverines inhabit the coniferous forests, preying on small mammals and birds. They will also eat carrion and have been known to bring down reindeer. Wolverines have a reputation for destructiveness, and they are reputed to eat more than any other carnivore. Because of this, they are known as the "glutton" although the name is probably exaggerated.

The wolverine is one of the most—if not the most—powerful and ferocious mammals. Although small compared to many of the large carnivores such as the bear, they are so ferocious they can drive other predators and even bears from their kills. Whenever the wolverine appears in our life, our passion for life and assimilating it will grow along with an increased ability to absorb, to eat up all that comes our way. This can be used beneficially or detrimentally. Being a glutton for knowledge is much healthier than being a glutton for food.

Wolverines have many of the qualities associated with the badger. Like the badger, the wolverine is a symbol of the wild. The wolverine is a carnivorous animal, and thus in what it eats, it becomes a keeper of that animal's medicine and power. The wolverine, like the badger, is a keeper of the secret stories of other animals.

The bold and ferocious wolverine never surrenders and teaches us not to do so. The things we desire, the things that can benefit our life, should be pursued with an almost gluttonous appetite. The wolverine spirit stays strongest when it is honored through silence, discretion, and a ferocious appetite for what is truth.

KEYNOTE

- **ferocious drive and appetites**
- **persistence**
- **keeper of hidden stories**

WOLVERINE
A carnivorous mammal of the genus *Gulo* (*G. luscus*); the glutton.

Are we not persisting?

Are we honoring the power of what comes to us?

Are we incorporating it into our lives?

Are we sharing too freely our secrets because we are being a glutton for attention?

Zebra

KEYNOTE

- **agility not strength brings success**
- **individuality within group settings**

ZEBRA
(Equus zebra)

Any of several African equine mammals, allied to the horse and the ass, but conspicuously striped black or blackish on a white or buffy ground. There are three species, rapidly approaching extinction. The true or mountain zebra (*Qquus* or *Hippotigris, zebra*) of the mountains of Cape Colony has the body and legs striped but the belly plain. **Burchell's zebra** (*E. burchelli*), of which there are several varieties inhabiting the plains in central and eastern Africa, has the body and belly striped, but the legs plain or nealry so. **Grevy's zebra** (*E. grevyi*), the largest species, inhabits mountains of northeast Africa. It has the stripes on both body and legs, narrower and more numerous, and has the ears long and fringed with hair.

➤ Zebras stand out on the African plains like fish in a glass bowl. Although they are the lion's main prey, they flourish because they have adapted.

There are two main types of zebras, plains and mountain, and they both live in small herds consisting of a single male and eight to ten females. In herds that are somewhat permanent, the females bond and even groom each other. All male groups are formed from the bachelors, and in both groups, status is based upon age and how long they have been in the group. Dominance is dependent upon agility, not strength

The striping of the zebra is a form of camouflage, and you may wish to review the information on it from Part One. In the herd, one zebra will not stand out and the lion or other predator may hesitate a vital second in its confusion. All zebra patterns are different, but the only ones to whom it really matters and recognize them as different are other zebras.

Often for those to whom the zebra is a totem or messenger, blending into the crowd will usually work best in endeavors. There should be no fear of losing one's identity in the crowd as each one is truly different. Zebras teach us individuality within group settings.

Zebras have intricate social behavior, with a great variety of expressions, which can show us ways of working and understanding group dynamics and communications more clearly. They help us in working in a group more effectively—especially by various vocal expressions and body language.

A zebra's major predator is the lion, and thus it should be studied as well. A few moments inattention by the zebra is all a lion needs to get within striking distance. In order to escape, the zebra must rely on their speed and agility. It is also possible that the lion may be confused by the stripe pattern if it runs into the herd.

Zebras seldom fight, but when they do, it is usually in a battle for the harem at the beginning of mating season. In cases of attack by a predator, sometimes they must fight as well. If flight is truly impossible, a zebra stallion can kick hard enough to knock out the lion's teeth or even kill it. But always it tries to rely on its agility and speed first.

**Zebra
(cont.)**

This is a reminder for those to whom the zebra is a totem. When the zebra appears, examine your relationship to various groups in your life. Do not confront directly unless there is no other choice. Use your mental agility to work around problems and obstacles, especially if it is in the form of other people and competitors.

MOOSE DOG

"The horse was introduced to this continent by the Spaniards when they arrived in the 16th century. Within two centuries they had been acquired by almost every people. As there was no Indian word for horse, and it carried its burdens like a dog, it was usually name d Elk Dog, Spirit Dog, Sacred Dog, or Moose Dog."

From Richard Erdoes and Alfonso Ortiz, *American Indian Myths and Legends*, (New York: Pantheon Books, 1984), p. 53.

Are you losing your identity?

Are you not asserting your individuality?

Are you confronting rather than relying on more indirect methods?

Are you trying to bull your way through obstacles when agility and subtlety will do?

Part IV

Kingdoms of Insects and Arachnids

Go to the ant, consider her ways, and be wise.
PROVERBS 6:6

*One should pay attention to even the smallest crawling
creature for those too may have a
valuable lesson to teach us.*
BLACK ELK

CHAPTER 10

Dialects of the Creepy Crawlies

Insects are one of the most ancient and plentiful creatures upon the planet. Three-fourths of all creatures alive are insects, with as many as 200,000 for every single human being. Although they have a bad reputation and humans tend to think of them as unpleasant pests, they are truly fascinating and amazing creatures.

They are found in every environment upon the planet. Although small, they have learned to thrive. They are the most adaptable group of animals on Earth. They have succeeded in surviving because of their adaptability and variety.

In the entire animal kingdom, only insects have six legs. All insects have two antennae, and most adults have four wings. Their sense organs are usually found between their eyes. They have developed thousands of ways to take advantage of every possible food and habitat. This has led to tremendous variations in colors, shapes, and characteristics within the insect kingdom.

Arachnids (spiders, ticks, scorpions, etc.), arthropods (centipedes and such) and worms are sometimes included with the insect kingdom but are not true insects. Spiders are the most commonly known arachnids, and like insects, they are all arthropods, which means they are animals with jointed legs and a hard outer skeleton. Arachnids differ from insects in that they have

Insects and arachnids are the most adaptable animals on earth. Their adaptability has enabled them to survive and has led to tremendous colors and shapes within the insect kingdom.

four pairs of walking legs, no antennae, and no wings. Most arachnids are carnivorous, although they often have no jaws.

In essence, these creatures are known as the creepy-crawlies, but I like to refer to them as the "mini-beasts." These include the spiders, snails, and other types of invertebrates. This group of animal life is very adaptable, living equally well on land, water, air, and even in deserts and on mountain peaks. Thus they are all natural "shapeshifters" in some way.

Shapeshifting

➤ The mini-beasts and insects are mostly creatures that go through metamorphosis. Change is essential to life, and all of the shapeshifters teach us how to flow with our changes. Like water, which will adapt its flow to the environment, the insects teach us how to adapt and change in the most creative and productive ways possible. Change ensures growth; it helps us to shed the old so that we can express the new. If we resist change and the natural flow, our life becomes stagnant, like water trapped.

There are distinct stages for most forms of metamorphosis. There is the egg stage where we give birth to a new idea, project, or quality. From the egg, there is a larva stage, a stage of feeding and strengthening to develop a solid foundation. Ideas and projects in this stage must be shaped and developed. Then there is usually a cocoon or even chrysalis whose differences could be explored, but for our purposes, this is the stage of reorganization because there are cellular changes. This stage serves as a reminder that in the creative process, we do what we must and can do and then we let the creative project take its own natural course. From this stage comes a new life, a new expression of life. In the insect kingdom that new life usually has wings with all of its symbolic associations.

Flowing like water, shifting our shapes and patterns of life, is the key to creativity and manifestation. The animals of this group help us to understand and work this process within our own life. Whether an insect, a spider, or a centipede, through the shapeshifters and other mini-beasts we learn to draw upon the waters of life for new birth and creative flow in all things.

Arachnids and Spiders

➤ Arachnids comprise another large group of the "creepy crawlies." Spiders are the most commonly known, but scorpions, ticks, and mites also comprise this group. When I teach workshops, two groups of animals are usually the most feared: snakes and spiders. Snakes are discussed in the section on reptiles, but spiders are right up there with them in generating fear in humans.

Most traditions taught that our fears and doubts will take the form of an animal, and only when we come to terms with them, do we truly become whole. Only then are we able to walk through life without casting a shadow. Most traditions also taught that the animals we fear are our totems.

I often try to ease the fear of individuals and help them sleep a little more peacefully at night through a better understanding of spiders and by sharing some spider trivia. Spiders serve a viable function in nature. They help to control the insect population. In order to do so effectively, they must be numerous as well. In fact they are so numerous that it is estimated that we are never more than three feet from one. (For some reason, this particular bit of trivia never seems to ease fears nor bring pleasant dreams.)

The truth is that arachnids and other strange animals generate fear many times because of their strangeness. True, they are not animals that we can cuddle up to, but they have magnificent qualities and abilities. When they show up as

messengers in our life, they provide amazing insight and assistance.

If there is an insect or arachnid that generates fear, remember that knowledge always helps to dissipate it. Go to the library. Go to the children's section of the library and get a children's book on the animals that you fear. Most children's books will provide the outstanding characteristics of the animal and will try to do so in a non-threatening manner. They will help to move you past the fear.

And always keep in mind, that if our messenger is an animal we fear, we are not required to cuddle up with it. Remember, though, that it has qualities that can truly benefit us in some way in our present life situations.

All spiders have certain qualities in common, just as all insects do. They all spin silk, but they do not all create webs. Spider silk is one of the strongest substances in nature, and it has a variety of uses. It is used for creating egg sacs, ballooning (floating to a new area), draglines, and snares. Try and determine the use of the silk in your particular spider encounter and it will help you in areas of your life. Do we need to keep our creative ideas and projects cloaked as in an egg sac? Do we need to let the winds take us where they will as in ballooning? Do we need to snare the opportunities around us?

Most spiders encountered in the Northern Hemisphere are web spinners. Web spinners teach us some simple lessons. The reason spiders do not get caught in their own webs is that only some of the silk threads are sticky. Those that go around the circumference have the sticky. Those that go directly out from the center, have no sticky. Knowing this is a clear message. If any spider is showing up in our life, do NOT take the roundabout way of dealing with things or you will get entangled. Be straight, direct.

Web spinning spiders are also great econo-mists. They spin their web—they do their work—and then they let the food come to them. They remind us that if we do our work, the re-sults will come.

Spiders have eight eyes, but they do not see very well. They have fibers on their legs that are sensitive to subtle movements. When spiders show up as messengers, to not trust what you see. Trust what you feel.

Spiders, like insects, also go through transfor-mations. Their growth is not in the form of metamorphosis, but in shedding its exoskeleton. Like snakes they shed what they have outgrown, and most spiders will shed four to twelve times before they reach maturity. This molting is often a reminder that we too must shed what no longer suits or fits us and our life.

All spiders are poisonous, but for most the bite is nothing more troublesome than a bee sting, unless there is an allergic response. Some spiders though are dangerously poisonous. Sev-eral of these will be discussed in detail in the coming dictionary. Most venomous animals have lessons in healing and toxicity around us. They sometimes awaken our own healing energies or point out a need to cleanse and purify some area of our life. They almost always reflect a change in the chemistry of our body and our life.

Notes

CHAPTER 11

Dictionary of Insects and Arachnids

Insects and arachnids are often likened to the element of water. Anything of water implies fluidness, emotions, and changes. Water is the natural shapeshifter, shifting as it flows and conforming to whatever contains it. Because of this, the animals associated with the spiritual aspects of this element are often the insects and arachnids.

All insects go through metamorphosis in order to live within their environment, changing their appearance completely with each stage of their lives. Like water, through these animals we learn to adjust the flow of our life, to take on the form that is most suitable for where we are.

The insects and arachnids are combined here because they both are often spoken of as "creepy crawlies." They are one of the most plentiful groups of animals upon the planet, and yet the most misunderstood. Regardless of the insect that appears within our life, it will be saying something about changes around us.

Many creepy crawlies—especially the spiders—possess a unique jaw that is sometimes modified into pincers as with scorpions. They all teach us in some way about grasping and digesting on many levels. Spiders often feed on live prey, reminding is to focus on the present and living for our nourishment on both physical and spiritual levels.

This chapter includes information about the following insects and arachnids:

- black and yellow argiope
- black widow spider
- brown spider
- caterpillar
- centipede and millipede
- cicada
- cockroach
- cricket
- daddy longlegs
- earthworm
- firefly
- flea
- fly
- jumping spider
- ladybug
- leech
- mosquito
- moth
- orb-weaver spiders
- scorpion
- silkworm moth
- slug
- snail
- stick bug (walkingstick)
- tarantula
- tick
- wasp
- water spider
- wolf spider
- woolly caterpillar

Black and Yellow Argiope

KEYNOTE

- engineering bridges between realms
- new dimensions

Are we ignoring our impressions and our feelings?

Do we need to open more strongly to new realms, dimensions and creative endeavors?

Do we need to explore our own creative insights and inspirations?

➤ This large and conspicuous spider is typically found in gardens and shows us that even where we pamper our plants, wonderful opportunities to open to new realms and inspiration occur. It is often a reminder that we may be missing or ignoring conspicuous openings to new realms and dimensions within our life.

Black and yellow colors were often associated with the angelic spirit nown as Auriel, the tallest of the archangels, who had eyes that could see across eternity. This particular angelic being was known as the protector and guardian of the Faerie Realm. In this role of Nature guardian, Auriel often appeared in the colors of black and yellow.

When these colors appear in nature, in plants, or animals, it is often a reminder of the closeness of the Faerie Realm and the opening of doors and and bridges to new realms and dimensions. This is especially reflected in the black and yellow argiope.

When you find this spider in your garden on a sunny afternoon, it will usually be hanging head down in the center of the web. It almost has the appearance of the tarot card, The Hanged Man, which reflects looking at things with a new perspective. When this spider appears, we need to take a different perspective in order to succeed at what we are doing. New realms and dimensions will open for us if we look for them in the right way, often a reverse perspective or approach, often something that we may not have ever tried. As scary as it may seem, it will work successfully.

Because these spiders do not see very well, we will often feel the presence of the other worldly beings or Fairie Realm more strongly before we ever actually see them. But when this spider appears as a messenger or totem, it heralds a time of greater contact and greater intuitive recognition of the spirits of Nature. Subtle psychic perceptions will become stronger and clearer than ever before.

Black Widow Spider

➤Among spiders, the black widow spider is the High Priestess, the Dark Mother, weaving new fates for those who cross her path. Her magic and power is great, but she is also dangerous.

All spiders are rich in lore and myth around the planet. They are the master weavers, weaving illusion, the life span, alphabets, and languages and even magic. They signal an awakening of our creative energies.

Spider shows up when we need to balance and work between past and future, physical and spiritual, male and female, waking and sleeping. Spider shows us how to weave today the dreams we want fulfilled tomorrow, teaching the magic of creation and how to use it to weave our own fates. The appearance of spider always heralds opportunities for three kinds of creativity within our life.

The magical ability to spin silk reminds us of our own power at this time to spin new creations. Spiders reflect the magic of assertion, reminding us that only by asserting and expressing our creative energies are we empowered.

And finally, the magic of the spider's web links past and future, death and rebirth, waxing and waning—all reflected by the web's spiral, reminding us there is a creative rhythm at play we may not recognize, but one which will bring balance and polarity.

Spiders are one of the oldest and most amazing creatures. Even though they have eight eyes, they do not see very well, although the tiny fibers on their legs are sensitive to the slightest movement. If spider has shown up in your life, do not trust what you see. Trust what you feel.

All spiders spin silk, although not all spiders weave webs. Spider silk is one of the strongest natural substances upon the planet. In the Northern Hemisphere, most spiders encountered are web spinners. Spiders do not get caught in their own webs because they secrete oil on their legs

KEYNOTE

the bite and weaving of a new fate

Black Widow Spider
(cont.)

and only some of the threads have sticky on them—the threads that go around the circumference of the web. Those that form the spokes, moving directly out from the center are not sticky. This is a clear message. Do not deal with things in a roundabout fashion or you will get entangled. Be direct. Straightforward.

The black widow spider does a great deal of her weaving in the dark and out of sight. She reminds us of how to express our creative energies. Do not be afraid to employ them in seemingly inaccessible areas. Weave your creative threads in the dark and then when the sun hits them, they will glisten with intricate beauty.

The black widow spider also reminds us to trust the subtle perceptions we experience. There is more depth and more activity beneath the surface. The black widow reminds us to use our creative opportunities and by doing so, we take our Fate back within our own hands.

All spiders are great economists. They spin their web; they do their work. And then they sit back and let the food come to them. Most spiders show us how to weave our energies so that the rewards of our efforts will come to us. The black widow spider reminds us to be patient, to stop pushing for our rewards. By pushing we are wasting efforts. She reminds us to let the benefits come to us in the time that is best for us.

Poisonous spiders, especially those that are dangerous to humans, are few. Yes, most spiders have poisons, but few are truly dangerous.

In the U.S. and Canada, fatalities from wasp and bee stings far outnumber those from spider bites and scorpion stings, and the bites of most of those large enough to penetrate the skin produce no harm at all.[1]

---

[1] Herbert Levi. *Spiders and their Kin.* (Racine, WI: Western Publishing Company, 1990), p. 16.

Widows are the best known and largest of the cobweb weavers, and there are a number of species of them in the U.S., Europe, the Near East, and South America. Adult males wander in search of females but do not feed or bite. They court the female by plucking the threads of the female's web. Females rarely leave their web.

Cobweb weavers are usually sedentary, hanging upside down in the center of irregular shaped webs or hiding in a crevice at the edge of the web. One of the best known of this group is the black widow spider. It is common to outhouses, trash sites, and dumps, and the spider hangs in the web, which she locates under objects. It is found in most warm spots around the world. Black widows are recognized by the hourglass marking on their underside. In North America, many spider bites are from black widows.

While the males do not bite, the female will if molested or surprised. The initial bite may go unnoticed and may not even hurt, but there are subsequent effects. Some of these are severe abdominal pain resembling appendicitis. There will also be pain in the muscles and in the soles of the feet. Sweating will occur and eyelids will swell. Antivenom is available in places where bites occur frequently and symptoms are also relieved by calcium gluconate. The appearance of the black widow is often a reminder that the changing of our fate has already been initiated, even though it probably went unnoticed.

All venomous animals have lessons to teach us about the chemistry of our body and detoxifying ourselves or some aspect of our life. They remind us that the chemistry of our life and our fate is changing. If we are ignoring our new fate, the bite of it will be felt soon.

Black Widow Spider (cont.)

Are you hesitating to weave your dreams into reality?

Are you taking advantage of creative opportunities?

Are you feeling stuck and out of balance?

Is it time for you to start writing, drawing and creating?

Are you going in multiple directions rather than focusing upon a central goal?

Are you becoming self-absorbed?

Are you focusing on others' accomplishments and not on your own?

Are you not following through completely?

Brown Spider

KEYNOTE

slow healing of wounds

➤ Brown spiders, such as the brown recluse, have been known since the 1930s to cause severe illness; but it was not recognized until the 1950s that the brown recluse itself was found to be toxic. This spider commonly lives in houses on the floor or behind furniture. Most bites occur because the spider rests in clothing or towels.

In severe cases of bite, a red zone appears around the bite, although the bite is not always initially noticed. Eventually, a crust forms and falls off. The wound grows deeper and sometimes does not heal for several months.

Often when the brown spider appears, it is time to examine a close personal relationship. There may be hidden hurts, and we may find ourselves in a situation in which we may be wounding another or another may be wounding us. The initial bite, hurt, or betrayal may go unnoticed, but it will become increasingly apparent in a relatively short time. Emotional hurts or wounds will grow deeper over several months before healing occurs.

Remember that most bites from the brown recluse occur because it is in clothing. If we find ourselves or our lives being wounded and poisoned, we should look to who or what is closest to us. We may be sharing things that could come back to bite us. We may need to be a bit more private and reclusive ourselves.

Are we nursing old wounds?

Are we not letting go of the past?

Are we refusing to heal, by picking at old wounds?

Are others around us nursing old wounds or picking at them?

➤ Caterpillars have often been associated with luck in some form or another. In England it was considered good luck if one creeps upon you and you toss it over your shoulder. If kept in a small bag and worn about the neck, the caterpillar would cure the whooping cough.

In insects, the eggs hatch to become larvae. This is the second stage of metamorphosis. The larva is the caterpillar of butterflies or moths, and during this stage it feeds to gain strength and achieve a new foundation before the chrysalis or cocooning stage begins. In the egg and larva stage of our life's activities, we give birth to new ideas and new creativity. They are then worked with, shaped, and honed into a foundation that will allow a new expression of life. Caterpillars represent new birth and new foundations. They are a symbol of good luck in the early stages of new endeavors.

Caterpillars use their feet to "taste" the plants first and make sure they are suitable. For this reason, caterpillars remind us to test the waters a little first before jumping in. Caterpillars are very fussy eaters, usually restricted to one food plant or one group of related plants. When the caterpillar appears, it is best to focus only upon one idea or one group of associated ideas and projects for our greatest success at this time.

Caterpillars usually signal a need for gentle and quiet approaches to our activities and endeavors. They can also signal a surprise or gift about to be offered to us, one that can be beneficial to our future if we take advantage of it. Caterpillars herald a time of good news, new birth, and creative inspiration, signaling a time to get ready to start a new project or initiate a new endeavor.

Caterpillars come in a variety of shapes and colors, reminding us of the many possibilities and promises of life at this time. Their shapes and colors help protect them from predators. Some

Caterpillar

KEYNOTE

- **good luck**
- **new birth**

CATERPILLAR OF
SWALLOWTAIL BUTTERFLY
(*Papilio asterias*)

The elongated wormlike larva of a butterfly or moth; also, any of the similar larvae of certain other insects, as the sawflies and scorpion flies. Caterpillars have strong biting jaws, short antennae, three pairs of true legs, and several pairs of abdominal fleshy legs (prolegs) armed with hooks. Some are hairy, others naked. They usually feed on leaves, fruit, or other succulent parts of plants, and are popularly called worms, as the cutworm, cankerworm, cottonworm, silkworm.

Caterpillar
(cont.)

Are we trying to do more than we should?

Are we scattering our endeavors, trying to feed on too many things right now?

Are we hanging onto what or whom we have outgrown?

Are we being lazy and not working toward our goals?

Are we trying to skip stages within our endeavors, or are we looking for shortcuts?

Are we brushing aside help and offers of help?

Are we lacking self-discipline or letting others distract us from our tasks?

of their forms make them appear as if they would be hard to swallow. Other colors warn predators they may be distasteful if eaten. The appearance of the caterpillar reminds us to be cautious in starting our new endeavors. We should protect and disguise them as much as possible as we pursue them. If we do so, we will see rapid growth and we will experience the birth of a new foundation.

Caterpillars can also indicate obstacles within our path. They may even indicate that a person or persons are blocking our growth or serve as a reminder that we must look at things and people around us realistically at this time. Failure to do so will slow down our progress.

When it first hatches, the caterpillar is tiny, but it grows so quickly that it must replace its skin. Most species of caterpillars molt four times, but some shed their skins every few days to make room for a bigger body. If the caterpillar has shown up, we may be refusing to shed the old that we have outgrown. Not doing so will prevent and hinder all new efforts and endeavors. The caterpillar reminds us that new growth cannot occur unless the old is shed.

➤ In China, the centipede is the archenemy of the snake. Many folktales tell how the centipede saves a person when a snake attacks or how its appearance warned individuals snakes were near.

To the Chinese, the centipede is also considered one of the five noxious creatures because large centipedes (yan-yu) are poisonous: "If their dried seed falls into what you are eating, you will die."[2] Efforts to expel them from human communities were performed on the fifth day of the fifth month, thus a time of power. It was also believed the cock could destroy them, and thus it should be studied as well.

"Hundred leggers" and "thousand leggers" are arthropods like insects and arachnids, part of thousands of many-legged creatures. The name means 100 legs and 1000 legs respectively, but they do not really have that many. Most centipedes have 15 to 23 pairs of legs, one for each segment of the body. Millipedes have two pairs of legs on each body segment. Young millipedes are born with three pairs of legs, but the number of segments and legs increase with each molt.

Legs provide stability and enable forward movement. Animals with legs a predominant feature often show us how to increase stability and move forward in our endeavors more successfully. For those whom the millipede is a messenger, successful movement in all endeavors will come with age. These are often "late bloomers."

Like insects but unlike spiders, centipedes and millipedes have a pair of antennae. All creatures with antennae reflect increasing psychic sensitivities and perceptions. Because they are also nocturnal, it will be important to pay attention to dreams when the centipede appears as a messenger. Dreams will become increasingly prophetic and clairvoyant, providing great insight and inspiration. Many centipedes are also blind, and

---

[1] Wolfram Eberhard. *Dictionary of Chinese Symbols.* (New York: Routledge, 1991), p. 59.

Centipede and Millipede

KEYNOTE

- movement into new psychic connections and relationships

- protection against psychic deceptions

CENTIPEDE
(*Scolopendra cingulata*)
Any of the numerous myriapods of the order or subclass Chilopoda. They are of elongated and flattened form, with numerous segments each with a single pair of legs; and they are of active, predaceous, and chiefly nocturnal habits. The single genital aperture is situated posteriorly. The largest species, sometimes eight or ten inches long or even more, inhabit tropical countries. Their anterior legs are modified into poison fangs with which the larger species can inflict painful but not usually serious bites. They are useful as destroyers of insects.

Centipede and Millipede
(cont.)

this can be a reminder to trust our inner perceptions and not outer appearances. Trusting in our higher perceptions will help us succeed in our endeavors and activities.

When male centipedes find a female, they touch antennae, and the male then follows the female. For those to whom the centipede appears, relationships are often based upon strong initial psychic connections not easily explained in other ways. When the centipede appears, it is not unusual for a strong psychic connection to occur with someone new shortly thereafter.

Both need damp environments, the millipede more than the centipede, For those to whom either is a messenger, it is important to have their own creative environments. Damp environments are symbolic of creative, psychic, and emotional areas. Finding an environment, supportive to their creative and psychic sensibilities, will be necessary for their health and well being.

Although both are many-legged creatures, there are some unique differences. Some centipedes produce silk, usually only used during mating and to capture prey. They are active predators of insects, spiders, and worms. Their front pair of legs acts as claws and all have poisonous glands in their jaws used for paralyzing and killing prey. Centipedes often remind us to be careful of what we say and how we say it.

Millipedes are found under stones and in moist soil and leaf litter. They avoid the light, feeding upon various plant materials and soft decomposing plant tissues. They discharge strong-smelling secretions that may be repellent and poisonous to other animals.

Centipedes and millipedes alert us to new psychic environments and connections and to new and previously unrecognized psychic relationships. They also appear to alert us to any possible pitfalls within those relationships. Theirs is the energy of quiet protection in psychic exploration.

➤ In France, cicadas are given at weddings and house warmings for good luck and for peace in the home. In China, the cicada symbolized immortality. A cicada of jade was laid in the mouth of the deceased. The symbol of a cicada on a hat symbolizes a man of honesty in China as well.

Cicada are fairly large, sap-sucking insects that feed mainly upon trees. Their long beaks easily penetrate the bark of smaller branches to reach the sap inside. The eggs are laid in the soil, and the nymphs take sap from various roots. They remain underground for several years (seventeen years for one American cicada) and they come up only when it is time for the adult to break out of its nymphal skin. Because of this, the cicada's appearance always reflects happiness from the past resurfacing within our life.

The cicada's presence heralds a stirring of forgotten, child-like joy. It can indicate the happy meeting of an old friend from the past. It can indicate the meeting of someone who will seem like an old friend to us. The cicada's appearance always means a gift, an opportunity, or an offering that along with being surprising will also touch the heart with happiness.

Cicadas are difficult to see when sitting on the bark, but the males give away their presence through incredible calls. A small membrane on each side of the body vibrates very rapidly, giving off a high-pitched whistle to attract the female.

When the cicada appears, our energy has changed. We find ourselves more attracted to and by the opposite sex. It is nothing that can readily be seen or detected, but its appearance usually indicates that invitations, offers, and proposals (sexual and otherwise) can be expected. And they will come unexpectedly! It is not unusual to begin having past life experiences as well. We begin to see the relationship of people and situations of the past and their positive effects and results within our present. Cicada heralds a time

Cicada

KEYNOTE

happiness from the past

CICADA
(*Tibicen pruinosa*)

A genus of large homopterous insects with a stout body, wide blunt head, and large transparent wings....The cicadas are often called *locusts*, and are noted for the prolonged shrill notes of the male insect, produced by vibrating membranes of special sound organs on the under side of the abdomen.

The larvae live under ground, and in some cases at least...require long periods to develop.

Cicada
(cont.)

Are we rushing our growth?

Are we locked into old patterns?

Are we refusing to dig ourselves out of the rut we are in?

of new happiness and renewed happiness with old ties.

When the eggs become nymphs within the soil, they remain there until it is time to become an adult. Using their powerful front legs, they dig themselves out of the soil to mate and continue the cycle. When the cicada appears, sometimes it may indicate what we have been trying to hatch may be delayed. It doesn't mean that it won't succeed, but it might be delayed.

Any delays will test our strength and endurance, but cicada reminds us to not overreact. Now is the time to be still, to be patient. Remember that some cicadas live in the ground for 17 years before coming to the surface. The cicada promises ultimate success as long as we do not give up.

Sometimes the cicada can also indicate that we are living in the past. We refuse to move past old issues and old people, rehashing the same things over and over again. The cicada warns that if we don't move from the past, our present will never change. Cicadas and all insects teach the importance of change. Cicada warns us about being lost in the past and things of the past that are stifling and can reflect that a relationship, while it may have been beneficial at one time, may no longer be suitable for us.

Cockroach

KEYNOTE

- survival
- sensitivity to changes in the environment

➤ Cockroaches are flattened insects with long spiky legs and very long antennae. Some can reach three inches in length (8cm.), and many can fly. Most species of cockroaches live within the tropics. Even the domestic cockroach that most people are familiar with in this country is a tropical species that has established itself in heated buildings.

Cockroaches are scavengers, coming out at night to feed on dead animals and fallen fruit and foods. Thus they always teach us how to use what we have available to us, what we have laying about us. They remind us to clean out the dead and.useless aspects of our lives.

Since they have learned to survive in spite of many efforts to eradicate them, cockroaches are one of the most adaptable of animal species. They remind us to be flexible and adaptable in whatever environment we find ourselves and teach us that we can adapt to outside pressures.

The antennae of cockroaches are very sensitive. Besides these long feelers, some also have a smaller antennae on their back. Many people try to step on cockroaches to kill them and find that this is usually unsuccessful. This antennae spike on their backs is sensitive to subtle changes in pressure and able to detect the changes in air movement as the foot descends so the cockroach can scurry out of danger. When the cockroach appears as a totem or messenger, our own sensitivity to subtle changes will be magnified. Trust what you feel, regardless of appearances. It will be critical to successful maneuverings in whatever environment we find ourselves.

Cockroaches lay eggs in purses, which the females will carry around with them for a time. For cockroaches there is no pupal stage. This may reflect a loss of childhood for those to whom this creature is a totem. Often cockroach people find that they have had lives in which there is a premature movement into adulthood, taking on adult responsibilities early in their life. Sometimes the cockroach's appearance indicates having to take on major responsibilities early on in projects and endeavors at home or in work.

Although often seen as a disgusting animal, the cockroach is a gifted teacher in the art of survival and successful adaptability, especially in environments that may seem a bit hostile.

Cockroach
(cont.)

COMMON COCKROACH
(Stylopyga orientalis)

Any orthopterous insect of the family Blattidae, many species of which are troublesome pests in houses and ships, esp. in warm climates. They are usually nocturnal in habits, and of flattened form with the head strongly bent down under the thorax. They antennae are long and many-jointed. They often have small wings or are without wings, esp. the females. They can run with great rapidity....
The cockroaches are an ancient group, dating at least from the Carboniferous.

Are we taking not adapting and using what is available to us?

Do we need to take advantage of the little things around us?

Are you ignoring the subtle changes around you?

Are you taking on responsibilities prematurely?

Are you hesitating taking on the responsibilities you need to succeed?

Cricket

KEYNOTE

- sensitive intuition
- power of belief

EUROPEAN HOUSE
CRICKET

(*Gryllus domesticus*)

Any of the saltatorial orthopterous insects constituting the family Gryllidae, noted for the chirping notes produced by the males by rubbing together specially modified parts of the fore wings. Unlike the grasshoppers, they have the fore wings flat above and sharply bent down at the sides, and in typical crickets the antennae are long and the ovipositor is long and spear-shaped.

➤ Crickets have an abundance of myth and folklore surrounding them, almost all having to do with a stimulation of intuition and the power of our beliefs. In China the cricket is considered a summer animal symbolizing pluck and a fighting spirit. In fact, ceremonial cricket fights were once staged to awaken such a spirit in their human captors.

In England and parts of Europe, to find a cricket upon one's hearth was a sign of great good luck for the home. Although some superstitions speak of a cricket in the home as a foreboding of death and bad luck, such teachings were rare. The opposite is the more common interpretation.

Crickets in the home were often thought of as the familiar that watched over and guarded the home's occupants—especially against bad spirits. In the 1800s many people believed that crickets were lucky to have about the house and would do no harm if treated well. Bad luck would befall only those who harmed this creature. In most traditions, it is best to leave the cricket alone. To remove it from the house or to kill it would bring bad luck

There are several thousand species of crickets around the world. They are also known as *bushcrickets*, and although they are related to the grasshopper, they have had a distinct symbology. They have been kept as pets. many believing them to be the reincarnation of relatives. They have been considered a familiar by some and the devil by others. Their singing was believed in parts of Europe to herald good luck. To do them harm was unlucky, while to honor them brought good fortune.

While some species do sing in the day, most crickets are mainly nocturnal. The appearance of cricket heralds an awakening of sensitivities and the finding of light within the dark. This is primarily because of their nocturnal activity and their darker coloration. They are perceptive within the dark times and are able to use whatever light is available to them. Their appearance reminds us to trust our own intuition, as it is much more accurate than we may believe. Dreams will become more clairvoyant, and cricket reminds us that we can truly rely on our dreamtime perceptions.

Crickets come in a variety of types, colors, and sizes. Katydids are noted for their loud songs and usually indicate a power time of late summer and autumn. The North American snowy tree cricket is also known as the "thermometer cricket." You can estimate the temperature by counting the number of chirps in 15 seconds and then adding 40 to it.

Crickets are distinguished from grasshoppers primarily by their long antennae, which reflect our heightened sensitivity. They further remind us to trust our own intuition and our own expressions of light, even if different from others. Now is the time to believe in and rely upon our long range perceptions and insights. We should trust in what we have always believed.

The male cricket sings by rubbing its wing bases together. Their calls are often shrill, but it is a call that is connected to mating. The song of the cricket is a song of good cheer, especially in relationships, a reminder to trust in our beliefs and perceptions about the other people within our life. If cricket is singing within our life, now is the time to be of good cheer. Our believing is about to be rewarded, and the song they are singing is of success and pleasures ahead.

THE WORM DANCE

Some birds have a way of tricking worms to the surface by tapping or pecking at the ground. If the soil is damp, you can entice worms to the surface by performing the worm dance. Gently stamp your feet, making sure you don't keep moving them or you might tread on the worms. Continue for about five minutes until the worms stop popping up.

Cricket
(cont.)

Are we not seeing things properly?

Are we denying our own beliefs?

Have we forgotten how to believe?

Is it time to get some new beliefs?

Are we exaggerating what we perceive?

Are we not hearing the true songs of the people around us?

Do we need to listen to what is not being said as much as to what is?

Are we not holding true to our beliefs?

Are others?

Most crickets live on the ground. Some can fly, but many have no hind wings. Some have no wings at all. If cricket has appeared, we may need to stay balanced and grounded when exploring or working with our intuition and psychic abilities. Our belief system may be a bit askew. It is not unusual to find a cricket appearing at times for professionals in the psychic or metaphysical field when conscious efforts are not being made to be balanced and grounded.

Most crickets molt at least once, and a cricket may warn us that it is time to shed old beliefs that are no longer suitable. It can warn that the psychic energies of ourselves or others may be over-stimulated and exaggerated at this time. Beliefs and ideas are more likely to be distorted and embellished, and this should be taken into consideration before taking any action. Perceptions may lack depth and there may even be some deception about what is being perceived. Others may be trying to make us believe something that is not entirely true or to which there is incomplete information. The cricket should stimulate some self-examination.

➤ Several insects and spiders have been known as the daddy longlegs. Although the name is associated with the crane fly, it is also associated with a member of the spider family. It is this latter to which we are referring here. The spider has long, skinny legs, giving it a graceful appearance. Its presence always indicates the weaving of a deeper relationship. Native to many climates, males and females are commonly found together (a rarity among most spiders), reinforcing the idea of deepening relationships.

The most commonly seen type in the U.S. is a species known as the *cosmopolitan cellar spider*. When startled, its body and web shake so rapidly that both the web and spider seem to disappear. Part of this spider's magic is the lessons of invisibility (or the illusion of it) for protection.

The daddy longlegs, as with all spiders, spins silk. When it appears, something new is being spun in a relationship, usually with a loved one. New harmony and balance are strong around us and our activities with others right now. Where there is one daddy longlegs, another is usually very near by, and this characteristic indicates that our success in endeavors now is achieved best by working with another person or other persons.

Its long legs are its significant characteristic. Legs on insects and arachnids serve a variety of functions. They enable movement. They are sensory limbs. They are sometimes used to grasp and hold food and prey. The spider's appearance now indicates that what we sense about a new relationship—personal or business—is what we hope. Now is the time to move and grasp it. It is a wonderful time to start something new.

The eyes of most insects and arachnids have multiple lenses, some as many as a thousand. Their compound eyes enable them to see in many directions at the same time. The appearance of the daddy longlegs always indicates a greater vision of what is happening on many lev-

Daddy Longlegs

KEYNOTE

weaving deeper relationships

Daddy Longlegs (cont.)

Are we letting pride hinder us?

Are we not seeing our relationship as it is?

Are we working in the wrong way to weave it into something more than what it is?

els—what may only be superficially noticed, if at all, by others. Daddy longlegs indicates increased awareness of what is going on around us, with greater ability to move in response to our perceptions. We must trust what we perceive is going on behind the scenes. That is why the spider has appeared now.

When the daddy longlegs appears, we can expect a surprise. New understanding, creativity, and ideas are flowing now, especially in relationships. Now is the time for deeper exploration of them. Doing so brings greater harmony and goals will be reached.

All spiders have tremendously heightened sensibilities. Although there is often fear of them, only a few species are actually poisonous, and most help in controlling the other insect pests that can be bothersome. Anytime a spider shows up, we may need to get a handle on our fears, to be more direct in dealing with them.

The daddy longlegs is a delicate spider, although most spiders are. Spiders are always a combination of gentleness and strength, for they have learned to combine both in order to survive. If daddy longlegs has shown up, we may need to balance gentleness and strength. We may be acting too timidly or too intensely, especially in an important relationship.

The daddy longlegs can indicate a loss of balance in a relationship. It may indicate that we are or someone around us is being too much of a perfectionist, maybe even maintaining inappropriately an all-or-nothing attitude. The daddy longlegs reminds us that disagreements are unimportant and focusing upon them will create unnecessary obstacles. It is time for someone to make the first move in resolving the problems. By doing so, they will all shortly disappear. We can then step over the obstacles and accomplish our goals.

➤ Although earthworms are not insects, they do fall into the general concept of what many shaman traditions called the creepy crawlies. They are legless animals with long cylindrical bodies. There are many types of worms, which are classified into a number of unrelated groups. The annelids are the segmented oones and are usually what most people think of when they think of worms. The earthworm belongs to this group.

When the earthworm appears, issues of working over old ground become prominent. This includes examining the past, including past lives for their effects on the present conditions.

The bodies of worms are muscular and segmented. The blood, digestive, and nervous systems run through all segments. Earthworms live in the soil, and they are constantly churning up the ground as they swallow soil and excrete it as worm casts. Earthworms digest decaying plant matter. Their numbers vary from 13,000 to seven million per acre. They are essential to plant growth and oxygenation of soil.

Worms tunnel beneath the soil. Their tunnels can reach a depth of five feet. They actually eat their way through the soil in search of dead plant material. The matter that passes through them is pushed toward the surface where it forms worm casts. With two million worms living within an area the size of a football field, a huge amount of earth can be shifted. They remind us that if we continue our efforts, no matter how slight they may seem, we are reshaping the earth around us.

When the earthworm appears, it is time to work over all we have been experiencing, a time in which we must examine and digest what has occurred in our life. In this way, we can determine what must be cast off, what is no longer beneficial or suitable for us. This is necessary to let in some fresh air and open up to new growth.

Worms don't usually come to the surface except at night, when they are not in danger of be-

Earth-worm

KEYNOTE

working old ground

COMMON EARTHWORM
(*Lumbricus terrestris*)

Any of numerous oligochaetous worms of the genus *Lumbricus* and many allied genera, found in damp soil. They have a cylindrical body, tapering at each end, and consisting of numerous segments, which are without appendages, though they bear minute bristles. Earthworms are hermaphroditic and oviparous, and undergo no metamorphosis. They feed by swallowing earth and digesting out the nutritive matter, what remains being deposited on the surface of the ground near the opening of their burrow. They are thus useful in loosening and bringing the deeper parts of the soil to the surface. On account of their use for bait in fishing, they are often called *angleworms*.

Earthworm
(cont.)

*Are we ignoring the past
and its effects upon
the present?*

*Are we not examining
and working through
things carefully?*

*Are we not digesting
and accepting what
is occurring?*

*Do we need some fresh
air in our activities?*

*Is life bogging down and
becoming constipated?*

*Are we afraid to start
new endeavors?*

*Are we letting what seems
to be a large task
intimidate us and
prevent us from acting?*

ing eaten. For those to whom worm appears, this is a reminder to be cautious about putting ourselves in a vulnerable position. There is a time and place to do so and it must be chosen carefully.

When the earthworm appears, we often find ourselves wanting to be alone. It appears often in times of turmoil as a reminder that we need to reassess and work over carefully what has been going on so that the changes we make will be beneficial and not result in repeating old patterns. Earthworms can help us in past life exploration.

Earthworm reminds us that it is time to take stock before making another decision. We must not react too hastily. Any sorrows that are occurring, any break-ups in the soil of our life, are essential to our future growth, even though difficult. Earthworm reminds us to work over the old thoroughly before moving on to the new.

Each segment of the earthworm has a few short bristles, which help it to move through the soil. The bristles must have something to push against in order to move. This is why it cannot move on a sheet of glass. Earthworms remind us of how the past (including past lives) influences our present and our future. Unless we recognize and acknowledge the past, we often repeat our mistakes. Earthworms can indicate that we are not learning from our past mistakes.

The earthworm always reminds us to use courage to see things clearly and thoroughly now. No matter how difficult it can be to face the realities of life, the earthworm reminds us that new growth and new hope await us.

Firefly

➤ Fireflies, often called lightning bugs, are magical symbols of inspiration and hope. They are the promise of accomplishment through hope and efforts. They remind us that we have laid the appropriate groundwork and from it will spring great reward. In the traditional tarot, they would be associated with the Star card.

Fireflies are small beetles that give off light, usually from the hind end. They may light up while flying or while resting in vegetation. The blinking or flashing of the lights is performed for short periods, and each species has a distinct rhythm. For the most part, the flashing rhythm is performed to attract a mate, who responds with a corresponding rhythm. It is part of the mating ritual that will extend the life of the species. The males perform aerobatics, making light patterns that are answered by the females, each species producing its own characteristic recognition patterns. These patterns are remarkably precise. A male emits a pulse of light that, after an exact interval, is answered by a female of the same species. Only if the timing and response are correct will a male fly over to visit a female.

The larvae of the firefly are flattened, luminous, and segmented. They are usually called glow-worms. They are often a reminder of the inner star we are developing or the promise of the star that is on the horizon for us.

For those to whom the firefly appears, it is time to trust in our own rhythms—physical and spiritual. Our hopes will begin to manifest, and our ability to inspire will grow. Fireflies remind us that there are others who will respond to us and who are like us. They flash with similar creative rhythms. They will make their presence known soon, and they will make our life more creative and healthier.

Fireflies generate light without heat, a process of chemistry and physics that is still baffling to science. Whereas most electric bulbs waste 97%

KEYNOTE

spiritual inspirations and hope

AMERICAN FIREFLY
(*Photuris pennsylvanica*)
In popular language, any nocturnal winged light-producing insect. They are mostly beetles belonging to two familes, Lampyridae and Elateridae, and hence are more correctly termed *fire beetles*, which name is, however, usually applied only to the large tropical species of the last-mentioned family... The ordinary fireflies are small, rather elongated, flattened, soft-bodied beetles of the family Lampyridae, the common North American species belonging to the genera *Photinus* and *Photuris*. They produce a bright, soft, intermittent light, without sensible heat, from an organ in the lower part of the adomen. This organ appears to be a specialized part the the fat body, and is supplied with nerves and abundant tracheae. The light is supposed by some to be caused by oxidation of a substance secreted by the cells. In many of these beetles the female is wingless; in some the larva is luminescent. These wingless females and larvae are popularly termed *glowworms*.

Firefly
(cont.)

of their energy in heat, a firefly concentrates 90 percent of its effort into light. The glow emerging from so tiny an animal is sufficient to read a printed page, reflecting wonderful opportunities to make the seemingly impossible a reality, inspiring wonders that will be flickering and manifesting around us.

When the firefly appears is a wonderful time to jot down all of those creative ideas that are flickering in our mind through this time. We needn't worry about what to do with them now, for just by taking them out of the mental realm, their creative force is released into our life and they will provide inspiration that will affect us for a long time in the future.

The firefly looks ordinary during the day, but by night they sparkle, flickering like a star. They hold the promise of accomplishing our goals. Spiritual gifts are awakening. We are on the right path, and there are strong spiritual forces around us. When fireflies appear, people begin to reassess their former opinions and perspectives. We begin to shine and sparkle. Opportunities to fulfill dreams, to inspire wonder, and to awaken greater hope will begin to flicker strongly within our life.

The firefly can indicate a variety of misjudgments or warn of their possibility, especially in dealing with those of the opposite sex. The female of one large predatory species has learned to mimic the female signals of a smaller species. When the eager males arrive, they are quickly eaten. It is important to be sure that those around us are not mimicking what is true rather than what we hope to hear. Or, we may be focusing

Animal

INSECT MOTHERS

Very few insects actually care for their young. The eggs are laid and then are left to hatch and develop on their own.

A unique exception is the Australian female harlequin bug. She guards her eggs against pests and predators.

Wonders

upon the wrong path or perhaps we are working with the wrong people or socializing with a crowd that is not healthy for us. We may be letting others (through their negative opinions) prevent the success of our creative endeavors.

The firefly should also get us to take a look at our health habits, particularly at what we are eating. Adult fireflies eat very little. They have learned to generate and draw energy from around them for their purposes. It would be wise to examine what we are eating and how much because this affects our health and our spiritual creativity.

Remember that fireflies remind us that positive hope is a critical component to fulfillment and accomplishment

Firefly
(cont.)

Are we being too pessimistic?

Are we holding on to a sense of hopelessness, that all is lost?

Are we trying to force movement along the wrong path?

Are we not acting upon our creative ideas or even acknowledging them?

Are we not taking advantage of the spiritual gifts available to us?

Are others misleading us, giving us false hopes and false inspirations?

Flea

KEYNOTE

Irritations and aggravations will increase until we make necessary changes

DOG FLEA

(Ctenocephalus canis)

Any of certain wingless blood-sucking insects having a hard, usually laterally compressed, body, and extraordinary powers of leaping.

Do we need to be more selective in our life choices?

Are we allowing others to drain our vitality?

Are we draining others?

Do we need to let others feed us for a while?

Are we carrying others too much in life?

Do we need to allow others to carry us for a time?

Is there something we are itching to do but are afraid to?

Are we locked into what we know rather than opening to change?

➤ Fleas are one of those animal species that people always assume is a pest. We must be careful not to assume that an animal is a pest simply because we can not see its purpose or viability. Often times the things, which irritate us or make us itch in life also motivate us to make changes that may be difficult but are important to make nonetheless.

Fleas dig themselves firmly into their host's skin with tiny barbs on their mouth. Then they suck blood from the host's bloodstream. Some fleas are fairly selective, only feeding upon certain species.

The host's life cycle often controls that of the flea. When rabbits become pregnant, hormones in their blood trigger the female flea to reproduce. About the time the baby rabbits are born, the flea eggs hatch and transfer to the rabbit's babies. When the flea appears, we may be carrying others too much, or we may need to allow others to carry us for a time.

Fleas are one of the most adaptable and least destructible animals on the planet. Sensory organs enable them to detect the subtlest change of body heat or smell. They have tremendous leaping ability. They can clear 120 times their own height. Some species can survive for years without food, waiting for a host to come along to feed upon. When fleas appear, it is time to move on and make some new leaps. We may need some new blood, some new inspiration in our life.

When fleas appear there is usually a need for change that we are ignoring. The problems will increase until we make the changes or eliminate the cause of our irritations. We may be hesitant to do something we're itching to do. Or perhaps be are being driven by the the philosophy "better the devil we know than the one we don't." Fleas remind us that we must assert ourselves and change what is irritating us or some aspect of our life.

Kingdoms of Insects and Arachnids

➤ The fly is one of those insects that has often been considered a great pest. The questions most often asked is "What purpose or benefit does a fly serve?" The truth is that scientists don't know, but this is also not known about most animals in nature. Humans often assume if an animal or insect is bothersome, that animal is truly a pest, and should be destroyed. Humans know more about animals than at any other time in our history, but when we compare it to what we do not know, that knowledge is a miniscule amount.

The fly is an animal of great disparity in what it means in various traditions. It was often considered a sign, but most interpretations are based on superstitions rather than actual knowledge. For example, a fly in a drink used to be considered a sure, good omen for the drinker. The last fly of the winter in parts of Europe was often considered magical, a sure sign of good luck. When a fly hung around through Christmas, it was considered the "lucky Christmas fly," the herald of sure good luck through the New Year.

Flies come from a very large group of insects of over 90,000 species. The housefly is one of the world's most widely distributed species. It is a liquid feeder, but its diet varies enormously, ranging from dung to decaying matter. The housefly is an indiscriminate feeder, and so can infect, carrying germs from dung to food. Its larvae, which is legless, live in decaying matter.

The adult fly emerges in a week during warm weather, and in colder weather, two months. These seemingly unhealthy kinds of behaviors and environments are usually short-lived, a reminder that any unhealthy environments that we seem to be living in (at work, home or other environments in our life) will be short-lived. They remind us that we will be able to remain stable within those environments until we can emerge.

Unlike most insects, they have only one pair of wings. Their hind legs are pinlike and serve to

Fly

KEYNOTE

**stability
even within
indiscriminate
and unhealthy
environments**

HOUSE FLY
(*Musca domestica*)

A dipterous fly...which is found in all habitable parts of the world, and is the most abundant and familiar insect about human habitations during the warm part of the year. It lays its eggs in decaying substances (chiefly in horse manure); and in warm weather the larvae, or *maggots*, hatch out in a few hours and become pupas in about five days, and adult insects in about five more. The proboscis of the house fly is not adapted for biting, but the very similar *stable fly*...often found in houses and mistaken for the house fly, is able to bite.

Fly
(cont.)

balance the fly. They act like a gyroscope when flying helping to keep their flight stable, reminding us of the need for stability and that any movement we are either making or thinking of making will be more stable than we may realize. Flies further teach us how to maneuver and remain balanced when things are decaying or dying around us.

There are, of course, other species of flies that most people are familiar with. The horse and deer fly are larger species. They pierce the skin with bladelike mouthparts. The female feeds on blood while the male feeds on nectar. The male does not have the mouth parts that the female does. The blood the female lives on helps her to feed the eggs she will bear.

These larger members of the fly family remind us to be careful about what we say or do (biting responses or silence) in the situations around us, even in those that are unhealthy. The female reminds us that sometimes we must be bitey in some situations if we are to nourish our young or host things we will give birth to in some area of our life.

All flies have large eyes that display a wonderful metallic color, while the rest of the body is somber. For those to whom the fly is a totem or messenger, there is an innate ability—which should be drawn upon—to see the color of life and life situations no matter what the environment. It is a reminder to look toward the positive.

When flies appear, it is important to take a look at the issues that have been most on our mind in the past two weeks. If we have been secretive, we may be giving off subtle clues, like the carbon dioxide of the caribou. We may also need to look for and pay attention to the subtle clues around us. Flies are almost always messengers about very recent issues and problems.

➤ Some of the most attractive spiders are the jumping variety. Most have bright colors, often with iridescent qualities to them. All are small spiders and unlike most of their kind, they are active during the day, actually liking the sunshine.

Jumping spiders walk with an irregular gait, but they have a wonderful ability to leap upon their prey. They can jump many times their own length. They are unique among spiders because their fourth pair of legs is modified to enable a jumping ability, and for those to whom this spider appears as a messenger or totem, there is an opportunity coming that could showcase your own unique abilities in colorful ways.

To ensure its success when jumping, this spider secures a silk thread on which it can climb back in case it misses its mark. When the jumping spider appears, there is greater security in leaping upon new opportunities because even if the opportunity does not work out, there is a safety net somewhere.

When a male spots a female, it performs a little dance, hopping and waving the brightly colored legs to attract her attention. Again, this is a reminder not to hide away your talents. Give them the light of day. Perform a little bit. Your color and uniqueness will be noticed now.

When the jumping spider appears as a messenger, examine what you are or are not doing. Now is the time to see what you can do and how best to do it. Remember that the jumping spider always has a safety thread, so this is a wonderful time to stretch new creative boundaries.

Jumping Spider

KEYNOTE

safe time to leap upon creative and colorful opportunities

ONE OF THE
SALTIGRADAE
(*Attus*)

A family of stout, short-legged spiders with large eyes and great power of jumping; the jumping spiders. They do not spin webs to catch their prey.

Saltigrade—having feet or legs formed for leaping.

Are you looking before you leap?

Are you hiding away your unique talents?

Do you need to be a bit more colorful in your activities?

Ladybug

KEYNOTE

wish fulfilled

LADYBUG

Ladybird or ladybug is the common name for any one of a group of small beetles. They are rounded on the back and flat below. Their wing covers usually are marked with spots. As to colors, they generally are red or yellow with black spots, or black with white, red, or yellow spots. Many ladybirds hibernate, a common one sometimes coming forth in a warm room in midwinter. The beetles are long-lived and very prolific, of much benefit to agriculturist and horticulturists.

➤ The ladybug is a small beetle that fascinates most people. A great deal of folklore exists about it. Sometimes referred to as the ladybird beetle, it is always considered lucky to have one light upon us, and the killing of them was considered unlucky. Some traditions make wishes upon them, resting them upon the open palm. When they flew off, the wish was released to be fulfilled. Many believed that the ladybug would fly to one's true love. The appearance of the ladybug heralds a time of luck and protection in which our wishes begin to be fulfilled.

Ladybugs aid in pollination. They also control aphids, which attack plants and crops. A single ladybug can eat 50 to 100 aphids a day. Their presence signals a time of shielding and protection from many of our own aggravations and pests.

The adult lives from nine months to a year and a half, and this always indicates a time of luck within our lives of about equal length. The adults congregate in the fall to hibernate. In the spring, they emerge and lay eggs, and a female can lay as many as 800 eggs, reflecting the abundance of luck and beneficial flow being activated within our life, with the fall and spring being the most abundant times for such.

Ladybug's appearance signals new happiness, often with material gains. A renewed sense of well being occurs, and higher goals and new heights can be more easily attained over the following months. Worries will begin to dissipate.

Often the female ladybug has seven spots, but regardless of whether it is a male or female, the number of spots should be counted if possible since the spots often indicate the number of gifts and wishes that will be fulfilled in the future. Whether a wish for love, job, or the fulfillment of a dream, the ladybug signals a time in which there will be opportunity to pursue and capture our dreams in our lives.

Ladybug
(cont.)

A significant aspect of the ladybug is the red and black coloring, although there are other color variations, including yellow and black. This coloring serves as a warning to predators. If attacked, it squirts a chemical from its knees, which is distasteful to those that would try and eat them. This characteristic might indicate that someone or something is preventing the fulfillment of a wish at this time. We may need to give a strong, clear warning.

There are different kinds of ladybugs, and one kind beats its wings faster than a hummingbird. The ladybug can indicate that we are trying to push too hard and too fast in fulfilling our wishes and dreams. We still have to work for them, but we also must allow our efforts to unfold and manifest in the time that is best for us. The ladybug can warn us not to push too hard, that the wish will not be fulfilled at this particular time.

Are we not protecting our endeavors, our dreams?

Are we allowing others to dissuade us from our pursuits and loves?

Are we trying to do more than we are capable of at this time?

Are we limiting our wishes and dreams?

Are we trying to force our dreams into manifestation rather than allowing them to unfold in the manner best for us?

Leech

KEYNOTE

• allow the joy to flow

• purification and detoxification

MEDICINAL LEECH
(*Hirudo medicinalis*)

The typical leeches have a flattened segmented body of lanceolate outline, broader near the posterior end, and exhibit externally well-marked annulations, which greatly exceed the true segments in number....Leeches are hemaphroditic and the development is usually direct. Most of them inhabit fresh water, a few are marine, and some tropical forms are terrestrial. They progress by means of their suckers, looping the body like a measuring worm, or swim with an undulating movement.

Are we not expressing them freely?

Are we holding on to the past?

Are we stuck in old, outworn patterns?

Do we need to cleanse ourselves of past emotional issues?

Do we need some new blood, new vitality?

Are we afraid to flow with and enjoy life?

➤ In the Middle Ages, leeches were often used as a form of medical treatment for many diseases, including depression. "Blood letting" was a medieval process of attaching leeches to a host skin and was a popular remedy for many ailments, including melancholy. Although at one time scoffed at in modern society, the use of leeches by the medical community has resurfaced. When leeches appear, there are old, even past life issues resurfacing somewhere within our life.

Leeches are related to earthworms, and they have 33 segments with suckers at each end. Small leeches are found in ponds and streams. Almost all are predatory, sucking out all fluids or eating their host whole. They will gorge themselves to many times their size. They have usually been associated with cleansing and purification, used to draw out poisons and to stimulate the free flow of blood believed to be toxic or infected. Today we know that leeches, like vampire bats, secrete a saliva which contains an anesthetic and an anticoagulant by the name of *hirudin*, which prevents clotting.

Anticoagulants are blood thinners, and they are used in modern medicine to prevent embolism and to break down blood clots. Leeches are being used once more because of the hirudin they extrude. They are being employed by physicians in such things as reducing hematomas (accumulated pockets of blood).

Not all leeches feed on blood. Some eat small creatures such as worms and snails. Some are fish parasites. Those that live on warm mammal blood lie in wait in damp places and stay on the victim only long enough to gorge themselves. Their sharp teeth make a Y-shaped bite.

If a leech gets enough blood at one sitting, it can survive without food for a year. Blood is four-fifths water, and a leech will excrete water as fast as it sucks blood. Any animal that is linked to blood should stimulate an exploration of the symbolism of blood.

Blood is the life fluid, representing the flow of life energy, vitality, and joy. Anticoagulants thin the blood so it can flow more freely. When leeches appear, we might not be allowing our joys to flow freely.

➤Long before there was a long ago, a great giant was eating the Tlingit people. The people were so troubled by it that they gathered together, plotting to attack the giant when least expected. Together all of the people attacked, stabbing him repeatedly in the heart. The giant collapsed and as he lay dying, his voice croaked, "Though I'll be dead, I will continue to eat you and all other humans forever!" The last thing the people heard was the giant's cruel laughter as he died.

The Tlingit were so frightened at this prophecy, that they cut the giant into pieces and then burned the pieces in a great bonfire. When the fire died out, they took the ashes and scattered them in the wind. As they did, each particle turned into a mosquito, and from their midst came the giant's laughing voice, "Yes, I will continue to eat you until the end of time."

The female mosquito actually does the biting because she is feeding hundreds of eggs she is carrying around inside of her and the eggs require the protein that comes from the blood of mammals. When she bites and feeds, she will usually only live another 24 hours. The male is mostly harmless and feeds on plant juices.

Blood is the life force, a symbol of joy and vitality. It contains the life essence—past, present, and future. Blood infections, of which mosquito bites are, often reflect temporary things we are allowing to affect our vitality and joy. The key is

Mosquito

KEYNOTE

- **temporary irritations and attacks upon self-worth**

- **some temporary extra protection and covering will benefit you**

MOSQUITO
(*Culex pungens*)
Any of certain dipterous insects of the family Culicidae, having a rather narrow abdomen, usually a long and slender but firm proboscis, and narrow wings with a fringe of scales on the margin, and commonly on each side of the wing veins. The males have featherlike antennae, and the mouth parts are not fitted for piercing, but the females have slender antennae, and a set of needlelike organs in the proboscis with which they puncture the skin of fruits or animals to suck up their juice or blood.

Mosquito
(cont.)

Is something or someone aggravating you in your life?

Are you itching to do something but not acting upon it?

What is unresolved and so still irritates us?

Are others being insensitive to us?

Or we to them?

Is our individuality and self-worth being threatened?

Do we need to be more protective?

Are we allowing things to become too still and stagnant?

Do we need to seek out new creative projects?

that these things are temporary and should not be dwelled upon.

Mosquito bites are irritations of the skin and always have symptoms of burning or itching. As the skin, our protective outer covering, is our largest sensory organ, it is a symbol of our sensitivity and self-worth. All irritations of the skin should get us to ask questions about what is aggravating us, what kinds of unresolved issues are irritating us, and what kinds of things we are itching to do but failing to do.

Mosquitoes breed in quiet or stagnant water and this is one of their most significant aspects. When mosquitoes truly become pests, we need to take a serious look at the environment in which we are working and living. Perhaps we need to be more protective or ourselves. Perhaps we are becoming too still and stagnant.

When mosquitoes appear, irritations are short lived. We should focus on protecting our creative projects, our own sense of joy and accomplishments.

►When moths persist in flying around you, a letter will shortly be coming your way bringing important news. The size of the moth often determines the size of the letter and the importance of the news. This and many other superstitions exist around moths and their closest relatives, the butterflies.

The actual difference between moths and butterflies is not always clear and are relatively minor. Butterflies are diurnal, and most moths are nocturnal and because of this, they rely on different senses. The moth cannot rely on its sight, but has a highly developed sense of smell, which it uses at night. Most butterflies have clubbed antennae, and most moth antennae are feathery and threadlike.

Like their cousins the butterflies, moths also go through metamorphosis. Moths spin cocoons while butterflies create a naked chrysalis. The cocoon is a more sheltered, outer covering. This can often indicate a need to be more sheltered in our creative transforming activities and relationships when the moth is a messenger.

There are many thousands of moths throughout the world and they each have their own unique abilities and qualities. If you can identify the specific species of moth, it will be easier to become more clear in interpreting the meaning.

All moths have unique defenses. Some are able to emit sounds that confuse the echolocation of bats. Some are bad tasting. Several make clicking noises to warn their predators, while others flash bright colors to startle off predators.

Unlike butterflies, most moths are active at night. During the day, they find a place to hide and sleep. Around dusk they begin to awaken and look for food. As they feed, they come fully awake and they spend the night feeding and flying about. The male spends most of each night looking for a female to mate with. As dawn approaches, they seek out a safe place to sleep un-

Moth

KEYNOTE

- sexual activity, fertility
- increased relationships

LUNA MOTH
(*Tropaea luna*)

Any insect of the order Lepidoptera except those known as butterflies…The moths, which in some classifications form a suborder Heterocera, vary much in form, size, and habits, but are usually nocturnal or crepuscular, and the antennae, though of various forms (often featherlike), are rarely distinctly club-shaped, as in the butterflies, and the body is usually stouter and the wings proportionately smaller than in that group, and the colors less brilliant. Though the wings are held or folded in various positions when at rest, they are not kept erect over the body as with many bu tterflies.

Moth
(cont.)

Does the situation smell right to you?

Are you catching and following the scent of possibilities?

Are you ignoring what you are sensing?

Do you need to stimulate some new relationships?

til night comes again, and the search for food and mating can be continued.

The female moth raises her abdomen to protrude a pair of glands and releases from them a scent known as *pheromone*. She flaps her wings to send the scent out into the air to attract males. For many years, scientists were unable to prove that such a scent existed. It is found in such tiny amounts that scientists had to collect the secretions of a half million moths in order to amass an amount as small as twelve milligrams.

Moths are able to find each other by following a scent trail over great distances. Because they are active at night, they need this scent to find a mate. Moth totems and messengers usually indicate an awakening sense of smell. It will be the fragrance of the opposite sex that will most attract and discourage. Trusting in one's own outer and inner sense of smell will be important in relationships—sexual or otherwise.

➤ Orb-weaving spiders are found all over the world, and orb webs are often under great research. Their web is an engineering feat that is amazing. They are built by many species of spiders at night. First, a bridge is established, then the spider reinforces it by walking back and forth over it, adding more silk. Next, the spider drops down on a thread it has fastened to the center of the bridge and secures this vertical thread. It then begins spinning and tightening radii out from it. Spirals come next. The radii and spirals are often rebuilt each night.

Because of this construction feat, orb weavers teach us how to carefully and creatively weave and engineer what we need it order to capture what we wish. This can be a job, a dream, or even the solution to a problem. They teach us how to bridge past difficulties.

All orb-weaving spiders have poor vision and locate prey by feeling the tension and vibration in the threads of their web. When an orb spider appears, it is not a time to trust what we see but rather what we feel.

When prey gets caught, the orb-weaver spider quickly bites it and then carries it to the center or to the spider's retreat in a corner where the prey is eaten. Anything inedible caught in the web is cut out and dropped to the ground. Orb-weavers remind us to use the web to capture what we need, but it also reminds us not to hang on to that which we do not need.

Orb-weaving Spider

KEYNOTE

creative designs and successful engineering feats

Are we building the bridges and foundations necessary to capture or attain what we seek?

Are we hanging on to that which we no longer need or which no longer benefits us?

Do we need to become more creative in our approaches?

Scorpion

KEYNOTE

**dynamic
transformation
through secret
passions and desires**

SCORPION

(*Androctonus occitanus*)

Any of numerous arachnids,
of most warm and tropical
regions, constituting the
order Scorpionida, having an
elongated body divided into
a cephalothorax and a
segmented abdomen, the
posterior part of the latter
forming a narrow segmented
tail (generally carried curled
up over the back) bearing a
venomous sting at the tip.
There are four pairs of
walking legs and in front a
pair of limbs (pedipalpi)
bearing large pinchers, and
a pair of mandibles. They
breathe by lungs and are
viviparous. Scorpions are
nocturnal, and prey on
insects, spiders, etc., and
sometimes enter houses.
Some become four or five
inches long, a few even
eight or more. Their sting
is very severe, though rarely
fatal to man.

➤ The scorpion is sometimes referred to as the serpent from the Garden of Eden. In Egypt it was the symbol of darkness, for it brought with it the waning strength of the sun. In Greek mythology, it was the monster that caused Apollo's horses to run wild while in the hands of Phaethon. This is often a caution for those to whom the scorpion is a messenger. Unless we control our passions and desires and direct their energies appropriately, the transformations will occur in the midst of chaos.

In astrology the sign of Scorpio is represented by several animals—the scorpion, the eagle, and the phoenix. The Scorpio zodiac sign has been associated with transformation and rising to new heights and is known for its secretiveness and passions. It is a sign of mystery, long associated with sex, death, and rebirth. Those of this sign have great strength and an ability to inspire. They also can misuse their psychic and sexual energies.

Sex and death are often associated with the sign of Scorpio. These mysteries stimulate great passions and feelings, and both are vehicles of change. Within the sex act, the two partners exchange energy and neither is ever truly the same again. Death itself is a transformation of energy so that rebirth can occur. This is scorpion energy.

The scorpion is an amazing creature. It is an arachnid, but it is very different from spiders. Underneath the last legs are comblike structures called *pectines*. These are sense organs of touch. Scorpions do have two eyes in the center of the head, and usually more along the sides of the head as well, but they do not see very well. They rely on their sense of touch. When the scorpion appears as a totem or messenger, the sense of psychic touch will become increasingly heightened. Responses to touch will grow stronger as will the ability to touch others more intensely.

Scorpion
(cont.)

Most scorpions are nocturnal, and one of the most common ways of collecting them is through the use of a black light which makes them fluorescent in the darkness. This reminds us that light can be found within darkness if we channel our passions correctly.

The mating ritual of scorpions involves the male holding the female by the pincers and leading her back and forth. Eventually the male deposits a package of sperm, which the female picks up with an organ on her stomach. The young will ride around on the mother's back until they shed their skin for the first time. They then become independent and live a solitary life. It is thus not unusual, when scorpions appear, to find that periods of solitariness are intermixed with intense and passionate relationships and encounters in life.

Remember the scorpion promises transformation. Whether that transformation is calm or chaotic depends on how we use our energies.

Are we channeling our passions correctly?

Are we allowing our passions to override our common sense?

Do we need to balance our relationships with more solitariness?

Are we becoming too solitary?

Do we need to merge our physical passions with our spiritual passions?

Are we ignoring our psychic perceptions only to be stung?

Silkworm Moth

KEYNOTE

- fertility
- success
- fulfillment

SILKWORM
(*Bombyx mori*)

a. larva; b. pupa; c. adult
female; d. adult male

The larva of any of certain moths, which spins a large amount of strong silk in constructing its cocoon before changing to a pupa. The common domesticated silkworm is the larva of a bombycid moth...which is yellow and measures about an inch and a half across the extended wings. It is supposed to be a native of China, but has been domesticated for many centuries, and is no longer known in the wild state. Its cultivation was introduced into western Asia and Europe early in the Christian Era, and into America during the colonial period. It feeds on the leaves of the white and certain other species of mulberry and the Osage orange. Many varieties or races of the worm have been developed by Asiatic and European breeders, which may differ in the number of annual generations....In America unsuccessful efforts have been made to use commercially the silk of various native species.

➤ Moths and butterflies are not only similar, but also together they form one of the largest insect orders, a reflection of the abundant opportunities for transformation when members of either group appear. Moths, like butterflies, are ancient symbols of change. There are some subtle differences between the two. Most butterflies have clubbed antennae, and moths usually form a cocoon rather than a chrysalis. Moths also have a frenulum, which holds the two wings together during flight. The silkworm moth heralds a time of celebration and is a powerful symbol of fertility, success, and fulfillment.

The giant silkmoths or *saterniids* are among the most spectacular and beautiful, including species such as the Promethea and Luna moths. The silkworm moth during the caterpillar stage surrounds itself with a silken cocoon. In domestic forms, the cocoon can contain as much as 3000 feet (900 m) of unbroken silk, an amazing feat. Silk is a substance that is light and insulating. The appearance of a silkworm moth always indicates greater protection in all endeavors and signals a time of abundance and fulfillment, new life beginning on some level.

The male silkmoth has an exceptional sense of smell. Its feathery antennae are covered with small receptors, each of which contains two nerve endings immersed in fluid. Scents enter the hair through pores on its surface and make contact with a pheromone receptor cell. A male silk moth has about 60,000 sensory hairs on its antennae and three fourths of them are sensitive to only one substance, *bombykol*, the pheromone emitted by the unmated female. The faintest scent of it alerts any male within three miles. The male's antennae are so sensitive that it can detect one molecule. When moths appear, our own psychic sense of smell will become very acute.

Many tribes of the West (particularly California) used the cocoon of the giant silkworm moth

Silkworm Moth (cont.)

for rattles. A few pebbles were inserted into the cocoon, and several cocoons were bound to a handle and decorated. They have been used for healing, fertility, and for manifestation. When the rattle was used while singing a prayer, the individual would get what he or she prayed for.[3]

Moths and butterflies always reflect transformation. The emergence of the moth from the cocoon reflects the final stage—a new birth is occurring. What was hidden inside (our talents, gifts, and blessings) are coming to the surface. The appearance of the silkworm moth represents a time of creative fertility—sexually, financially, spiritually, and artistically. Joyous success, conclusions, and new births are abundant now. Our hopes will be fulfilled.

The domesticated silk moth is now unknown in the wild, and they have lost the ability to fly. When the silkworm moth appears, it may also be an indication that circumstances have changed around us. What had been good may begin to stifle unless we look to new directions to teach us how to fly once more.

All moths and butterflies reflect transformation. Transformation is essential to continued growth. The appearance of the silkworm moth sometimes indicates a resistance to change. We are weaving nothing new although the opportunities are there. We may be trying to milk too much from past efforts rather than initiating the new. It is time to move into new areas of endeavor.

The silkworm moth reflects our fertility. We may be inhibited, affecting our ability to be productive. The silkworm moth reminds us that the creative process includes, joy, hope, appreciation, and renewed effort.

Are we trying to do new things in old ways that no longer work?

Are we ignoring our creative opportunities?

Are we not taking advantage of opportunities to change?

Are we living off old success, afraid to pursue and produce new work?

Have we failed to appreciate the accomplishments of the past?

Are we feeling sorry for ourselves, refusing to pursue new interests?

---

[3] Pablita Perez Kelley. *"The Cocoon Shell Rattle."* (Sacramento, CA.

Slug

KEYNOTE

- **movement to the light**

- **increasing fertility and divination**

SLUG

(*Limax campestris*)

Any of numerous terrestrial pulmonate gastropods closely related to the ordinary land snails, but having the shell rudimentary and often buried in the mantle, or wanting entirely, and the body when extended on an elongated fusiform shape, the whole lower surface constituting the foot upon which the animal crawls. The slugs are not now regarded a natural group, but are considered to have descended from shelled snales of several different families....They secrete abundant mucus from the skin.

➤ The slug is a member of the snail family, but without the shell. They are essentially snails that have lost or almost lost their shells. The internal organs that are usually housed in the shell of a snail are packed into the body of a slug.

The slug is an ancient tool for divination, often considered sacred. Its slimy trail was guidance in life and in decisions. When placed within a flower, its trail was the sacred writing of a future marriage partner. It is a symbol of the male seed, the origin of life, the silent slow tendency of darkness to move toward the light.

The slug is related to the yod in the Hebrew alphabet, both being very similar in shapes. In Qabalistic traditions, the letter yod stands for the occult faculty of touch and of the sexual union. It is shaped like the sacred seed. In the Qabalistic Tree of Life, the yod is associated with the path of the Hermit, the Wayshower or the Adept.

When the slug appears as a totem or messenger, we are opening to higher vision. A new path is opening:

> This path (The Hermit Path) and its symbols and imagery place before us opportunities to become a new person. On a spiritual level this path stimulates a greater commitment to the spiritual life. We are setting energy in motion that proclaims to the universe, "I am ready to accept change in my life![4]

The slug's appearance reminds us that we will soon recognize and realize the illumination that is always present within us.

Slugs vary in size and they live in damp places. Some live entirely underground. They are most active at night or after a daytime shower. They move through hydraulics. This means rather than moving through the work of muscles against joints, they move through the interaction of

---

[4] Ted Andrews. *More Simplified Magic.* (Jackson, TN: Dragonhawk Publishing, 1998), p. 211.

Slug
(cont.)

muscles and fluid movement. The body fluids contract the muscles, causing the slug to stretch and push. As it relaxes, it becomes smaller, until the fluid advances once more through the muscles. Remember that the slug moves slowly but steadily, a reminder there are no shortcuts.

For those to whom the slug is a totem or messenger, care of the body joints will often be important. Exercising in pools and in activities that are not hard on the joints will be most beneficial. On a spiritual level, the slug is a reminder that the Biblical phrase, "Ask and it shall be given..." is active within our life. The slug reminds us that if we know the proper way to ask, we will begin to manifest that which we need or desire.

In the slug is the deception of appearances. Most slugs feed near ground level, eating decaying plant matter and even some worms. Many are excellent climbers, and this unexpected ability is a reminder that we can often do much more than what we may have thought physically and spiritually possible. Let others think what they will and then let them be surprised at what you accomplish and the heights you reach. The slug reminds you the magic to do what you wish is already present in spite of what others might say.

Slugs are *hermaphrodites*, containing both male and female organs, but they do require interaction with other slugs. There is a two-way exchange of sperm between the mating pairs and the eggs are laid soon afterwards. The eggs hatch almost a month later.

Hermaphrodites have both male and female sexual organs. Even though humans don't have both sets of organs, we are all a combination of male and female energies on other levels. Whenever the male and female are brought together on any level, a new birth results. When we do this within ourselves, we give birth to the Holy Child within. The slug reminds us that we are on the path to giving birth to our inner Holy Child.

Are you staying cloaked, afraid to come out and express your inner talents?

Are you trying to do too much too soon?

Are we not moving out on our own path?

Are we locked into the paths of others, rather than pursuing our own?

Are we ignoring our own illuminations?

Do we need to trust in our own ability to create?

Snail

KEYNOTE

protecting vulnerable emotions and spirit

SNAIL

(Macrocyclis concava)

Any of numerous gastropod mollusks; esp., when used without a qualifying term, one of terrestrial habits having a well-developed spiral shell into which the animal can withdraw for protection. Though not abundant in most parts of the United States, snails are very numerous in Europe and in most warm countries, and are often very destructive to vegetation.... Some are used as food (esp. in France), generally after feeding and fattening.

➤ Snails have often been associated with the death and the spirits of the dead. To come across a black snail was an indication that you would soon encounter the spirit of someone dead. To discover a snail indoors was a sign of death of someone close. Although these are superstitions, the appearance of snails often reflect that protective spirits are about.

Snails carry their home upon their backs. Their shell is their protection, acting in much the same way as a turtle's shell does. Since the shell encloses and protects, it keeps the snail's soft body from drying out and guards it against predators. As the snail grows, it lays down more shell, enlarging it at the entrance.

Snail's appearance often reflects a need to be more protective in some environments. Keep your guard up and your shell about you. By noting where you are and what you are more focused upon at the time of the snail encounter, you can usually determine where in your life this extra protection is needed. Think about whether you encountered the snail on the way to work or in a relationship. A snail's shell helps protect its soft, vulnerable body. It is often a reminder to protect our own vulnerable aspects.

Snails avoid predators by coming out mostly at night. This also helps prevent them from being dried out by the sun. If it is too hot or cold, the snail shuts its door and seals the entrance to the shell with a layer of hard mucus.

Snail people are often loners or perceived as loners. They are not very social and are often timid. Learning to trust is a big life lesson. Learning to balance protection and trust is an even more difficult one. When snails appear as messengers, it is usually a time to be cautious about exposing ourselves to environments that are not always nurturing and safe. Be careful of exposing too much vulnerability openly.

Snails make a tasty meal for any bird that can open their shell. The song thrush and snail kite are well known for this. Both should be examined by anyone for whom the snail appears. The song thrush bashes the snail against a hard stone to crack the shell. Those with snails as totems often have a hard shell that they present to the outer world, but they have hearts and feelings that are very soft and tender.

Most snails eat plants, but some are carnivores, eating other small creatures. Snails are also hermaphrodites. They have both male and female parts to their body. When mating, the snails stick together and shoot a "love dart" carrying sperm into the other snail. They can then both lay eggs.

Snails, like slugs, teach us to protect the inner child—the Holy Child within us. It is not unusual for those with snails as a totem to have had an early life in which the childlike sensitivities and energies were often discouraged or ridiculed. Thus a shell was built around the person to protect their sensitive and very tender hearts. Snails as messengers remind us that the Holy Child still lives within us. It is often a sign that it is time to bring that child out once more. Remember that all is possible to the Holy Child within.

When snails appear in our life as messengers and totems, they should stimulate us to look at the walls and shells we have built around us.

Are we remaining too closed in?

Are we exposing ourselves too much?

Are we being too sensitive?

Do we need to protect ourselves a little more?

Are we going to keep our Holy Child hidden away or bring it out so we can experience the magic of life?

Stick Bug (Walking-stick)

KEYNOTE

activity beneath the surface

STICK INSECT ON A TWIG
(*Diapheromera femorata*)
Any of various orthopterous insects of the Phasmidae, usually wingless, with a long round body, sticklike in form and color, and long legs, often held rigidly in such positions as to make them resemble twigs of the trees on which they live.

Are we discontent with what we are accomplishing?

Are we letting others know about and use our plans?

Are we being too impatient, trying to rush the success before the proper protection and foundation has been set?

Are we not trusting in our own inner voice relying solely on others?

➤ The stick bug is also known as the Walking-stick. There are about 2000 species, and some are the world's longest insects, reaching lengths of 14 inches. Their bodies are so thin and sticklike that they are almost impossible to see as they rest in bushes and trees. Their appearance always indicates that there is activity around us beneath the surface that we may or may not be aware of. If we remain still, making no movement or commitment, the proper course of action will make itself known.

The appearance of the stick bug is a reminder to be patient. We should continue what we have been doing, quietly camouflaging our endeavors. The stick bug indicates results are coming, but we must allow them to come in their own time. When we do, we will be in a better position to grab them and use them for our benefit.

The stick bug reminds us to focus on our own activities and ourselves. It is also an indication that meditation and prayer will bring much greater results and benefits now. There is something in the offing, but we must be able to recognize it. This is where personal stillness—meditative and altered states of quietness—come into play. There may even be signals of what is coming through the dream state.

Stick bugs are experts at camouflage. They hold still, keeping their legs and bodies in a position to resemble twigs. Their appearance is always a reminder to camouflage our intentions and our activities. We should keep them hidden beneath the surface. Most do their feeding at night, using the dark to further cloak their presence. Stick bugs also remain motionless around large animals, including humans, and are very difficult to detect. They remind us that for the greatest success in laying a strong foundation for our endeavors, we should use camouflage. We should not let others know of our activities. Present the appearance that nothing is happening, but prepare quietly and thoroughly for what we seek to accomplish and we will find ultimate success.

The appetites of stickbugs are great, and if their numbers are abundant enough, they can defoliate trees and bushes, especially oak trees. (The significance of oak trees should be studied by anyone for whom the stick bug appears.) Because of its appetite, when stick bug appears, our appetites may be getting our of hand and may be becoming too public. We may be letting the wrong people know of our goals and endeavors. Stick bugs can also warn of being too open and too trusting. An old adage speaks of strength through silence. Now is not a good time to let others know of our plans. Others may be undermining them or trying to steal them for themselves.

Sometimes the stick bug may indicate that we are holding our ideas too close to the chest. We may be thinking about them, making plans, but never acting upon them. We may be too distrustful and may need to open up to someone a little.

The Best Defense...

Being some of the smallest creatures on the planet has its drawbacks. In order to defend and survive, insects have adapted amazing defense mechanisms. One of their best defenses is disguise.

Some grasshoppers have heads that look like grass seeds, thus blending into the background. The praying mantis remains perfectly still, seeming no more than a part of the stick upon which it rests. Some treehoppers rest on thorny stems, taking a posture that resembles one of the thorns.

The way an insect defends and protects itself sheds light on things we can do to be more successful—especailly in endeavors where there is a great deal of competitioin.

Tarantula

KEYNOTE

**transformation through
heightened psychism
and feelings**

EUROPEAN TARANTULA
(*Lycosa tarantula*)

Any of several large
poisonous spiders. The true
tarantula is a large European
wolf spider…whose bit was
supposed to cause tarantism.
The tarantula of Texas and
adjacent countries are large
hairy spiders of *Eurypelma,
Avicularia,* and allied genera
of the family Theraphosidae.

Do we trust what we feel?

*Are we relying too much
on appearances?*

*Do we need to protect our
activities and ourselves a
little more aggressively?*

*Do we need to trust our
psychic impressions more?*

*Do we need to pay attention
to the subtle activities
going on around us?*

➤ In southern Italy, there is a popular folk dance that has circular directions and quick foot movements, which seem to reflect the convulsive movements in humans that are bitten by a spider. This dance, the tarantella, is named for the spider believed to cause these convulsive movements, the tarantula.

Tarantulas are part of a group of spiders known as the *hairy mygalomorphs*. Most live in the ground, though some do live in trees. Their eyes are very sensitive, but they hunt mostly at night by touch. They are very sensitive to vibrations and movement around them. They can live 10-20 years, and usually when a tarantula appears as a messenger or totem, it will be important in our life for a long period of time.

Tarantulas do spin silk but they do not create webs. They usually dig a burrow or hole in the sand or soft earth and hide in the bottom of it. Tarantulas have fibers on their legs and bodies that are sensitive to touch and rely heavily on this sense. When they feel something walking about their hole, they jump out, grab it, and pull it back into the hole. They are sensitive to the subtle activities in their environment, and they teach us how to be more aware of them as well.

If tarantulas have appeared in your life as a messenger or totem, it is important to trust your own feelings. Even though they have eight eyes, they do not see very well, relying mostly on their sense of touch. Trust what you feel, not what you see. If you do so, you will find yourself more successful in all of your endeavors.

When frightened, tarantulas will rear up and shed the hairs on their stomach, flicking them off by their legs. These hairs are very irritating to skin, and it is a defensive measure. It becomes a distraction and enables the tarantula to escape. If we find ourselves or our activities threatened in some way, we should find a way to distract the source of threat or irritation.

Female tarantulas experience molting after maturity, shedding their outer form, much in the manner snakes shed their skin. Males do not molt. Often when the tarantula appears, it is time to shed the old in some way. Do not follow the same patterns or trust the senses relied on before.

➤ The tick is an arachnid, meaning it has four pairs of legs. The first pair is modified to function as a cutter, enabling the creature to slice the skin. It has a chemical in its saliva that dissolves tissue so that it can embed its mouthparts into the skin. The saliva can transmit diseases such as typhus and Lyme disease.

Ticks are large members of the mite family, and all are external parasites of reptiles, birds, and mammals. They molt and wait in foliage ready to attach to any animal that brushes past. They attach themselves to their host only with their mouthparts, and they feed only on blood. Most drop off their hosts after feeding. Because of this, they often reflect imbalance in some aspect of relationships.

All ticks feed on blood, Blood is the life fluid, and it often symbolizes the vitality and joy of life. Animals that feed on blood or cause blood infections should be examined in light of what we are allowing to affect our own vitality and joy in life.

Some ticks do spread disease. The most recognizable in recent years is Lyme disease, named after the town in which it was first discovered. Lyme disease is an infection of the blood in which early recognition and treatment with antibiotics is needed to prevent more difficult problems. Maybe this is a reminder that if we have problems with others affecting our joy in life, early recognition and treatment may be critical to our future health. All ticks require us to examine our relationships.

Tarantula
(cont.)

Tick

KEYNOTE

unbalanced relationships

ARGAS
(*A. talaje*)

Any of numerous arachnids of the order Acarida but larger than the ordinary mites, which attach themselves to man and many animals and birds, and suck their blood.

Are those around us feeding off of us in some way?

Are we feeding off others in some inappropriate manner?

Are recent relationships and friendships a matter of convenience and one sided?

Are we allowing ourselves to be used or are we using others?

Do we need more vitality in our life?

Are we being to reclusive and not socializing?

Are we allowing others to infect our vitality?

Wasp

KEYNOTE

- **protective nourishment and role fulfillment**

- **dreams fulfilled through practical efforts**

TARANTULA KILLER
(Pepsis formosa)

Any of numerous aculeate hymenopterous insects generally characterized by having a slender body, the abdomen attached by a narrow stalk or petiole, well-developed wings, and (in the workers and females) a more or less formidable sting. They belong to many different famiies and include species of social as well as of solitary habits. Wasps exhibit great variety in their nesting habits and food, but unlike the bees, are largely carnivorous, in many cases provisioning their nests with caterpillars, insects, or spiders, killed or paralyzed by stinging, for their larvae to fee on.

➤ The wasp is a stinging insect that belongs to the same group as bees and ants. Just as with bees, wasps live in differing societies. There are social and solitary species, and regardless of the species, they all provide their offspring with some kind of animal feed. The type of prey can be anything from aphids, flies, caterpillars, spiders, and even bees.

The wasp stinger paralyses the prey, not killing it so it does not rot. In this way the wasp grubs can feed upon the prey until they are fully-grown. Because of this, the wasp can teach us to sustain ourselves on the nourishment we do have. They help us to recognize it and use it fully.

There are social and solitary wasps, and the particular kind will tell us something about our social activity or lack of it. Solitary wasps include black wasps and a variety of black and yellow. They often dig tunnels in the ground or in rotten wood. Some wasps, such as the potter wasps, build nests of clay. Typical social wasps are hornets and the black and yellow species so prominent in late summer. The common wasp and yellow jackets are also social, with organization like the bees in many ways.

With social wasps, the queen hibernates through the winter and then begins her nest in the spring. Wasps make paper nests from scraping fence posts and dead wood with their jaws and chewing them to a pulp. Some are found in hollow trees or hanging from branches, but most are found underground. Six-sided cells are built for the first group of grubs.

These first grubs grow into workers, enlarging the nest and feeding later grubs. They also feed the queen while she continues the egg laying. Males and new queens appear in the late summer. Egg laying falls off, but mating is carried on by them. The workers have less work to do and so can be more troublesome at this time of the year. They die in the fall, along with the old queen and males, leaving the newly mated queens to hibernate and carry on for the next year.

As with bees, there is tremendous symbolism to the wasp and all of its activities. It teaches the lesson of fulfilling one's role and responsibilities, revealing how to construct and nurture our dreams. The six-sided cell is a geometric shape associated with the heart. The grubs are the things of the heart that must be nurtured and hatched in solidness. Dreams without practical preparations are more likely to fail and die. Dreams motivate us, but their fulfillment is based upon work.

Wasps have a cycle of power ranging from spring to fall. Late summer it is stronger. Wasps have a tendency to become more aggressive in the late summer and early fall. And this cycle is usually at play for those to whom the wasp is a messenger.

Wasp

(cont.)

Animal Wonders

INSECT BUILDERS

Humans can learn much from how animals build things, including homes and storage areas. Insects are some of the greatest builders.

The nest of a potter wasp is made of clay and looks like a small clay pot. Before it lays its eggs, it stores some caterpillars in it to feed the young when they hatch. Army ants use their own bodies to build bridges. Water spiders spin diving bells so that they can breathe and hunt under water. Which came first, human buildings or their animal teachers?

Are we feeling paralyzed in the pursuit of our goals?

Are we building from the ground up?

Are we working solitary or for the group?

Are we fulfilling our tasks?

Are those around us doing their parts?

Are we pursuing our dreams in a practical manner?

Are we getting too aggressive in our pursuits?

Water Spider

KEYNOTE

- lucid dreaming
- comfort in new environments

WATER SPIDER
(*Argyoneta aquatica*)

An aquatic European spider…which constructs beneath the surface of the water a bell-shaped structure of silk, open beneath and filled with air which the spider carries down in the form of small bubbles…. Any spider that habitually lives on or about the water, esp. the large American species (*Dolomedes lanceolatus*) which runs rapidly on the surface of water.

Are we ignoring our dreams?

Are we not indulging our creative and artistic inspirations?

Are we getting lost in dream worlds?

Do we need to become more practical and grounded?

➤ The water spider actually lives under the water most of the time. It is an ordinary looking spider. While most female spiders are larger than the male, in this species the female is smaller. It lives on small water animals, insects, and larvae.

The water spider must breathe air, even though it lives in the water. It adapts to the watery environment by constructing a small diving bell out of its silk, which it attaches to stems and leaves of water plants. The water spider then traps a bubble of air from the surface between its hind legs and dives to the bell with it, repeating the process until the bell is filled with air. The spider lurks in the bell until a small water animal, insect or larvae swims near it, and then it captures and eats it. Because of this, the water spider can show us how to adapt to environments we wouldn't normally think we could survive in.

Many spiders show us how to move and live between worlds. The web is a bridge between worlds, and all "tween" places are places where our world meets and intersects with other dimensions. The water spider awakens lucid dreaming, where we become aware while dreaming that we are dreaming. When this occurs, we can change the dream or leave it entirely. A lucid dream is a half step from a conscious out of body experience, and the appearance of the water spider will open the doors to these happenings.

The water spider also teaches us how to live in environments that otherwise would suffocate or drown us. It teaches us that we can survive successfully and creatively in environments that may seem alien and can show us how to move between worlds and dimensions.

The water spider is also a wonderful totem for helping individuals who may have a fear of water or swimming. It is an excellent totem for those who are into scuba diving.

Wolf Spider

➤ The wolf spider is one of many species of spiders. They get their names because, like wolves, they run their prey down instead of snaring it as so many other spiders do.

Wolf spiders are among the most common ones. They are small to medium, usually with bodies no longer than an inch or legs about the same size. They are found most often among leaf litter, but they will dig small burrows and often line them with silk to rest in. They hunt during the day, although in warmer climates they will also hunt at night. Those to whom the wolf spider appears as a messenger or totem will find greater success during daytime activities.

Wolf spiders eat small insects, which they chew to a pulp and suck through their mouths. This type of behavior is highly symbolic, reminding us to get the most of what presents itself to us.

Unlike most spiders, the wolf spider has acute eyesight. Most spiders are sensitive to touch and movement due to fibers on their legs and have very poor eyesight, reflecting a need to trust how we feel rather than what we see. Wolf spiders, on the other hand, see well and teach us to pay attention and recognize what we see and feel.

Female wolf spiders carry their eggs about with them in a ball of silk held on to with their jaws or attached to spinnerets. This adaptive behavior helps protect their eggs from other insects and spiders. In this way, the mother's fangs remain unencumbered while the eggs develop. When the spider senses that her eggs are about to hatch, she cuts through the tough sac enclosing them. The spiderlings clamber out and climb up her legs. They drag silk lines that catch on specially adapted hairs on the mother's back. The young then ride on the mother's back for several days.

This should remind us to keep our creative projects or endeavors tight within ourselves un-

KEYNOTE

- pursue opportunities
- digest past experiences

Are we not truly digesting our experiences?

Are we chewing on things of the past too much, while not getting any benefit?

Wolf Spider (cont.)

til ready to be truly hatched. Don't speak of them or show them prematurely to others. Doing so can be disastrous since it may dissipate their power and even prevent their ultimate success. We must protect our projects and be able to defend them while they develop, and even after born or initiated, we must watch them carefully in the early stages.

Wolf spiders teach us how to spot and pursue our opportunities and then to make the most of them. When they show up in our life, they are reminders to take advantage of all that presents itself, to fully digest and absorb the creative juices within their opportunities.

"BEES DO IT..."

Many insects are essential to pollination. Bees and butterflies are the most commonly recognized.

As the insects gather nectar, they inadvertently pollinate flowers, plants, and trees. Pollen from the flower's male anther sticks to the legs of the insect and brushes off on the female stigma of the next flower it visits.

Often when insects appear as messengers we find ourselves stimulating the creativity and fertility of those we touch...often without realizing it.

Wooly Caterpillar

➤Farmers have often used the woolly caterpillar to determine the severity and closeness of the coming winter. This caterpillar is the weathercaster, the animal that reveals changes in the climate. When the woolly caterpillar appears, there will occur a change in the climate of our life.

This caterpillar hibernates and then spins a cocoon in the spring. Adult moths emerge in two weeks and lay eggs in clusters. These eggs hatch, the caterpillars grow, pupate, and emerge as adults. These adults then lay eggs from which emerge and grow the woolly caterpillars seen in the autumn. These offspring of this second generation are the ones who hibernate as caterpillars.

The woolly caterpillar is most common in the fall, seen scurrying on the ground, usually searching for a place to hibernate. When this caterpillar appears, fall may be a time to pull back and hibernate a little, waiting for spring before we emerge fully. Its appearance is often an indication that this rhythm will work best for our projects and us. Any project not completely reaching maturity and fruition by the fall should be held over until the spring for the most benefit. Any other time frame will be premature and possibly fruitless.

When you touch a woolly caterpillar, it curls up like an armadillo, protected by its dense covering of stiff bristles. They are difficult to pick up because the bristles make them slide out of the grasp. When the woolly caterpillar appears as a messenger, especially in the fall, it is time to trust in the changes that are coming. Even though they may be unclear, and we can't quite get a grasp on the particulars of the changes, trust that they are coming and will benefit us.

KEYNOTE

- forecasting
- a change of climate for future generations

Are you ignoring the signs you have been receiving?

Are you preparing for the changes, even though they have not fully defined themselves?

Are you protecting yourself in the midst of the changes?

Is it time to change the climate of your life?

Part V

Kingdom of Reptiles and Amphibians

Who knoweth the spirit of man that goeth upward, and the spirit of the beast that goeth downward to the earth?
ECCLESIASTES 3:21

Never say there is nothing beautiful in the world anymore. There is always something to make you wonder...
ALBERT SCHWEITZER

CHAPTER 12

Exoptic Language of the Ancients

Reptiles are one of the most ancient groups of animals upon the planet. There are over 6000 species of reptiles, with lizards and snakes making up the largest quantity of them. Crocodiles and alligators, along with tortoises and turtles, comprise another large component of the reptile kingdom. In some cases they are distantly related to the dinosaurs that once walked the Earth. Most, though, evolved from amphibians more than 300 million years ago.

Reptiles are distinguished from other animals by distinct qualities and characteristics. Their body temperature changes according to the environment in which they are. They are cold-blooded. Mammals have an internal thermostat, but if reptiles get cold, they must seek out warm places. This is why snakes and other reptiles are often seen basking in the sun. It is also why they are associated with the element of fire. Reptiles also have scales that protect them, and most reptiles have at least one full lung.

Amphibians are included among The Ancients because most reptiles evolved from them. These include frogs, toads, and salamanders. They have similar adaptive characteristics to reptiles, but amphibians have actually lead a double life. Their time is divided between the land and water, and many go through their own metamorphosis. Frogs go from tadpoles to frog, from a gill breather to a lung breather. Salamanders breathe partially through their skin. Unlike reptiles, though, amphibians have no fur, feathers, or scales. They will usually have toes at some stage, but no claws.

Most reptiles and amphibians lay eggs, although a few species of lizards and snakes give birth to live young. Only a few reptiles will actually care for their young. For most amphibians and reptiles, once the eggs hatch, the young must survive on their own. Because of this, reptiles and amphibians teach us about enterprises, survival, self-sufficiency, and self-reliance.

All reptiles and amphibians are cold-blooded and this is very symbolic. Whenever reptiles show up, there will be increased sensitivity to the environments in which we find ourselves. Reptiles and amphibians teach us to be selective about what environments we expose ourselves to.

Amphibians, like a variety of reptiles, will shed their skins as they outgrow them. The shedding of skin is tremendously symbolic and further relates this group to the element of fire. Fire burns away the old so that the new can be born, an ancient symbol of transformation, resurrection, and rebirth. This same process is reflected in the shedding of the skin by amphibians and some reptiles. As a group, they are symbols of change and transformation within our life. They provide insight into the death and rebirth process occurring around us and how dramatic, intense, productive, and creative it is.

Reptiles and Amphibians and the Initiation of Fire

➤ Fire has always been regarded as something mysterious. The manner in which smoke rises and melts into the air was considered magical. It is an ancient symbol of passion, spirituality, sexuality, and transition—as are most of the animals found within its grouping.

Like water, fire is both creative and destructive. The element of fire is found within all life, and many societies had special initiatory rites associated with it. The initiation or "baptism of fire" encompasses trials of strength and balance. Through these we learn to see what must be burned out, what is no longer beneficial, so that the new can be born. It is the discovery of our relationships with others and what they teach us about ourselves. The relationships may create change and turmoil, but these are the fires of experience.

The cycle of life, death, and rebirth is part of the element of fire. It is a creative process that has its own balance within it that is ancient and misunderstood. It is often reflected in the image of the *ouroborous*, the snake swallowing its own tail. All of the animals of this element teach us how to work with this cycle in some way.

The spirits of the element of fire are traditionally known as salamanders, not because they look like them, but because when seen within fire, their bodies tapered into the flames like the tail of a serpent or salamander.

Ancient and misunderstood like fire, reptiles and salamanders were chosen as the animals to represent this element. Like fire that adjusts to its environment, reptiles are cold-blooded. Their environment directly affects their body temperature. Through these animals we learn to keep our creative fires strong, giving them new birth and new expression in whatever environment in which we find ourselves.

Reptiles and the Empathic Response

➤ The response of reptiles and amphibians to their environment because of their cold-bloodedness links reptiles as totems to empathic responses. In humans, empathy is a heightened form of feeling. It is one of the most ancient of the healing arts, but also one of the most difficult to control.

With empathy, the body becomes a barometer for what is being experienced. Experiences register upon the body as if they are the individual's own. For example, most hypochondriacs that I have counseled have been empathic. The aches, pains, illnesses, etc. that they "know" they have have been picked up psychically from others they have been around. They do not really have the illnesses, but their own psychic sensitivity causes the illnesses to register upon their body as if truly their own.

For those to whom reptiles and amphibians appear as totems and messengers, it will be important to be aware of this tendency. You will become more sensitive to the environments in which you enter, more likely to be affected by them for good or bad. If you are in a partying group, you may find yourself as the one with the lampshade upon the head. If it is a depressed group, you may find yourself the most depressed or even suicidal. There will be a greater potential for taking on the temperature or energy of the environment in which you find yourself. Vigilance, control, and maintaining your own personal space will be important.

For those to whom the reptiles and amphibians are messengers, empathy will need to be understood more fully. Empathic individuals need to pay attention to and honor what they feel. This is not always easy to do. We have not been trained to honor our intuitive aspects. Someone or something may appear to be O.K., but with the empathic individual it won't be until the actual touch occurs that a true assessment

of the person or situation will crystallize. Remember that reptiles and amphibians have highly developed feeling natures.

Reptiles and amphibians teach us that if we do not honor what we feel, it will likely get us into trouble. Most of the time, the impressions we get, no matter how strange, will be correct. Trusting those feelings is part of what all reptiles and amphibians teach us.

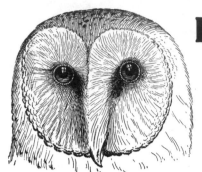

Notes

CHAPTER 13

Dictionary of Reptiles and Amphibians

All reptiles and amphibians have certain qualities in common. They are, of course, cold-blooded, which means the temperature of their surroundings affects their body temperatures. Because of this, when reptiles and amphibians appear there is always greater susceptibility to be affected or to affect our own environments on some level. Only a study of the specific species will helps us understand the exact message as it applies to our life.

Amphibians differ a bit from reptiles. They have a naked skin. For many the skin will shed as they grow, but the old one is often eaten. Water is absorbed often through the skin, moisture being important to their breathing. Oxygen and CO_2 are also exchanged through the skin. As amphibians mature, they go from being gill breathers to lung breathers. Like reptiles, they are also cold-blooded and easily affected by their environment.

In this chapter, you can find specific information about the following reptiles and amphibians:

- basilisk
- chameleon
- cobra
- copperhead
- corn snake
- cottonmouth
- crocodile
- frog
- garter snake
- gecko
- Gila monster
- green anole
- horned lizard
- iguana
- Komodo dragon
- milk snake
- newts
- painted turtle
- python
- rat snake
- rattlesnake
- salamander
- sea turtle
- skink
- snapping turtle
- tadpole
- toad
- tortoise
- tuatara

Basilisk

KEYNOTE

- **dragon energies about**

- **guardianship and wonders**

BASILISK

(*Basiliscus mitratus*)

Any of several tropical American lizards of the genus *Basilicus*, of the iguana family. This genus is remarkable for a membranous bag rising above the occiput, which can be filled with air; also for an elevated crest along the back, that can be raised or depressed at will.

➤ The basilisk is an iguana lizard of tropical America, named after the basilisk dragon, a dragon of great virulence. It was cobralike and often depicted as a terrifying creature. It could breathe fire and spew a deadly venom and could even kill with a single look from its eyes. If a human laid eyes upon the basilisk before the basilisk laid eyes upon the human, the human would live. Otherwise the human died.

Much of the lore of the basilisk dragon is symbolic. The perception that it could kill with a single look probably had more to do with the shock of seeing something so strange and powerful. The death was often symbolic of the death of some aspect of the person's life. He or she would never be the same.

As frightening as the basilisk dragon was made to appear, it had many magical qualities:

It's skin could repel snakes and spiders, and silver rubbed with its ashes would become gold. Crystal would reflect its deadly vision and venom. It has been said that the eyes are the gateways to the soul, and it is through the basilisk form of the dragon that we learn to read the true soul of individuals by looking into their eyes. This dragon has the knowledge of how to use the eyes to entrance and control.[1]

In the America tropics, a basilisk can grow to be two feet with a long tapering tail. Unlike its namesake, though, it is only dangerous to birds and rodents, although it will also eat some vegetation. When this lizard appears in our life, we can truly expect an awakening of dragon energies.

The basilisk has a crest that runs down its back and neck. Lizards with crests along the spine usually the heightening of the sensitivities of their corresponding chakras. For the basilisk,

---

[1] Ted Andrews. *Enchantment of the Faerie Realm* (St. Paul, MN: Llewellyn Publications, 1993), p. 183.

we can expect that our inner vision—that ability to see into the souls of others—and our power of expression will increase. We must learn to control these abilities, for dragon energy is strong and vocal expressions will be experienced more intensely. Things said lovingly will be felt more lovingly. Things said to cut and hurt will hurt more deeply.

Basilisk
(cont.)

If danger approaches, the basilisk will run away on its long hind legs. This skilled runner can even traverse water for short distances without sinking. Dragons are fantastic creatures of great wonder. Theirs is the force of strength and spiritual power through which the impossible becomes possible. The basilisk's ability to run on water is a reminder of this.

Are we being too aggressive?

Are we ignoring our perceptions?

Are we confronting and fighting when we should be avoiding?

When the basilisk appears, the dragon energy is alive within our life. New realms will open, including more tangible experiences associated with the Faerie Realm. The climate of your life will change. The basilisk is the guardian and a keeper of the creative force of life. Higher perceptions and intuitive abilities will awaken in ways not even imagined. When the basilisk appears, we must learn to control our intensities.

Are we not guarding our creations?

Are we not taking advantage of opportunities for change?

Have we forgotten that we can starve as much from a lack of wonder as we can from a lack of food?

Chameleon

KEYNOTE

news of changing environments

COMMON CHAMELEON (*Chamaeleon vulgaris*) of North Africa, Syria, etc.

Any of a group of peculiar Old World acrodont lizards having a laterally compressed body, prehensile tail, and opposed digits. They are very slow in their movements, but can shoot out their tongue for a distance nearly equaling their length to catch insects. The skin is covered with small granules; the eyeballs are very large and are moved independently of each other, but the lids are fused together, leaving only a small central opening. They are remarkable for the changes of color of the skin, which depend on the temper and passions of the animal, as well as on surrounding conditions....From it's power of living for long periods without food, the chameleon was formerly supposed to feed upon air.

➤ True chameleons are some of the most fascinating of all lizards. Chameleons can change color in response to changes in light, temperature, and emotional state. The color change is partly camouflage and partly a mood communication. The appearance of the chameleon heralds news of a changing environment—news and changes that will be good.

The eyes of the chameleon can rotate, moving independently of each other. This enables it to detect food or dangers more clearly and rapidly. Whenever the chameleon appears, our own spiritual sight is going to become more independent, more active, and more beneficial to us. We will begin to see things coming from any direction more clearly, and we should trust what we perceive.

When chameleons see an insect or other prey within their range, they shoot out a tongue that is longer than their own body. The insect gets caught on the sticky tongue tip and is whipped back into their mouth. Such an attack can occur within a second, and it is a reminder that we must act immediately and quickly when opportunities present themselves. The appearance of chameleon alerts us to coming opportunities so that we can partake of them when they appear.

Some chameleons lay eggs and others give birth to live young. Regardless of how they are born, within a day of being born or hatched, the young begin catching prey. When chameleons appear, opportunities and gifts that present themselves should be snatched and acted upon within a day or the opportunity may be lost. Although they are slow moving, chameleons respond quickly and immediately to food that presents itself. Chameleon's appearance now alerts us to follow that example.

The male has three rigid horns, one projecting from the nose and the other two from between the eyes on the forehead. The male and female have prehensile tales and powerfully engineered toes for clutching and climbing.

Chameleons are slow moving animals. Rarely do they move more than one leg at a time and they anchor it firmly before moving the next leg. When the chameleon appears, we may be trying to move too quickly. We may be getting ahead of ourselves, and we need to slow down and make sure we are firmly anchored before acting or responding. We should wait until the offer is made before we act upon it. We should not rush anything now.

Chameleons do change their color according to mood, often as a signal to other chameleons. For example, an angry chameleon can almost turn black. When the chameleon appears, the moods of those around us and our moods are likely to change, sometimes dramatically. Because of this, we should not commit ourselves fully or completely until we see how the moods are going to change, especially in regards to new endeavors. The mood change that is likely to occur will create an uncomfortable relationship.

Chameleon
(cont.)

Are we becoming too sensitive to the environment?

Are we seeing or reading things that are not there?

Are we acting too hastily?

Are we not staying grounded and balanced as we follow new pursuits?

Are we hesitant to act on opportunities?

Are we ignoring signs?

Cobra

KEYNOTE

**swift, sudden
decisions and actions**

COBRA OF EGYPT
(*Naja haje*)

A very venemous snake (*Naja tripudians*) of the warm parts of Asia, especially abundant in India. It sometimes reaches a length of five feet, but is usually much smaller, and is very variable in color. When excited, it expands the skin of the neck into a broad hood by a movement of the ribs. It is of sluggish disposition, seldom biting except in self-defense, but often enters gardens and houses, where (especially at night) it is likely to be trodden on. In India alone it causes over 5,000 deaths annually. The name is extended to other related snakes, as *Naja haje* of Africa, and the *king cobra*.

➤ In India and Sri Lanka, the cobra is sometimes referred to as naja or naga. The cobra is associated with the serpentine type of dragon, also known as a basilisk. In lore, the basilisk was very cobra-like, breathing fire and having deadly venom that could kill with a look of its eyes, but from it one could learn to read the inner soul of any person. When the cobra appears, we can expect an awakening and heightening of our own intuitive vision that will enable us to make swift decisions and take quick actions that will benefit us tremendously. Now is not a time for hesitation.

Most cobras are medium sized snakes and when frightened or excited, rear up. Movable ribs spread the skin behind the neck until it forms a flattish hood. Anyone who comes too near the cobra in this state is likely to be bitten. When the cobra appears, we should keep our senses alert because the likelihood of unexpected opportunities is about to take place. Opportunities to strike in business are very near, and we should be ready.

Taking advantage of these unexpected opportunities may seem impulsive to others, but we should trust our own instincts. What may be foolishly impulsive for others will be successfully impulsive for us right now. This is further reflected in the fact that cobras will often guard their eggs, a reminder that we must guard our endeavors until ready to act, and then act upon them swiftly.

Indian snake charmers try to make people believe that it is the song of their flutes that cause the cobra to dance, but the cobra is actually following the movement of the flute and not the music. When cobra appears, we should be alert to subtle movements and signs. We should not be distracted by what others might say. It is a time to trust in what we perceive regardless of appearances. If we do so, we will be a strong position and we can respond in the most beneficial manner for us.

The venom of the cobra contains poisons that affect the nervous system. Victims may experience heart failure and breathing failure in as little as fifteen minutes. Some cobras attack by spitting venom directly into the eyes of the victim, causing blindness for a time. The cobra often heralds a time to keep our eyes open and be alert. We may be blind to what is occurring around us or to our opportunities. We may be allowing fear and doubts to prevent our taking appropriate actions.

However, the cobra sometimes reflects a time to withdraw and to not act impulsively. This is further reinforced by the fact that sometimes cobras will play dead when threatened or frightened. If we are not sure how to react, we should not react at all. We should make sure that we have all of the facts straight, that we are clearly seeing everything before we take action.

Cobra
(cont.)

Are we not acting when the opportunities present themselves?

Are we acting to hastily and without thinking?

Are we disorganized and not able to see all of the facts?

Are we feeling uneasy?

Are we oversensitive right now, taking affront inappropriately?

Are we being too trustful?

Too distrustful?

Do we need to protect our endeavors a little more closely?

Is there a hidden poison around us—emotionally, mentally, or spiritually?

Copper-head

KEYNOTE

- **aggressive healing and change**

- **auric vision and sensitivity**

COPPERHEAD

(*Agkistrodon contortrix*)

A poisonous snake allied to the rattlesnake, but without rattles, found in most parts of the eastern United States. It becomes about three feet long, and is coppery brown above with dark transverse, somewhat hourglass-shaped markings. It is viviparous and inhabits chiefly damp places, and is quicker and more aggressive than the rattleshake.

➤ The copperhead is a poisonous snake related to the rattlesnake. It has a coppery head from which it gets its name, and it also has hourglass-shaped body patches. The hourglass is a reminder of the lessons of most snakes—the continuing cycle of life, death, and rebirth. It is sinuous and fast, growing to 30 inches or more. The head is broad and roughly triangular due to the venom glands, one of the distinguishing physical features of most poisonous snakes.

The copperhead has a pit between the eyes and nostrils that is very sensitive to heat, helping them to find and strike at warm-blooded prey. When the copperhead appears, our own sensitivity to others will increase. We will sense the auras of others—which reflects their true essence—more easily and clearly.

Around all things that have an atomic structure is an energy field called the aura, which is composed of electrical and magnetic energy frequencies and it also has thermal aspects. Learning to see and feel the aura will often alert us to opportunities and dangers. When the copperhead appears as a totem or messenger, we will become more sensitive to the auras of others. We will feel and see them clearly, and our perceptions of those individuals will become increasingly based upon those accurate perceptions.

When snakes attack, they do so quickly. They raise themselves up and strike hard and true to the mark. When encountered, many poisonous snakes will alert and warn, and even move out of the way if they feel they will be disturbed. The copperhead rarely moves on. It will stand its ground, expecting the intruders to go around it. If disturbed, it will attack rather than move. The copperhead brings a message of standing one's ground, even if only based upon a "feeling." And if need be, do not hesitate to strike in defense of oneself. In time, that feeling will prove itself out and standing your ground will be confirmed as having been the right thing to do.

All venomous snakes have lessons associated with healing and toxicity around us. They sometimes appear to awaken our own innate healing energies and abilities. They also appear to herald the need to cleans and purify some area of our life. They reflect a change in the chemistry of our body or our life situation—not necessarily for good or bad but just a change.

Most vipers or poisonous snakes give birth to live young and one of the mysteries of the copperhead is that twice as many males are born as females. The male energy is associated with the electrical, assertive aspects of life. When the copperhead appears, it is usually an indication we need to get more assertive and aggressive in our healing and other activities. If the copperhead has appeared, we should take a look at the process of death and rebirth in some area of our life, particularly associated with healing.

Are we not asserting our energies as strongly as we should?

Are we not striking?

Are we giving up our position rather than standing our ground?

Are we ignoring our perceptions of others, even though there is nothing tangible to base them on?

Are we striking out when we shouldn't be?

What needs to be healed?

Corn Snake

KEYNOTE

- easier movement
- a lifting up

➤ There are two ideas as to where the corn snake got its name. One is that it was named because it is often found in cornfields and corncribs. Another theory is that its name reflects the similarity of its belly markings to the checkered patterns of kernels on Indian corn. Either way, it is wise to study the significance of corn as a plant totem for even more insight to this animal.

Corn snakes are part of the rat snake family, and thus it should be studied as well. It is one of the more colorful members, and they are also known as the red rat snake because they usually have reddish-brown or crimson blotches. These are the colors of the earth and soil with a lot of iron in it. Sometimes this can be a reminder to examine our intake of iron in our own diet.

The corn snake is a constrictor, and like many such snakes, it can hiss and vibrate its tail when cornered. It is found in woods and open country and feeds mostly on mice, but occasionally eat frogs, lizards, birds, and eggs. Like all rat snakes, it lays eggs, usually in rotted logs and stumps.

All rat snakes are excellent climbers and every member of this species teaches us how to climb to new heights or are signs that we will soon have or be in the midst of opportunities to climb. Their climbing ability is improved because they have specially shaped belly scales which curve upward where they meet the sides, giving the snake better traction. This often indicates we will get our feet underneath us and be able to move a little more easily than what we may have in the recent past.

Do we need to set our sights a little higher?

Are we not climbing or taking advantage of opportunities when they appear?

Do we need to hold onto and squeeze all we can from what we have?

Are we grateful for what we have?

Are we allowing ourselves to stay in a rut when a new path would be easier?

Cotton-mouth

➤ Swamps are often considered places of fear, danger, and mystery. They have been associated with haunting and wandering specters. Swamps are places where strange creatures abound that are rarely understood. They are places of decomposition, where there is a breaking down of the old and a building up of the new. They are often the doorways to the Underworld.

The cottonmouth, sometimes known as the water moccasin, is a snake of the swamps and marshes. It gets its name from the white insides of its mouth, which it opens and shows as a warning display. Gaping is a display of threat.

The cottonmouth is a thickly built, venomous snake that is dark and not strongly marked. It is more vicious than many other snakes of its kind, swamp snakes that feed on fish and frogs. Among vipers, only the cottonmouth is an important fish eater, although it eats a variety of other prey.

As with all venomous animals, there are associations with healing and the detoxifying life. They often reflect that the chemistry of our life is about to change. When the cottonmouth appears, there is usually an underworld initiation about to occur. Most traditions teach the crossing of the Underworld to get to some transformative state of being. The Underworld is connected to the place of birth, the land, heritage, and all of its powers and magic. It is returning to the chemistry of our true essence.

Initiations are beginnings, new births:

> The Initiation of the Underworld, deals with dangerous interactions; but they only destroy the inflated personality, the fear-riddled mask that tyrannizes our individuality...Understanding initiation is not gained by reading books, though intellectual clues and stimulus are useful, but by a change of direction.[2]

WATER MOCCASIN
(*Agkistrodon piscivorus*)
A poisonous snake...of the southern United States closely related to the copperhead. Above, it is dull dark chestnut brown, barred with black; beneath, is black, blotched with yellowish white. It reaches a length of about four feet, is found in or near the water, and feeds largely on fishes.

*Are we truly wishing
to heal our lives?*

*Are we looking
to transform?*

*Do we put on displays
showing form but no
substance?*

*Do we need to attack our
fears more aggressively?*

*Are we ready to face our
greatest fears and
awaken our
greatest gifts?*

---

[2] R.J. Stewart. *The Underworld Initiation* (Northamptonshire, GB: Aquarian Press, 1985), p. 68.

Cottonmouth
(cont.)

The Underworld Initiation links the inner and the outer through our physical body and our physical life environment.

The cottonmouth is a guardian and guide through the underworld, the place where we face our fears, masks, and shadow selves. This animal of the dark gods and goddesses functions as a catalyst, initiating the experience that will transform us.

Most snakes can swim quite well, and the cottonmouth is one of the best. In fact, it is the one viper that is normally associated with water and is well adapted to this environment. The eyes and nostrils are located toward the top of the head so that it can breathe and see while it swims along the surface of the water. It has keeled scales, which help it to swim. Because of this, it becomes both guardian and guide as we delve into new realms and tap deeper waters.

When the cottonmouth appears, an initiation is at hand. Opportunity to cross into strange lands will occur in some area of our life. In many ways, it is a crossing of faith and fear.

Animal Wonders

ALLIGATOR NESTS

For the Florida alligator, nest-building is a simple matter of creating a pile of mud and swamp vegetation with a few swipes of the female's powerful tale. She then lays and buries the eggs within. While she does patrol the nest to prevent the eggs from being eaten, once the young are hatched, they are entirely on their own.

Crocodile

KEYNOTE

**primal strength
and creation**

CROCODILE OF THE NILE
(*Crocodilus niloticus*)
Any of several large, thick-skinned, long-tailed, aquatic reptiles of the genus *Crocodilus*; also, in a wider sense, any reptile of the family Crocodilidae or order Crocodilla....True crocodiiles are found in the waters of tropical Africa, Asia, Australia, and America....It reaches a length of 12 feet, but some species of other countries become much larger....The eggs are laid in the sand and hatched by the sun's heat. They are found chiefly in fresh water, but some enter or frequent brackish or even salt water. In some localities they are dangerous to man.

➤ The crocodile family includes the largest of all living reptiles. They live in tropical parts of the world and have an ancient and mixed symbology and mythology associated with both destruction and birth. They are the devourers and mothers. Crocodiles in particular are associated with the Great Mother, for they are excellent mothers, a rarity among reptiles. The appearance of the crocodile indicates the presence of primal strength and creation, the mothering forces.

Although cold-blooded, crocodiles rarely let their body temperatures vary much. They come ashore at sunrise to bask in the sun and then they cool off in the water as the sun becomes hotter. They float low in the water, with little more than eyes and nostrils showing. When crocodile appears, it heralds a time of balance within all environments within our life. The balance may come unexpectedly, but it will come as a result of our own efforts, strengths, and creativity. It is time to trust our instincts in what will work.

The Nile crocodile breeds when 5 to 10 years old and the males will fight for breeding territories. The female will dig a huge pit and can lay up to 90 eggs. After four months, the eggs hatch, and the mother crocodile takes the hatchlings in her mouth down to the water, guarding them from other predators. When the crocodile appears, we should watch over and protect the things we give birth to for at least a four-month period. We may get assistance from others or assist others in some new births.

Our instincts will be very accurate and strong in regards to whom or what we can trust. Our creative energies are fertile now, along with practical applications. This is the time to trust what is right for us, our home, our children, and our endeavors. We have the opportunity to tap very primal creative energies. New birth and initiation are near, as is the strength necessary to accomplish them.

Crocodile
(cont.)

Are we ignoring our instincts, our intuition?

Are we missing creative opportunities?

Are we being too emotional about what we have created?

Are we trusting those we shouldn't?

Are we being too domineering?

Are we unbalanced and too open?

When the young crocodiles begin to develop within the eggs, they begin to squeak. The mother hears them, answers them, and helps them to hatch. She then assists them to the water, carrying them in her mouth. If crocodile has appeared, it is time to heed our primal instincts or we may miss the calls of new creative opportunities.

An adult crocodile captures its prey by lying in wait near game trails and water holes. It then comes out of the water, seizing its prey in its powerful jaws, dragging the prey under water, trying to drown it or knocking it out with its whipping tail. The crocodile may even grip the prey's body in its jaws, rolling over and over beneath the water, tearing into it. The crocodile may indicate that we are not taking advantage of our opportunities or our impulses. We may also need to be careful of things that are hidden and unexpected, especially in environments that usually nourish us. There may be reason for distrust. If we are not careful, we may be in danger of being dragged into or under in some way.

➤ Frogs have a tremendous mythology and lore about them. They have been associated with the Faerie Realm and Egyptian goddesses and gods (Herit, Isis, and Osiris). To some peoples of the Amazon, they call the rains and influence the climate. In Europe they are frequently associated with healing. Whenever frog appears, we are entering a time of new beginnings. The creative energies are awakening, and it is a time for new birth and new starts.

Frogs are amphibians, meaning they spend part of their life in the water and part upon the land. They are found everywhere within the world except Antarctica. All frogs go through metamorphosis, and their appearance reflects a time of transformation for us as well. From the eggs come tadpoles or polliwogs, From the tadpoles come frogs. They go from being gill breathers, living within the water (polliwog stage) to being lung breathers upon the land and the water (frog stage). Because the polliwog resembles the male spermatozoa, frogs are the heralds of abundance and fertility on all levels. Frog's appearance can signal a possible birth or pregnancy for someone close to us.

The frog heralds an ideal time to initiate new starts in business. It is a wonderful time to explore and seek out a new career, job, or way of life. The appearance of the frog is a reflection of the maturity and transformation from the polliwog stage. It is time to hop into new areas of endeavors. It is beneficial to accept invitations and offers.

Frogs are keenly attuned to sound. They possess a very sensitive tympanic organ, and their element (water) is a tremendous conductor of sound vibrations. Their croaking is a means of attracting a mate. If frog has appeared, we should listen for new opportunities and know that our ability to persuade and influence people to par-

Frog

KEYNOTE

- fertility
- new beginnings

LEOPARD FROG
(*Rana pipiens*)

Any of numerous tailless leaping amphibians of the genus *Rana* and other more or less nearly allied genera. The term is not a definitely limited one. A typical frog differs externally from a typical toad (genus *Bufo*) in its more aquatic habits, smooth skin, webbed feet, much greater agility in leaping and swimming, as well as in certain anatomical characters, but many intermediate forms occur which are called by either name....The ordinary frogs feed on small fishes, worms, etc., and lay their eggs in water, in large clusters inclosed in a jellylike secretion. The young hatch out as tadpoles, in which state some species pass a year, or even more, before assuming the adult form.

Frog
(cont.)

Are we ignoring new opportunities?

Are we mired in the mud of our day-to-day life?

Do we need to dive into some fresh waters?

Are we becoming bogged down in emotions and not transforming them?

Are we becoming too mundane?

Are re repeating old patterns and mistakes rather than moving onto new things?

Are we resisting change and hesitant to use our own creative forces?

ticipate in new beneficial endeavors is very great right now. Frog's appearance heralds an awakening of the unique and creative powers of our own voice.

Outside of the breeding season, the frog is a solitary creature, living around marshes, ponds, and damp woodlands or grasslands. As adults, they always remain semi-aquatic. When frog appears, the old waters we have been working and living in may be becoming stagnant and dirty. It is time to clean them up. There may be something murky about what we are trying to initiate or with whom we are associating.

The frog can indicate a need to take a serious second look before initiating anything new or starting with someone new. This does not mean to give up the possibility of change and new starts, but we may need to plan further before proceeding. Rather than starting now, a delay or temporary canceling of our endeavors may be best at this time. Frog may indicate a need to re-examine offers from others and can herald that solitary efforts are more productive now than partnership or group endeavors.

Animal

POLLUTION TESTERS

Amphibians are like living pollution testers. They reveal much about the health of the Earth because they are so sensitive to such a wide variety of environmental poisons. That's because they live part of their lives in water and part of their lives in damp soil. Thus, they are exposed to both land and water pollutants. They also have no scales to protect them. A study of the amphibian life within an environment will reveal tremendous insight into pollution problems affecting the area and other indigenous wildlife.

Wonders

➤ Garter snakes are probably better known than any other snake. Thirteen species can be found throughout the U.S. and Canada. They are not poisonous and often have yellow, red, or orange stripes running down their body.

Unlike most snakes, the garter gives birth to live young rather than laying eggs. Snakes that give birth to live young, are strong messages. They remind us that we do not need a time to incubate our ideas. We should act on them and immediately get them off and running as quickly as possible.

The young garter snakes are born in litters of 20 to 50 or more. When the garter appears as a totem or messenger, it often indicates a tremendously creative time. Ideas and inspirations will flow, and it will be important to act on as many of them as possible.

In the first few months of their life, garter snakes have a very heavy death rate, due mainly to predators and starvation. This reinforces the idea of initiating and acting upon as many creative ideas as possible, even if those ideas may seem premature. The first few months will see a heavy toll on them, but those that do take will survive and grow. A garter snake can live for twelve years in the wild. Some of the ideas and endeavors will not make it initially, but others will, and the percentages will work in your favor.

Most garter snakes are fairly docile, but they will eject an unpleasant fluid from vent glands when captured. It is not unusual for those to whom the garter appears as a messenger to have problems with indigestion and gas when stressed.

Garter Snake

KEYNOTE

act on as many ideas as possible

Are you acting on your ideas or keeping them to yourself?

Are you allowing stresses to hinder your creative efforts?

Are you too worried about failing that you do not even put forth strong efforts?

Gecko

KEYNOTE

**do what must be
done in struggles**

GECKO

(*Platydactylus muralis*)

Any lizard of the family
Geckonidae. The typical
geckos are small, more or less
nocturnal, animals with large
eyes and vertical elliptical
pupils. Their vertebrae are
amphicoelous and their toes
are generally expanded and
furnished with adhesive disks,
by which they can run over
walls and ceilings. They are
numerous in most warm
countries....Though often
considered poisonous, they
are absolutely harmless and
are useful in destroying
insects.

*Are we too involved to see
what is going on around us?*

*Do we need some
emotional objectivity?*

*Do we need to detach
ourselves from things of the
past so that we can have
harmony in the present?*

Are we being too defensive?

*Are we hesitating to take
the proper action?*

*Are we not asserting
ourselves strongly enough?*

*Are we asserting ourselves
too aggressively?*

Are we being too sensitive?

➤ Geckos are wonderfully attractive lizards, usually recognized by their large, lidless eyes with
vertical pupils, much like those of cats. These
nocturnal animals are the only lizards that have
their own bark or call whose voice can be heard
clearly. While most are docile, they seldom hesitate biting when provoked and their appearance
tells us to do what we must in all struggles.

When gecko appears, there is usually opposing energies or strife already at play within our
life. Its appearance now is a signal that we should
not be docile or passive. The situations around us
now demand clarity in regards to how we feel and
how we act. Now is the time to be firm in all responses. If there is competition and opposition,
we should respond sharply. If we do, our efforts
will be rewarded and we will be less likely to encounter that kind of opposition and strife again.

Geckos are nocturnal, hiding in crevices and
such during the day. At night they feed on insects. It is important to pay attention to dreams
when gecko appears, as the dreams will often
bring insight as to the sources of conflict and
strife around us. It is common to have dream
conflicts, and the people in the dreams show us
with whom the conflicts are arising during the
day. Dreams now will likely reveal the pests we
must confront.

Geckos are great exterminators of insect pests,
and in parts of the world are kept in homes specifically for that purpose. When gecko appears, it
is time to do what we must to restore order and
bring conflicts to an end in the home. It is time
to handle the in-house pests. If we are firm and
clear, we can resolve it all. Gecko reminds us that
the stress and conflict will only get worse unless
we take action. Gecko teaches us the importance
of righteous anger and the need for proper responses to the causes of that anger.

The tails of most geckos break off easily. This
is an adaptation they have developed to fend off

predation. When the tail breaks off, the gecko can scramble to safety and will eventually grow another in its place. When the gecko appears, we may not be able to resolve the conflicts and strife that are going on currently. It may be best at this time to detach entirely from the people and situation, if only for a short time. We may need to accept that things are not going to get any better or be resolved at this time. Sometimes it is necessary to separate us or part of ourselves from others for our own good or the good of others. This detachment will at least help us to have a little more harmony in our life.

➤ The Gila monster is one of only two poisonous lizards in the world. Its name comes from the Gila basin in Arizona where this lizard is plentiful. It can measure as large as two feet. It has a large blunt head, a thick tail, and a stout body that is mainly black with pink and yellow patches.

They spend much of their time burrowed in the sand and under rocks by day. Because they move slowly, they cannot catch fast moving prey and feed on rodents, eggs, baby birds, and such. If food is scarce, their own body fat can yield the nourishment they need to sustain them. They have been known to live two to three years without a meal. Because of this ability to go without food,, the Gila monster is a sign to maintain our control and beliefs, and they will sustain us as long as is necessary.

The Gila monster heralds a time of greater discretion in using our resources, especially in forthcoming endeavors. This is a time to protect our own affairs but not to overextend ourselves beyond our means. We should hold on to what we have, but reserve any pushing toward new things until a more appropriate time. Otherwise, we may leave ourselves short. We have what we need to preserve and maintain our present status,

Gecko
(cont.)

Gila Monster

KEYNOTE

maintaining control and beliefs

GILA MONSTER

(*Heloderma suspectum*)

A large stout lizard...with a rough tuberculated skin and thick tail, found in the arid regions of Arizona, New Mexico, etc. It is dull orange and black in color and of sluggish but ugly disposition. It sometimes attains a length of about two feet....The bite of these lizards is venomous, the poison glands, unlike those of snakes, being in lower jaw. They are believed to be the only poisonous lizards.

Gila Monster
(cont.)

Are we not maintaining control of our environment?

Are we being impatient and exposing ourselves prematurely?

Are we or those around us more vulnerable right now?

Are we not showing gratitude and appreciation for what we already have?

Are we bending under adversity, refusing to fight back and protect what is ours?

Have we not prepared properly?

Are we overextending our affairs and ourselves?

but any attempts at expansion now will tap our reserves and could create shortages.

Gila monsters do have poisonous glands in the lower jaw. The poison is not injected, but may enter a wound when the Gila monster bites. Their poisonous bite is deadly and is used mainly for defense. Although usually slow and clumsy, Gila monsters can twist their heads, bite swiftly and hang on tightly. When it appears, it is a time to maintain and defend our position strongly. This is not a time to show weakness, and if necessary we should strike hard and swift. By doing so we protect what is ours. The Gila monster is a reminder to protect our beliefs as well as our possessions, but we should do so with discretion. Only if actually attacked should we defend—and then as strongly as we can. By doing so we protect our affairs and our possessions and we persevere.

The desert and steppe climate in which Gila monsters are found reveals a significant aspect of their behavior. They cannot take the extremes of heat found within these environments and thus they take refuge during the day under rocks and buried in the sand until cooler times of the day when they emerge and hunt. When the Gila monster appears, we must be careful not to get out of sync with a rhythm of life that is more beneficial for us. We may be trying to force something that is not healthy or suitable, and we may get burnt in the process. This is not a time to expose ourselves inappropriately.

The Gila monster may reflect a time to pull back. Initiatives now are not likely to succeed if there is not complete preparation for the tasks at hand. Gila monster warns to pull back and try and sustain ourselves, taking time to prepare ourselves fully if we truly wish to succeed. Any display of weakness now could be detrimental. This is a time for self-preservation—to cover all of our bases.

➤ When growing up, I remember going to the circus and seeing chameleons being sold, but what was promoted as a chameleon was actually a green anole. The green anole is a common member of the lizard family, related specifically to the iguana. They do have the ability to subtly alter their coloring according to temperature, humidity, and even emotions. The main color changes are green to brown. They have been kept as pets and given as gifts in different parts of the world as symbols of harmony and peace for the household. They represent a new foundation in relationships—personal and business.

The green anole is wonderfully adapted for climbing. They can run and climb straight up, straight down, and even sideways. They can teach us how to move in whatever direction is necessary in order to accomplish what we must, especially in establishing or restoring harmony in the home. They remind us that there are always things we can do.

The toes are the reason for their ability to climb. They are flattened and have tiny ridges on the bottom. The ridges themselves are covered with tiny hooks, which enable them to hang on and to move over surfaces that would not seem possible. The anole reflects the ability to move into areas that would not seem accessible or safe to others.

The appearance of the anole heralds a time of harmony and personal satisfaction. The task has been done well, and now is the time of harvest. Now is the time to enjoy the fruits of our labors. A new foundation of peace is being established around us.

The anole also has a pineal eye, a rudimentary third eye on top of the head through which it senses lightness and darkness. This pineal eye sets the anole's biological clock. For the greatest harmony and peace, we should trust our own inner rhythms and highly developed perceptions.

Green Anole

KEYNOTE

harmony and peace

Are we not adjusting to the environment very well?

Do we need to change our colors or direction?

Are we being overly confident?

Are we not showing our gratitude?

Do we not trust our impressions?

Are we allowing others to disrupt our harmony or spoil things for us?

Are we being careless in our judgements?

Green Anole

(cont.)

Harmony comes now through trusting our own perceptions rather than perceptions of others.

Anoles have throat fans (a stiff rib of cartilage attached to the throat that the anole can flare outward) that make its head look larger. The throat fan is usually a bright orange or red and a strong male will use it to claim territory and the right to mate with local females. The green anole may reflect that someone is intruding into our territory and we should be cautious no matter how their motives may seem. Being careless now about people and activities could rob us of harmony, peace, and personal satisfaction in our work and home.

All anoles are territorial to some degree, and when the anole appears, a new direction or a change to new territory may be in order for our greater success. Our talents and skills may be wasted in our present position, and we may not be able to build the castle we want at this time in this place. We should not be overly confident, and we should look for alternatives. This is especially true if we have been feeling unappreciated as of late. We should remember that anoles can move in any direction if they need to.

➤ The horned toad is a unique creature. In fact the only other animal like it is found in Australia. The horned toad is not really a toad at all, in spite of its appearance. It is a lizard, and more than a dozen species are found in desert lands of North America. Horned toads drink dew and hunt insects, especially ants. For those to whom this is a totem or messenger, the study of ants will also benefit you.

The head and neck are protected by spines. Lizards with ruffs and spines often indicate a heightening of their corresponding chakras. All sensitivities will be heightened——physical, emotional, mental, and spiritual.

Horned toads are very expressive. Some puff up when angered. Others flatten themselves out. When frightened, they may squirt a thin stream of blood from the corners of their eyes. It is thought that the blood will irritate the eyes of an enemy. They will also lift themselves high on their legs and hiss threateningly. Most of their behaviors are bluffs, as these animals rarely bite

For those to whom this animal appears as a totem, it will be important to express the emotions. Keep in mind too that your emotions may easily be read by others around you and so camouflaging them will be more difficult. Emotional displays will be more effective than actual confrontations. The horned toad always reflects a heightening of emotions and a need to protect them more strongly.

Horned Toad

KEYNOTE

protect your sensitivities

HORNED TOAD
(*Phrynosoma cornutum*)
Any of certain small harmless insectivorous lizards consituting the genus *Phrynosoma* of the family Iguanidae, or of the closely allied genus *Anota*. These lizards have several hornlike spines on the head, and a broad, flat body, covered with spiny scales. They inhabit the dry, sandy plains of the western (esp. the southwestern) United States, and Mexico.

Are you letting others know how you truly feel?

Do you need to protect your sensitivities more strongly?

Are we being too sensitive or not sensitive enough?

Are you keeping your emotions bottled up?

Iguana

KEYNOTE

- breaking down and simplifying of life
- climb for new goals

IGUANA

(*Iguana tuberculata*)

Any of several large tropical American lizards constituting the general *Iguana* and *Metopoceras*. The best known is I. *tuberculata* of South and Central American and parts of the West Indies, which attains a length of five or six feet. It is greenish and blackisk in color, more or less speckled and barred. The neck and back bear a high serrated crest, and there is a large gular sac (which is not dilatable) having a serrated margin. In habits it is inoffensive and entirely herbivorous, and it is esteemed as food. It is partly arboreal and frequents the vicinity of water.

Are we hanging on to things that no longer nourish us?

Do we need to simplify what we are doing in life?

Are we not learning from our past mistakes and thus are repeating them?

➤ The iguana is one of the largest groups of lizards, and all lizards are animals of great subtlety. Most have long tails to help balance and serve as defense mechanisms. Many, like the iguana, have ruffs and crests about their head. Most iguanas live on the ground, but can be excellent climbers. Some do live in trees, thus the significance of the tree, as a symbol for life should also be examined.

Common iguanas are herbivores and rely on bacteria in their gut to digest plants. This two-stage process is very symbolic for those to whom the iguana appears. First, nematode worms in the iguana's gut break down the plant food. Then bacteria break down the cell walls of the plant, releasing nutrients, absorbed by the iguana. This reflects the importance of learning to break things down to their essentials before trying to "digest" or use them.

Newly born iguanas have none of these digestive aids because the eggs and spores are incorporated in adult droppings. So the mother deposits droppings near the nest where the offspring are likely to eat them as their first meal. Then, suitably prepared, the young iguanas move on to their proper diet.

Iguana people usually have to go through the waste of others in order to find the nourishment in their own life—be it physical or spiritual. They are able to draw upon the mistakes of the past to build more fully for the future.

Iguanas are great climbers and have healthy appetites. When they appear, they remind us of our goals and dreams we may have forgotten. Our appetites for more than what we have will increase, as will opportunities to pursue them. We will be able to climb past our present circumstances if we choose to.

When iguanas appear as totems and messengers, they help us to break down the things that are no longer beneficial. They remind us it is time to simplify our life.

➤ The Komodo dragon is the largest living lizard. Found within Southern Indonesia, males can grow to 8 feet and weigh as much as 200 pounds or more. Females grow to about 7 feet and can weigh 150 pounds of more. Although around 5000 still live in the wild, only about 350 of them are breeding females. Because of this, they are considered threatened. They are solitary, powerful, and can move quickly over short distances. If Komodo dragon has appeared, now is the time to trust in our own strong survival instincts and move ahead. Now is the time for quick decisions, changes, and actions.

The dragon of lore is a creature that controls the climate, of Nature or of our life. When Komodo appears, it is this same fiery dragon energy that is being awakened. If we want to change the climate of our life, now is the time. The creative energies are strong, the impulse is there, and now is the time to act upon it. We must remember, though, that dragons and the dragon energy were never meant to be slain but to be controlled and directed. Its appearance heralds a time of new adventures and journeys, physical and spiritual, that will help us to control and direct our creative forces in the future.

The Komodo dragon can live as long as 100 years and its appearance reflects that the changes we make will be long lasting. We will experience their effects for some time to come. If we act now, the benefits will last a long time. If we fail to act, the opportunity may not return again for a long time as well.

Komodo Dragons lay 20 to 40 eggs at a time, with an incubation period that lasts approximately eight months. When Komodo Dragon appears, we will usually see a window of approximately eight months in which acting upon our impulses and instincts will work powerfully for us. We can use those impulses to initiate changes or complete what also needs to be ended. Either

Komodo Dragon

KEYNOTE

strong survival instincts and impulses

Komodo Dragon

(cont.)

Are we letting disputes hinder us?

Are we not acting decisively?

Is there jealousy about?

Are we not responding creatively to situations and opportunities?

Are we hesitating too long?

Are we speaking inappropriately to or about others?

way, we must act while we can, and as a result we will discover the primal creative power within us.

Komodo dragons are very powerful, and they usually hunt by ambush. One bite will usually kill. The bacteria in their saliva are so virulent that if the bite itself does not kill its prey or enemy, the blood poisoning that results from it will. When the Komodo dragon appears, everything we do will take on greater force and power. Because of this, we must be careful how we use our vocal power or allow others to use theirs on us. Words spoken more gently and lovingly will touch the heart. Words spoken more harshly will rip the heart out. Everything takes on greater force. We must be cautious of speaking inappropriately or too poisonously. If we suspect others of speaking in such a way about us, we should trust that suspicion but respond only when the time is right.

The Komodo dragon has a powerful tail, which it uses for defense. It can whip a crushing blow very quickly. When it appears, we may be using undo force or responding too strongly too soon. We should also be wary of others around us who, though facing us, may be trying to crush our endeavors or us with a quick unexpected whip of their tails. We should look for others trying to undermine our activities, frustrating our efforts.

Milk snakes get their name from the absurd folk belief that it milks cows, taking large amounts in the process. The milk snake is part of the king snake family. Like most non-venomous snakes, they kill prey by constriction. They usually feed on rodents, lizards, and other snakes.

Milk snakes also feed on two poisonous species: the rattlesnake and copperhead. They can feed on the venomous snakes because they are partially immune to the poison. When the milk snake appears, we will find ourselves increasingly less sensitive to the poisons of others around us. Attacks are futile, and although they can be distracting, any negative words or actions of others will cause no permanent harm to our life or us.

The banded pattern of the milk snake often causes it to be mistaken for the venomous copperhead. This often indicates you should let others think you are as "poisonous" as you may appear. It will ultimately work to your benefit.

Milk snakes are found in woodlands, rocky hillsides, grasslands, and suburbs. They are secretive and not usually seen in the open except at night. When the milk snake appears, it is important to be secretive about your activities, even if others tend to misinterpret them. All will come to light soon enough, if and when it ever becomes necessary. When the milk snake appears as a messenger, we should examine how we are letting others affect us.

Milk Snake

KEYNOTE

- secret immunity to the poisons of others
- immunity from poisons around us

THUNDER SNAKE
(*Carphophiops amoena*)
The milk snake. A reddish ground snake...of the eastern United States.

Are we being too sensitive to the bites and barbs of others?

Are we being too open about our activities?

Do we need to appear stronger and "more dangerous"?

Are we not acting out of fear of poisonous threats?

Newts

KEYNOTE

• **creative inspirations, ideas, and endeavors**

• **the return home**

NEWT

Any of various small salamanders, aquatic at least for a part of their existence; an eft or triton....In America, commonly , a salamander of the genus *Diemictylus*, of which *D. viridescens*, in the eastern United States, and *D. torosus*, on the Pacific slope, are common species.

Are you not acting on your ideas?

Do you need to come home and get back in touch with whom you truly are?

Are you ignoring your upbringing and your foundations?

➤ Newts are part of the salamander family, and thus the salamander should be studied as well for further insight into their meaning and significance within our life. Their eggs are laid in the spring and after the adults spend three or four months in the water. Water is the creative element, and it is not unusual for those to whom the newt is a messenger or totem to have actively creative and artistic early lives. Many of the creative inspirations that are such a normal part of their existence, though, may not be getting the expression they deserve.

The newt larvae leave the water to spend two to three years on land as an unusual form called the red eft. When the eft returns permanently to the water, it changes colors and develops a swimming tail. Some newts skip this eft stage, and just remain in or near their home waters.

When newts appear, this same cycle is at play within our life. There is a two to three month period of immersion in creative energies, followed by a period of two to three years of developing those energies outside in the real world. The return home is permanent, but almost always successful.

When the newt appears, it heralds a time of successful ventures in creative and artistic endeavors. There is a promise of success in doing and acting upon what is truly you. It will have the feel of finally coming home—of returning to whom you truly are.

➤ Painted turtles are some of the most common and widespread of turtles and most of their time is spent in or near water. Hardy and adaptable, they are found wherever there are ponds, swamps, ditches, or slow streams where they feed on water plants, insects, and other small animals. The appearance of painted turtle now indicates that our efforts are about to be rewarded. If we continue with what we have already set in motion, we will win. Its appearance is a sign of good news coming. Its message is power through faith and effort.

Their broad, flattened, smooth-edged shells easily identify painted turtles. The edges are marked with red, yellow, or orange, as is the skin of its head and limbs. It sometimes appears as if someone has spilled paint upon them or actually painted them. Painted turtles can teach us the importance and significance of color. Its appearance now reflects new color coming into our lives. Relationships will get better and our efforts will be rewarded. Healing will take place and new opportunities will arrive soon.

Painted turtles often gather together, and if approached quietly, they can be seen sunning themselves on logs and rocks. If we are involved in group efforts and projects, the painted turtle heralds eminent success for the group. If we continue the efforts, the good news will come, and the benefits will be longstanding and widespread. Its appearance also reflects that the group will work well together.

Males are smaller than females and both have long nails on their forefeet. The females will lay six to twelve eggs in a hole dug with their hind legs. The eggs hatch in two to three months, though some of the young may not emerge until the following spring. When painted turtle appears, we can expect our faith and efforts to be rewarded within two to three months if we continue our efforts. We must persist. The painted

Painted Turtle

KEYNOTE

faith and efforts rewarded

SPOTTED TURTLE
(*Chelopus guttatus*)

Orig., any marine reptile of the order of subclass Chelonia; a sea turtle; now, any reptile of that group; a tortoise, in the broadest sense of that word. Besides the bony shell (composed of an upper convex shield, or *carapace*, and a lower flattened shield, or *plastron*) which incloses the trunk, and into which in many species the head, limbs, and tail may be withdrawn, and the toothless horny beak, the Chelonia have many anatomical peculiarities and form a group which was already differentiated in the Triassic. It now occurs in most parts of the world except the colder regions, and comprises land, fresh-water, and marine forms. All are oviparous, and most of them bury their eggs in beaches and sand banks, the young digging their way out when they hatch. Turtles develop slowly, and some live to a great age. Some are herbivorous, but the majority are carnivorous. The flesh of many, as the green turtle and the diamond-back terrapins, is esteemed as food.

Painted Turtle
(cont.)

Are we trying to strut our colors too soon?

Are we trying to accomplish too much too soon?

Are we not putting forth enough effort? Is someone trying to take our color from us?

Are we letting the little things pressure us, not trusting in our own innate, hardy abilities?

Have we lost faith in our work and ourselves?

turtle is very hardy and reminds us that if we can persist and have faith, we will very soon succeed.

In the north, during the winter the painted turtle will dig itself into the sand or ground to hibernate while insulated. Being cold-blooded, they are susceptible to the outside temperatures and influences, but they are very hardy. If the painted turtle has appeared (especially during cold times), we may be giving up too soon. Things may not be gelling or working out the way we anticipate, but delays are temporary. We need to rebuild our faith.

The painted turtle can be a reminder not to force anything at this time. The group we may be working with may not be compatible and its efforts may be scattered and dissonant. Because of this, there is increased pressure and work. We may need to pull back, bury ourselves in the sand for a bit, and try again at another time. If we continue to try and force things now, the walls and obstacles could damage our faith in our abilities. The timing is off right now.

➤ The python is unusual among most snakes. While most snakes simply lay their eggs in a safe place, then abandoning them to take their chances, there are some pythons that not only protect their eggs, but also incubate them as well.

After laying them. The female coils around them and begins to shiver. These rhythmic contractions can raise her body temperature as much as seven degrees centigrade (thirteen degrees Fahrenheit). She may even gently shuffle the eggs in and out of the sun. Although several other species of snakes guard their eggs, only the python incubates them. This may be because other species lack the massive muscle power required to generate warmth.

The python is a powerful constrictor that squeezes and strangles its prey. Then, as with all snakes, it swallows the prey whole, head first. The snake teaches us how to take in knowledge and power. The python reminds us that we are already powerful, but we may need to incubate that power until the appropriate time. When the python appears, you will be able to digest and swallow whatever comes your way.

The python embodies all of the traditional meanings and significance of snakes, but it also heralds a time to reflect on the transformations so they can truly be processed.

My personal lesson in shedding the old came from a nine-foot Burmese python by the name of Monty at the nature center where I once worked. I went to open his cage as I always did when I arrive, to let him out to roam and move around a little. I could not see him in the cage, and when the door opened, he fell out. He had been leaning against the door, sleeping.

Startled from his sleep, he struck at the empty air as he fell out through the opening. I knelt down and reached in to his coiled body to pull him all the way out. As I reached in, his head curled around, and he struck, biting hard on the

Python

KEYNOTE

- **time to incubate your activities**
- **be patient**

Are you acting without thinking?

Are you trying to give birth too quickly?

Are you not absorbing and understanding all that is truly going on?

Do you need to grasp and cling more tightly to what is dearest to you?

Python
(cont.)

outside of my hand! I snapped my hand back, eyes wide with surprise.

As I pulled my hand back, he released, and blood dripped from the bite to the floor. I couldn't believe it! Monty had actually bit me! I never would have expected it and for days I didn't understand. Then it slowly became clear.

When the python bit me, I was shocked. I had not expected it at all. When I took time to reflect on its significance, I began to understand its meaning on many levels. The python had just gone through a shedding, and so it was stressed. My opening the door had surprised it. I moved too quickly in trying to bring it out of the cage, and I wasn't paying attention to the physical signals it was demonstrating.

At that time in my own life there was a great deal of stress. I was in the midst of shedding (completing) a new book project for the publisher. I was stressed from a lot of travel, and so my own sleep was a bit disturbed. I was ignoring my own physical signals of stress. And I wasn't taking needed time to heal and rest myself.

The following week the snake was still feisty towards me, but I had begun to slow down a lot of my activities. I began to take more time for myself. By the second week after the bite, the python was responding like his old self to my handling him. I was also feeling more like my old self again.

There were other, more personal significances to the experience which I won't relate here, but from just a superficial level, the episode was a strong reminder that like the snake, I need to have regular times to shed the old. I must take time to rest and heal.

Rat Snake

➤ Rat snakes are found around the world. They are adaptable, fast, and active. Slender and agile, they can be either diurnal (daytime) or nocturnal (nighttime). They have the typical snake characteristic of large eyes at the sides of the head and nostrils at the side of the snout. They actively seek out prey and strike accurately when they find it. When the rat snake appears, there will be acceleration and movement in all of our affairs and activities. We can expect the movement to continue for some time.

All rat snakes are active hunters and constrictors. They attack quickly. Upon spotting prey, they raise up a bit and strike quickly, hard and true to their mark. When the rat snake appears, it is time for us to do so as well. Now is the time to accelerate our own movements. We should strike immediately while we can. Being powerful constrictors, rat snakes are reminders to hang on tightly once we strike.

Rat snakes have scales that are slightly keeled or ridged, enabling them to climb more easily over rough surfaces, even trees. Rat snake's appearance heralds a time of movement and progress, regardless of the terrain we are in. Our goals are within reach and we will be able to move even more closely to them or even capture them soon. Progress is assured as long as we assert and accelerate our efforts.

All snakes have highly developed senses. Most snakes can see somewhat well, but they usually do not rely on that sense. They are attuned to the subtlest of vibrations that they pick up through their body, and they smell through their tongue. They have at the roof of their mouth what is called a *Jacobson's organ*. The tongue flicks out, captures air particles, and brings it to the roof of the mouth. In this manner, they sense whether there is food, danger, etc. about them. When the rat snake appears, it is best not to trust what we see initially, but what feels or smells right to us.

KEYNOTE

acceleration and movement

Are we hesitating to act when the opportunities present themselves?

Are we not striking sharply enough?

Are we not hanging on tightly to what we have?

Have we bitten off more than we can chew?

Are our appetites too big for our stomach?

Do we need to slow down and shed some of the old before striking for the new?

Are we being too impatient in our endeavors, trying to lay too many eggs too soon?

Rat Snake
(cont.)

If we trust what feels right and then strike at whatever that is, we will be more successful and see quicker progress within our life.

Most snakes are seasonal breeders, and the rat snake is usually able to breed by its second summer, although it does not truly reach maturity until its third or fourth year. The female snake is capable of storing the sperm inside to delay fertilization until a more appropriate time. If the rat snake has appeared, we are likely to see some delays in our progress. This is not a time to be impatient or premature in our endeavors. We should maintain control and wait for a more appropriate time to strike out. Undo force could disrupt our plans. Often, the second year of our endeavors is when progress most often occurs.

The rat snake swallows its prey whole, headfirst, unhinging its jaws in order to do this. The rat snake can indicate that we are trying to take in too much at this time. We may have literally bitten off more than we can chew or swallow. We probably need to adjust our goals a little at this time, especially our time frame.

Animal Wonders

SELF-SACRIFICE

Lizards usually rely on speed and agility to escape predators or other dangers. When this doesn't work, the tail can be sacrificed.

A predator may grab for the lizard, its paw or mouth landing on the lizard's tail. The predator is soon surprised as the tail breaks off and the lizard runs to safety. The lizard then begins growing another tail in its place.

➤ A young man was walking through the woods in winter, and he came across a rattlesnake, stiff with cold on the path. Feeling sorry for the snake, he placed it inside his coat to help warm it. As he continued his walk, the rattlesnake began to warm up and move. The young man stopped and as he opened his coat to let the snake out, it coiled and bit him sharply on the cheek.

The young man was stunned. As the snake dropped to the ground, it turned, and looked back at the young man. He sat down upon the cold ground, the poison already moving through his body. "Why did you bite me," the young boy asked. "I picked you up and warmed you inside of my coat so you would not die."

The snake paused and then spoke, "You knew what I was when you picked me up." And the snake slithered away.

The rattlesnake has a tremendous amount of myth associated with it. Among the Native American traditions, it is the healer, transformer, and the spirit of life and death. All snakes have certain qualities in common and these should be studied.

All venomous animals teach us something about the toxicity and poisons in our life. They help point to paths of healing for us. Of none is this truer than with the rattlesnake.

The rattlesnake is not truly an aggressive snake. It will warn before striking and will move out of the way if possible as long as it has not been startled. Its rattle is scales from previous sheds that remain on the tail. The rattlesnake reminds us to be alert to warnings and to alert others before we strike.

Rattlesnakes move around during the cool hours of the night. Extreme heat is deadly to them, and when the rattlesnake appears, you will find yourself becoming more nocturnal, or you may find that your nighttime dreams become more lucid and real. The rattlesnake opens the

Rattle-snake

KEYNOTE

- healing
- transformation

RATTLESNAKE
(*Crotalus horridus*)
A poisonous snake of a yellowish-brown color and having a series of horny joints at the end of the tail which make a rattling so und, when the name.

Rattlesnake

(cont.)

Are we ignoring the toxicity of our present life situation?

Do we not trust what we perceive?

Do we need to shed the old and move into the new?

What new realms are opening for us?

Are we ignoring our inner visions and dreams?

doors between life and death, and dreaming is one phase of our movement between worlds.

Because it is a guardian and a guide between life and death, there will be increased spirit activity in our life. We will sense the presence more frequently and clearly than we ever realized possible.

The rattlesnake has a sidewinding motion to its movement. It also has a special sense organ; a small pit in the head, that reacts to heat put out by other creatures. This is how it senses its prey. On a symbolic level, this reflects an increased sensitivity to the auras of others. You will start seeing them and feeling them more strongly. Trust what you feel around others, no matter how strange those feelings.

The rattlesnake is a symbol of healing and transformation, and when it appears as a totem or messenger, we can expect opportunity for healing our life and transforming our world.

➤ Salamanders, like frogs and toads, are amphibians. Their long bodies and tails are the reason many people mistake them for lizards. Unlike lizards, though, they have moist, smooth skin with no scales, rounded heads, spots or strips on their bodies, and no claws on their toes. They also move more slowly than lizards and can be found under logs and rocks.

Most salamanders lay eggs in the water that hatch into larvae with gills. The larvae eventually develop into salamanders that breathe through lungs, often by gulping air. Some even breathe through their skin. This unusual respiration reflects the unique inspiration and assistance we will experience.

When salamander appears, as with all amphibians, there is transformation about. The difference is that the salamander reflects assistance coming for that transformation from somewhere outside of us, either through an unexpected person or through a unique resource within our environment that inspires a creative and successful approach.

Salamanders are very sensitive to their environment and all changes within it. If salamander has appeared, it is important to maintain or develop a more compatible relationship with our environment and those within it. Harmoniously cooperating with our environment and its resources (including the people within it) is key to our success. Answers and solutions will be found within our environment, often in unexpected ways.

Male salamanders court the females with special displays, then deposit packets of sperm, which the females collect. When salamander appears, someone will be giving us the knowledge and support we need to be more productive and fertile. There may be a temporary partnership, a temporary courting, but any seeds planted from

Sala-mander

KEYNOTE

unique inspiration and assistance

SALAMANDER
(*Ambystoma punctatum*)
Any of numerous amphibians of the order Urodela, which superficially resemble lizards, but are scaleless, being covered with a soft, moist skin. Most of them are small, and somewhat terrestrial when adult, living in moist, dark places, but the majority pass through an aquatic larval stage during which they breathe by gills. Certain chiefly aquatic forms are called *newts*. The salamanders are perfectly harmless and feed on aquatic worms, insects, and other small animals.

Salamander
(cont.)

Are we feeling stifled?

Are we unable to breathe freely in our work or relationships?

Do we need some fresh air, some fresh inspiration?

Are our efforts toward change being wasted?

Are we being overly confident in our own creative abilities, ignoring those around us?

Are we using all that is available to us?

Are we expecting too much from our environments, business or personal?

Are we not looking close enough and seeing what could benefit us?

Are we only looking at the superficial?

Are we ignoring the resources available to us?

this will prosper We should plant as many of them as we are able.

Salamanders are nocturnal, avoiding direct sun, thus the help and assistance that we need for successful changes and endeavors will likely come from sources not readily apparent. We will find unique cooperation and assistance in things and from people not normally recognized. They will stimulate creativity and improve our chances for success.

Salamanders tend to live in wet or moist places, although some do live entirely within the water. The moisture is critical to their ability to breathe and if salamander has appeared, working and living within a creative environment with cooperative and supportive creative people is critical to our health and life. If salamander has appeared, a new direction may be needed and warranted. Our present environment—business or personal—may be suffocating us and affecting our overall health and productivity. This is especially true if there has been a frequency of blocks in our path recently.

Salamanders rely largely on scent and sight to find food, and those living on land only eat moving prey, such as worms or slugs. Our senses may be askew and sources we believe to provide inspiration and nourishment may not do so. We should check things and people carefully before proceeding with them.

➤ Turtles have existed almost unchanged for over 200 million years, but there are many varieties, each with its own unique qualities. The marine or sea turtles are different from and larger than pond or land species. Within this grouping there are five main types, the two most common and larger being the leatherback and loggerhead. If sea turtle has appeared, we can expect success and achievement if we persevere.

Sea turtles have a flatter carapace or shell than other types of turtles, and their limbs have evolved as flippers. These characteristics enable them to move more smoothly through the water. When sea turtle appears, our progress in things creative will become smoother. We will encounter much less resistance to our efforts. Goals will be attained.

Breeding females will flop clumsily onto sandy beaches to lay the eggs. When the eggs hatch, the baby turtles must scramble down to the sea by themselves. They are at the mercy of crabs, gulls, and other predators. Most do not survive. When the sea turtle appears, it is an indication that our perseverance is about to be rewarded. The worst is over, and as long as we maintain our courage and persistence, we will shortly succeed. The sea turtle is a powerful signal that the future looks very good in all endeavors, especially business.

All shore areas and beaches are doorways between the human world and the spirit world, the Faerie realm in particular. The sea turtle is especially the keeper of the doors between dimensions, and its appearance heralds a time of new wonders and rewards if we maintain courage. New dimensions are opening for us.

The survival skills and strategies of sea turtles are amazing. They have acute hearing, and they sense subtle vibrations in the water through their skin and shell. The appearance of sea turtle reflects a heightening of our senses, and they

Sea Turtle

KEYNOTE

persevere to achieve

LEATHERBACK
(*Dermochelys coriacea*)
The largest sea turtle... distinguished by its flexible carapace, composed of a mosaic of small bones embedded in a thick leathery skin. It occurs in all warm seas, but is most common in the Atlantic, and sometimes weighs over a thousand pounds.

Sea Turtle

(cont.)

Are we not persisting in our efforts?

Are we allowing minor setbacks to prevent further efforts?

Do we need to act with more courage?

Are we not hearing and sensing what we should about our endeavors?

Have we taken on too much?

Not enough?

Are we trying to accomplish too much at once?

Are we giving up too easily?

Are we afraid to "come ashore" and give birth to that which we desire?

remind us to trust our senses in our pursuits. If we do, we will be rewarded.

Sea turtles rarely come ashore. Although graceful in the water, they are very clumsy on land. If sea turtle has shown up, we should examine whether we are trying to accomplish and achieve in an environment that is not suitable for us. We need to look for more suitable surroundings for our pursuits. We may be out of our element.

Because sea turtles come ashore to lay their eggs, they are a reminder that we are living in a creative environment. But there must be a practical expression of that creativity. In this way, the sea turtle alerts us to find a balance between practicality and creativity. Both aspects have to be considered if we are to be productive. We must plan more carefully and be patient. Sea turtles lay dozens of eggs at a time so that some will survive the high rate of predation. Sea turtle warns that we may be relying too strongly on one or two possibilities. We need to expand and increase our productivity.

➤ Skinks make up one of the largest groups of lizards. Many are smooth scaled, and some have no limbs. Skinks are good at burrowing, and some spend most of their lives underground. They are the only lizards that most people in the U.S. have ever seen. Skinks can always be recognized by their smooth, flat scales.

Particular species of skinks are identified by their specific markings which are usually the lines running down them, such as the five-lined skink, four-lined skink, and so on. Examine the numerological significance of the number of lines, and it will help you decipher more specific interpretation of the skink message you are receiving.

Skinks mate around May and give birth about six weeks later. They hibernate in the winter. When skinks show up, our most fertile time and the best time to uncover the hidden is late spring and summer. In winter, it is best to pull back from our digging and exploring efforts.

Because skinks are ground lizards, they all burrow at some point. Burrowing animals teach us how to dig beneath the surface of things in our life. When the skink appears, we will find it easier to uncover hidden things going on around us.

Skink

KEYNOTE

- **dig beneath the surface**

- **hidden will be uncovered**

SKINK
(*Scincus officinalis*)
Any lizard of the family Scincidae, a large group of pleurodont lizards, mostly small, with stout scales, and a slightly notched tongue covered with scalelike papillae. They usually prefer dry sandy places, and many burrow in the sand. Though most have well-developed limbs, in some the limbs are reduced or wanting.

Snapping Turtle

KEYNOTE

- approach with wariness

- strong quick responses when necessary

SNAPPING TURTLE
(*Chelydra serpentina*)
Either of two large and voracious American aquatic turtles…so called from their habit of seizing their prey with a nap of their jaws. They are: (1) The common snapping turtle…which occurs east of the Rocky Mountains from Canada southward to Ecuador, reaching a length of over two feet and a weight of from 20 to 50 pounds; and (2) the alligator turtle. Both have a strong, musky odor, but are extensively used as food.

Are we speaking too strongly?

Are we chewing on others inappropriately?

Are others doing so to us?

Are we allowing what others say to eat at us?

Are we afraid to bite into our opportunities?

➤ All turtles have great myth and lore about them. They are symbols of the earth and serve as guardians to the doorways of the Faerie Realm. In some traditions they reflect sexuality and fertility. The turtle is one of the oldest reptiles and thus has some of the most ancient mythologies surrounding it. These should be examined to gain deeper insight into the turtle that has appeared in your life.

The snapping turtle and its relative, the giant alligator snapping turtle, are some of the more dangerous members of this species. They are very temperamental and they display a vicious temper. They have a powerful jaw that they use to capture and eat fish, small waterfowl, and even muskrats. These should be studied too if the snapper has appeared in your life. They have a sharply toothed rear edge to their shell, often coated with green algae to disguise its presence in the water.

Snapping turtles are fresh water turtles, and their most outstanding feature is their jaw. The mouth and jaw are powerful symbols. It is the place of digestion and speech. The snapping turtle is an animal that must be handled with care. When it appears as a sign or totem, we should approach things around us with a little more caution. We should also be prepared to bite—to grasp—with quick responses. Snappers have tempers, and we may need to deal with issues of temper in others or ourselves. Whenever the snapping turtle appears, we need to examine what we are saying and how we are saying it.

➤ Tadpoles are the immature or larval stage of frogs and toads. When they appear in our life as totems or messengers, we should closely study the information on frogs and toads. They reflect the same energies, but in a developing stage. Things are just beginning to develop.

Tadpoles resemble the spermatozoa. Their appearance often heralds the presence of new possibilities for us. We are either in the midst of creative and fertile situations or will soon have opportunities to immerse ourselves in such. Sometimes the presence of tadpoles heralds a physical fertility in which an actual pregnancy can manifest. If we are aware of this, extra precautions should be heeded.

Frogs themselves are heralds of abundance and fertility, and in the polliwog or tadpole stage they often reflect the development of that fertility. When tadpole appears as a messenger to lovers and couples, pregnancy can and may have already occurred.

The tadpole will go through metamorphosis. Its fins will become legs and its gills will become lungs. Regardless of what our current position is, a metamorphosis is promised. We will move out of the pond, coming into our own in time.

Tadpole

KEYNOTE

possibilities for fertility and new birth

TADPOLE OF FROG

An aquatic, water-breathing, immature or larval stage of most amphibians, during which they possess gills and a long tail bordered above and below by a fin membrane. The change to adult form in frogs and toads is a rather rapid metamorphosis with many internal changes, loss of gills, and absorption of the tail. In salamanders it is much less marked.

Are we trying to rush our growth?

Are we trying to do more than we are capable of?

Are we finding appropriate outlets for our fertile and creative energies?

Are we allowing them to develop on their own?

Toad

KEYNOTE

**inner strength
and resources**

EUROPEAN TOAD
(*Bufo vulgaris*)

Any of numerous tailless leaping amphibians of the genus *Bufo* and other more or less nearly allied genera, esp. those of the family Bufonidae. Like *frog*…, the term *toad* is not a definitely limited one, and there are many amphibians to which either name is applied. The typical toads are generally terrestrial in their habits, except during the breeding season, when they seek the water. They have a short, squat body, comparatively weak hind legs, and are covered with a rough warty skin in which are glands that secrete an acrid fluid. Most of the species burrow beneath the earth in the daytime and come forth to feed at night. They eat insects, worms, slugs, etc. and are hence most useful to man.

➤ Amphibians have at least a 50-million year head start on reptiles, but these first land animals never became completely independent of water, except for adult toads who are well adapted to life on land. Although maligned and falsely credited with causing warts, they are amazing creatures, and they do behave differently from frogs.

Frogs divide their time between land and water, and toads live in places that are much drier than frogs. While frogs have a slick skin, toads hace a skin that is rough and a bit warty. Toads are less streamlined than frogs and their hind legs are shorter, limiting them to hopping or walking rather than leaping. The appearance of toad now heralds a successful time of drawing upon and using our inner resources.

Toads, like frogs, have a wide and varied mythology and symbology. They are associated with healing, money, and prophecy. In parts of Europe, its appearance warns of the presence of an enemy. To see a toad crossing or by your path as you are walking was a good omen, foretelling good luck and money. The presence of toad heralds a time of seeing things and people more clearly. It reminds us to use our strength of character and inner resources now and we will be blessed with solutions to problems and inner strength.

True toads know how to protect themselves and their movements. If need be, they are gifted at burrowing, playing dead, inflating their bodies to look more threatening, and even exuding poisons through their skin to help deter predators. They have many resources and abilities available to them. When the toad appears, it is a reminder to draw upon and use all of our skills. We have all of the resources necessary to accomplish our tasks at hand, but we must bring them out and use them. Toads remind us that with our skills and abilities, we are always in a stronger position than others may realize. They herald a time of personal advantage in endeavors and conflicts, and they embody the promise of success, achievement, and recognition through our own abilities.

Toads hibernate on land, among leaves in ditches and under stones and such. In the spring, they make their way back to their favored ponds where large numbers congregate. These migrations take place at night. If the toad has appeared, we may have gotten away from our roots and our strengths. We may be forgetting what brought us to where we are now. We may be taking for granted the skills we have developed to succeed. The toad is a reminder not to forget the past.

Toads and frogs have amazing tongues that are attached to the front of their mouths instead of the back. A frog's tongue can dart out and capture small insects and small moving creatures. The toad may indicate that we are missing or ignoring opportunities that are presenting themselves. We may be hesitating to act and use our abilities when the opportunities present themselves. We may be allowing fear to hinder us. When toads appear, it is important to perform some self-examination.

Toad
(cont.)

Are we being indecisive?

Are we hesitating when opportunities arise?

Are we letting fears prevent us from acting?

Are we ignoring the past and the skills that brought us to where we are now?

Are we being impatient and trying to leap further than we are capable right now?

Do we need to be more protective?

Are we not trusting in our own resources or ourselves?

Tortoise

KEYNOTE

movement through pressures

BOX TORTOISE

A name loosely applied to any turtle, but more correctly restricted to particular members of the turtle family. The true tortoises are land-turtles, represented in the United States by the wood-tortoise, the box tortoise, and the burrowing turtles of the southern states. They feed upon plants and fungi. Their shell usually is highly arched, with the hard plates showing concentric markings.

➤ Tortoises are land turtles with blunt, club-shaped feet very different from the web-shaped feet of aquatic species of turtles. Although the box turtle is also a land species, they are usually found in or near water. Land tortoises still look much like their very early ancestors when the age of dinosaurs was young. Though slow and plodding, the tortoise heralds movement, even with all of the pressures upon us now.

When tortoise appears, we have usually been experiencing many changes and many burdens, and although it may not seem so, its appearance now indicates that the dawn is slowly approaching. It reminds us to carry on, moving and facing things steadily and slowly in our endeavors. The tortoise has been around a long time, and it reminds us that though the responsibilities have been great, we will succeed in time.

Land tortoises tend to have high domed shells and toes with claws for digging. Daily they warm themselves by basking in the sun and then feeding on leaves, flowers, and fruits for the most part. They move slowly, following this same basic routine. If they need to they can reach normal human walking speed. Tortoise reminds us that we must continue on; we must keep digging, no matter how sluggish and slow. They remind us that we never face anything that we cannot handle. Theirs is a life of slow, methodical movement, and we should follow that pattern when life becomes hectic and overwhelming around us. They remind us to slow down and focus on the essentials.

The tortoise is ancient and heralds a time of getting in touch with and trusting our primal senses and rhythms. It is time to recognize that abundance and growth do not have to be obtained quickly and immediately. Nature's rhythms will work for us in the time and manner that is best if we allow them to. If we trust that, we will understand the reasons behind the lessons and pressures we have been experiencing. We will then move through them with greater understanding of the big picture and larger patterns at play.

Tortoises have a very slow metabolism, and their appearance may indicate that our own pressures are too great, especially if we are feeling pressures at home and work. We need to slow down. Life may be getting too hectic.

Whether large or small, land tortoises are among the longest living groups of animals. When they appear, we may be trying to live life in the fast lane, and it will unsuccessful for us. They remind us that we have plenty of time to accomplish what we wish, and we must not be impatient. The tortoise teaches that time is irrelevant, especially when examined from the spiritual perspective. Progress is made one step at a time. We must get back to basics and use our skills in the right way.

Tortoise
(cont.)

Are we being impatient with others or ourselves?

Is life becoming too hectic?

Are we trying to do too much too soon?

Do we need to slow down a bit and focus on the essentials of life?

Do we need to reexamine our goals?

Are we taking on other people's problems and ignoring our own progress?

Are we letting the burdens of others slow our own movement?

Are we taking on more than we can handle?

Are we ignoring our responsibilities and obligations?

Tuatara

KEYNOTE

- slow down
- patience until the time is right

TUATARA

(*Sphenodon punctatum*)

A large iguanalike reptile…formerly common in New Zealand, but now confined to certain islets near the coast. It is the only surviving rhynchocephalian. It reaches a length of two and a half feet, is dark olive-green with small white or yellowish specks on the sides, and has yellow spines along the back, except on the neck.

Are we following our own rhythm or that of others?

Are we rushing?

Are we just procrastinating?

Are we getting impatient?

➤ The tuatara is the last remaining member of a reptile family, distinct from lizards, turtles, and snakes. Although lizard-like, they are not actually lizards. The tuatara reptile is a breed of its own, completely unique among reptiles because of the shape of its head. This species is 200 million years old, and its ancient ancestors died out more than 65 million years ago. The tuatara can live up to 100 years, and today it lives primarily on New Zealand's north island.

Their metabolism is extremely slow, and they have a reputation for being slow-moving in all things. Some reports state that they occasionally go without breathing for an hour or more, and they have been know to fall asleep while chewing food. The female takes 3-4 years to build enough energy to produce a clutch of about six to fifteen small eggs.

Mating usually takes place in summer, and the female stores the sperm in her body for about ten months before fertilizing her eggs. At first the embryos develop rapidly, but then slow down during the winter. The young hatch, sometimes 15 months later, the longest incubation period of any reptile.

It is not unusual for those to whom the tuatara has significance to be slow moving, probably to the point of being aggravating to others around them, but they do eventually accomplish what they set out to do. If the tuatara has come into your life, do not allow yourself to be rushed. Set your own rhythm, regardless of the pressure around you.

You may be in the midst of a three to four year period of having to follow your own rhythms, even though others around you may seem to be accelerating in their lives and accomplishing many things. The tuatara is the animal of the "late bloomer" and its appearance is a reminder that you will blossom, but in your own time.

The appearance of the tuatara can also signal a slowing down or delays of activities in your life. Delays that do come, although unwanted, will be for the best. Look for a ten to fifteen month delay that will ultimately leave you in a much better position. The tuatara as a totem or messenger reminds us to go at our own speed. The tuatara promises success but in its own time and way.

Animal

PRENATAL CARE

Reptiles and amphibians have some of the most amazing and innovative prenatal care behaviors. Such methods enable the young to have a better chance of survival and thus sustain the species:

- Turtles bury their eggs in a hole so they will need no camouflage.

- The lace monitor lizard lays its eggs in termite mounds. The termites repair the damage, leaving the lizard eggs safely inside for near perfect incubation conditions. At the right time, the mother returns and digs the eggs out.

- The male Darsin's frog releases his young from his vocal sac where he has carried them since early tadpole stage.

- Some pythons are able to raise their body temperature through shivering and thus incubate their own eggs.

- Painted turtles hatch from their eggs in autumn. They spend their first winter in their nest to emerge in spring healthier and able to go off on their own.

- Many frogs and toads carry their eggs on their backs. The courting pairs do fancy loops in the water to get the fertilized eggs on the mother's back.

Wonders

Part VI

The Kingdom of Sea Life

*Mythology is the womb of man's initiation
to life and death.*
JOSEPH CAMPBELL

*As dolphins surface and begin to flip
their arched backs from the sea, warning the sailors
to fall-to and begin to secure the ship...*
DANTE
The Inferno

CHAPTER 14

The Depths of Sea Life

The world of sea life is filled with great mystery, power and magic. Some of our most ancient myths revolve around the world of the sea and its creatures.

Many traditions tell how all life sprung from the primal waters of life. Water is the creative source and the creatures that live within the watery realms can guide us to our most primal creative energies.

In the Hindu tradition, the fish is Vishnu the savior. He used the form of the fish when he saved humanity from the flood and founded a new race. The golden fish was Varuna who controlled the power of waters. In Buddhism, fish represented freedom from restraint of desires and attachments. Buddha was the Fisher of Men. Jesus in Christianity was the fisherman. In Christianity the fish symbolizes baptism, immortality, and resurrection. In the Chinese language, the words for fish and abundance are homophones (words that are pronounced alike), and so the fish has come to represent wealth, regeneration, and harmony. Also in China, the mother goddess Kuan Yin has a fish as one of her emblems. In Scandinavia, fish was eaten on the Feast of the Great Mother. The day of the feast was Friday, a day of the week named for the goddess Freyja.

One of the most ancient images is that of three fishes sharing one head. It was a symbol of

divinity, and variations of it were found in Egypt, Mesopotamia, Persian, France, and among the Celts. This symbol of the three fishes even became common among the early Christians who adopted it from these earlier pagan traditions.

Water is an archetypal symbol for birth, death, and creativity. It is the formless containing potential form and possibilities. It is the realm of dreams and the astral, the home of emotions, intuition, and inspiration. Through the watery element and the creatures within we find healing, psychic ability and heightened powers. Fish and animal life of the water were considered a sacramental substance. It has been a part of all mystery religions. It was associated with the worship of all moon goddesses, all goddesses of the water and the underworld.

Water is purifying, and it has rhythm and movement. It represents time and change. The crossing of any water source was often seen as a change in consciousness and even an initiation.

The watery realms have always been sources of great mystery, each with its own unique spirits and energies. Reefs and shoals were often objects of religious awe and were personified as giants and aquatic monsters, home to fantastic creatures such as dragons and mermaids. The sea life surrounding them was considered their children. Reefs and shoals were symbols of enchantment and also possible obstruction of our destiny.

Other watery realms had their own mysteries and wonders. The oceans and seas were older than anyone knew. They always changed, and yet they were always the same. Civilizations could come and go, but the great seas were always there. From the great seas came life-sustaining foods, and yet many experienced death through the seas. Water was always shifting, with no beginning and no end. Ponds, lakes, and rivers had their own spirits as well, each unique to their en-

vironment. A study of the specific environment will provide even more insight.

Fish and sea life commonly represent independence, potential, and possibilities. A solitary fish sometimes represented a solitary lonely person. Fish swimming down symbolized the involution of the spirit, while fish swimming up symbolized the evolution of spirit. This means that even though we can make some generalizations, only a study of the particular species will truly help us define the meaning and significance of the particular animal. There are lessons though that all sea life and fish can teach us.

➤ The common ancestors of all vertebrates, fish are some of the most fascinating creatures in the world. They have developed the ability to adapt to all aquatic environments, and thus they are teachers to us of the skills we need to adapt more effectively to our own environments, no matter where the waters of life take us. Fish help us discern how deep the waters are around us and how clear. They reveal the strength of the currents present within our life and life situations and how to swim with them or against if necessary.

Fish have four main characteristics that enable them to adapt and live within their watery realms. If we have fish appearing within our life, a study of how they adapt themselves will help us to adjust our own behaviors and actions in order to more effectively succeed in the waters surrounding us, no matter how churned up they may get.

Lessons
of
Fish
Adaptations

1.
FISH ARE
STREAMLINED.

➤ Streamlining allows easy passage through the water. Their fins provide guidance, helping them to steer more effectively. The quality of fish is often a reminder to do one of two things. It can indicate a need to do some streamlining in our life. This has nothing to do with changing our bodily shape. Rather it has to do with the amount of activity in our life. Maybe there is too much going on. We may be trying to do too many things by ourselves. The appearance of fish is a reminder to slow down and streamline the number of activities in which we are involved. We are very likely doing too many things at once.

The appearance of fish may also reflect the opposite of this. Have we streamlined our life too much? Are we cutting out too many activities and people? Are we refusing to involve ourselves in lifeæto dive into new creative activities? Our fears of failure, of not being good enough or creative enough, or of drowning in them probably have basis in reality.

2.
FISH HAVE
DEVELOPED
SCALES.

➤ Scales of fish are covered with mucous that lubricates the fish's body and protects it from bacteria and other infections. Individuals with fish as totems will need to keep their skins moist. On a physiological level fish people often fall into one of two categories—either being more susceptible to bacteria infection or very resistant to it. Even those that are more susceptible easily overcome. Most colds and such are picked up through touch, and those to whom fish appear need to be cautious of this at times.

On a less physical level, the appearance of fish often indicates that there is innate protection around us. If the fish is connected to negative situations in our life, it is an indication that we do have some innate protection, and we will be able to maneuver in these waters without becoming infected with the negativities of the environment. On the other hand it may indicate that the waters

around us are beginning to infect us, and we might want to change environments. A little study and contemplation on the situation around you will reveal which it is. In this contemplation, trust your emotions as water and the creatures that are associated with it are always linked to our emotions on some level.

Scales were often symbols of great significance. Scaly patterns on beings and creatures were often considered mythical, as in the case of mermaids and other fantastic creatures of this realm. Scales are for protection and defense. When fish appear, we will find ourselves more protected as we open to the mystical and netherworlds.

3. FISH ALSO HAVE GILLS.

➤ Gills are a physiological adaptation enabling breathing in the watery environments by providing the means for fish to take oxygen from the water and absorb it into the bloodstream. This reflects much about how fish remind us and teach us that we can find oxygen and creativity in what appears to be the most suffocating of environments.

You will find yourself increasingly able to function in environments that others would find stifling. It is not unusual to find others making such comments as "I just don't understand how you are able to (work, live, etc.) there." Fish are often a good reminder that we can be creative in all we do, wherever we are.

Fish can also teach us new breathing techniques to help us in every aspect of our life. This includes breathing for health, for stimulating lucid dreaming and for aiding in the development of conscious astral travel.

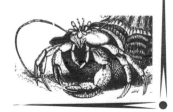

4. FISH ALSO HAVE GOOD SENSES.

➤ Fish have excellent eyesight, but even in deeper waters, the senses of fish are very acute. Fish have strong sense of smell and extremely acute hearing. When fish and sea life appear, we should study which sense is strongest, because it is always indicate that sense will awaken more fully.

Water is a great conductor for sounds, sounds carry further and more clearly in water. With sea life, we will experience some phenomena associated with hearing. They are often an indication that clairaudience or the hearing of spirit will awaken or get stronger.

Often times, when clairaudience begins, we begin to experience spirit more clearly in our dreams. Spirit will talk to us in our dreams, and we may even wake up thinking that we have heard someone in our room. Once the adrenaline settles, and we realize there is no one there, we assume that we were just dreaming it all. Sleep though is an altered state, and all altered states make us more sensitive. What has occurred is that we were at a point between waking and sleeping, and thus were experiencing the voice of spirit.

Sea Life and the Initiation of Water

➤ Water is the creative element of life. Many myths speak of how all life sprang forth from the great spiritual waters. Water is also destructive; thus it is a source of life and death. It is purifying, and has rhythm and mood. It represents time and change. Water adjusts to the environment, flowing around and over objects. Adjusting its flow according to the environments. It shifts as it flows. Anything of the water implies fluidness, emotions and changes. It adjusts, flowing according to the environment. It is the natural shapeshifter, taking the shape of whatever contains it. Because of this, the animals associated with this element teach us about adaptability and the flow of life. Through the animals of water we

learn to adjust the flow of our life, to take on the form that is most suitable for where we are.

Water has a life of its own, always shifting. Inherent within the element of water are lessons also associated with the emotional aspects of life. Through water we learn to creatively express and use our feeling nature. We learn to use our psychic and creative abilities uniquely, giving them the expression most beneficial for us.

Those with a predominance of the water element and its associated animals usually require intense emotional involvement in life. They also need the presence of water within their life for balance to replenish their energy and for healing. Going to the seashore will have a recuperative and strengthening capacity, awakening the ability to shapeshift our lives through our creative intuition and imagination.

►Water is often considered the womb of life, the source of rebirth, and it is a symbol of all that we dream of manifesting. It is the home of dreams and the ethereal realms of life. Thus the creatures of this realm help us to awaken to our dreams, making them more vibrant and important. The fish and sea life guide us when the waters of our own life become murky.

Water has a life of its own. It is a world in which many fantastic creatures and beings exist. There are many spirits of the waters and seas, and they often take the form of the creatures found naturally within them. And inevitably, when a sea creature becomes a totem there will occur greater contact with the spirit realm of life.

Water has often been the most traveled route into the dream world, into the Faerie Realm and into new life. Water links us to the astral dimension where spirit beings operate more actively. The creatures of waters help us in connecting with these subtle realms. Natural ponds, wells,

The Womb of Life

seashores and creek beds are open doorways and magical places. The creatures of these realms awaken our own belief in magic and wonders.

Anything of the water implies connection to fluidness, emotions and the feminine aspects of life (the creative, intuitive and imaginative powers). Through the creatures of the waters we open to the initiation of water. We learn to use the emotions creatively and productively. We develop our intuition and creative imagination. We open ourselves to healing and the development of our psychic natures. Through them we will always experience a rebirth on some level, in some area of our life. We learn to re-emerge from the womb more empowered.

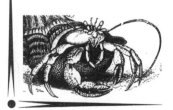

CHAPTER 15

Dictionary of Sea Life

All creatures of the waters have certain amazing characteristics. These characteristics reflect the creative opportunities that exist within the waters of our own life. Each has had to adapt to part of the watery environment that is very different from our own. Thus all fish and sea life teach us how to be ever more creative in adapting to our life circumstances—for our health, our growth, and our spirituality. Through them we learn creative and beneficial ways to express and use our emotions—no matter how different our life environments may have been from other people.

In this chapter, you can find specific information about the following sea life:

- angelfish
- barracuda
- bass
- carp
- catfish
- clam
- coral
- crab
- crayfish
- damselfish
- eel
- electric eel
- goldfish
- grouper
- jellyfish
- moray eel
- mussels
- octopus
- salmon
- sea anemone
- sea horse
- shark
- squid
- starfish
- stingray

Angelfish

KEYNOTE

- **guardianship**
- **unexpected assistance**

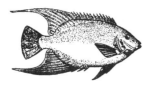

ISABELITA
(Holocanthus ciliaris)
An angel fish...colored
orange-red, sky-blue,
and golden, common in
the West Indies.

➤ Angelfish come in both freshwater and marine varieties. All species of these popular aquarium fish have narrow bodies and are brilliantly colored. Their name comes from their delicate bodies and the winglike pectoral fins.

Angelfish always indicate the presence of angels in our life and the appearance of a guardian angel. Although this guardian angel may be in spirit form, more often it is someone in our physical life who is like a guardian angel to us, providing surprising, unexpected, and very welcome assistance to us. The appearance of the angelfish may also indicate opportunities for us to become guardian angels to someone around us.

Angelfish feed on small water animals. They have small mouths that contain many crushing teeth. Some have slender snouts for sucking prey from crevices. This is a reminder that we will have to put extra effort into what we take into our life. It has links to discrimination and discernment. Sometimes the angelfish may remind us that we need to be more discriminating in what we do to avoid problems.

Discernment is like a guardian angel that keeps us out of trouble. It is important not to rush or allow us to be rushed into anything. It also reflects that any troubles that arise will have a resolution if we look for it closely enough and be true to ourselves.

Angelfish are connected to sea angels. These are the water spirits, mermaids, and mermen. They awaken in us our psychic natures, and through them we learn to be more nurturing and healing. Angelfish always reflect opportunities to be a guardian to someone close. Any assistance given will be rewarded in kind.

Are you ignoring opportunities to help others?

Are you resisting the help and assistance of others?

Is it time to explore new healing alternatives— particularly associated with color therapy?

Are we rushing into things?

Do we need to discriminate a bit more before taking action?

Baracuda

➤ With a jutting lower jaws and a set of fangs, the barracuda is a fierce looking and sometimes fierce acting fish that has a voracious appetite. It usually charges through schools of prey fish, snapping its jaws. Sometimes it even herds the prey fish. Often this is a reminder to take advantage of what presents itself.

KEYNOTE

**learning to go
our own way**

When barracuda are young, they travel in schools. As they get older, they become more solitary. When the barracuda appears, it is often an indication that it is time to break away from the group. It is time to go off on our own—to follow our own path.

GREAT BARRACUDA
(*Sphyraena barracuda*)
Any of several voracious pikelike marine fishes allied to the gray mullets, constituting the genus *Sphyraena* and family Sphyraenidae. The great barracuda…of the West Indies, Florida, etc., is often six feet or more long and as dangerous as a shark. In Cuba, its flesh is reputed to be poisonous.

While scuba diving in Eleuthra in the Bahamas a number of years ago, I had some unusual experiences with a barracuda. Every time I was in the water, what I am sure was the same barracuda, was extremely aggressive toward me. This was at a time in which I doubted my decision to leave teaching to pursue a writing career. What I didn't realize at the time was that part of its message for me was to break away and follow my own solitary path.

These experiences with the barracuda began to make me a little paranoid. I could not get into the water without the barracuda coming after me. It wasn't until late in this diving trip that I realized (through the reminding of my wife) that it was my necklace and medallion that was attracting it to me.

Barracuda hunt by sight, and they will attack any flashing metallic object. Barracuda often remind us not to be flashing our personal things at this time or presenting ourselves to others too strongly. It is more likely to aggravate rather than impress. They are reminders to just do what we need to do for ourselves without a lot of fanfare.

Are we still following the group?

Are we not doing things in our own unique way?

Are we trying to accomplish things in the same old way?

Are we trying to be too flashy in our efforts?

Do we need to just focus on basics and go about our own business?

Are we ignoring the flashes we are getting about our pursuits?

Bass

KEYNOTE

balance and union of the male and female and other extremes

STRIPED BASS

(Roccus lineatus)

An anadromous serranoid fish…native of the Atlantic coast of the United States, but common also on the Pacific coast, where it has been introduced. It is olivaceous above, yellowish silvery on the sides and below, and marked with numerous longitudinal black stripes. It is highly esteemed as a game fish and as food, frequently reaching 20 and occasionally 100 pounds in weight.

Are we restricting ourselves too much?

Are we spreading ourselves too thin?

Are we being too assertive?

Are we being too passive?

Are we ignoring our intuitive and creative aspects?

Are we being too nurturing?

➤ The bass is a sportfish with the size and appearance of the salmon, even though they are not related. Common bass eat prawns, shrimp, crabs, and small fish. Although often thought of as just a common sport fish, it does have great significance when examined.

One of the relatives of the common bass is a hermaphrodite, with both male and female sex organs. Other bass are intersexed, changing from male to female or vice versa. This type of sexuality is often important to the survival of species.

Hermaphrodites have had a great mysticism about them in many traditions. The male and female together was always considered sacred and magical. Because they were believed to be neither male nor female, they were thought to be intermediaries between worlds and able to walk between both. Their appearance often indicates new opportunities for balance when faced with opposition. We will find greater opportunity and ability to operate in distinctly differing environments in our life.

When the male and female join in any form, there is new birth, and the bass is an indication of new birth on some level. While some may worry that it may indicate some expression of bisexuality at play within the individual's life, it more often reflects a need to balance the male and the female in some area of our life, providing opportunity for new birth if we will act upon it.

Bass lay eggs in great quantities—as many as 10,000. Of these, only one percent will actually survive. Bass are reminders to be as fertile as possible. Bass people often have their hands in a multitude of projects and activities. They all won't work out, but a percentage will and those that do enable growth. When the bass appears as a totem and messenger, we should examine the balance in our life. If we truly desire a new birth in our life on any level and in any area we must harmonize the masculine and the feminine.

Carp is one of the most widespread fish. The goldfish is a member of the carp family, and it should be studied as well. Many believe that carp originated in the Far East, and there is a tremendous amount of mythology surrounding this fish. Anyone to whom carp appears should study past life connections to various Asian traditions, particularly the Japanese and Chinese.

In China, carp are often depicted in pairs, and they are symbols of marriage, union, and fertility. They are also a symbol of literary eminence and perseverance in one's studies. When the carp achieved its goal and learned all it needed in life, it "leaped the Dragon's Gate" and became a dragon.

In other traditions it had just as eminent interpretations. In Japan, the word carp is a homophone for word "love." It was often a symbol for the Samurai, representing courage and endurance. In Judaism, it was considered the food of the blessed, and it is often spoken of in relation to the Waters of the Torah. During the Renaissance, the carp was associated with Aphrodite, love, and fertility.

The carp is a muddy bottom dweller, living in shallows where there are plenty of water plants. They feed mainly on mud dwelling animals. They have sensory barbels under its chin that help it in finding food in the mud. The carp holds the promise of success in love and achievement in spite of the muddy waters around us. We must be patient and continue feeding, even if it seems as if we are doing so blindly.

The carp has many taste receptors lining its mouth and throat, and even more around the lower parts of their gill arches. Each receptor has a cluster of cells with tiny bristles. Carp grub about for food in the bottom mud, and they use their array of taste buds to sort out the edible from the inedible. Usually when the carp appears, a refinement of our tastes will increase or

Carp

KEYNOTE

blessed love and achievements that will last

MIRROR CARP
(*Cyprinus carpio*)

A soft-finned, fresh-water, physostomous fish....It inhabits ponds and sluggish streams, feeding chiefly on vegetable matter, and sometimes living to a great age and attaining forty pounds or more in weight. It is exceedingly prolific and tenacious of life. The carp was originally from Asia, whence it was early introduced into Europe, where it is extensively reared in artifical ponds and is esteemed as food. Within a few years it has been introduced into America and widely distributed by the government, but has proved a nuisance in many localities, destroying the natural growth of water plants and increasing to such an extent that other and more valuable fish cannot exist. It is rapidly extending its range. In American it is not generally considered fit for food.

Carp
(cont.)

take place and we will learn to separate that which is good for us from that which is not.

Carp have a reputation for having very long lives; however, the length of their lives is often exaggerated. They can live as long as 50 years, but the average lifespan is 17. The seventeenth card in the tarot deck is The Star, a card whose meaning often reflects the mythical symbolism of the carp. It is the card of future accomplishment, of inspiration and hope.

When the carp appears as messenger and totem, opportunities for achievement are on the horizon.

Animal

PERILS OF REPRODUCTION

Many animals risk death to reproduce, the instinct to keep their species alive being tremendous. This is found among all types of animals, but it is most evident among life associated with the sea:

- Sockeye salmon come in from the Pacific and travel up North American rivers to breed and die.

- Grunion risk death on California beache s to lay and fertilize eggs which stay buried in the sand for two weeks.

- Every two to three years green turtles take an epic journey of over 1200 miles to mate onshore on Ascension island in the middle of the South Atlantic.

- On Christmas Island red land crabs make an annual pilgrimage to the shore to breed, risking death on the journey and drowning upon arrival.

Many believe that such instinctive behaviors teach stamina and the pursuit of goals. They may even be reminders that we are capable of much more than we may have imagined.

Wonders

Are we neglecting the opportunities that are presenting themselves?

Are we ignoring how our tastes and desires are changing?

Are we allowing ourselves to be mired in the mud and not rise to new occasions?

Are we ignoring what is no longer beneficial for us?

Catfish

➤ Catfish are bottom dwellers with whiskerlike barbels around their mouth. Barbels serve a purpose of sensing. Many fish that live close to the bottom have taste sensitive organs that complement their nostrils in searching for food.

Catfish have poor vision and rely almost entirely on taste-sensitive filaments that hang from their mouth. When catfish appear, we may need to separate out what will benefit us and what truly will not.

There are two main types of catfish—armored and naked. The armored are most often found in South America, and they have a bony armor on them. This often indicates that we will be protected from the words of others or it can also indicate that we may need to protect the words we speak and write. The second type is the naked and has a variety of forms and habits. These are the kinds most people in the US encounter and their appearance often reflects a greater sensitivity to the words of others.

The appearance of the catfish usually indicates a greater sensitivity to all spoken and written words. Words spoken to us or about us are likely to have a much stronger and deeper impact—for good or bad. Words we speak will have a much stronger and deeper impact upon others—for good or bad.

Catfish as totems and messengers remind us of the need to discern, especially in speech. Speak what you feel in a tempered manner and you will see results.

Do we trust what feels right to us?

Do we only trust what we see and not what we feel?

Do we need to speak out?

Are we speaking too openly and harshly?

KEYNOTE

- **words will have greater impact**
- **our tastes are changing**

CHANNEL CAT
(*Ictalurus punctatus*)

Any of various fishes, some of which have apparently been so called on account of some fancied resemblance to a cat, as in their teeth, their ferocity when caught, or from having barbels about the mouth likened to the whiskers of a cat; esp., any of the numerous physostomous teleost fishes composing the large family Siluridae....The Siluridae are scaleless or in some cases partly covered with bony plates; the posterior dorsal fin is adipose, and the head is provided with long tactile barbels....Though many are marine, the majority inhabit fresh waters, and many species attain a large size. Many are important food fishes, though their flesh is not of the finest quality.

Clam

KEYNOTE

- examine sexuality and relationships
- partnerships

QUAHOG OR ROUND CLAM
(*Venus mercenaria*)

Any of various bivalve mollusks, esp. of certain edible species. The two xommon clams of the Atlantic coast of North America are the round or hard clam, or quahog…having a thick shell of rounded outline, most abundant from southern New England southward and the long or soft clam (*Mya arenaria*), having a thin elongate shell and long siphons, whose range extends farther north, and which burrows in the land or mud, where it is taken by digging at low tide. The quahog does not burrow and is usually taken with rakes.

➤ Aphrodite is the goddess of love. Born from the ocean foam, she is often depicted standing upon an open clam or oyster shell. The water is an ancient symbol of the source of life, fertility, and sexuality. The open shell is a sexual symbol for the opening of the woman's vagina. And any time that clams or oysters appear as messengers, there are energies of sexuality and issues of relationships at hand.

The clam is a mollusk or mussel, and giant clams can be more than four feet in width in the Indo-Pacific reefs. There have been many stories of giant clams snapping shut on the legs of unwary swimmers, but not one has ever been verified. Besides, they close their shell too slowly to ever trap anyone.

The giant clam has a light-sensitive mantle that lines its shell. When a shadow passes over it, it begins to close its shell. When the clam appears as a totem, it is time to examine our relationships. When the clam appears in the beginning of a relationship, it is the first sign of a shadow or something that is not quite right. We may need to close up and not go any further.

Aphrodite was the guardian of truth in relationships—personal and otherwise. She demanded the ideal and expected it. If clams are appearing, we may need to make sure that we are being as open and truthful as those to whom we are linked in various relationships in our life.

Are we being too open to others in relationships—especially sexually?

Are we too closed, afraid to open up?

Is there seduction going on around us that we should be more aware of, sexual or otherwise?

Are others trying to seduce us in other areas of our life?

Do we need to be open to new partnerships?

Coral

➤ Coral is part of a class of sea creatures often called "flower animals." Sea Anemones are also part of this group. Coral live in colonies, usually in tropical seas and are surrounded by and supported by a hard chalky skeleton. The skeleton protects and insulates the coral. In the human body, the skeleton protects our nervous system, which is our primary communication system.

Coral catch small swimming animals with their tentacles, often a reminder that we have to extend ourselves if we wish to thrive. Coral reproduces in two ways. It has the capacity for sexual reproduction, the colony producing its own eggs and sperm cells. Often this is a reminder that our personal endeavors are protected and that those around us will help in our creative efforts. The second way of reproducing is asexually by budding, and thus we may be seeking help when it is not truly needed. We should examine what is needed or not, but either way, coral holds the promise of new growth.

Since many believed coral would prevent sickness and frighten away evil spirits, it has often been used as a preservative against dangers. Many amulets and charms of protection were made from coral, particularly those for infants.

Coral comes in varying shades of color, and a study of color can help us pinpoint more specifically the importance of the coral in our life. Coral often only become white when it is dead, and if white coral is about, our projects are not likely to take off for us at this time. Our efforts will seem to die, coming to naught.

Coral is always a sign of protection for that which we have given birth to. This may be an actual child or our personal creative projects, which are like our children in many ways. It can also reflect a need to be more protective of the child within. Coral reminds us that there is protection around us, but children need some exposure to grow and mature.

KEYNOTE

protection and expansion of family, children, and creativity

MILLEPORE
(*Millepora alcicornis*)
The calcareous or hornlike skeleton of various Actinozoa and a few Hydrozoa (the millepores); also, the entire animal which produces this skeleton. The corals are mostly compound animals the individual polyps of which arise by budding; and the colony in many cases has a branching, treelike form.

*Is our family—
our colony—protected?*

Are we hesitating to act upon new ideas, afraid they may be too soon exposed?

Is it time to expose our creativity?

Crab

KEYNOTE

hidden and protected sensitivity

BLUE CRAB

(Callinectes sapidus)

Any crustacean of the order Decapoda...distinguished by the short, broad, and usually flattened carapace, the small abdomen, which is curled up beneath the body, and fits into a groove or depression under the thorax, and the short antennae; also, any of various other crustacea....

The true crabs have the anterior pair of limbs modified into large pincers, and in some...the posterior pair take the form of paddles. Crabs can walk in any direction on land without turning, but usually move sideways.

Are you being overprotective of your emotions?

Are you not protecting your emotions and sensitivities enough?

Are you becoming more psychically sensitivity?

Is it time to come out of your shell?

Is it time to go back into your shell a little more?

➤ In China there was once a belief that crabs of jade existed in the world. Every fourteen days (the period between the full and new moon) a jade crab that brought hidden good luck and repelled evil could be gotten out of a sacred well.

The crab is a crustacean, a form of life of which there is about 4500 species. Almost all have hard shells. The hermit crab is an exception with a soft shell. True crabs have five pairs of legs. Not all are necessarily visible. The front pair has pincers for picking up food. Their tails are small and they vary in what they eat.

Animals with shells on their back help us to hide and be protected, but they can also indicate that it is time to come out of our shell a bit more. An examination of the various situations in our life will help us to determine whether we should be more protected and hidden or come out of our shell.

In Western astrology, the crab is an animal associated with the sign of Cancer, an animal of the water with the qualities of sensitivity, shyness, and self-protection. It is an animal whose trust must be earned.

Hermit crabs have a symbiotic relationship with sea anemones and for those whom the crab appears, a study of anemones should also be pursued. Hermit crabs actively encourage anemones to live on their shell, since the anemone's long stinging tentacles give it some protection from predators. If an octopus threatens the crab, the crab moves the anemones to the lip of its shell for maximum protection.

A boxer crab defends itself with a sea anemone held in each of its specially adapted pincers. Because these pincers are occupied with defense, the crab must use another part of its walking legs, modified to feed itself. If crab has shuffled into your life, it is a good time to examine issues of sensitivity and reclusiveness.

➤ Like the crab, the crayfish is a crustacean with its head and thorax covered with a shell. Crayfish (also known as crawfish and crawdads) are fresh water crustaceans that look like miniature lobsters and are found throughout the world except in Africa.

Crayfish hide by day under stones or in holes in the bank. At night they come out and hunt for food. As with most crustaceans, they can teach us about coming out of our shells. They have a protective shell on their back, which they carry with them, and even though they hide, if they wish to eat, they must move from their hole or out from the stone. They remind us that things do not get done unless we move.

Crayfish have a pair of strong jaws and two smaller pairs of jaws. The thorax has three pairs of appendages, which pass food to its jaws. Thus crayfish are well adapted to capture whatever food is within their reach. Their stout pincers enable them to capture and hold prey. Crayfish serve as a reminder to come forth in spite of fears we may have and teach us that in spite of our fears, we must move and act.

A crayfish has four pairs of legs for walking and on its abdomen are other limbs called *swimmerets* that are used for swimming, which it can do well and fast. The crayfish can even swim swiftly backward to escape an enemy. Again, a reminder that even if we encounter dangers or threats in our coming forth, we are capable of backing out of most troubles we will encounter. But for the most part, when crayfish appear, it is time to move forward.

Are we hiding, afraid to act upon our ideas?

Are we expecting things to get done but not doing our part?

Are we hiding our abilities from others?

Are we afraid to try?

Are we forgetting that we have our own shield on our back to help protect us in our endeavors?

Crayfish

KEYNOTE

- **do not hide from fears**
- **now is the time to try**

AMERICAN CRAWFISH
(Cambarus affinis)
Any of numerous crustaceans of the family Astacidae, closely resembling the lobster, but much smaller, and found in fresh waters. Some of them attain a length of six inches and are esteemed as food. The North American species are numerous....

Damselfish

KEYNOTE

aggressive defense

Are you permitting others to intrude into your territories?

Do you need to defend and assert your authority over what is truly yours?

Are you being too aggressive?

Are you being too defensive?

Are you attacking when there is no reason to?

➤ The small but aggressive damselfish is a brilliant colored fish found near coral reefs. It will attack and eat smaller fish and defend its territory aggressively against any perceived intruders or threats.

On several diving trips to the Island of Bonaire, I was always amazed at how aggressive they were when I was snorkeling or diving in their areas. They demonstrated no fear and would try to bite. They are so small that they could not hurt humans, but their bites would sting and there was no doubt that they meant business. Several even came tapping my mask.

Damselfish remind us to show no fear, but to defend what is ours, regardless of the obstacles or opponents. Their message is not one of passivity, but active defense. Their aggressiveness continues until the perceived threat is gone. Damselfish remind us that there are times when we must defend what is ours.

FISH MILK

The many young of the brown discus fish do not face the same feeding problems of other fish. Their parents exude a substance that provides offspring with the nutrition they need, much like mammals' milk.

Eel

➤ In Europe, there are many folktales and myths about how eels sprang from mud, dew, and even the hairs of wild horses dropped onto the water. In England, to wear an eelskin garter while swimming would prevent cramps. Eelskins could also cure rheumatism.

In the Chinese legend of the Flood, a mythical emperor called up the waters while in the form of an eel. Yet another Chinese belief:

> If a snake is eating an eel, you should wait until only the head is still visible and cut it off; if you carry this head about with you, your income will be assured and you will always win at games.[1]

Adult common eels hatch somewhere at sea and travel some 4000 miles to breed, setting off from lakes, rivers, and ponds in Europe. Some even wriggle across fields and ditches to streams and rivers flowing to the Atlantic Ocean.

They swim at such a great depth that scientists are unable to locate them. Eel larvae are so dissimilar to the appearance of adults that it was years before they were linked. Arriving in Europe in winter, they gather in estuaries and change into miniature gray or black adults, known as elvers. Filled with an urge for fresh water, they start their swim upriver. The females migrate further inward into waterways where they will live for the next five to eight years. Then one autumn, they seek the salt water again to mate.

The eel is often an animal associated with male sexuality because of its shape. In Chinese, the word *eel* is often used for *penis*. In Japan, to call someone a "yellow eel" was to call him a homosexual. When the eel appears, greater sexuality and attraction to others will occur—males and females. Some of the attraction may be sexual, but it is not limited to this.

KEYNOTE

great depths and epic journeys of transformation

COMMON EEL
(*Anguilla anguilla*)
Any of numerous voracious, elongated, snakelike teleost fishes constituting the order Apodes....They have a smooth slimy skin (often without scales) and are destitute of pelvic and sometimes also of pectoral fins. The common eels of Europe and North America are important food fishes. They have minute scales embedded in the skin. The European form (*Anguilla anguilla*) and the American (*A. chrisypa*) are scarcely distinguishable. They ascend fresh-water streams, but descend to the sea and to deep water to breed, and pass through a peculiar larval stage in which the body is compressed and transparent. These larvae were formerly regarded as a different family of fishes, called Leptocephalidae.

---

[1] Wolfram Eberhard. *Dictionary of Chinese Symbols.* (New York: Routledge, 1986), p. 90.

Eel
(cont.)

Are we holding onto the past, afraid to let go?

Are we ignoring the opportunities to transform our lives?

Are we afraid of our own creative and sexual energies?

Is it time to travel and seek out the mysteries?

Often the eel brings an awakening of the kundalini energy, the "serpent creative life force" within us, the force of life that allows for our greatest transformation. A study of the kundalini process will be of great benefit to those whom the eel appears as a messenger or totem.

The young eels look so different from their adult counterparts, that for years scientists did not realize the connection. When the eel appears as a totem or messenger there will a great journey ahead. It will be so transforming that even our family may not recognize us through the changes.

When the eel appears as totem or messenger, we will be going into a spiritual journey of great depth and distance. The opportunities to do so will soon appear. We may find ourselves traveling to distant places and exploring new depths that will transform us. What we were may not even be visible at all. We will have grown stronger. We will be spiritually and physically transformed.

Electric Eel

The electric eel is not truly related to eel at all, but is actually from a species of freshwater fish called *knifefish*. They have a long anal fin from their throat to their tail. They have small eyes with blood vessels to help absorb oxygen into their body through their eyes, aiding them in seeing better in the mud and muddy waters.

Electric eels have a large electrical organ under their skin from head to tail that can generate as much as 550 volts, enough to stun a horse. They use this organ for defense and to generate electrical pulses as beams to sense their way through the murky environments.

Electric eels teach us to see our way through the murky waters around us. When they appear, it is often at times when life is getting murky. Their appearance reminds us to trust our own senses in feeling our way through. It may seem blind, but they remind us that as "scary" as it might be, it will work out and we will find ourselves moving into clear waters. The electric eel is a message that you will see yourself clear, and its appearance is a wonderful opportunity to develop trust in your own intuitive perceptions.

Electric eels are also reminders that we should not hesitate to defend ourselves quickly and strongly—to strike with the speed of electricity and the strength of lightning. It is not unusual for electric eel people to be afraid of striking out too hard—even against enemies—for fear of hurting them too greatly. The eel reminds us that if we do not strike strongly if threatened, the threats will continue. William Burke once wrote, "Evil prospers when good people do nothing." When the electric eel appears, we must strike, otherwise the old patterns will return and grow worse.

KEYNOTE

- **trust perceptions when life is murky**
- **defend strongly**

ELECTRIC EEL
(*Electrophorus electricus*)
An eel-like physostomous fish…of the rivers of the Orinoco and Amazon basins, the most powerful of electric fishes. It becomes six feet long, and is said to be able to disable large animals by its shocks. The electric organs are situated along the posterior ventral part of the body.

Are you afraid to move because you cannot see where life is heading?

Are you not trusting in your own abilities to move to cleaner waters?

Are you not trusting and acting upon your intuition?

Are you allowing yourself to be bullied and not responding?

Are you not defending yourself or those around you?

Are you being passive and not taking any action?

Are you not trusting in your own abilities?

Goldfish

KEYNOTE

peace and prosperity

➤ The goldfish, a member of the carp family, is the most widely domesticated of all fish. For those to whom the goldfish appears, a study of carp will be of great benefit as well.

The Chinese bred the first domestic goldfish, including fancy breeds as well. Ponds with goldfish are good feng shui, helping to balance the home's energy, inviting peace and prosperity.

Goldfish and salmon have lateral lines on their body. These are outer signs of a special sensory system used by them to detect the movement of other animals in the water close by:

> The lines consist of canals containing cells receptive to pressure changes in the surrounding water. Any other animals nearby causing movement of the water are immediately detected by this system.[2]

Are ignoring the signs we are being given?

Do we need to respond more quickly when we get a "sense" of things?

Is it time to focus more on prosperity?

Goldfish remind us that the opportunities are present. When goldfish appear, we will find ourselves detecting subtle movements around us and can respond accordingly. In business, this will help in prosperity and in relationships and will help in creating harmony. When the goldfish appears in our life, there is a need to focus on our sense of peace and prosperity.

---

[2] John Palmer, ed. *Exploring the Secrets of Nature.* (New York: Reader's Digest Association, 1994), p. 326.

Grouper

➤ Large groupers with their gapey mouths with many strong, needle-sharp teeth have a reputation for stalking scuba divers. This gaping is not a threatening posture, but actually serves to increase blood flow around the grouper's body, giving the fish more energy in case it must make a quick dash away.

In more ancient tales, they are the guards and watchers over the kingdoms beneath the sea where the merpeople live. Some legends speak of how mermaids and mermen will take the form of a grouper to swim near humans and learn more about them. It is not unusual when groupers appear in our life to have their appearance followed in a short time by dreams of the merfolk, which is a sign of our awakening to hidden realms.

There are many species of groupers, one of the most unusual being the soap fish, named because it will exude slime when startled or frightened. The slime is then beat into a foam with thrashing movements. Some groupers are hermaphrodites with both male and female sex organs. Still others are chameleon-like, changing their colors rapidly to blend into their environment, a trick they can teach us.

Groupers teach us how to disguise what we are doing or feeling. They teach us to disguise our activities a little to accomplish our tasks, especially when curious about something. Groupers remind us to protect and disguise what we are exploring until we are sure the doorways are safe and protected. Now is the time to act upon what we are curious about, but like the grouper, we should do it cautiously.

KEYNOTE

- **disguise and hide**
- **opening to new realms of curiosity**

RED GROUPER
(*Epinephelus morio*)
Any of numerous serranoid fishes of warm seas constituting the genera *Epinephelus, Mycteroperca*, and certain allied genera. Many are important food fishes of the coasts of Florida, the West Indies, Central American, etc., some attaining a length of two to three feet, and one species, at least, much more.

Are we rushing in to things too quickly?

Are we not hiding what we are doing?

Do we need to be more protective of our studies?

Do we need to learn more about the wonders of the Faerie Realm?

Although doors may be disguised or hidden, do we need to seek them out anyway?

Jellyfish

KEYNOTE

- growth through defined division of labor

- caution when working with spirits

JELLYFISH

(*Callinema ornata*)

Any of various marine free-swimming coelenterates having a more or less transparent body of a jellylike consistency; a medusa.... They swim by the contraction and relaxation of the umbrella or its marginal part. Many have long extensile marginal tentacles, which, on account of the stinging hairs they bear, often cause great annoyance to bathers.

Are you or someone around you playing with the "ghosts" and spirit communication?

Are you taking it as serious as you should so you won't get stung?

Are you trying to do everything yourself?

Is it time to reorganize?

Do you need to get more assistance and divide the labor in your life?

➤ Many tales exist about jellyfish. These range from them being the spirits of sailors lost at sea to giant members, able to swallow entire sailing ships. When seen in the water, they often appear as the spirits drifting in the waters.

Jellyfish are part of a group of animals called *coelenterates*. The typical jellyfish is shaped like an umbrella, and most have between four and eight tentacles. The body of the jellyfish is 99 percent water, but they can still be very venomous and have a great many stingers.

For those who are involved in psychic and spirit communications, caution is necessary when the jellyfish appears as a messenger. It may seem harmless and even fun, but it is easy to get stung. Extra caution is needed in working with the spirit realm.

The Portuguese man-of-war is one of the largest and most dangerous of the jellyfish. In actuality, it is not a single fish, but a complex colony made up of individuals. The core of the colony is an animal in the form of a floating balloon. Trailing from it are its tentacles that can extend up to 70 feet, each being an individual animal called a *zooid*.

Every tentacle is armed with powerful stinging cells known as *nematocysts*, whose sole function is to capture prey. The threads or tentacles, carrying venom, shoot out their barbs to paralyze fish. The tentacles then retract, hauling the prey up to digestion cells below the balloon-like float. The food is ingested and diffused throughout the colony.

This colony develops from a single fertilized egg. All colony members then are genetically identical. They are a remarkably coordinated superorganism and primarily the jellyfish can show us how to become more organized in our labors. Doing so will help insure success.

➤ Morays have a bad reputation for threatening or attacking divers which is a totally unearned reputation. Yes, they do have large sharp teeth that are often displayed because they need a continuous flow of water through their mouths in order to breathe. For those with this animal as a totem, there may be a greater need for intake of water on a regular basis for health benefits.

Over 100 species of moray eel are usually found around coral reefs. Because of this, coral should also be studied by those with this animal as a totem or messenger.

Morays have a symbiotic relationship with certain kinds of shrimp. Morays allow them to feed occasionally on the damaged tissue and parasites in their jaws. For most people to whom the moray comes as a messenger, there will be an unlikely partnership formed. It will be an on-and-off-again type of relationship, but it will benefit both—as unusual as it may seem to others.

Morays like to lurk in crevices and holes in the reef, and it is not unusual for moray people to like lurking and watching from the edges of activities. They are observant, and they teach us to be more observant of what is going on around us so we can take advantage of opportunities when they appear before us. Morays teach us to be ever more observant, to stand aside and watch for our opportunities.

Moray Eel

KEYNOTE

**observe from a
safe position**

MORAY EEL
(*Muraena helena*)
Any of a number of voracious and pugnacious, often brightly colored eels, constituting the family Muraenidae. Their gill openings are small and round, the pectoral fins as well as the ventrals are wanting, the back of the head is elevated, and the jaws are usually narrow and bear strong knifelike teeth. They occur in all warm seas and are especially common in crevices about coral reefs.

Are we too out in the open?

*Do we need to be a
bit more reclusive?*

*Are we paying attention
to what is going on
around us?*

Mussels

KEYNOTE

**strength in attachments
and perseverance**

➤ After starting life as free-floating larvae, young mussels or *spats*, eventually settle on suitable rocks and spend their lives anchored there. It is not unusual to find that those for whom mussels appear are soon to find the attachment and anchor themselves in it—be it a personal relationship, a new home, or an occupation. These always indicate strong attachments that are difficult to break once formed.

A mussel secretes from its foot a sticky substance that hardens in contact with seawater to form a thick thread made up of a mass of filaments. These threads are so strong that only the roughest of seas can tear the mussel away from the rock. For those for whom mussels are prominent, it is usually a sign to stand firm no matter how rough things may seem to get around you.

Mussels cannot go in search of food, so they are often found below the low tide mark where they are able to feed constantly. Mussel people have a unique ability to find a home or job that will provide them long-time nourishment.

Mussels take in about ten gallons of seawater a day, filtering out the plankton. This reflects the ability to filter through the difficulties to find the nourishment necessary to survive, whatever is necessary to withstand and hold on.

They efforts are usually rewarded. The fan mussel is anchored to the seabed by golden threads that were once harvested and made into the cloth of gold. This is a reminder of the gold that awaits those who persevere in their efforts.

A small silvery fish, known as a bitterling, remarkably lay their eggs in fresh water mussels, providing excellent protection for their eggs. Female bitterlings grow and egg-laying tube that trails behind her. She inserts her eggs through this tube into the respiratory tube with which the mussel draws in water. She repeatedly nudges the mussel's mouth until it gets used to it and then she lays her eggs. The male bitterling swims past and releases sperm, which are inhaled by the mussel and fertilize the eggs in its gill chamber. For a month the eggs develop in the shell, then the young bitterlings swim out of the breathing tube into the river. The mussel spawns at this time, and the mussel larvae hitch a ride on these bitterlings until they are ready to settle.

Mussels

(cont.)

Animal

SEX IN THE WATER

Fish try to take advantage of every mating opportunity, even going so far as changing sex or playing both sexual roles.

• Hamlet fish play both sexual roles, taking turns laying eggs and fertilizing them. They stimulate each other to release more eggs and sperm.

• Blueheaded rasses of Atlantic coral reefs begin life, hatching as males; some then develop into females.

Fish that are hermaphrodites often teach lessons of balancing the male and female roles and energies in our life, of learning to bring together opposites in creative ways.

Octopus

KEYNOTE

intelligence and camouflage

COMMON EUROPEAN
OCTOPUS

(*O. vulgaris*)

An eight-armed cephalopod. They have a large head armed with a strong beak, and small oval saclike body, and the eight arms are more or less united at the base by a membrane and are usually provided with two rows of suckers by means of which they cling to their prey or to other objects. Octopuses ordinarily live on the bottom among rocks, but they are also able to swim after the manner of other cephalopods. There are numerous species, mostly of rather small size, and usually timid and inoffensive.

➤ In the Pacific Northwest, among the Nootka, is the tale of Octopus Woman who had eight long braids. She walked along the shore collecting clams. Raven saw her and flew over to try and bother her, thinking it would be great fun. He repeatedly kept asking a single question, though he knew the answer, "Are you digging for clams?" Octopus Woman never answered.

When Raven poked his beak into her basket, knowing full well that it would aggravate her more, she suddenly stood up. The eight braids became arms and with four of them she grabbed Raven. Holding him tight with the four arms, she used her other four to grab onto a rock at the shoreline. Holding Raven tight in front of her, she began saying repeatedly, "Yes, Raven, I am digging for clams. Yes, Raven, I am digging for clams..."

She held him tight, repeating this sentence as the tides came in. Raven struggled, apologizing until the water engulfed them and Raven died. Crow would eventually bring Raven back to life, but he never bothered Octopus again.

The octopus appears in various dragon or whale myths. It appears in Cretan art, and is related in some ways to the spider web and the spiral of life. Both the octopus and the spider are reflective of the mystic center and the unfolding of creation.

In Jules Verne's *Twenty Thousand Leagues Under The Sea*, a giant octopus attacks the ship. Though a tale of fiction, the intelligence and power the octopus applies is most amazingly. The octopus is one of the most intelligent animals. It is a cephalopod, soft but strong, with a bulbous body and eight arms.

The bag-shaped body (mantle) contains a remarkably well-developed brain and nervous system. The eyes of an octopus can adapt to rapid changes in light as it moves from depths to near the surface. They easily learn to discern shapes, remember events, and carry out certain techniques.

The octopus is a bottom dwelling animal, hiding in crevices during the day. It does most of its hunting at night, often reflecting that the nocturnal energies and rhythms are likely to be more productive for those to whom this is a messenger or totem.

The eight arms are significant. In traditional numerology, eight is the number of power, money, and authority. The octopus shows us how to get what we want in intelligent and efficient ways, reminding us of how much more we are capable of accomplishing than others accomplish at this time. The octopus can even grow a new arm if it damages one.

The octopus can change its color to blend in with its surroundings in less than a second. It can distinguish colors by their light sensitivities and can also mimic the texture of the terrain it are crossing. It uses stealth to capture its prey. This often heralds the need to be stealthy and intelligent about our own endeavors. We should camouflage what we are doing until we have it within our grasp.

The female can lay as many as 150,000 eggs, a reminder of the many different creative things we may become involved in when the octopus appears. The female will not leave her nest during the time it takes for the eggs to hatch, which can be from four to six weeks and she does not eat while guarding her eggs. Many starve to death during this time. When the octopus appears in our life, we must remember to take care of ourselves while we work. We should not immerse ourselves so deeply in our tasks that we forget to take care of ourselves.

The octopus is a rather messy animal whose lair is often recognized by the pile of discarded

Are we acting without thinking?

Are we neglecting daily responsibilities?

Are we doing too much thinking and not acting upon the ideas?

Are we being too open about what we are doing?

Do we need to be a little more cautious and camouflaged?

Octopus
(cont.)

shells outside of its entrance. It is almost as if the octopus is so wrapped up in its task and thinking that it can't be bothered with mundane household labors. This same characteristic of "messiness" is often found with those to whom this animal is a totem. The octopus teaches how to use our intelligence, stealth, and ability to camouflage our activities to succeed and thrive.

SCHOOLING

Many fish swim in schools for protection, moving in tight groups as they search for food. Often even if a predator threatens, the fish will stay in a tight bunch rahter than scattering, coordinating their movements as they try to escape.

This is often considered a selfish response—each fish trying to put others between itself and the approaching danger.

➤ Among the Celts, the salmon was a sign of sacred wells and healing waters. Its presence symbolized foreknowledge of events. Among the Haida of the Northwest are tales of Salmon Boy who was a healer and taught the people about the circle of life and death, of giving and receiving. He revealed the power in transformation.

In the spring and early summer, sockeye salmon begin a journey of a lifetime. Born six years (a six-year cycle is at play when the salmon appears) earlier in the headwaters of North American rivers, they now respond to a strong and long-remembered scent of their home waters. From the coast, they surge upriver to their birthplace (approximately 1500 miles).

They leap over obstacles, including waterfalls, until they reach their goal. They mate in the shallow waters of their birth, laying thousand of eggs in gravel. Afterwards they die, energy spent. Their offspring live, inheriting, and carrying on the ancestral lineage. Both male and female salmon grow to maturity at sea. The time at sea ranges from one to four years, depending upon the species. Identifying the species will help you to identify the cycle that is at play in your life.

Fish have a sixth sense that enables them to detect the presence of other animals in their environment. Salmon have a lateral line that is an outer sign of a special sensory system, enabling them to detect pressure changes in the water around them. Any other animal movement is immediately detected.

For those to whom the salmon appears, there will be increased ability to get a "feel" for others in the environment. This is especially important in areas of healing, giving the salmon person the ability to detect subtle changes in the bodies of those around them.

By the time they reach the freshwater breeding grounds, both males and females have undergone remarkable changes. The males will now

Salmon

KEYNOTE

- **pilgrimage and coming home**
- **success through persistence**

SALMON
(Salmo salar)
A large soft-finned fish…living in the sea near the coasts, and ascending, for the purpose of spawning, many European and American rivers tributary to the northern North Atlantic. Its size, gameness, and beauty, and the excellence of its rich and characteristically flavored flesh, which is of an orange-pink color when cooked, make it the most highly esteemed of game fishes. It attains an average weight of 13 pounds. Though the salmon enters the streams in the spring or summer, the eggs are laid in the fall, and the young remain for a year or two in fresh water before descending to the sea.

Salmon
(cont.)

have a hooked jaw that they use to defend and protect their mate. The female will have changed as well and be filled with eggs.

When the salmon appears, we need to take a look at the pilgrimage we have either been on or have been considering taking. Our life will never be the same. We will be transformed. There will be a feeling of predestination in regards to a spiritual journey.

Are we persisting so rewards will come?

Are we giving up before the transformations?

Do we need to take a pilgrimage—time away to mature?

Is it time to return home, to get back to our roots?

Do we trust what we feel?

Are we ignoring our spiritual journey?

> The seashore is a mystical place. It is an ancient "tween" place between the land and the sea, a place where the sea spirits often manifest. The seashore is a doorway to other realms that may seem to be filled with wonders, but the wonders also have dangers. The anemone, as a flower of the water fairies, is an animal that heralds wonders and dangers ahead.

Tidal pools are extremely magical spots. They are places where the water separates from the sea. Thus they are a doorway by which water spirits enter and exit from the Faerie Realm to the mortal realm of humans. They are places of magic, wonders, and even dangers for the unaware. The seashore is a place washed by the rising and falling of the tides. Many creatures find it a good place to sit and wait for food to come to them. The battering waves require special adaptations. This is especially true of the sea anemone.

Though it has a flowery name and mythology, the sea anemone is a beautiful and deceptive creature. Found in rocks of shallow waters in tidal areas, its colorful petals are lures that are capable of killing other sea creatures. On each of its tentacles are thousands of harpoon-like cells. Each harpoon has a poisoned end and is attached to the anemone by a thread. Sea anemones kill small fish by firing hundreds of these harpoon-like threads from their tentacles. When it is time to move on, their fertilized eggs hatch and become free-floating larvae to be carried off in the ocean until they settle on new rocks. There they anchor themselves and the process begins again.

When the sea anemone appears, things may not be as they seem and we should proceed a little more cautiously. There are likely to be hidden dangers and hurts about.

Sea anemones often indicate the opening of new doors in our life, but we should not rush through them. The environment will not be what

Sea Anemone

KEYNOTE

- new tides
- realms and doorways of wonder and danger

SEA ANEMONE
(*Actinoloba dienthus*)

Any of numerous, almost invariably solitary, and often large and beautifully colored, polyps of the order Actinaria.... Their form, bright and varied colors, and numerous tentacles surrounding the mouth often give them a superficial resemblance to a flower. They develop no skeleton, and rarely reproduce by budding or fussion. They prey on small animals that they catch with their tentacles, which are armed with stinging cells.

Sea Anemone
(cont.)

Are we rushing in too quickly?

Do we need to be more cautious?

Are we recognizing new tides and rhythms within our life, realizing it may be time to move on?

we think. This doesn't mean that the environment is bad, just not what we think it is. Overconfidence and rushing in under assumptions will create troubles.

The anemone is an essential to much life in the sea. The clownfish, immune to the anemone's poison and thus safe among the anemone's tentacles, feeds on minute plants and animals. Although the anemone can live without the clownfish, the clownfish would not last long on their own without the anemone.

Sometimes sea anemones attach to hermit crabs, a compatible relationship for both. Hermit crabs will use sea anemones as protection from predators, and the anemone will use the crab to move around to find food. When it changes its shell, it takes the sea anemone with it, prodding it onto the new shell. For those with the sea anemone as a totem, a study of the hermit crab is in line.

It is not unusual for those to whom the sea anemone appears as a totem or messenger to develop some new and unusual relationships. These will be mutually beneficial. These may even be relationships with beings from the Faerie Realm—from the "tween times and places." The sea anemone is sign of new realms that will entice us.

➤ One of my most cherished scuba diving experiences was on the island of Bonaire in the Caribbean, approximately 50 miles off the coast of Venezuela. On one of the dives, our guides took us to a small coral reef where sea horses were found. We were permitted to hold the tiny creature gently in our hands. And it filled me with a true sense of wonder!

Sea horses and sea dragons are some of the most unusual looking creatures. They are actually related to the pipefish. They swim upright, and they use their tail to anchor themselves around supports. The sea horse resembles the knight on the chessboard, but that is not the true reason for its keynote.

The sea horse is encased in rings of body armor. Like the armor of ancient knights, it provides protection. The knights were individuals who lived under a code of chivalry. They were trained in fighting and in courtly behaviors and protected the young and women. When the sea horse appears as a totem, our own sense of chivalry will be awakened. We will see a time of romance, with opportunities for chivalrous behaviors to come forth.

The sea horse is the best known example of male pregnancy. A female sea horse lays several thousand eggs into a male's pouch, where he fertilizes them and protects the embryos until they hatch. The lining of the pouch secretes a nourishing fluid that feeds the growing young. After about two weeks, a brood of sea horses is expelled by constrictions of the pouch.

When the sea horse appears, there is usually a dynamic two-week cycle of creativity. It is a powerful time, especially for males to be creative and productive. Often the "Mr. Mom" qualities and opportunities manifest. Responsibilities are often switched in the household.

Sea Horse

KEYNOTE

knightly codes and chivalry

SEA HORSE
(*Hippocampus hudsonius*)
Any of a number of small lophobranch fishes... related to the pipefishes, having the head and fore part of the body suggestive of the head and neck of a horse. They are covered with rough bony plates, and the tail is prehensile.

Is it time to reverse the roles?

Do we need to be more responsive to our partner's needs?

Are our behaviors coarse and inappropriate?

Are we trying to direct our paths too much rather than trusting in the knightly quest?

Are you providing the protection and support that you can?

Do we need to take on the role of protector?

Sea Horse
(cont.)

In the case of the sea horse, the female does the courting. Thus for women, it is an ideal time to court the choice in male, and males should allow the female to seek them out and court them. The male carries the young and eventually sends the offspring out into the world.

Sea horses have a long association with the merfolk, spirits of the waters. These beings are the incarnate beauty of the sights and sounds of the sea. Encounters with them could enrich or endanger, depending upon how prepared and balanced we are. They often take mortals into their favor and are strong faithful protectors. They are also the guardians of women. Often when the sea horse appears, we will find ourselves in opposition of guarding someone close, usually a woman or child. Trust in your ability to do so. The sea horse is a reminder that you are more than capable of the task.

The seahorse drifts with the current, as the knights often rode the countryside more from inspiration than purpose. When the seahorse appears, it is a time to look toward knightly behaviors.

➤ Probably no other animal generates more fear and wonder in the ocean environment than the shark. It is the supreme predator, a hunter that is relentless and ferocious. Though often thought of as an instinctive killing machine, it is now believed that they learn to hunt by experience.

It has so many magnificent qualities that it is difficult sometimes to determine its true keynote. It is an ancient animal (with relatives over 500 million years old), and its appearance awakens a time of primal energies and sensory abilities.

There are different types of sharks, ranging in size and behaviors. Identifying the individual shark and studying it will enable you to more specifically define its meaning for you. All sharks, though, do have some qualities in common.

A shark's skeleton is made of cartilage rather than bone, and unlike boney fish, it does not have a swim bladder to keep it afloat and buoyant. To prevent itself from sinking, it must continually swim. For those to whom the shark is a totem, staying busy and active will be most beneficial. It is not unusual to find work-alcoholics with shark totems, but it is not a problem for them. Their continual busyness is what helps them to thrive.

Shark cartilage is being marketed as a healing remedy, even for such things as cancer. One of the reasons this is so is that most sharks do not have problems with cancerous conditions. Cancer is a condition that eats away at people. The key, though, is not in eating the shark cartilage. More likely it is learning to attune and resonate with the shark's spirit energy so that we are not eaten up by our problems that aggravate dis-ease.

All sharks have tremendously acute senses. Its sight is crucial to finding prey at the surface, silhouetted against the light. It has greatly enhanced vision in murky depths. A shark's eyes can adapt to rapid changes in the amount of light as it moves through various depths. When the shark

Shark

KEYNOTE

**heightened senses
with relentless
ferocity in pursuits**

THE MAN-EATING SHARK
(*Carcharodon carcharias*)

Any of numerous elasmobranch fishes which conform more or less nearly to the ordinary fishes in the fusiform (not flattened) shaped of the body and lateral position of the gill clefts, as distinguishsed from the greatly flattened rays and the grotcsquely shaped chimaeras…and from some of the more primitive extinct elasmobranchs. The sharks are mostly marine and, though widely distributed, most abundant in warm seas. They are usually of medium or large sizc, the largest existing fishes (30 to 40 feet long) being of this group….

Sharks have a tough, usually dull gray, sometimes conspicuously spotted skin, which is roughened by minute tubercles. The tail is strongly heterocercal and the snout is produced beyond the mouth, which generally has formidable teeth. Though some feed chiefly on shellfish, most are very active, voracious, and destructive to other fishes, and the larger ones are often dangerous to man.

Shark
(cont.)

Are we ignoring our senses?

Are we not discriminating?

Are we biting into the opportunities that present themselves?

Are we keeping our eyes open for new possibilities?

appears as a messenger, we will see the silhouettes of possibilities beyond the surface. Keeping focused upon them will help us to claim them. Even a little distraction now could cause us to lose the opportunity.

By far the shark's strongest sense is that of smell. Most of its hunting is done through smell, and most of its brain is taken up with the sense of smell. It can smell prey, especially blood, from several miles away. Its sense of smell enables it to pick up even the faintest traces of blood in the water and follow them to their source.

When the shark appears as a totem or messenger, our own sense of smell will become acute. We should pay attention to the subtlest impressions we get especially the ones we would normally discard as "ridiculous." It will be as if you can read people by their smell—able to tell more about them than if you had long conversations.

The sense of smell is linked to discernment and discrimination. When the shark appears, it is time trust what smells right for us. Our own ability to discern and discriminate will be greatly heightened. With sharks comes the ability to respond powerfully and ferociously in response to those discernments. Doing so will protect us and enable us to accomplish tasks seemingly impossible. We will find ourselves able to take advantage of fleeting opportunities.

The tiger shark has been responsible for more fatal attacks on humans than any other shark. It will eat anything, including humans, something that is not done by other sharks. Other species may bite and kill humans, but they won't actually eat the remains.

Since the movie *Jaws*, many myths and fears have evolved about the great white shark. It is one of the largest and stays to the open waters, coming in shore only when the shallow seas are near deep water. If the great white has come into your life, it may be time to move temporarily from the deeper water to more shallow to accomplish what you are after. Sharks remind us that in the waters of life sometimes we must attack things with greater relentless and ferocity. We must trust our own instincts above those of others.

Squid

KEYNOTE

- shapeshifting
- body language

SQUID
(*Ommastrephes illecebrosus*)
Any of numerous ten-armed cephalopods having a long, tapered body, and a caudal fin on each side....They have the shell reduced to an internal chitinous structure shaped like a pen.

➤ Squid and octopus have some of the most highly developed eyes of all invertebrate animals. The structure of their eyes is similar to our own. Unlike humans eyes, though, the squid will move the lens forward and backward like the lens of a slide projector.

The squid can use polarized light, a rare ability to make out the shape of its focus very clearly even in low light conditions. Combined with its speed and natural aggression, it is an efficient hunter

Squids have an expressive body language. They use light, color, and form to communicate with each other. They have sacs of pigment in their skin that allow them to express a mood or change their appearance. While the squid lies in wait, it changes color to blend in with the surrounding, becoming almost invisible.

When the squid appears, we should pay attention to what is being communicated in the body language of others around us, as well as by our own. When squids appear as messengers, our ability to read the moods of others will become quite accurate. Trust in it.

Are we revealing more than we should?

Does the body language of others belie what they say?

The Kingdom of Sea Life

➤ Starfish have no right or left, only top and bottom. On its underside is a mouth and small suction cups. There are over 200 varieties of starfish, each with their own unique qualities and colors. They are named for their five star-shaped "arms," although some have more than five.

Starfish living in the darkness of the ocean are quick to find the remains of dead fish that fall to the bottom of the sea. They can detect waterborne chemicals given off by rotting food and they are able to follow scent trails being carried in the slow moving currents of the ocean floor. Individuals for whom the starfish appear often are very sensitive to the true emotions of others surrounding them no matter how they are shielded and disguised by the individuals.

With no eyes or ears, the starfish is dependent upon its sense of touch and smell, which are acute. When the starfish appears, it will be important to "follow your own star"—your own scent—to what you desire. Others may not think there is anything in it for your efforts. Trust your own instincts. Your ability to discern new opportunities and possibilities will be increasing.

Starfish digest in an unusual way. They cling to their prey (mainly mussels, which should be studied) and as soon as they find a soft spot, they turns out their stomachs through their mouths. The stomachs come out and onto the soft spot of the mussel and begins to digest it. When done, starfish pull their stomachs back inside themselves. Doing things in your own unique way, no matter how strange it may seem to others will usually work better for you. This is part of what starfish teaches.

Just as lizards can regrow a limb, a starfish can regrow an arm that has been bitten off as well. Even if we fail in our own unique endeavors, we will regain anything that is lost and still be able to

Starfish

KEYNOTE

- perceiving emotions
- following your own unique way

ONE OF
THE ASTEROIDES
(*Echinaster sentus*)

They are characterized by being unattached, having a star-shaped or pentagonal body, the rays or arms (usually five in number) hollow and containing prolongations of the coelom and alimentary and other viscera. The skeleton consists of calcareous plates and ossicles somewhat loosely united, often allowing the arms great freedom of movement. The mouth is on the lower surface, and is not provided with jaws or teeth…the anus is often wanting or functionless, undigested matter being thrown out at the mouth.

Are you following the crowd?

Are you ignoring your own emotions or those aroundyou?

Are you not paying attention to the emotional signs you are getting?

Is it time to try some thing different?

Starfish
(cont.)

continue.

For starfish people, there is no gray area usually. Things are black and white, up or down. To follow what one knows is right for himself or herself is difficult, but it brings its own rewards. It opens stars of possibilities.

Stingray

➤ Stingrays are relatives of the sharks. They have flattened, flounder-like shapes with long whiplike tails that have a stinger or poisonous spine attached. Stingrays have electro-receptors on their snout by which they accurately detect buried food. Some generate and emit low level electrical pulses that help them to guide and recognize food and danger. Often,when stingrays are totems or messengers, people get tingling sensations to alert them to the presence of danger, treasures, etc.

A network of nerves informs the stingray of the position of each part of its body wherever it is swimming. For those to whom the stingray is a totem, there is a natural gracefulness, a sense of never being lost. This individual is usually confident in maneuvering and operating in whatever environment in which he or she is found. For those to whom the stingray is just appearing, the ability to maneuver gracefully in new environments will need to be developed.

When the stingray appears, trust in your own inner guidance. Trust in your own ability to find what is beneath the surface. Do not be afraid to whip that tail around to protect your own dance in life. It will be much smoother and more graceful than you imagine.

KEYNOTE

- **gracefulness in maneuverings and moves**
- **staying on course**

STING RAY
(*Dasyatis sabina*)
Any of numerous rays of the family Dasyatidae.... Some species reach a large size, and some, esp. on the American Pacific coast, are very destructive to oysters.

Are you hesitating to make the moves that are necessary?

Conclusion

Sharing the Wonder

*There is nothing in life too terrible or too sad
that will not be your friend when you find the right
name to call it by, and calling it by its own name,
hastening it will come up right to your side.*

KOBA IN
LAUREN VAN DER POST
A Far Off Place

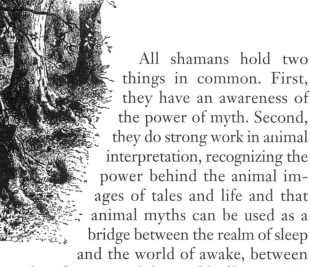

All shamans hold two things in common. First, they have an awareness of the power of myth. Second, they do strong work in animal interpretation, recognizing the power behind the animal images of tales and life and that animal myths can be used as a bridge between the realm of sleep and the world of awake, between the realm of nature and the world of humans. In more ancient societies, shamans were the keepers of sacred knowledge of animals and nature and were linked to the rhythms and forces of nature. They were held in high esteem and recognized as true shapeshifters who were able to walk the worlds.

Shamanism

➤ Shamanism is an experiential growth process and involves becoming the master of your own initiation. In shamanism, the individual ultimately answers to no human or totem and is alone with the supernatural. Yes, he or she maintains a true sense of belonging and connectedness to all life, but the individual is able to visit the heavens and the underworld. The individual is able to learn from all life forms.

A person usually becomes a shaman by one of three methods:

- by inheriting the profession,

- by a special calling, or

- by a personal quest.

TED ANDREWS

The process of following that personal quest and unfolding the innate powers begins with two steps. The first step is the overcoming of preconceived notions and limitations and is comparable to what Edgar Cayce taught: "There is as much to unlearn as there is to learn." The most difficult part of this step is seeing through the illusions of our lives.

Becoming the shaman practitioner develops a strong sense of not truly belonging to reality. We are often taught that we should belong to something. Many people spend their whole lives attempting to belong and most of the time it leads to disappointment. The animal-wise shaman must develop an individuality that is strong and by working through animals, we then can learn that we are able to be alone without being lonely.

The second step in the shaman quest is building a bridge between our world the more subtle realms of life. This involves unfolding our intuition, creativity, and creative imagination. Here, we learn to visit the heavens and the underworld by means of an axis, which may be the image of climbing a tree, being carried or led by an animal, by becoming a bird or animal, following a cave through a labyrinth, or any number of other possible images. Ancient societies employed mythic imagination to facilitate this step.

This means that we must now move beyond the orthodox treatment of mythic imagery (including that of animals) as found in modern religion. In today's world these images and their association to outer reality are held in fixed, unchangeable dogma, but they have grown stale and have lost their ability to touch each of us uniquely. We must restore the experiential aspect to the mythic images of life and transform our usual perceptions through an epiphany with Nature.

As much as I love writing, teaching is where I often find my greatest fulfillment. No matter

what workshop or subject I present, no matter what the subject of my book, all are centered around two of my strongest beliefs:

- WE ARE NEVER GIVEN A HOPE WISH OR DREAM WITHOUT ALSO BEING GIVEN OPPORTUNITIES TO MAKE THEM A REALITY.

- WE CAN STARVE AS MUCH FROM A LACK OF WONDER AS WE CAN FROM A LACK OF FOOD.

In the world around us, there are myriads of wonders, but unfortunately we often get so wrapped up in our day to day life that we forget about them or don't even recognize them. It is through the animal kingdom, through the multitude of wonders found in nature, that we can experience renewal. Every sojourn into Nature offers an epiphany for the heart and soul. And if only for a little while, let us open our heart to it and see what glories unfold.

Exercise

> ## BENEFITS
> - increases awareness that we share the world with all living things
> - gifts us with animal encounters that fill our hearts with blessed wonder

The Silent Walk

The silent walk is a powerful exercise for attuning to nature and the myriad of wonders within it. This is potentially the most powerful exercise we can perform as it is an act of sacred sharing, honor, and openness.

The skill lies in walking in silence, abandoning all words, vocalizations, and any trappings of civilization that are likely to make un-naturelike noises. The silence and harmony of this activity, especially when performed at dawn or dusk, creates an increasing awareness that we share the world with all living things. And ultimately, it will gift us with animal encounters that fill our hearts with blessed wonder.

This exercise should be performed at dawn or dusk because these are sacred times, times in which the spiritual and physical intersect, times when the human and the animal walk through similar corridors. These are times in which animals are often more active and visible.

Prepare for this by giving yourself at least a half-hour of meditation time prior to the walk when your focus is on the quiet attunement to Nature. Choose a location that is somewhat secluded where there will be no traffic. Old country roads that are seldom traveled and overgrown are good. Choose a park or nature center that has trails that are easily followed. Plan on walking a half-hour to forty-five minutes out and then turn around and come back.

Animals sense the energy of a single person or a group, thus the preparatory and solitary medi-

tation. Animals recognize disharmony and even unconscious and unintentional disrespect. If they feel a peace, a harmony that is soft and unthreatening, they do not run away or hide. The animals encountered or experienced may move away at your approach, but they do so without the frantic fear that they demonstrate most often when humans approach. They may retreat a few steps at a time, stopping to look over their shoulders, just to satisfy their curiosity. It is important to continue on at these times, slowly and calmly, or if you do pause, resist staring and avoid any broad or sudden movements. Keep the eyes lowered and do not look directly at the animals. Staring will be interpreted as a threatening posture. If we avoid this, we will increasingly sense a growing kinship with the animals. Remember that we are entering their world—not as outsiders or possessors of the land but as distant relatives—co-inhabitants.

This exercise requires control, sensitivity, and a subtle appreciation. It will enhance attunement to the presence of animals not readily encountered or readily visible. Through experiencing Nature in silence, we discover everything is an expression of the Divine Life—including ourselves. One of Nature's greatest gifts is her endless willingness to teach us about ourselves and our possibilities. Through sacred silence, we experience the wonders and beauty of animals more intimately, and we begin to realize that every creature mirrors the magnificence of our own soul.

TED ANDREWS

The Animal's Saint

St. Francis of Assisi is the guardian and patron saint of all animals. His love of Nature and all creatures has been an inspiration for many—including me. St. Francis was born in 1181 in Assisi, Italy, of a wealthy family. His life changed dramatically after being taken prisoner during a military expedition and spending a year in jail.

After he was freed, he became severely ill, but it was during his sick time that amazing revelations came to him. Soon after his recovery, he left his home to live as a hermit and began administering to the poor and to all creatures. His teachings spread, and in 1209 Pope Innocent III officially sanctioned the Franciscan Order.

In 1221, St. Francis left the Franciscan Order and withdrew from the outer world. He spent his last years in remote places, nearly blind and in poor health. During this period, he composed the "Canticle of Creatures" which today is more commonly known as the "Hymn to the Sun." St. Francis considered all Nature as a reflection of God, calling all creatures his brothers and sisters. In this poem, he gives praise to God for the wondrous works of Nature.

St. Francis died on October 3, 1226, and was canonized two years later by Pope Gregory IX. In 1979, Pope John Paul II recognized St. Francis as the patron saint of ecology. Today, on October 3rd every year, an increasing number of churches celebrate the Feast of St. Francis with masses and ceremonies to bless the animals which—one of the few times animals are truly welcomed into churches and honored for their sacredness.

Several years ago, because of our teachings and work with animals, my wife and I were invited to participate in a celebration and blessing of animals at Camp Chesterfield Spiritualist Center in Indiana in honor of the Feast of St. Francis. We brought the hawks that we use in educational programs with us.

At the end of the service, my wife and I stood—each with a hawk—on either side of the center aisle, forming a sacred doorway. Owners with their pets then passed between the hawks to receive blessings and healings from the ministers. Each animal was also given a St. Francis Medalion to wear upon its collar. It was a simple ceremony, but powerful and most beautiful and the amazing thing was that all of the animals got along.

Although I have participated and performed in many church services and other rituals over the years, this was one that is the dearest to me. Animals have been the gateway to blessings and healings many times in my life. My participation in this simple ceremony enabled me to be a gateway for them so that they could be blessed and healed in turn.

Canticle of Creatures

(OR HYMN OF THE SUN)

by Saint Francis of Assisi

Most High, All powerful, God of Goodness;
To Thee be praise and glory, Honor and all thankfulness
To Thee alone, Most High, are these things due,
And no man is worthy to speak of Thee.

Be thou praised, O Lord, for all Thy creation,
More especially for our Brother the Sun,
Who bringeth forth the day and givest light thereby,
For he is glorious and splendid in his radiance,
And to Thee, Most High, he bears similitude.

Be Thou praised, O Lord, for our Sister the Moon, and for the Stars:
In the heavens,
Thou hast set them bright and sparkling and beautiful.

Be Thou praised, O Lord, for our Brother the Wind,
For the air and for the clouds, For serene and for tempestuous days,
For through these dost Thou sustain all living things.

Be Thou praised, O Lord, for our Sister the Water,
For she giveth boundless service, and is lowly, precious and pure.

Canticle of Creatures

(cont.)

Be though praised, O Lord, for our Brother the Fire,
Through whom Thou givest light in the night hours,
For he is beautiful and joyous, vigorous and strong.

Be Thou praised, O Lord, for our Sister Mother Earth,
Who doth nourish us and ruleth over us,
And bringeth forth divers fruit, and bright flowers and herbs.

Be Thou praised, O Lord, for those who show forgiveness
    through Thy love,
And that do endure sickness and sorrow,
Blessed are they that do suffer in lowliness of spirit,
For by Thee, Most High, shall they be exalted.

Be Thou praised, O Lord, for our Sister Bodily Death,
From whom no man living may escape.
Blessed are they who shall be found doing Thy most Holy Will,
For the second dying shall work them no evil.
Be Thou praised and blessed, O Lord, in endless thanksgiving,
    and served in all humility.

ANIMALS IN THE NATURAL WORLD

Andrews, Ted. *Animal-Speak*. St. Paul: Llewellyn Publications, 1993.

Angell, Madeline. *America's Best Loved Wild Animals*. New York: Bobbs-Merrill Company, 1975.

Austin, Elizabeth and Oliver. *Random House Book of Birds*. New York: Random House, 1970.

Benyus, Janine. *Beastly Behaviors*. New York: Addison-Wesley, 1992.

Buettner, Gudrun. *Familiar Reptiles and Amphibians of North America*. New York: Alfred Knopf, 1997.

Chinery, Michael, ed. *Kingfisher Illustrated Encyclopedia of Animals*. New York: Kingfisher Books, 1992.

Carrier, Jim and Bekoff, Marc. *Nature's Life Lessons*. Golden: Fulcrum Publishing, 1996.

Clement, Roland. *Living World of Audubon*. New York: Grosset and Dunlap, 1974.

Cornell, Joseph. *Sharing Nature with Children*. Nevada City: Dawn Publications, 1979.

Domico, Terry. *Bears of the World*. New York: Facts On File Publications, 1988.

Farb, Peter. *The Insects*. New York: Time-Life Books, 1962.

Farrand, John, ed. *Insects and Spiders*. New York: Alfred Knopf, 1997.

Harlow, Rosie and Morgan, Gareth. *175 Amazing Nature Experiment* New York: Random House, 1991.

Hines, Bob. *Fifty Birds of Town and City*. U.S. Department of Interior Washington D. C.

Huxley, Anthony. *Green Inheritance*. New York: Doubleday, 1985.

Johnson, Sylvia. *The Wildlife Atlas*. Minneapolis: Lerner Publishing,

Kinney, Karen, ed. *Insects and Spiders*. Alexandria: Time-Life Books,

Levi, Herbert, and Levi, Lorna. *Spiders and their Kin*. New York: Golden Press, 1990.

Limburg, Peter. *What's in the Name of Birds*. New York: Coward, McCann and Geoghegan, Inc., 1975.

_____.*What's in the name of Wild Animals*. New York: Coward, Mc and Geoghegan, Inc., 1977.

Mackenzie, John. *Birds of Prey*. Minocqa, WI: North Word, Inc., 198

Mattison, Chris. *Encyclopedia of Snakes*. New York: Facts On File, Inc. 1995.

Moenich, David. *Lizards*. Neptune City, NJ: T.F.H. Publications, 199

Palmer, John. *Exploring the Secrets of Nature*. New York: Reader's Digest, 1994.

Peterson, Roger. *How to Know Birds.* Boston: Houghton Mifflin, 1957.

Rezendes, Paul. *Tracking and the Art of Seeing.* Charlotte, VT: Camden House Publications, 1992.

Seidensticker, John and Lumpkin, Susan. *Great Cats.* Emmaus, PA: Rodale press, 1991.

Sequoia, Anna. *67 Ways to Save the Animals.* New York: Harper Perennial, 1990.

Snead, Stella. *Animals in Four Worlds.* Chicago: University of Chicago Press, 1989.

Tanner, Ogden. *Urban Wilds.* Alexandria: Time-Life Books, 1975.

Terres, John. *Audubon Society Encyclopedia of North American Birds.* New York: Wings Books, 1980.

Weidensaul, Scott. *American Wildlife.* New York: Gallery Books, 1989.

Wood, Peter. *Birds of Field and Forest.* New York: Time-Life Books, 1977.

Zim, Herbert and Smith, Hobart. *Reptiles and Amphibians.* New York: Golden Press, 1987.

MYSTICISM OF NATURE

Andrews, Ted. *Discover Your Spirit Animal* (audiocassette). Dayton, OH: Life Magic Enterprises, Inc., 1996.

_____. *Enchantment of the Faerie Realm.* St. Paul: Llewellyn Publications, 1993.

_____. *How To Meet and Work with Spirit Guides.* St. Paul: Llewellyn Publications, 1992.

_____. *Magical Dance.* St. Paul: Llewellyn Publications, 1992.

_____. *More Simplified Magic.* Jackson, TN: Dragonhawk Publishing, 1998.

_____. *The Animal-Wise Tarot.* Jackson, TN: Dragonhawk Publishing, 1999.

_____. *Treasures of the Unicorn.* Batavia, OH: Dragonhawk Publishing, 1996.

Arnott, Kathleen. *African Myths and Legends.* New York: Oxford University Press, 1989.

Baskin, Wade. *The Sorcerer's Handbook*. Secaucus: Citadel Press, 1974.

Caduto, Michael and Bruchac, Joseph. *Keepers of the Animals*. Golden, CO: Fulcrum Publishing, 1991.

_____. *Keepers of the Earth*. Golden, CO: Fulcrum Publishing, 1988.

Campbell, Joseph. *The Way of the Animals*, Vol. I & II. New York: Harper and Row, 1988.

_____. *Mythologies of the Primitive Hunters and Gatherers*. New York: Harper and Row, 1988.

Christa, Anthony. *Chinese Mythology*. New York: Peter Bedrick Books, 1983.

Cirlot, J.E. *Dictionary of Symbols*. New York: Philosophical Library, 1962.

Doore, Gary. *The Shaman's Path*. Boston: Shambhala Press, 1988.

Edroes, Richard and Ortiz, Alfonso. *American Indian Myths and Legends*. New York: Pantheon Books, 1984.

Frazer, James. *The Golden Bough*. New York: Collier Books, 1922.

Godwin, Jocelyn. *Mystery Religions in the Ancient World*. San Francisco: Harper and Row, 1981.

Hall, Manley P. *Secret Teachings of All Ages*. Los Angeles: Philosophical ResearchSociety, 1977.

Hamilton, Edith. *Mythology*. New York: New American Library, 1942.

Hope, Murray. *Practical Eqyptian Magic*. New York: St. Martin's Press, 1984.

Ions, Veronica. *Indian Mythology*. New York: Peter Bedrick Books, 1983.

Manes, Christopher. Other Creations. New York: Doubleday, 1997.

McLaughlin, Marie. *Myths and Legends of the Souix*. Lincoln, NE: University of Nebraska Press, 1990.

Nicholson, Irene. *Mexican and Central American Mythology*. NewYork: Peter Bedrick Books, 1982.

Nicholson, Shirley. *Shamanism*. Wheaton, IL: Theosophical Publications, 1987.

Opie, Iona and Tatem, Moira. *A Dictionary of Superstitions*. New York: Oxford University Press, 1989.

Osborn, Harold. *South American Mythology*. New York: Peter Bedrick Books, 1983.

Parrinda, Geoffrey. *African Mythology*. New York: Peter Bedrick Books, 1982.

Piggott, Juliet. *Japanese Mythology*. New York: Peter Bedrick Books, 1982.

Poinsias, mac Cana. *Celtic Mythology*. New York: Peter Bedrick Books, 1983.

Sams, Jamie and Carson, David. *Medicine Cards*. Santa Fe: Bear and Company, 1988.

Spence, Lewis. *Myths of the North American Indians*. New York: Dover Publications, 1989.

Sun Bear and Wabun. *The Medicine Wheel*. Englewood Cliffs: Prentice-Hall, 1988.

Sympson, Jacqueline. *European Mythology*. New York: Peter Bedrick Books, 1987.

Tyler, Hamilton. *Pueblo Birds and Myths*. Flagstaff, AZ: Northland Publications, 1991.

Waring, Philippa. *Dictionary of Omens and Superstitions*. Secaucus: Chartwell Books, 1989.

- B -

* indicates **Animal Wonder**

* indicates **Animal Wonder**

* indicates **Animal Wonder**

* indicates **Animal Wonder**

* indicates **Animal Wonder**

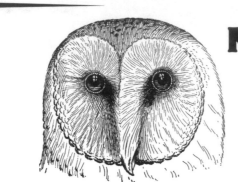

Notes

Notes

* indicates **Animal Wonder**

The Crane Report

How can you tell the diffference between good psychics and the "not so good" ones?

The Crane Report might provide some answers. The premier issue contains a book excerpt from *Psychic Protection* by Ted Andrews called "Distinguishing Psychic Junk" Ted has over 25 years experience in doing psychic readings for individuals and advises us that the best way to tell the legitimacy of a psychic is to have a face to face reading.

In "The Unusual" article, Becky Wendorf, an intuitive reader and bookstore owner, describes what it is like to do a reading and how readers relay information. Becky describes several readings and talks about how clients works as hard as readers do.

The "Questions to Ask a Psychic Reader" provides a list of questions to ask psychics or metaphysical professionals before enlisting their services. Some of the questions include: "How do you use your psychic skills to help me reach my goals?" and "What is your approach to a reading?"

The Crane Report

| Winter 1998 | Premiere Issue | $1.50 |

Distinguishing Psychic Junk
by Ted Andrews

Dear Friends,

As more people begin to explore metaphysical topics, they need someone or some place to turn for the "truth" about the products or services they'd like to purchase.

We know—we've been there too. In our own spiritual struggles, we've found some answers to our questions in the books written by Ted Andrews, an internationally recognized teacher and mystic.

To our delight, Ted has joined us in our efforts to publish a "consumer report" for the metaphysically minded. Since all journeys begin with a single step, we wanted to share our first effort with you.

Enjoy!

Let us know what you think!

Everyday on TV, in magazines and newspapers, there are ads for psychic consultations. For anywhere from three to six dollars a minute, we can have our fortune told. We can learn who our true loves are and how to attain our wealth from "master psychics."

A half-hour consultation on most psychic phone lines can cost as much—if not more than $150 dollars. Sure, some offer as much as "ten free minutes" in their ads, but the ten free minutes must be distributed over five or more calls, which ultimately will cost the client hundreds of dollars with no way of determining the legitimacy of the psychic or the sponsoring company. Plus, there are no guarantees.

An increasing number of professional psychics are working for the psychic phone lines. Some because they do not have to really prove themselves; they can remain anonymous. On the other hand some do the phone lines because it enables them to work out of their home.

(continued on page 4)

Feature   **Article**

Excerpted from *Psychic Protection* by Ted Andrews

Would your customers like to receive our newsletter?

If you enjoyed this newsletter and would like to carry it in your store, let us know. Suggested retail price is $1.50.
Wholesale prices available in quantities of ten.

About Our Name

To the ancient Chinese, the crane was the Messenger of the Gods, an intermediary between haven and earth. Our logo is the Sandhill Crane who populates our region in the summertime, but winters in Cuba, California's Central Valley, and across southern states from Arizona to Florida.

As the totem of our newsletter, we are working with Crane to celebrate all creative resources, keeping them alive through proper focus and attention.

A Consumer Report for the Metaphysically Minded

Write or call for a FREE sample copy of the newsletter.

The Crane Report
P.O. Box 158
Hitterdal, MN 56552

or call 218/962-3202

TED ANDREWS

Meeting Your Spirit Animal

(audiocassette)

SIDE 1:
Discover Your Spirit Animal
(music only)

SIDE 2:
Discover Your Spirit Animal
(music and guided meditation)

From the best selling book "ANIMAL SPEAK"

Discover Your Spirit Animal

Ted Andrews

50 minutes
Retail: $10

available through all major distributors and all major bookstores

ISBN 1-888767-05-7

Animals reflect our spirit. They are out teachers, our guardians, our companions, and our totems. They remind us of the majesty of life. They restore our wonder at the world. They reawaken our lost belief in magic, dreams, and possibilties.

Animals have much to teach us. They reflect the potentials we can unfold, for every animal is a gateway to the phenomenal world of spirit. This powerful exercise has been used to guide thousands to a better understanding of the spiritual and magical purpose of the animal spirits within our lives. It combines music and meditation to open the heart more fully to Nature.

Music and words composed and performed by Ted Andrews.

**Also by
Ted Andrews**

The Animal-Wise Tarot

⭐*Runner-Up
1999 Visionary Award* for
BEST SPIRITUALITY BOOK!*

All traditions taught the significance of Nature—particularly of the animals crossing our paths, whether we are awake or dreaming. Use The Animal-Wise Tarot to develop your intuition, strengthen your connection to the animal world, and to find the answers to your most puzzling questions in life.

Whether an experienced tarot enthusiast, a shamanic practitioner, or a novice to psychic exploration, this tarot's clarity and ease of use will be a refreshing surprise. Anyone can use this tarot effectively from the moment it is opened and you will find yourself becoming truly animal-wise!

*The ANIMAL-WISE TAROT
contains 78 full-color cards
of actual animal
photographs and a
248-page soft-cover text.*

* Visionary Awards presented by the Coalition of Visionary Retailers at the 1999 International New Age Trade Show.

DISCOVER THE LANGUAGE OF ANIMALS!

The Animal-Wise Tarot

by Ted Andrews

$34.95 USA

ISBN 1-888767-35-9

AVAILABLE FROM
DRAGONHAWK PUBLISHING
P.O. BOX 1316
JACKSON, TN 38302-1316

About the Cover Artist

Native American Images
by

JAMES OBERLE

James Oberle's art reflects his Cherokee Ancestry. His portraits of Native Americans contain a reverence of the spirit, which extends from the beginning of people on this continent to the present day. His art shows how they enrich our lives through their wisdom, traditions, and achievements. The faces displayed in Jim's art captures the strength and enduring character of Native peoples.

Jim's art is housed in many fine galleries and private collection throughout the United States. The Miami Valley Council for Native Americans uses his original designs. He produced commissioned pieces for First Frontier, "Blue Jacket Outdoor Dram" (1992, 1994, and 1995). His original art, the *Heartbeat of Turtle Island*, has been included in school textbooks and teacher manuals. The Ohio Humanities Council featured his piece *Spirit of the Panther* in 1998.

Jim's artistic abilities have been recognized by national publications, including Native Peoples Magazine. He received first place as an Individual Artist from the Dayton Culture Builds Community in 1998. He has exhibited with nationally known America Indian artists Johnny Tiger, Jim Yellowhawk, and Rex Begay. Him served as the Art Director for the Inter-tribal Arts Experience from 1990-1993.

Jim is a native of Dayton, Ohio. He and his wife, Gilda who acts as his manager, have four children and five grandchildren.

For information on obtaining prints of the cover art *Wolf Dreamer* and other pieces by James Oberle, contact:

James Oberle
Native American Images
135 South Sperling
Dayton, OH 45403
(937) 253-4680
gloheaven@aol.com

About the Author

Ted Andrews is an internationally recognized author, storyteller, teacher, and mystic. A leader in the human potential, psychic, and metaphysical fields, he has written over 20 books which have been translated into as many different languages. Ted has been involved in the serious study of the esoteric and occult for more than 30 years, and brings to the field a very extensive formal and informal education.

Called a true Renaissance man, Ted is schooled in music, h y p n o t h e r a p y, accupressure, and other holistic healing modalities. He has composed, performed, and produced the music for ten audiocassettes, and is a continuing student of the ballet and kung fu. Ted also has many years of hands-on experience with wildlife rehabilitation, possessing state and federal permits to work with birds of prey. He conducts animal education, storytelling programs, and metaphysical seminars throughout the United States.

TED ANDREWS

Notes